From Apocalypse
to Way of Life

From Apocalypse to Way of Life

Environmental Crisis in the American Century

Frederick Buell

ROUTLEDGE
New York   London

Published in 2003 by
Routledge
29 West 35th Street
New York, NY 10001
www.routledge-ny.com

Published in Great Britain by
Routledge
11 New Fetter Lane
London EC4P 4EE
www.routledge.co.uk

Routledge is an imprint of the Taylor & Francis Group.
Printed in the United States of America on acid-free paper.

10 9 8 7 6 5 4 3 2 1

Library of Congress Cataloging-in-Publication Data

Buell, Frederick, 1942–
    From apocalypse to way of life: four decades of environmental crisis in the U.S./Frederick Buell.
        p. cm.
    Includes bibliographical references and index.
        ISBN 0-415-93407-9 (Hardback)
    1. Environmentalism—United States. 2. Environmental policy—United States. I. Title.
        GE197 .B84 2003
        363.7'00973—dc21

                                                                                            2002012439

To Nicholas, Alexander, Jill, and Andy

CONTENTS

ACKNOWLEDGMENTS

I am indebted to a number of my colleagues for their encouragement during the years I worked on this book. In particular, I am grateful to Nancy Comley (whose consistent help and support I especially appreciate), David Speidel, and Steven Kruger. I also have significant intellectual indebtedness to a large number of people who shared their expertise, interests, and commitments with me. A multiyear interdisciplinary seminar, "The Human Place in Nature," sponsored by the Nathan Cummings Foundation provided an ideal forum for exploring the impacts of recent environmental changes on politics, philosophy, and culture; I owe much to its convener, Charles Halpern, its moderator, James Hillman, and its members, including Mermer Blakeslee, Jackie Brookner, Edward Casey, Sandy Gellis, Jeff Golliher, Ned Kaufman, Julie Mankiewicz, Paul Mankiewicz, Margot McClean, Andrew McLaughlin, Gene McQuillan, Nina Sankovitch, and Mark Walters. I owe similar debts to Stanley Aronowitz, and Michael Menser and the C.U.N.Y. Center for the Study of Culture, Technology, and Work, and to Burton Pike, friend and colleague for many years. I am grateful to John Barry for his generous and illuminating comments on a version of this manuscript, as I am to my brother, Lawrence Buell, for his unfailing encouragement, generous intellectual exchange, and comments on one chapter of the book—all parts of a relationship much richer and more multifaceted than most siblings enjoy. David McBride, my editor at Routledge, has far exceeded this author's hope for meaningful collaboration on this project; I am indebted to him not just for his steady encouragement and expertise but also for his insightful commentary on several versions of the manuscript. My deepest debt is to Andrew McLaughlin not just for reading and valuably critiquing drafts of this book but for years of collaborative work and dialogue on environmental and environmental-political issues, specifically on globalization and the environment; with him I enjoy a rare connection, one that couples intellectual passion with genuine personal friendship. My most personal debts are to my children, Nicholas and Alexander, who are knowledgeable about and living through the issues raised in this book, and to my wife, Jill, who has made them a part of her teaching for years.

I have received important institutional support from a number of different sources. I thank Queens College and the City University of New York for supporting my research through a number of different programs, including their collaborative incentive and scholar incentive programs. I thank the American Council of Learned Societies and the Nathan Cummings Foundation for support on a project that proved relevant to this book. And I gratefully acknowledge support from the National Endowment for the Humanities that allowed me to complete the book. Portions of this book have appeared previously, and I thank the journals and their editors for permission to use this material. Material from Chapters 2, 3, and 4 appeared first in *symplokē* 9:1–2 (2001), pp. 45–73, and are here reprinted by permission of the journal. Portions of Chapter 2 also appeared in "Nationalist Postnationalism: Globalist Discourse in Contemporary American Culture," *American Quarterly* 50:3 (Sept. 1998) and are here reprinted with permission of Johns Hopkins University Press. Portions of Chapters 1 and 7 and the Appendix appeared as "Conflicting Conceptions of Nature in Popular Discourse, Environmentalism, and Social Theory," *Found Object* 9 (Fall 2000), and are here reprinted by permission of the journal.

PREFACE: THE DECADE OF CRISIS

In 1962, Rachel Carson warned of ecological disaster in progress. Though not the first to raise the specter of imminent human-made environmental crisis, Carson's book, *Silent Spring*, had a decisive effect. It led the way in making concern about environmental crisis a national issue. By the 1970s, Robert Gottlieb writes: "the mood of environmental crisis seemed more and more overwhelming." Environmental crisis seemed to be written for all to see "in such disparate events of the late 1960s as the burning of the Cuyahoga River in the center of Cleveland, the eutrophication of Lake Erie, and the dying birds washed up on the oil-slicked shores of Santa Barbara."[1] In exactly this spirit, Senator Gaylord Nelson, originator of the idea of the first Earth Day (1970), argued that the environmental crisis "was the most critical issue facing mankind," making "Vietnam, nuclear war, hunger, decaying cities, and all the other major problems one could name . . . relatively insignificant by comparison."[2]

Concern about environmental crisis, however, was just part of the postwar environmental movement that Carson helped inaugurate and the 1970 Earth Day helped celebrate and consolidate. In that movement, utopian enthusiasm and optimistic reformism overshadowed environmental apocalypticism. People committed themselves to a wide variety of causes, such as "ecology," green lifestyles, ruralist back-to-the-land movements, and wilderness appreciation and protection: concern about environmental crisis in no way canceled out exuberance and hope. But neither did hope nullify concern about crisis; in fact, the two motives intensified each other. New perceptions of nature's potentially irreversible deformation intensified peoples' impulses to experience, protect, and cherish nature and work to ensure a viable future for human society.

Historians of the post-Carson environmental movements' political activism and cultural enthusiasms have concentrated, for the most part, on the hopeful or the hope-bringing side. As is only natural, commentaries on the environmental movement seek, while chronicling challenges and set-backs, to direct the movement toward solutions.[3] But just as important as telling the story of changing forms of activism is a second story: that of how environmental crisis and alarmed human concern about it has also devel-oped and substantially changed since the time of Rachel Carson. Though much has been (and is daily being) written about what constitutes environ-mental crisis, most of it is devoted to urgent present assessments and warn-ings. Little has been written that surveys how and why these assessments and warnings have changed over time. The result is that people tend to speak of *the* environmental crisis—as if "it" were a clear, stable, and ahistorical con-cept. To do so, however, is unfortunate, because it suppresses the complexity, diversity, and dynamism of accumulating environmental problems. It also ob-scures an equally important story: that of how the impact of these problems on U.S. society has changed—and dramatically deepened—over time.

The truth is that, since Rachel Carson, environmental crisis has rapidly evolved and substantially changed in form, not just in nature, but also in human discourse about it. Announcing itself as apocalypse, environmental crisis has been debunked, has resisted debunking, has been reworked, and has been dramatically diversified and expanded, resurfacing in unusual new forms. The world (as of the writing of this sentence and presumably also the reading of it) has not ended; eco-apocalypse hasn't happened. Yet people today also accept the fact that they live in the shadow of environ-mental problems so severe that they constitute a crisis. And this shadow is in many ways far larger than the one Carson described. Carson's small-town-American "silent spring" has become the much more diverse and compre-hensive set of problems known, ominously, as the global environmental crisis. A history of crisis thought that fully incorporates both the apparent failure of previously forecasted apocalypses and the continuance and even deepening of alarm is a necessity today. This book seeks to fill that need.

Though far narrower in focus and findings than today's sense of crisis, re-sponses to proliferating environmental problems in the 1960s and 1970s were fiercely urgent and apocalyptically final. If the ecology movement had led people to a new kind of appreciation of nature, analyses of what threat-ened nature were clothed in fearful and sensational terms. Carson's book started this trend off: it was anything but understated in its pictures of envi-ronmental catastrophe. Her book's famous preface, "A Fable for Tomorrow," depicts a "small town in the heart of America" which has been mysteriously "silenced." This is a place from which birdsong and animal cry have been mysteriously erased; a place in which a mysterious blight has swept away the farm animals, killing chickens, cattle, and sheep and leaving the remaining ones virtually barren. What brings all this death is the pervasive poisoning of the environment with synthetic chemicals in a process Carson pictures as creepily silent: everywhere a "white granular powder" still lies on the land in patches, weeks after "it had fallen like snow upon the roofs and the lawns, the fields and the streams."[4]

If a silenced spring and a poisoned earth thus became her trademark nightmares, Carson also did not shrink from bringing people into the loop. After describing the poisoning of ecosystems, Carson depicts human beings as exposed to conditions that go (as one chapter title puts it) "Beyond the Dreams of the Borgias." For example, Carson makes the peacefully domestic suburban world of consumerist America—the society that emerged from the 1950s—seem a toxic minefield. A "few minutes' research in any supermarket" yields, for Carson, abundant evidence of a new "birth-to-death contact with dangerous chemicals" for Americans. The insecticide section contains chemicals (in "homey and cheerful" packaging and displays) that, if dropped to the floor by child or careless adult, could splash people "with the same chemical that has sent spraymen using it into convulsions."[5] Mothproofing material contains DDD (a close relative to DDT); insecticide contains chlordane. Carson then couples her gruesome rendering of domestic life with an equally upsetting and much more prolonged analysis of environmentally caused cancer. Her summary—a quotation from an unnamed "investigator"—is fearfully simple. People today live in "a sea of carcinogens."[6]

Though never equaled by any subsequent nonfiction or fiction, *Silent Spring* helped spark a small tsunami of catastrophe rhetoric in environmental science and screeds and in popular literature. Thomas Disch introduced a collection of short fiction, *The Ruins of Earth*, by remarking that, while 1950s' concerns about nuclear holocaust had been successfully black-boxed ("one had learned to live with the bombs largely by looking the other way"), environmental crisis was different: "now, in 1971, it isn't possible to look the other way."

> It is the daytime, suburban side of existence that has become our nightmare. In effect the bombs are already dropping—as more carbon monoxide pollutes the air of Roseville [the suburb where Disch attended high school, but another instance of Carson's "town in the heart of America"], as mercury poisons our

waters, our fish, and ourselves, and as one by one our technology extinguishes the forms of life upon which our own life on this planet depends. These are not catastrophes of the imagination—these are what's happening.[7]

Targeting other problems, Harry Harrison wrote "Roommates," the story that became first his novel, *Make Room, Make Room!* and, later, the film *Soylent Green*. In the story, Andy Rusch, a policeman, dwells in a tiny apartment with his girlfriend, Shirl and a roommate, Sol; in this grotesquely overpopulated, environmentally and socially decayed New York City of the future, space is so short that everyone is forced to live packed together with people assigned to them by the Welfare Department. Heat is also at a premium; food is unnourishing and scarce (weedcrackers, kofee, and, if you're lucky, soylent burgers), so that many Americans suffer from kwashiorkor, a deficiency disease. Even water is tightly rationed and fiercely fought over. But the deepest nightmare is population. Everywhere there are people, teeming, crowded together, fighting for breathing room, at each other's throats in a battle for dwelling space.

At the end of the film made from the novel made from this story, emphasis shifts from nausea at overpopulation to a keening lament for the extermination of nature and a horrible revelation about how the earth's population has come to feed itself. Andy, played by Charlton Heston, gazes in distress through the window of a chamber of the voluntary suicide center in which his beloved friend Sol, played by Edward G. Robinson, awaits death. The allure and consolation that bring people into the euthanasia center come from the chance to view old films of the planet's vanished natural loveliness, its last untainted fields, forests, flowers, and fauna.

Forcing his way into the center, Andy watches along with the dying Sol the gorgeous old footage. In this scene, all of Charlton Heston's memorable ability to portray pain and agony via dazzling white teeth, muscular jaws, and sweat-beaded forehead is displayed to advantage. For the last remnants of nature are preserved now only in technicolor virtual form on film; viewing them heightens immeasurably both their beauty and the pain of their loss. After this remarkable and influential scene—one that impacted subsequent crisis depiction strongly—the revelation that immediately follows, the unveiling of the movie's central dietetic mystery, is almost an anticlimax. The discovery that soylent green (the descendent of the story's tasty soylent burgers) is in fact the recycled flesh of the visitors to the euthanasia center is not quite the shocker it is supposed to be.

Philip Wylie's novel, *The End of the Dream*, expanded the field considerably. It does not just depict *an* environmental crisis; it chronicles an ongoing, prolifically diversified, multiform global environmental and social meltdown—a meltdown that becomes, the novel maintains, irreversible in 1971 (the year before the book's publication). 1971 is when "people switched off the grimly growing news about their endangered environs" and "an infantile majority became lunatic."[8] Set in the mid-1990s, the novel depicts an earth ruined and human population decimated by an astonishing variety of environmental problems.

The novel's depiction of these problems has quite a lot of lively variety to it, ranging from the comic-grotesque to the spectacular. On the comic-grotesque side, additives in a brand of frozen TV dinners prove to have a fatal chemical flaw. They produce explosive gas when processed in the mammalian intestine. Victims are, first, the elderly Edith Greetlan's beloved dog Tumsie; when the dog makes the mistake of passing gas too close to an open flame, it explodes. Mrs. Greetlan herself explodes later that night, as does, shortly thereafter, Father Trentchel, an Episcopalian minister who "one day . . . eased his flatulence by breaking wind as he was standing with his back to a blazing fire."[9] When a fourth incident occurs—to a prize pig this time—the fact that the animal is so valuable instigates an investigation, and the dangerous food additive is quietly withdrawn from the shelves, without, of course, the real reasons for the recall being revealed.

More pathetic, though also grotesque, is a tragedy on the Little Dwain River in Kentucky. There parents are forced to watch their children die, thanks to release of boiling water from a supposedly safe upstream reactor. As their father remembers it:

> They couldn't see to row back. Come on 'em too fast. We couldn't go out to them. Not even stay on the pier. They was screaming—bein' steamed to death, o'course. Cooked alive. Took ten minutes, maybe more, before they even began t' quieten down.[10]

Still more spectacular is the explosion of (not just the fire in) the Cuyahoga River outside Cleveland—"an explosion so cataclysmic it was attributed to an atomic bomb."[11] What happens is that, frustrated by failed attempts actually to clean up this industrial sewer—labeled a "fire hazard" for its propensity to burn—industry and government instead develops an ingenious chemical film to cover it, sealing the pollution below. Thus the river is far more vigorously polluted than previously—and with supposedly no visible effects. The book also chronicles an attempt by industry to reengineer all rivers this way—as industrial sewers, thereby lessening the strain on the land. Problems occur only when an occasional great bubble of volatile toxins erupts through the film. Near Cleveland, as ill luck has it, a larger bubble, vastly more volatile than usual, forms and rises to the surface. It explodes, registering a force at "ground zero" of 21 kilotons.

The book's most dramatic event results from a still different environmental problem in New York. It comes at holiday time, when the city's merchants are hoping, after some bad years, for a record-breaking sales season. Ignoring reports that an extraordinary air pollution event was in progress, the mayor and his counselors decide to go ahead with their plan to put two thousand extra city buses on duty to ferry the anticipated huge crowds of shoppers in and out of Manhattan. People respond to the lure, even though breathing the air is painful: "every ensuing inhalation added misery . . . [and] people passing in their thousands were coughing, choking, eyes and noses streaming, handkerchiefs held to filter out some portion of the pollutants" (p. 139). The novel's hero, Will Gulliver, encounters the resulting meltdown head on. Leaving his workplace, he looks downtown through the dim haze—visibility is less than a block—as he hears an odd sound, something like "a whispered scream" that in seconds becomes "a roar."

> What I saw was almost incredible. The crowd on my side of the street at a distance of four blocks and beyond had become dwarfed. It took a moment to understand that incredible phenomenon. It was as if everybody had suddenly become two feet tall. And this strange endwarfing was spreading. The standing masses were serially shortening—and then it was plain.
>
> They had fallen.
>
> They were falling like wheat cut by an invisible reaper, one that was approaching. They were, I knew, dead.[12]

Unable to get back into his office building, Will turns to run with the mob uptown, realizing that what has happened is the generation of "a lethal concentration of nitrogen oxides, NO and NO_2, mainly" and that it will reach the spot where he stands in a minute or less. As he flees, "the voice from the south was now terrible, a roar and scream of fear from thousands of throats."[13] Gulliver makes it to Central Park, then back to his Park Avenue apartment; he is one of the lucky ones, as huge numbers of shoppers and rescuers lie dead in cross streets, at the wheels of their cars, fire trucks, or ambulances. The city smells "like a battlefield"; over a million two hundred thousand people die.[14]

Doubtless, to most, imagery of such extreme ecological and social melt-down would seem out of date today. Some might consider these garish images with the indulgent amusement that outlandish fashions of several decades ago can inspire, the amusement that later generations feel at recall-ing the strange old worlds that people somehow once so naively lived in. Though the imagination of disaster very much persists, old disasters quickly age. Others might come to a still harsher judgment. They might well conclude that the apocalyptically minded called nature to its last party, and no guests came. Indeed, recounting the sometimes hysterical warnings that didn't come true, skeptics have argued with some influence that the problem was not with the environment but with those who raised the warning—the victims of what was called (among other things) the Chicken Little syndrome.

Still, despite all the debunking of past warnings, concern about environ-mental crisis persists. Indeed, the stories that fill the newspapers today are, in some ways, more disturbing than anything Wylie imagined. Open water at the North Pole; state-sized chunks of ice shearing off Antarctic glaciers; four mil-lion acres of Alaskan forest dead as a probable result of climate change, caus-ing underwriters to refuse fire insurance coverage to nearby residents; acute water shortages predicted for an increasing number of people in the world during the new century—stories like these make contemporary environmen-tal problems seem graver and more soberingly real than anything in Wylie's fiction. The earth seems stressed past its limits, and human futures seem in-creasingly constricted and constrained; concern with crisis has not simply disappeared into the background like smoke from a fanatic's gradually expir-ing campfire.

As I shall argue in this book, just the opposite has happened. The smoke has grown more persistent and omnipresent even as a well-organized ideo-logical fire brigade has sought to smother its plumes while ignoring the fire producing them. For even as it has been effectively contested and denied, a sense of unresolved, perhaps unresolvable, environmental crisis has become part of people's normality today. Faith in effective action has diminished at the same time that the concern about the gravity of the crisis has sharpened. Debate about environmental crisis has suffused itself more widely than be-

fore throughout American culture and society and become entangled in
the routines of more and more daily social and cultural controversies. No
longer an apocalypse ahead, critical environmental problems and constraints
help construct society's sense of daily normality. Far from going away, environmental crisis has become a regular part of the uncertainty in which people
nowadays dwell.

In taking readers through the story of how crisis has been formulated and
denied yet has deepened, diversified, and domesticated itself as a part of ordinary life, I hope this book will do for them what it did for me in writing it. I
hope that the book will make readers feel that, though looking environmental
crisis seriously in the face may risk turning one to stone, regarding crisis in a
serious and sustained fashion is as imp ortant to the maturation of American
society as capturing Medusa's head was to Perseus' maturation personally. He
needed that head to attain his adulthood. So does American society today: facing and understanding how and why people are so rapidly changing their terran
environment is fundamental to any credible and mature understanding both of
society and culture today and of the legacy it is leaving future generations. And
perhaps such understanding is more possible to reach today than it was during
the 1970s, when a direct, eye-to-eye encounter with crisis in its most apocalyptic form was vigorously pursued. Looking more slowly at environmental crisis
in the mirrors of politics, science, history, sociology, philosophy, and literature
may help preserve us, as Perseus' shield did him, from turning to stone, from
being frozen either politically or psychologically, by what we contemplate.

But taking environmental crisis seriously in this way is, of course, not easy.
And people, collectively, have decades of uneasy denial and worsened conditions to overcome. Accordingly, regarding crisis in these mirrors will initially,
at least, be difficult. Indeed, many may come to feel that society today resem-
bles less the young and ardent Perseus contemplating Medusa than it does the
faux-youthful hero of Oscar Wilde's famous fable, *The Portrait of Dorian Gray*,
standing in front of a picture of himself, the curtains that had been concealing
it pulled temporarily aside. For U.S. society today, like Dorian Gray, does not
seem overtly to exhibit the stigmata of a life led so wrongly. Only an artful portrait of it shows how far the process has gone. Apparently healthy but no longer
innocent and perhaps fairly far advanced toward exhibiting openly what the
picture shows, contemporary viewers may well feel how difficult it is to look
closely at such an image without closing the curtain quickly and trying to walk
away.

Part I

Contesting Crisis

CHAPTER 1

The Politics of Denial

Every country had its companies lost in skepticism about climate change. But in the USA the scale of the collective denial was unique. There was something primitive, even frightening about it.
——Jeremy Leggett, *The Carbon War*

Changed my view of the world, very enlightening. I believed most of the environmentalist agenda before I read this book without any critical thinking [sic]. *This book has converted me from a worry wart about the environment to much optimism about the world's future. . . . I highly recommend it. The logic of it makes so much sense.*
——Comments by "a reader" of Julian Simon's *The Ultimate Resource 2*, posted on Amazon.com, August 2, 1997

Something happened to strip environmental crisis of what seemed in the 1970s to be its self-evident inevitability. Something happened to allow environmentalism's antagonists to stigmatize its erstwhile stewards as unstable alarmists and bad-faith prophets—and to call their warnings at best hysterical, at worst crafted lies. Indeed, something happened to allow some even to question (without appearing ridiculous) the apparently commonsensical assumption that environmentalists were the environment's best stewards.

The most important explanation for these events isn't hard to find. In reaction to the decade of crisis, a strong and enormously successful anti-environmental disinformation industry sprang up. It was so successful that it helped midwife a new phase in the history of U.S. environmental politics, one in which an abundance of environmental concern was nearly blocked by an equal abundance of antienvironmental contestation. Prophets rushing into the public space bearing environmental warnings like lanterns held high found themselves suddenly in a very crowded square, one now jammed with antienvironmental spokespeople also waving lanterns. If formerly too little information had hampered environmental activism, now too much information achieved the same end. According to Samuel Hays, who carefully chronicled American environmental politics between 1955 and 1985, the public drive for environmental change had been "neutralized" by the 1980s, blocked by an increasingly organized and elaborate corporate and conservative opposition.[1]

Despite scientific evidence and even, in a number of cases, virtual scientific consensus to the contrary, issue after issue was contested. The ozone hole was denied and trivialized, food and population crises were debunked, and global warming was hotly denied, doubted, and dismissed as unproven. Even the most sacred of environmental cows was vigorously attacked: voices were even raised in defense of DDT, arguing that Carson-inspired hysteria eliminated a chemical essential to preserving public health from diseases like malaria.

Environmentalists, in turn, were stigmatized as extremists. Even to mention environmental crisis meant being called "Chicken Little," or "doomster," or "doomsayer." Ronald Bailey, in his book *Ecoscam: The False Prophets of Ecological Apocalypse*, went for this particular jugular with even more ferocity than did his predecessor and model, Julian Simon. Bailey put a different spin from Thomas Disch's on the filiation of environmental crisis from fear of nuclear apocalypse. "Modern ecological millenarians, impatient with waiting for the flash of thermonuclear doom, now claim there is a 'global environmental crisis' threatening not just humanity, but all life on earth."[2] Anything but respectable scientists or responsible citizens, environmentalists were both pathological fanatics (they were contemporary millenarians) and ill-motivated manipulators of the innocent public. Bailey thus coined a new term for them. They were "apocalypse abusers"—a disreputable group that presumably used and misused apocalypse like others did alcohol or dangerous drugs.

Environmentalists were also entirely wrong, Bailey asserted. Along with making *ad hominem* attacks, he proceeded to marshal supposedly scientific evidence to show how wrong environmentalists were. In doing so, Bailey joined a large and surprisingly well-organized movement of such writers. For, along with sneering at environmentalists, crisis debunkers began the "counterscience" movement—a movement devoted to countering the findings of environmental science with the creation of a body of antienvironmental science. It grew so galling and influential that one of its targets, Paul Ehrlich, in collaboration with his wife Anne, sought to answer it in a book significantly entitled *The Betrayal of Science and Reason*; and environmental scientists and organizations generally recognized that they had to grow adept at quickly refuting disinformation as well as at researching issues and uncovering new information.[3]

Bailey's book showed all the earmarks of the "counterscience" movement, as the Ehrlichs described it. Filled with an abundance of statistics and apparently well documented, its facts and statistics were nonetheless highly unreliable; more revealingly, it was threadbare when it came to documentation of respectable scientific sources. It clothed its nakedness instead with references to fellow counterscience writers, most of whom were not scientists but antienvironmental journalists, economists, and ideologues. Further, it was a book gestated not in peer-reviewed academia but in the hothouse of right-wing and conservative think tanks—those recently invented and well-funded institutions dedicated not (like previous think tanks) to objective research but to the dissemination of ideologically driven "knowledge."

Along with being extremist and wrong, environmentalists weren't even stewards of the environment any more. Instead, a rather different sort of person was. The list of "real" environmental stewards came to include not only specific corporations—ones that claimed to be green in products and processes—but also, astonishingly, free-market capitalists and even grassroots antienvironmental activists. If you asked, in the wake of the 1970s, who was looking out for the environment, everyone's hands went up—including those of the antienvironmental right and the nation's most polluting corporations. And when the hands went up, it would be harder than ever before to tell who was who. For the crowd included many wolves in sheep's clothing, folk with name tags reading "Global Climate Coalition" (an industry lobbying organization dedicated to sandbagging global-warming reforms and winner of the infamous Scorched Earth Award presented at Kyoto) or "National Wetlands Organization" (an organization of developers).[4]

All of this debunking and abuse took its toll on environmentalists. Crisis talk, surprisingly, became almost as much a problem for environmentalists as it was a weapon against environmental disregard. Thus Theodore Roszak, a writer with old commitments to the environment but also with a sharp eye for what was timely and popular, backed off from crisis talk as a real political negative for environmentalists. He did this even though he was angry about the "plain [*sic*] vicious . . . new antienvironmental counterattack" environmentalists were subjected to. He portrayed this uncommonly nasty attack feelingly, but then he replicated it strangely himself, asserting that environmentalists' "habitual reliance on gloom, apocalyptic panic, and the psychology of shame takes a heavy toll in public confidence."[5] Having made this observation, Roszak let loose with a bashing of doomster environmentalism that might well have come from Bailey's pen—an analysis of it as a neo-Puritan pathology—while proposing his own solution, a "new psychological sensitivity" that could dip down into "the passion and longing that underlie many of our culture's seemingly thoughtless ecological habits."[6] Perhaps Roszak suffered from a subtle version of the Stockholm syndrome. But whatever the cause, Roszak's aversion to the environmental politics of crisis as politically naïve only drove him to be still more politically naïve himself. He ended up recycling as fact an important aspect of the very conservative rhetoric of dismissal that he himself had just finished critiquing.

But conservative antienvironmental rhetoric was crafted from the start as part of a larger package. It cannot be discussed in isolation from the broader stream of right-wing political discourse. One cannot separate the antienvironmental rhetoric from rhetoric about society, culture, and the economy; for conservative antienvironmentalism in the 1980s was part of what was carefully made to seem a comprehensive movement in American political culture. I mean the new conservativism, or the right-wing, or Republican "revolution," as partisans called it; more critical observers described it as "authoritarian" or top-down "populism." Emerging into daylight with the "Reagan Revolution," it reached a new kind of high-water mark with the congressional "Republican Revolution" of 1994. It is important to remember just how dynamic this movement was, now that it has lost much of its angry-outsider populist edge and become, with George W. Bush's presidency, less a movement than a mainstream, established, institutionalized political ideology.

The 1980s and nineties movement and the issues it encompassed showed all the earmarks of what was in fact a complexly compound creation. The movement was composed of a sometimes dissonant but always highly diverse set of partisans. It included mandarin intellectuals supported by conservative think tanks as well as members of angry-outsider populist groups organized often in top-down fashion and supported by expertise and aid from mainstream corporations and political organizations. It included, of course, those corporate networks and political organizations; it also folded in Christian fundamentalists and moral-majoritarians; football dads (as opposed to soccer moms); corporate libertarians and cyberlibertarians; local activists committed to a wide variety of issues, such as tax relief and withdrawing support from public schools; and talk-back radio-show hosts stirring up the likes of these about still further issues, such as the right to life and the scandalous dominance in U.S. public life of homosexuals and "hairy-legged" feminists. Right-to-life activists and extremists got in there too, and topping off the mix was the odd motorcycle gang and militia unit. The movement's equally diversified portfolio of issues included education reform; free-market fundamentalism styled as economic revolution; advocacy of a "common culture" based on hostility to advocacy of diversity; hostility to big government; moral crusading (with a special preference for the unborn); progun legislation; and virulent antienvironmentalism.

But the movement's peculiar rhetorical genius was to unite these issues and factions under what seemed to be a single banner, to portray itself to others and (above all) to its own constituencies as a single "movement." Arguably as diverse as the rainbow coalition, it managed to appear, at least for a time, as a single, dynamic movement of "the people." To be sure, this collective unity frayed at times—the division between old-fashioned conservatives, the new far right, and the diminished Republican center could become a difficult abyss to negotiate politically. But during the 1980s and into the early 1990s it cohered sufficiently for the Reagan and Republican revolutions to seem indeed revolutionary, phases of a genuine social movement dedicated to bringing about sweeping political and ideological change. It seemed a movement of the people, not politics as usual.

By arguing that the conservative movement was carefully crafted and not simply spontaneous, I do not mean to conjure up some vast right-wing conspiracy. I mean instead to give its creation its proper due, as one of the major events of U.S. political and cultural life in the last three decades. And the very notion that its hodgepodge of constituencies and issues in fact cohered into a single, spontaneous movement was itself part of this strategic accomplishment. The antienvironmentalist Ron Arnold articulated the strategy best as it emerged with Ronald Reagan and matured (with growing pains) during the time of the first Bush administration: "Then I read *People, Power, Change* by Luther Gurlick and Virginia Hayne, and their analysis helped me to realize that in an activist society like ours the only way to defeat a social movement is with another social movement."[7] To defeat the legacies of left social movements—from the New Deal to the racial, social, and environmental activism of the 1960s and 1970s—the right started one of its own—a backfire to meet and counter an existing fire. By the late 1970s and 1980s, the conservatives had captured the "social movement" field so thoroughly that theirs seemed to be *the* new social movement, one that replaced the previous, left-oriented ones and appropriated their mantle of future-oriented, visionary outsider-hood with a mission.

But intentionality alone, no matter how well funded, could not have launched a social movement. Enabling conditions needed to be in place, and indeed they were. Two historical factors in particular made this radical transformation of American political culture possible at the end of the 1970s. The first was a sense that the United States had suddenly entered a rapid decline—that the nation was rapidly losing pride and position externally and affluence and stability internally. This decline seemed to show up in a wide variety of areas: in global power and prestige; in global economic strength; in internal economic strength; in social stability and morality; in cultural unity and educational excellence. The second historical factor was similar: the older social movements—the ideologies and groups that had shaped policy in these areas for some time—had institutionalized themselves and aged. In the face of this new sense of crisis, many of the solutions proposed by the existing liberal-left social movements seemed no longer to be solutions but could be made to seem part of the problem.

This double whammy occurred across a wide spectrum of economic, cultural, social, and environmental fronts. Many in the United States came to feel that the nation was both slipping from its position of global centrality and was in disarray at home: the "American Century" was ending almost as it had begun, and the United States was in danger of slipping into Third World status. Michael Omi and Howard Winant tallied up many of these anxieties. The United States "suffered the humiliating 'losses' of Vietnam, Nicaragua, and Iran in the 1970s"; since the oil crisis in particular, it seemed that the United States "was being 'held for ransom' by the OPEC nations, which controlled 'our' vital energy resources." Soon slippage from the top of the economic global heap became a chief preoccupation: "once the world's creditor, [the United States became] its chief debtor; once the chief exporter of manufactured goods, it was now their main importer."[8]

This loss of power was as much fretted about as an internal economic decline as a decline in international power. Along with the oil crisis, "inflation . . . surged to unprecedented levels," and the "problem of 'stagflation,' which Keynesian policies were helpless to overcome, came to seem a permanent feature of U.S. economic life."[9] Thus the New Deal legacy came to be seen as another problem, not the solution: "the state was unable to act as its New Deal lineage obliged it to do, to solve or at least ameliorate economic problems. . . . Thus arose the fiscal crisis of the state." This was a crisis that "manifested itself on local, state, and national levels. The near bankruptcy of major cities, the property tax revolt (exemplified by California's Proposition 13 tax-cutting initiative), and the soaring federal deficit provided further fuel for the crisis and growing antistatist sentiment."[10] All of this sense of disarray was ratcheted into still higher gear when, by the 1980s, Japan seemed to be replacing the United States as the world's economic power, and the United States seemed to be slipping into a Third World identity. U.S. executives hastened to ponder *The Art of War* and Japanese corporate organizational techniques; a wider spectrum of folk—even many of those facing job cuts and downsizings—felt that the rhetoric of slippage and the assignment of blame for that slippage to the state (i.e., big government) was anything but exaggerated.

Next, economic crisis seemed to be coupled with social and cultural crisis. Thanks to continuing reactions against the "tide of radical collectivism" unleashed in the late 1960s by race riots and cultural nationalism (pioneered by the Black Power movement), attempts to foster cultural diversity in school curricula and through affirmative action seemed to some (mostly but not exclusively conservative whites) a problem rather than a solution. Once again, old social gains could be styled as new problems, and the New Right came to argue that:

> During the 1960s and 1970s, the state was recklessly allowed to expand and intervene in every aspect of social life; it came to dictate social policy with disastrous results. In particular, it acceded to racial minority demands and gave minorities privileged access to jobs and social services. Ed Davis, a new right cult figure and former Chief of the Los Angeles Police Department, put it this way: "I always felt that the government really was out to force me to hire 4-foot-11 transvestite morons."[11]

As with post–New Deal domestic economics and with racial politics, so with environmentalism; it too aged as a social movement and came to be seen as part of the problem. As the decade of environmental crisis unfolded, environmentalism seemed to score many gains. The 1970s saw "an extraordinary range of legislative initiatives, regulatory activities, and court action," including the passage of the 1970 National Environmental Policy Act (establishing the Environmental Protection Agency, or EPA), the 1970 Occupational Safety and Health Administration Act (establishing Occupational Safety and Health Administration, or OSHA), 1970 Clean Air Act, the 1970 Resource Recovery Act, the 1972 Water Pollution Control Act, the 1972 Federal Insecticide, Fungicide, and Rodenticide Act, the 1976 Resource Conservation and Recovery Act, the 1976 Toxic Substances Control Act, and the 1980 Comprehensive Emergency Response, Compensation, and Liability Act (better known as Superfund).[12]

These very gains, however, became the source of new problems; environmental crisis began to turn, paradoxically, into the crisis of environmentalism. As a consequence of gaining power, the environmental movement throughout the 1970s and 1980s became increasingly professionalized and less like a populist movement. Mainstream natural environmental organizations (such as "Big Ten," a group of national environmental organizations consolidated in the early 1980s to oppose Reagan-era changes) identified themselves with the Washington policy process and lost touch with grassroots activism. For its part, grassroots activism, in the form of impatient, direct-action-oriented groups like Earth First! and passionately local antidevelopment, environmental justice, and antitoxics organizations, saw mainstream environmentalism as a problem, not an ally. As the national organizations grew in terms of staff and financial resources, they became absorbed, Robert Gottlieb notes:

> by the operation and maintenance of the policy system itself. A revolving door between staff positions in the mainstream groups and government and industry positions cemented those connections, while the groups' advocacy role, focused especially in terms of crucial lobbying and litigation functions, became more and more centered on keeping the system intact.[13]

At the same time as its successes were distancing the environmental movement from its recent radical past and its grassroots base, these successes meant increased vulnerability to attacks by opponents. Environmentalists' gains could be made to seem to the larger public as problems, not solutions. What once seemed like creative tools to protect the environment—such as the use of the Endangered Species Act to protect whole areas and ecosystems from development—were used to make environmental protection appear wrongheaded or outrageous. When a lowly species like the snail darter threatened to stop a huge dam project, environmental protectionism was presented as extremist; the issue became still more incendiary when the spotted owl threatened both the timber industry and local property owners desirous of turning their land (or, in the case of the timber industry, government land) to some profit. Soon "fried spotted owl" was featured at prologging demonstrations, and bumper stickers asked "Are you an environmentalist or do you work for a living?" as people bought the industry's line that environmental protection (not corporate behavior) was what was threatening their jobs.[14]

As Paul and Anne Ehrlich argue, such reversals revealed a Catch 22 built into environmental politics. Successes risked increasing political resistance more than building a stable, satisfied constituency. Increasing regulation in an already regulated society created sharper resistance. Worse, while early gains in energy efficiency and reduction of toxic emissions were not only easy but also yielded significant results *and* made sense economically (they helped reduce costs), later gains were much more difficult, costly, and small. Once the first round of improvements had been carried out, then, controlling environmental decay in the face of growth meant stepping still more heavily on still more toes. Discursive meddling also quickly became part of the Catch 22; as time passed, people forgot that the conditions they enjoyed were the result of earlier gains won by the environmental movement. People became ripe for disinformation. Critics claimed that environmentalists' warnings had been hysterical; the end of the world didn't come. Worse, thanks to short public memories, the very corporations that had been in fact dragged into the public limelight and forced to reform themselves against their will began to claim that they, not environmental activism, were responsible for the gains.[15] Look, we, the corporations, did this; we're the true environmentalists.

So the stage was set for something to happen—and it did.

Perceived crisis and the aging of older social movements made an opening; a comprehensive and strategically crafted right-wing countermovement rushed in. Its heterogenous coalition sought to unite a wide variety of interest groups and actors broadly across cultural, economic, and environmental issues. It was, of course, a popular movement, a revolution, anything but a horde of special interests pursuing politics as usual. As different voices contributed their words to the rising din, a set of different battlegrounds were laid out: these became the scenes for launching what were widely called the "culture wars," what were occasionally called the "economic wars," and what we will call the "environmental wars." For these three different "wars," the right crafted rhetorical weaponry that was remarkably similar—and it used this fractal self-similarity to help create the impression that it was mounting a unified movement with a coherent social program to renew America, not just advancing a shopping list of different political positions.

In what follows, I consider the rhetoric that accompanied and advanced this deep sea change in public discourse. In Appendix 1—a section I recommend to only the hardiest of readers—I give a brief account of the organizing and institutional activity that lay behind that rhetoric. This chapter concerns what has been said; the appendix concerns the construction of institutional and other mouths with which to say it. I elaborate the rhetoric to identify it for all as discourse that is neither original or truth-seeking, but always in service of one goal: checkmating environmentalism. Sometimes memorable because of its sheer panache, it is always carefully scripted, intentionally partisan rhetoric. It is also virtuosically polyphonic. Though its linguistic range is not perhaps as large as St. Paul's—it doesn't speak simultaneously in the tongues of men and angels—it does encompass a considerable range of voices nonetheless. It reaches across the gulf between the media-savvy, expertise-rich talking head on a highbrow television show to the hectoring vulgarity of Rush Limbaugh–style talk-back radio-show hosts.

Five large-scale rhetorical shapes emerged and were deployed (with little modification) across a full spectrum of high-profile cultural, economic, and environmental issues. For the most part, they emerged in sync with each other, but there was a bit of development over time. None of these rhetorical shapes ought to be surprising in and of itself; they were implementations of tried and true national rhetorical strategies. But they were deployed with noteworthy consistency and success. Succinctly labeled, the five were: 1) *outcasting opponents*; 2) *respinning the past*; 3) *returning to roots*; 4) *hyping a new paradigm*; and 5) *dividing the opposition*. Applied similarly to the cultural, economic, and environmental wars, they helped create what was, with apologies to William Blake, a fearful synergy.

The first three strategies were tightly linked to each other and were devoted to capitalizing on the historical opportunities described above. The right identified their opponents as having run to a variety of excesses, thereby weakening the nation and creating what was, in fact, a national crisis. Accordingly, the right began to nurture a whole ecology of abuse, abuse dedicated to *outcasting its opponents*. This abuse was then tied to the second strategy: *respinning the past*. For, having identified left-liberal social movements as ones that had created the national decline, the right then respun them as betrayers of national traditions, not outgrowths of them. Equally, conservatives respun themselves; conservatives weren't wealthy, narrowly interested defenders of class and race privilege; they were courageous advocates of democracy, freedom, openness, and fairness. They were, in short, the real stewards of the American legacy. Thus, to pick just one example, thanks to the linguistic alchemy of right-wing ideologues, what were formerly seen as "public-interest organizations" were now "special-interest groups," even as new corporate-funded, right-wing ideology factories eluded identification as propaganda machines and called themselves "think tanks," so that their research, publications, and pronouncements would be taken instead as serious research in pursuit of truth.

It almost seemed that the goal of these outcastings and respinnings was to be as dazzlingly contrarian as possible; the goal was not just to revise the old pattern of left-versus-right oppositions, but to reverse them outright. Perhaps there was a pursuit of *sprezzatura* in this enterprise, for it was with contrarian panache that the old social activists were respun as the new tyrants and the old tyrants were respun as the new victims. And the logic took a further, genuinely astonishing step. As the right styled itself as representative of the "real Americans" held hostage by an un-American and tyrannical left, it clamored after victim status, and it did this even as it aggressively sneered at the left for having an obsession with victimology. In this way, society's true victims were no longer the culturally, racially, sexually, and politically different; the helpless, the poor, the exploited; or the defenseless environment and its biota. No, they were, startlingly, the partisans of the right—a group that included the erstwhile oppressors, the white male, the wealthy, and the corporate establishment. Much abused and long-suffering, these new victims had had enough: they were now ready to reclaim their legacy, to reassume their roles as stewards of the American traditions and values the left-liberals had made a hash of. Thus *outcasting opponents* and *respinning the past* became almost seamlessly interwoven with another old trope of fundamentalist nationalism: *returning to roots*. Possible? Plausible? Let's go to the videotape—to a survey of the rhetoric as it was deployed first in the culture wars, then the economic wars, and finally the environmental wars.

To pick just one notorious example from the culture wars, the momentum of the civil rights era was sharply countered. The idea of righting old wrongs in an attempt to make American political and civil ideals work for a racially and culturally diverse nation suddenly changed. Implementing these ideals by restructuring education and culture or, most notoriously, by social reengineering via affirmative action suddenly became the problem, not the possibility. Those who advocated those measures opposed the very ideals they said they stood for—equality of opportunity—and were revealed as un-American, a fifth column within the nation. Worse, they held genuine Americans hostage: whites, not blacks, were now the victims of discriminatory laws.

Outcasting opponents and *respinning the past* thus became powerful forms of rhetoric for conservatives in the social and cultural arenas as the "culture wars" were vigorously launched. These controversies felt important; they were on everybody's lips, even though today, just a few short years later, the great hoopla is hard for all but a minority of veterans to recall, let alone get agitated about. But then there was crisis indeed. In conservative rhetoric, the United States was repeatedly dangerously disunified by multiculturalism; the nation was exposed to the risk of becoming a Third World country, one that was culturally as well as economically backward. Like a Third World country, the United States was supposedly becoming riddled with ethnic conflict fomented ignorantly or intentionally by multiculturalists. Multiculturalists, accordingly, were styled by conservatives uniformly as advocates of racial and ethnic separatism; they were surly, bigoted, aggressive, Afrocentric black nationalists, low-on-the-bell-curve reverse racists who were concertedly dumbing down America.

It didn't matter at all that ethnic separatism and old-fashioned nationalism were notions that most thoughtful/mandarin multiculturalists also opposed; it didn't matter that the very term "multicultural" meant, on its face, an embrace of cultural complexity rather than the simplification of separatist ethnic or racial pride. If abuse worked, go with it. Matters were also not helped when a Japanese prime minister commented about how backward and undereducated people in the United States now were and attributed this to the presence of America's minorities. In 1986, Prime Minister Nakasone Yasuhiro announced that the United States contained "many blacks, Puerto Ricans, and Mexicans, and on the average America's level [of intelligence] is still extremely low"—thereby asserting with blatant clarity pretty much the same thing U.S. conservatives had been saying, sometimes in slightly more coded messages, at home.[16] In the eyes of the rising new global power—as Japan was seen and saw itself, briefly, at that time—the United States was rapidly becoming part of the multicultural Third World. Multiculturalism did not just breed internal division; it was responsible for U.S. slippage not merely from global preeminence but from membership in the First World.

All these fears—coupling devolution at home with loss of geopolitical position abroad—were augmented by the new global awareness prompted by the end of the Cold War. The new global spectre was not the second, "red" world, but a Third World full of Beiruts and Rwandas, a world of blasted infrastructure and ethnic violence. Multiculturalism, conservatives were not shy in implying, represented the royal road to such conditions, and America had started down it. In this spirit, Samuel Huntington raised at least my eyebrows by claiming, in his book *The Clash of Civilizations and the Remaking of World Order*, that multiculturalism's "rejection of the [American] Creed and of Western civilization was the end of the United States of America as we have known it. It also means the end of Western civilization"—sentences that did not lack in apocalyptic fury, even though they came late in the media circus of the culture wars.[17]

Helping to foment this disunity were, of course, the tenured radicals. If ethnic activists were the mob, these folk were Robespierres, totalitarians in radicals' clothes. Figures such as George Will, President Bush *père*, and Richard Bernstein styled multiculturalists (as opposed to foreign powers) America's worst enemies, said they were working to end free enterprise and freedom, and claimed (astonishingly!) that they were comparable to the Spanish Inquisition and the French Reign of Terror.[18] This professoriat conspired to bring the Spanish Inquisition to America in the form of "political correctness"—a phrase that was a creation of some genius, as it gave the flavor of boot-on-the-neck Stalinism to what was, in many cases, less a matter of restrictive ideology than mere possibility-creating decency. Now that the nation's racial and ethnic heterogeneity was showing up in the schools and universities—now that student bodies were becoming more multicultural—people needed to find language and forms of politeness to facilitate the discussion of literary, historical, scholarly texts that not only depicted but frequently also symptomized and even embraced past cruelties. How should one understand Conrad's *Heart of Darkness* in racially sensitive America if one is black—or if one is a white teacher with students of color one cares about? Though there were excesses on the left as well as the right, issues might often boil down to whether an elementary schoolteacher, asking students to come to school in costumes they would have worn at the time of the first Thanksgiving, was observing the best principles of her profession when she told her several black students they had to come as slaves. Respinning soon made pedagogical reforms aimed at solving problems like these turn, with alchemical magic, into tyranny, even as stripping minority and non-Western authors from college courses was seen as liberty.

Reinforcing this attack—and linking bureaucrats on the public payroll, lovers of excessive regulation, to those seeking to consolidate tyranny rather

than promote liberty (like school choice)—was the vigorous critique of cultural illiteracy led from the top by William Bennett, Reagan's secretary of education, and a cadre of scholars publishing on U.S. secondary education. If the
universities had bred the multicultural philosophers, the schools carried out
their mandate to dumb down America, making it culturally illiterate in the
name of diversity.

In this situation, the real Americans—those lining up behind conservative
banners—had become outsiders in their own country. The real Americans
were today the victims—the victims of multiculturalists' cultural disunifica-
tion. Thus respinning the past, the new conservatism appeared as anything
but the old enemy that liberal activists had firmly described and decried—
monocultural vested interests committed to the un-American and unprincipled
values of intolerance, racial and ethnic barriers, and economic inequity. No,
the new conservatism was not the old oppressor of old victims. It emerged
as: 1) the oppressed, not the oppressor, a new coalition of abused but noble
victims, true Americans held in bondage; and 2) the defender, not transgres-
sor, of American values, *the* contemporary representative of equity of access,
choice, and a genuinely common culture. Rewriting history was thus part of
the process. FDR's legacy had aged and needed to be undone, and even so apparently grotesque a villain as Joseph McCarthy was scrubbed up and repositioned by some as an unfairly demonized crusader against what was, after all,
a real communist infiltration. While many of these outcastings and respinnings would have seemed unthinkable as part of mainstream discourse just
ten years previously, they became not just imaginable but part of legitimate
discourse. The strategy of going with the left-liberal flow and then turning it
against itself—accepting and then respinning left-wing techniques and even
values, mounting a countermovement to defeat a movement—proved an extremely potent form of political *aikido.*

The conservative embrace of victimology and virtue and its respinning
of the past were in fact so potent that not only whites were attracted to its banner. As Angela Dillard, the chronicler of "multicultural conservatism" has argued, "multicultural conservatives share in the narrative deployed by so many
conservatives in the past, which depicts them as marginalized and persecuted
by a liberal cultural, political, and media elite."[19] Multicultural conservatives
also complained "of having been silenced by a stringent orthodoxy"—the
"powerful civil rights establishment that has determined who is allowed to
speak in the name of African-Americans, Latinos, Asian-Americans, women,
and homosexuals, as well as how they are permitted to do so."[20] The existence

of this group then helped nonmulticultural conservatives "to lay claim to the goals of the civil-rights movement," something Dillard rightly labeled "a tricky bit of revisionism."[21]

The culture wars got, perhaps, the most media attention; much more fundamental, however, were the economic wars. Again, the New Deal legacy was identified as the problem, not the solution, and as something that repressed the American spirit of entrepreneurialism, holding it hostage to bureaucracy, regulations, and a vast (and growing) social welfare constituency. Perhaps the culture wars were emphasized to draw attention away from this core issue, one that, in many ways, was the hardest of all to sell. For, as economic revolution first emerged with Reagan, "greed is good," privatization of public services, union-busting, and unregulated capitalism without safety nets became watchwords of the hour. These positions required perhaps more legerdemain to restyle than any taken in the heat of the culture wars—though, one would have thought that bullying minorities in the name of a white majority restyled as victims was a pretty far reach. But the attempt was made and even carried through, so that even when "greed" was clearly the greed of the successful few, that did not matter: their gains would "trickle down" into the realm of the rest of us. The very name of the theory, "trickle-down economics," suggested it had a less-than-perfect ideological fit with democratic values. Joseph Lieberman, during his acceptance speech at the 2000 Democratic convention, put it in more realistic terms: it was the theory that to feed the birds you ought to feed the horse more oats. Still, it flew for a while—even as Republican opponents of Reagan (such as George Bush) and Reagan's own appointees (such as David Stockman) debunked it.

Outcasting and respinning liberalism were thus particularly crucial to the economic wars. Outcasting a variety of people on the left as antidemocratic— as stiflers of individual enterprise—and celebrating entrepreneurialism as the essential expression of democratic virtue was the message powerfully hammered home. Thus unions were attacked, the tyranny of regulation-happy bureaucrats and big government decried, even middle management became suddenly fat, lazy, and uncompetitive, and entitlement to lifetime employment became (astonishingly) an aberration, oppressive to the honest American entrepreneurial spirit and an outrage to all truly free people. Public employees were depicted in still more demonic terms, for they lazily swilled at the trough that honest taxpayers had to fill, a sad echo in the United States of Third World conditions, where public employment bought constituencies and civil peace at the price of national competitiveness. Worst still, at the bottom, a vast army of entitled, nonworking welfare recipients—people who were often brazen enough to be multicultural—held hostage those who wished to exercise their entrepreneurial freedoms by retaining their own earned income.

Many of the interests challenged by such an assault—unions, vulnerable white-collar workers, public employees, and even the antipoverty establishment—were once powerful, but the overarching atmosphere of crisis, the outcasting of them as enemies, and the respinning of conservative whites as victims succeeded in changing national dialogue and policy. The New Deal, the civil rights legacy of communitarianism, and the War on Poverty were all transformed into the ethos of a horde of bureaucrats and welfare cheats. Much was made of tax-cutting and deregulation; and much was made of outsiders breaking entrepreneurially into the economy, making it big, and creating a boom that buoyed up the whole economy. Though Michael Milken, the outsider junk-bond financier, became somewhat tarnished, endless stories were spun about what came out of certain garages in California and from people called, simply, Bill. In this way the economy was to be handed back to its proper stewards, democratic free-market entrepreneurs.

In the area of environmental politics we find something remarkably similar. The environmental wars had the same shape as the culture and economic wars. Those who were formerly seen as defending the environment were vigorously outcasted; those who were formerly seen as trashing it were turned into victims; and the spokespeople of these new victims were (quite astonishingly) turned, at least in their own rhetoric, into the true stewards of the nation's environment.

There have been few areas in which right-wing abuse was so fecund as with antienvironmentalism. How did the right revile environmentalists? Let us count the ways. They were first and foremost responsible for the economic crises of the 1970s and 1980s in America; in its magazine, *Policy Review*, the Heritage Foundation, a leading conservative think tank, called the environmental movement "the greatest single threat to the American economy."[22] Further, the Heritage Foundation estimated that "the cost of federal regulations to the economy . . . [has been] $500 billion a year, or $5,000 per household"; Newt Gingrich commented that U.S. environmental policies over the past two decades were "absurdly expensive" and that the U.S. EPA "may well be the biggest job-killing agency in the inner city in America today."[23] In the same vein, in 1992 President Bush *père* denounced "environmental extremists" for locking up national resources.[24] Ignored were all other factors, from the rise of competition from the Pacific Rim and the aging of American in-

dustry to financial meltdowns such as the savings and loan scandal, Reagan-
era government overspending, and Bush-era inaction in the face of recession.
Environmentalists were *the* problem.

But environmentalists weren't just the problem; they were the enemy.
Thus James Watt, Ronald Reagan's unfortunate choice for secretary of the interior, asked, after his first run-in with the "militantly moderate conservation-
ists" (Daniel Helvarg's characterization) of the National Wildlife Foundation,
if the "real nature of the extreme environmentalists" wasn't "to weaken America." As sinister as the multicultural Robespierres, environmentalists, in Watt's
dim perception of them, actively sought the destruction of the United States.
This characterization came before Watt was ousted from office for bragging
that a special commission convened to review his policies about coal sales was
diverse, because "we have every kind of mix you can have. I have a black, I
have a woman, two Jews and a cripple."[25] While Watt sneered at diversity politics as politically correct, others as quickly characterized environmentalism
as yet another manifestation of that same political correctness. Like feminism
and multiculturalism, environmentalism was inherently totalitarian, an enemy
to America's tradition of freedom. If feminism and multiculturalism tyran-
nized good Americans with charges of racism and chauvinism, environmentalism forced the still crazier charge of "speciesism" down those same good
peoples' throats.

In the same vein, Rush Limbaugh egregiously instructed his listeners that
"environmentalists fall into two categories, Socialists and enviro-religious fanatics. . . . With the collapse of Marxism, environmentalism has become the
new refuge of socialist thinking. . . . What better way to control someone's
property than to subordinate one's private property rights to environmental
concerns."[26] Environmentalists were, at the same time, medieval heretics and
steely-edged socialists lusting after people's private property; their commitments, apparently, really had nothing to do with the environment.

That environmentalists were Marxists, socialists, and even Stalinists was
repeated *ad nauseam.* It became, however, a little fuzzy in yet further dia-
tribes. These linked environmentalism to fascist authoritarianism. This mode
of discourse was widespread on the populist-redneck low end; it surfaced as
well on the academic left, which explored the florescence of the Green movement under the Third Reich. Few noted the dissonance involved in being
Marxist and fascist—and also a religious fanatic—at the same time.

But if the question of whether environmentalism was Stalinist or fascist
went unresolved, there was no debate about environmentalism as a form of

religious fanaticism. It all too clearly was. "Enviroreligious" extremism was forcefully denounced by Chuck Cushman of the National Inholders Association: "the preservationists have become like a new religion, a new paganism that worships trees and sacrifices people"—a strain of attack rhetoric that, according to Daniel Helvarg, Ron Arnold, founder of the antienvironmental organization Wise Use, traces back to John McPhee's *Encounters with the Archdruid*. McPhee quotes what Charles Fraser, the Hilton Head developer, said about environmentalism: "Ancient Druids used to sacrifice human beings under oak trees. Modern druids worship trees and sacrifice human beings to those trees."[27] But property rights activists and prodevelopment forces weren't the only people to speak like this; advancing the same sort of argument were conservative Christians, who became quite agitated at proenvironment education materials as "paganistic, satanistic, anti-Christian and [equally horrible to contemplate] anti-business." As Sharon Beder adds, they claimed that "the growing 'environmental education movement' is a recruitment drive intended to conscript young students into a pagan children's campaign."[28]

If this sounds fairly low-end, there were also a variety of more scholarly-sounding and thus high-end analyses of environmental extremism. Richard Chase, in a tome entitled *In a Dark Wood: The Fight over Forests and the Rising Tyranny of Ecology*, argued that environmentalists "are driven to recover the Garden of Eden" and that the environmental movement is (simultaneously) a continuation of Puritan extremism, for: "the Calvinist world of depraved humanity is now rediscovered as an environmental vision of human beings as the cancer of the earth, sinners raping the land and environment, who will pave the way for their own destruction."[29] Environmental extremists—committed communists, satanists, pagans, fascists, Stalinists, multiculturalists, and totalitarians—were also, the right maintained, extreme Protestants. Better, they were extreme Protestants twice over. Gloomy, moralistic, people-hating Calvinists, they were also apocalyptics, "doomsters" and "apocalypse-abusers." Clearly, the environmental pagan, *bête noire* of the conservative Christian, and the doomsaying Puritan, figure of ridicule (and if empowered) menace to the more secular and genteel, were villains that didn't really fit together easily. But if that were true, so much the better. Conservative surliness was large; it contained multitudes.

There was also something analogous but, again, fundamentally different and even contradictory offered for those who were interested not in theology but in culture. Charles Rubin, author of *The Green Crusade: Rethinking the Roots of Environmentalism*, recalled that he was once "green in judgment and cold in blood" (which means that, poor put-upon naïf that he was, he had once been an environmentalist) and admitted that "if at times my aspersions are caustic, it is because I have had to battle against these seductive ideas myself." He decried environmentalism for its "tendencies toward utopianism and totalitarianism," and because it was "heir to the antislavery and temperance movements and thus a part of the ongoing saga of evangelical reform that has characterized American history" (a tradition Rubin saw as running to excess).[30] Martin Lewis, author of *Green Delusions: An Environmentalist Critique of Radical Environmentalism*, similarly sniped at environmentalism's commitment to Arcadianism and Romanticism—to the way that, "especially since Rousseau, disaffected intellectuals have looked longingly to Arcadia as a symbol of the countryside left behind."[31]

Of course, environmental activists were also less elegantly labeled psychological and social misfits—woolly-headed, sentimentalist, nostalgic purists, be they traditional tree-huggers or antitraditional, countercultural "ecofreaks."[32] Worse, they were neo-Luddites and neoprimitives, sometimes out of principle, sometimes out of ingrained stupidity. Thus, as the science historian Robert Proctor reports, a director of New Jersey's Department of Agriculture called *Silent Spring*: "typical of that 'vociferous, misinformed group of nature-balancing, organic-gardening, bird-loving unreasonable citizenry that has not been convinced of the important place of agricultural chemicals in our economy.'"[33] These sentiments were then updated for a more stylishly contemporary, post-Carson doomsters by the conservative polemicist Edith Efron when she called environmentalists "chic-apocalyptic neoprimitives."[34] More sententiously, Berkeley professor of political science Aaron Wildavsky held that they suffered from an "Armageddon complex."[35] If that were not enough, they were also deluded purists, eager to mothball reality, pathologically in flight from recognizing that not just society but nature itself was not as pristine as they neurotically maintained. For, after all, as no less a figure than Reagan put it, trees polluted. In Reagan's mouth, this sentiment was perhaps the outrageous gaffe many people thought it was.[36] For others, however, it became an erudite antienvironmental cryptocommentary. For the oxygen trees produced was "pure" and "pristine" only according to your perspective; after all, that same oxygen had been a deadly pollutant to the earth's previous population of anaerobic bacteria. Nature was deadly and evolution was a competitive struggle; for the very trees that were to weak-minded environmentalists an instance of the pure and pristine were in fact the source of horrible impurity, of deadly toxic poison, to an earlier generation of oxygen-sensitive bacteria (bacteria with which conservatives, in a stunning instance of right-wing relativism, thereby rhetorically identified themselves). Antienvironmental discourse that sought to exculpate industry by labeling nature as the biosphere's chief polluter became, as Proctor painstakingly shows, a central plank of conservative antienvironmental science and polemics, particularly in the area of public-health regulation.[37]

In yet another remarkable contradiction, at the same time that environmentalists were so pathologically idealist, they were also smooth, worldly, fat-cat, elitist hedonists, pursuing their own delicate pleasures at the expense of the masses of real people. Totally unlike the populist Republicans, they were "elitist," "overwhelmingly white," "overeducated," and "urban" fat cats—or, to use a somewhat more specialized right-wing term of art, "pointy-heads" who never worked for a living—who didn't know anything about real work, real people, or real nature. As Bill and Barbara Grannell expressed it, environmentalists were "the elitists at the top driving Mercedes and BMWs and telling average Americans what to do."[38] Marvelously, though, environmentalists also managed at the same time to be middle-class—they were blindly selfish NIMBYs, a novel sociological category given to the world, suspiciously, not by a sociologist but by an antienvironmental public relations person. These not-in-my-backyard folks were not, of course, to be confused with their somewhat more extremist middle-class neighbors, the BANANAs (build absolutely nothing anywhere near anything), who supposedly took the same attitudes to an even more ludicrous extreme.

This does no more than sample the robust and outrageously internally contradictory ecosystem of outcasting that blossomed during the 1980s and 1990s. Why was it so large? Some, less committed to objectivity than I, might suggest that it was large simply because too many nasty, sneaky, and opportunistic people had too many personal axes to grind and too much think-tank and corporate grant money in their pockets. I think rather that the extreme sociodiversity of this ecosystem perfectly mirrored the heterogeneity of the conservative movement, the fact that it was a pastiche of actually quite dissonant interests, actors, and audiences. A flexible and varied—and, as long as nobody noticed, internally contradictory—stream of abuse helped unify diverse groups on the right. Further, the astonishing vehemence of that abuse has suggested to a number of different commentators that environmentalists were specifically chosen by conservative strategists to replace the "reds" as the enemy they could unite in abusing. Sadly deprived of this old target with the fall of communism and the end of the "evil empire," the right chose environmentalism to fill the gap.

   With such outcasting, then, environmentalists lost, in a remarkably short time, much of their former clout as celebrants of wilderness, openness, freedom, democracy, consciousness expansion, American nature, and joy in life. Abused as communists, fascists, pagans, Stalinists, Arcadians, utopians, Puritans, evangelicals, doomsters, pathological idealists, ecofreaks, selfish and manipulative elitists, and selfish and unintelligent middle-class home owners, they lost their status as public-spirited prophets of imminent dangers to a fundamental legacy for all Americans. Elizabeth Whelan, cofounder of the American Council on Science and Health, went so far as to dub environmentalists "toxic terrorists," for they were people who terrorized good Americans with their inflated stories of toxins and carcinogens and, worse, actually put the nation at risk. They created an atmosphere of doom, led Americans to focus on the wrong problems, and even (by, for example, banning chemical fertilizers and pesticides, necessary to keep food production up) sought to bring on economic and social crisis.[39]

   The "real" Americans then became their victims. Thus, Ron Arnold claimed: "Things are so regulated and restricted that people are sensing themselves as an oppressed class, and that's how you get revolutions. . . . Try telling a logger who's lost his job and house and whose neighbor is molesting his daughter because he has nothing else to do that he should remain nonviolent."[40] But then, in a still more dazzling bit of respinning, these victims became the actual environmentalists: "the Wise Use Movement," Sharon Beder reported, argued "that the true environmentalists are those who work in the environment rather than those environmentalists whom they characterize as living in the cities, divorced from nature's realities."[41]

   In their preface to *The Wise Use Agenda*, Alan Gottlieb and Ron Arnold greatly expanded this list of environmental stewards:

> They are the true guardians of the environment, the farmers and ranchers who have been stewards of the land for generations, the miners and loggers and oil drillers who have built our civilisation by working in the environment every day, the property owners and technicians and professionals who provide all the material basis of our existence.[42]

This was a stunning claim indeed—a set of categories into which literally anyone, including the hardworking folk who brought us Love Canal, could locate themselves. And corporations were quick to style themselves as environmental stewards for the benefit of an audience of consumers and voters. DuPont's CEO Ed Wollard coined the term "corporate environmentalism" in a 1989 speech shortly after the *Exxon Valdez* disaster. In it, he claimed "environmental groups can't solve any of these problems. Governments can't do it. Corporations have to do it."[43] Unfortunately, corporate green performance often meant not stewardship, but "greenwashing"—pasting a green image onto environmentally destructive production and consumer products.[44] But the broadest claims went still further: the ultimate environmental steward, for conservatives from Arnold and Gottlieb to Julian Simon, was free-market capitalism itself, the system that sustained the corporations. Thus the Ehrlichs, in their review of antienvironmentalist literature, singled out the astonishing claim that "unregulated capitalism is good for the environment" as one of its most insistently repeated themes.[45]

In the culture, economic, and environmental wars, then, groups were outcasted and the past was respun in markedly similar fashions. Older social movements were turned into un-American hostage holders, and "real Americans" were turned into victims. Then, as shown above, the right capped the argument by *returning to roots*—by restoring those real Americans and their traditions to their place of honor as true stewards of the U.S. environment. The image of Reagan, the cowboy Westerner, the nice guy, easy-going, yet (when necessary, as it was with unions, minorities, communists, and environmentalists) tough as nails, was crucial here; the cult of his public image did an enormous amount to make Americans feel an old health had been restored to the national community.

These three strategies play, of course, to nationalist feelings everywhere, but in the United States they appeal specifically to a couple of the nation's oldest myths/ideologies, ones that American Studies scholars love to point to. The first goes as follows: ever since the second-generation blues of the Puritan—in which the second generation felt it lacked the immediacy of the experience of grace which had inspired the first—a national taste was created for listening to warnings (first called jeremiads) that showed people how they had departed from their original high ideals and that asserted they were being punished for these defections. In some sense, when this structure of rhetoric and feeling resurfaces, the more the punishment the better, because that alone shows that Americans are still the elect nation and reminds them that their real spirit has stayed alive nonetheless under the ashes, ready to ignite again at the proper rededicating call. The second mythic structure is similar: ever since the Puritans' Indian wars, Americans have been horrified and fascinated by stories of people taken into captivity; the original stories were about people carried off into Indian (not Native American) captivity, suffering horribly from mistreatment by the "savages," and then being ransomed back or escaping. These, next to the Bible, were the Puritans' best sellers. Fear at and fascination with the idea that the nation was being held captive by demonized "others" started here, but, long before the 1980s, the host of "others" included the people's own government. Particularly in its populist rhetoric, the conservative revolution worked with the emotional resonances of this tradition. Thus the nation had disastrously departed from its mission, and the real Americans had fallen into bondage to liberalism, big government, environmentalists, and so on; in making modern jeremiads and captivity narratives, the right played upon a collection of old, powerful national emotions.

A fourth line of conservative rhetoric added a crucial further component; I call it *hyping a new paradigm*. A mere return to roots would leave out another important part of American mythology: America as the city on the hill, a light to all nations, the country of the future, the place where the new universal revelation will be/is even now being brought among mankind. That future is always in the process of being born when this structure of feeling is evoked; America is always young. What I shall call "new paradigm" rhetoric emerged in the last decades of the second millennium as the nation's most recent version of this old strain of feeling; it supplied what was necessary to fill this gap.

Perhaps one of the more outrageous respinnings of the Reagan years was the sense that, under the oldest president in history, the nation was young again; but this vein of conservative ideology—a return to roots masked as rejuvenation—was only that, and not an actual new paradigm. With Reagan, the closest thing to a "new paradigm" in policy was deregulation in the name of trickle-down economics, but this "paradigm" didn't last. Condemned by George Bush as "voodoo economics," it didn't outlive the Clinton's publicizing and promotion of a far more fundamental shift—the shift from national to global ways of thought and action. This shift *was* a new paradigm for a new era, and focusing on it allowed Clinton to reappropriate some energy from the right and to mount a counter-countermovement of his own against the conservative countermovement. Just how he did this is the subject of the next chapter; here it is necessary only to note that, when Clinton celebrated globalism, he helped make enthusiasm for the new crucial to mainstream U.S. political discourse.

But neoconservative rhetoric had by then also entered the new-paradigm field vigorously, moving beyond "trickle-down" to more comprehensive celebrations of the emerging "new economy"; this celebration became at last official in the Republican "Contract with America" of 1994 and Newt Gingrich's embrace of the Tofflers, the futurist authors of *Future Shock* and *The Third Wave*. This version of "new-paradigmism" had its roots in corporate-led enthusiasms about a new set of industries in which the United States felt it could be competitive and whose successes could assuage the public sense of shame felt during the 1970s. The failures of that time were made to seem painfully clear: the Fordist-era, mass-manufacture mentality (and the institutional structures that went with it) were all painfully outdated and old-think; indeed, the U.S. automobile industry itself (the place where it all started) had been producing not world-class but tacky goods. The new industries, on the other hand—postmanufacturing, post–smokestack industries, including the genetic engineering industry, the computer industry, and the postmodern global mass media—increasingly expressed themselves in futurist, new-paradigm rhetoric.

As corporate futurism became a virtual cottage industry, voices on the right increasingly invoked the future to prove that the New Deal was out. The New Deal had helped turn industrial modernization from a dynamic movement into a stagnant, overstructured, top-down, union-fettered, employee-entitled, smokestack-era, heavy-industrial mass-standard business culture—one that had adapted to the similarly overstructured government bureaucracies that fettered and regulated it. What people were witnessing instead in the new economy was the rebirth of American entrepreneurialism in a glitzy, new, privatized, downsized, spun-off, outsourced (without benefits), unregulated, weblike, boot-strapped, information-economy, postmanufacturing form. And when Communism fell and the whole world seemed to become capitalist, the new economy's national flood became a global, oceanic tidal wave bringing free-market fundamentalism to the entire world and thus inaugurating not just a national but a global renaissance. In conservative rhetoric, then, free-market economics became equated with the new global future rather than styled as a legacy from the past to be reclaimed.

Conservative/right-wing new-paradigm rhetoric came to support libertarian free-market fundamentalist positions, even though this very development helped disrupt some of the unity of the older conservative agenda. The battle for a common culture, for example, began to get less important; the idea of a "common culture"—a return to roots—was hard to style as a new paradigm, as opposed to moralizing old mossbackism. Also, new economic possibilities in the United States thrived not on national standardization, but on niche marketing, taste culture, and commodification of new waves of arresting difference, in-

cluding cultural difference, and the globalization of consumption and production increasingly recognized the polyculturality of the world's new consumers
and producers.

But if new-paradigm rhetoric did not prove kind to the cultural agenda of
conservatives, it was enormously useful to right-wing antienvironmentalism.
Global free-market fundamentalism authorized tearing down environmental
regulations almost as much as older appeals to national integrity seemed to
support creating them. Further, strange new antienvironmental "environmental" paradigms began to spring up in abundance. Thus Julian Simon revealed, among other things, that the earth's resources were infinite and that
the population explosion was no problem because it enhanced human creativity.[46] Others celebrated the capacity of new technologies to restructure
or (in some fantasies) virtually replace nature. In the more mandarin realm of
academic theory, new-paradigmism proclaimed that nature was "dead" or
"over" or "socially constructed" and was thus no longer an "other" to man. For
a longer look at how antienvironmental new-paradigm rhetoric flowered during the 1980s and 1990s, I refer readers to Chapter 7; the attitudes described
there are still very much in play.

The last, but not the least, component of conservative rhetoric was an attempt
to *divide the opposition* strategically to disunify its opponents. Once it had
labeled the positions and players of the old social movements as extremists,
the right proceeded to single out their most vulnerable and/or controversial
elements and make those small, loud, and often colorfully extravagant parts
stand metonymically for environmentalism as a whole. Doing this gave specific bite to outcasting rhetoric; further, it helped divide the opposition by setting more radical-intransigent and moderate-adaptive elements within it at
each other's throats.

This tactic had worked with multiculturalism, a movement that contained, in fact, a number of different perspectives ready to argue with each
other. Even though, as noted above, multiculturalism did not embrace but was
for the most part critical of racial separatism, all multiculturalists become,
in conservative rhetoric, separatist racial extremists, bigoted themselves.
They were advocates, therefore, of an America balkanized into separate
racial/ethnic groups, each inflated with an aggressive racial/ethnic pride
pumped into them by folk represented as crude ideologues with little
knowledge and less respect for actual history. To put it as the academy
might, such leaders espoused cultural essentialism, a disreputable view-

point; to put it in more mass-public terms, people like these were racist themselves—in fact, they were the real racists, conveniently replacing the right-wing white conservatives who traditionally occupied that role. This virtuosic respinning allowed right-wingers to assume the mantle of equity and antiracism even as they subtly propagated the old racial stereotypes of blacks as ignorant and violent. Louis Farrakhan seemed to fit that role admirably, as did, to a degree, Al Sharpton; behind the media treatments of both lurked the spectre of Willie Horton, of the notorious ad campaign crafted in support of the "kinder and gentler" president, George H. W. Bush. This respinning did not just outcast multiculturalism and promote conservativism; it also served to help keep already seriously disunified multiculturalists arguing with each other. It helped to widen the rift between those who sought to make multiculturalism a mainstream position and those who sought to make it the basis for more radical change.

Environmentalists, also a disunified and internally dissonant group, were treated in the same fashion. In particular, the right sought to style all environmentalists as nature fundamentalists—as people who sought the liberation from human oppression of an essentialized vision of nature. In fact, there were environmental groups that, thanks to their commitment to direct action, did stand in something of the same relationship to moderate environmentalism as Malcolm X stood to Martin Luther King. These arguably included Earth First!, Greenpeace, and the Sea Shepherd Society. But they were fundamentalists with differences the right ignored. Inspired by Edward Abbey, who coined the term "monkeywrenching"—and who famously remarked that he'd rather kill a man than a snake—they embodied a provocative humor that descended from the romantic urge to *épater les bourgeois* and the earthy, outrageous rhetoric and gestures of the Beat movement and the 1960s counterculture; they also incorporated something of the legacy of the peace movement, targeting things, not people. Thus, as Roderick Nash reports in *The Rights of Nature*, early eco-activists included the Chicago "Fox," who "plugged factory smokestacks and, on one occasion, diverted liquid toxic waste from a U.S. Steel plant to a location inside the chief executive's private office"; the "Billboard Bandits," who, like the heroes in Abbey's novel, *The Monkey Wrench Gang*, chainsawed billboards; and the "Bolt Weevils," who "dismantled electrical powerlines and blocked survey and construction crews."[47]

The right focused particularly on Earth First!—aided no doubt by assertions that an incident of tree-spiking in 1987 led to injury to a sawmill worker. They characterized it as a terrorist group and helped influence many, including the FBI, to believe that ecoterrorism was a significant new internal danger threatening the United States. In the process, the provocative humor that was also Abbey's legacy was overlooked by folk not known for much love of the gentle virtue; and outrages to environmental activists somehow didn't get quite the play that demonstrations by those activists did. (Thus few on the right objected when, in 1983, "a bulldozer operator, screaming 'I'm going to kill you!' literally buried the blockaders of a lumber road in a pile of dirt" and Earth First! leader Dave Foreman was "dragged a hundred yards behind a truck and suffered permanent knee damage.")[48] Equally, the emphasis on nonviolence and a commitment to target property, not people, on the part of the great majority of eco-activists went utterly unnoticed in the scrutiny of the right, which wished only to find domestic equivalents to Abu Nidal.

In his book, *The War against the Greens*, Daniel Helvarg argues that conservatives were so successful in persuading the FBI and local law enforcement that environmentalists represented a significant terrorist threat that crimes against environmentalists were ignored, while investigations of environmentalists as terrorists received high priority. Thus, for example, Helvarg argues that Judi Bari, injured when a pipe bomb exploded in her car, was unfairly pursued as a terrorist, not a victim.[49] Excesses like these might seem to have been rendered archaic today, thanks to the massive destruction of life as well as property when members of the al Qaeda network brought down the World Trade Towers and the small death toll, but large impact, of the subsequent anthrax attacks. But conservative attempts to equate environmental direct action with this sort of terrorism and to divide the environmental movement against itself continue. In the wake of the destruction of the World Trade Center, Senator Don Young (R-Alaska) said there was a "strong possibility" that ecoterrorists were responsible. Shortly thereafter, Scott McInnis (R-Colorado) tried to use these suspicions to widen an already existing split between moderate and grassroots/ radical environmentalism. McInnis wrote to the Sierra Club, Greenpeace, the League of Conservation Voters, the World Wildlife Fund, the National Wildlife Federation, Earthjustice Defense, and the National Resources Defense Council, giving them the deadline of December 1 to publicly "disavow eco-terrorism." Though McInnis was correct that organizations such as the Earth Liberation Front and the Animal Liberation Front had taken credit for damage to property after September 11, his letter to these eminently respectable environmental organizations was disingenuous. Neither he nor anyone else had thought to send such a letter to mainstream conservative organizations after the Oklahoma City bombing—or suggested doing so after the actual anthrax attacks that targeted

Democratic senators and media representatives and the copycat ones that targeted abortion clinics.[50]

But stigmatizing environmentalism as terrorists wasn't the only way conservatives sought to divide the environmental movement. For if the right
labeled some environmentalists as terrorist shock troops, it styled others as
their mullahs. Along with targeting direct activists such as Earth First!, the
right went after a group of philosophers as well—ecocentrics generally and,
more specifically, Deep Ecologists. Deep Ecology emphasized what the Nor-
wiegan philosopher, Arne Naess, who coined the movement's name, called
"ecological egalitarianism" or, as others specified it, "biocentrism" or "ecocentrism." Its central precept, Roderick Nash argues, "was the right of every form
of life to function normally in the ecosystem or, in Naess' words, 'the equal
right to live and blossom.'"[51] The right seized on views like these to characterize Deep Ecology as radical, an antihuman doctrine elaborated by dangerous
misanthropes, people who would celebrate the elimination of the human race
by the wounded earth (as an infected body cures itself of a dangerous virus)
and who define "human beings as an alien presence on the earth."[52] The latter
comments come from Al Gore, in what appears to me one of the few intem-
perate moments in *Earth in the Balance*, a book remarkable for its clear and
substantial outline of environmental crisis. The dismissal testifies, I believe, to
the effect of the rhetoric of the right. True, a few, such as Christopher Manes,
have notoriously called for elimination of humans to restore balance to a
human-dominated earth, but these were fringe statements as far as most Deep
Ecologists were concerned. By making the self-caricature stand for the movement, the right mightily assisted in the metamorphosis of a small cadre of
thoughtful philosophers committed to social change into a sinister force capable of toppling the state.

It should be no surprise, then, to find ecocentric misanthropes emerging as
stock villains in pop fiction. No less notable a writer than Tom Clancy makes
them the villains of his novel *Rainbow Six*—John Brightling, the billionaire
head of a bioengineering firm, and Carol Brightling, his ex-wife but really his
partner in a plot to decimate the earth's population with an engineered virus
named Shiva. Closet ecocentrics, they seek to "save the [natural] world" by getting rid of humans.[53]

In the novel's climactic exchange, Clancy writes an example of finely
honed philosophic repartee if there ever was one. The Brightlings are cor-
nered at last in a hideout in the rain forest by John Clark and his sidekick,
Domingo Chavez (a nice multicultural touch that), who ask them why they

were willing to slaughter their fellow humans. "To save the world!" Carol Brightling, more than a bit of a bitch (as independent women, as opposed to good wives, always are in Clancy), snaps back. "Okay," Clark responds, "let me get this right. You were willing to kill nearly every person on earth, to use germ warfare to do it, so that you could hug some trees?" "So that we could save the world!" John Brightling repeats for them all.

Not only does Clancy write dialogue much more awful than usual here, but he sacrifices his trademark skill at thrilling climaxes in which a stunning display of high-tech weaponry and expertise yields emotional catharsis in too-long-postponed righteous violence. For the villains in *Rainbow Six* are finally ludicrous. Rather than being bloodily exterminated, they are stripped naked in the jungle and told, with a nice imitation of Rush Limbaugh, "Okay, here's the score. You want to live in harmony with nature, then go do it. If you can't hack it, the nearest city is Manaus, about ninety-eight miles that way."[54] As urban elitists totally unfamiliar with real nature (which is, of course, as Clancy and his readers know, red in tooth and claw) at the same time as they are antilife eco-centrics, they won't, of course, last even a night. This isn't Clancy's finest hour as a writer but it is indicative of how large he thinks his audience of antienvironmental yahoos is.

Seeking to divide the environmental movement by caricaturing it as extremist and then making the caricature stand for the whole movement isolates the radical while setting moderates running for new sorts of philosophic cover. Thus perhaps Gore attempted to distinguish himself as a centrist from *those people*. But targeting Deep Ecology and Earth First! must be seen in a still larger context: it has been part of an attempt to discredit environmentalism by rebuking the entire wilderness tradition itself, particularly its preservationist (as opposed to conservationist) strain. This rhetoric portrayed wilderness activism as the core ideology for all environmentalism. Here, environmentalism was depicted not just as extremist but also as stupidly archaic; and in reducing environmentalism to wilderness activism, this rhetoric strategically ignored many of the movement's key components, ones already becoming important in the 1960s, such as engagement with toxics, pollution, food safety, and urban issues, and calls for both moderate and radical social change.

To be sure, U.S. environmentalism was vulnerable to such a reduction. Until recently, wilderness preservationism and conservationism were seen as the important sources of modern American environmentalism; public health, workplace safety, food safety, urban sanitation, and social reform were, by contrast, categorized as separate social, not environmental, issues. This emphasis on wilderness conservation and preservation was distinctively Euro-American; in fact, it came under fire from Third World environmentalists.[55] Though the U.S. movement in the 1960s and 1970s was much more complex, incorporating both many new and previously separately categorized issues, these changes did not prevent "nature" and "wilderness" even then from retaining their dominance in a number of ways. They continued to function as environmentalism's chief source of ethical norms, its primary source of symbolism, its guide to technological reform, and its measure of what needed protection. They continued to be the banner behind which a growing number of other issues marched—a status they have in many ways lost today. But changing this from a problem within environmentalism—a problem that could eventually lead to the creation of a more robust, diversified, and self-reflexive movement—to a problem *for* environmentalism was the work of the antienvironmental right, which sought, by scathingly satirizing the wilderness tradition, to drive a divisive wedge deeply into the environmental movement.

Caricaturing wilderness preservationism, then, quickly became a fruitful source of antienvironmental rhetoric, even as it was a means of driving wedges between environmentalists. Smearing the wilderness lover as a white, elite, urban, antihuman sentimentalist helped keep tensions between environmentalism and labor warm, slowing down recognition by both of common ground in workplace safety issues and anticorporate activism. Thus for working men, "the slogan 'No work, no food—Eat an environmentalist,' first heard in steel-producing communities during the 1973–75 recession and later in timber-producing regions, symbolized the potential fissures between environmental and worker constituencies."[56] Equally, environmental-justice and antitoxics activists emerged with the same mind-set, reacting against wilderness-based environmentalism with aversion:

> "Calling our movement an environmental movement," Lois Gibbs declares, "would inhibit our organizing and undercut our claim that we are protecting people, not birds and bees." Similarly, Richard Moore of the Southwest Organizing Project and Tony Mazzochi of the Oil, Atomic, and Chemical Workers Union, among others, have argued that people of color and workers are turned off by the environmentalist label, suggesting the term conjures up associations with middle-class and upper-class Anglo yuppie types seen as consumers of Nature or policy technicians.[57]

Today, both divides are rapidly being bridged; ecojustice is an increasingly important part of environmentalism's agenda in many areas, and labor and Greens have marched side by side in antiglobalization demonstrations.

If activists sometimes bought into right-wing caricatures of wilderness preservationism, so did academics. On this level too, such rhetoric helped widen rifts between potential allies. Probably the most celebrated recent instance of this came when the environmental historian, William Cronon, published an anthology called *Uncommon Ground* and initiated a debate about wilderness that has generated much subsequent scholarly controversy. The anthology's general drift, and particularly Cronon's essay for it, "The Trouble with Wilderness," sought overtly to rethink environmentalism to save it. Unfortunately, the book and Cronon's essay did, rhetorically, something very different.

In seeing the wilderness tradition as a social construction—a creation of society, not a fact of nature—and then characterizing that construction as serving extremely unattractive ends, Cronon's essay discredited and dismissed the wilderness tradition as white-racist, androcentrist, and elitist. Though Cronon's first move—seeing social construction where others had previously asserted facts of nature—was important and unexceptionable, his second move was unfortunate. As was the case with so much that skeptical academic theory touched, what was socially constructed was repudiated, not reimagined.

Cronon thus dismissed wilderness tradition rather than attempting to reshape and resituate its values and aims as a component of a new, more diversified, self-reflexive environmentalism. In doing so, Cronon's deconstruction risked replicating right-wing caricature. For example, a repeated charge in the book was that protecting wilderness meant allowing all other land to be trashed. Though the deconstructive logic sounds compelling, in fact, the opposite was the case: wilderness enthusiasms in the 1960s and 1970s were part of a movement that also worked for clean air and water and toxic dump cleanups, issues important for urban areas. Equally, Cronon's dismissal ignored the wilderness tradition's great potential for sponsoring a reshaped future legacy. Wilderness activism was, even as Cronon wrote, being absorbed into the biodiversity movement, and wilderness values (such as health and beauty) were being utilized to fight pollution and overdevelopment in suburbs and cities. Cronon's book thus seemed to give aid and comfort to the enemy. One of the headlines that followed its publication was "Wilderness Is a Bankrupt Idea"—a response suggesting that the book bought into and simply added, for many, to the heckling from the right.[58] Though Cronon was surprised and disturbed by the controversy his book raised among environmentalists, he could have avoided it had he been as complexly self-critical about his own discourse as he was trying to be about environmentalism's.

If ecoterrorism, ecocentrism, and the wilderness tradition clearly provided the right with ways to invalidate and disunify environmentalism, so did targeting environmental crisis. But there was a difference. The power that crisis elaboration had to mobilize a wide variety of people on a wide variety of societal, urban, and technological as well as nature-based issues made it the most important target of attempts to discredit environmentalism and divide environmentalists. Ecoterrorism was easy to condemn, and nature purism easy to satirize; both, however, involved limited constituencies. Environmentalism's discourse of crisis, bolstered by science as well as sentiment, was by contrast much more difficult to dismiss. At the same time, it was the most necessary to delegitimize: its constituency was the largest and most various, and it was the environmental discourse that offered the most forceful and telling critique of industrial capitalism.

Thus by the end of the 1970s, environmentalists were regularly and extravagantly vilified as pathological crisis-mongers, Chicken Littles, apocalypse abusers, false prophets, joyless, puritannical doomsters, chic-apocalyptic neo-primitives, sufferers from an Armageddon complex, and toxic terrorists: calling them this in serious social analysis and on talk-back radio alike, as noted above, became a big business. Also as noted above, the elaboration of counterscience became a well-funded and widespread enterprise. Under this withering fire, fault lines appeared among environmental advocates and theorists. Theodore Roszak was far from alone in deciding that crisis elaboration meant doomsterism and was thus a political liability for environmentalism. And other more academic writers, such as the Marxist geographer David Harvey, found philosophical and theoretical as well as important political reasons for dispensing with the discourse of crisis, a discourse he unsympathetically characterized as the "millenarian and apocalyptic proclamation that ecocide is imminent."[59] And if, for Roszak, Harvey, and others, crisis talk was retrograde and to be dispensed with, new environmental paradigms and theories were needed to fill the gap. The result was not a reconception of crisis in the face of new political circumstances but a jettisoning of crisis in favor of new environmental-political paradigms, ones crafted to take its place.

Political, philosophical, and theoretical perils do exist in the elaboration and use of environmental crisis, and I engage these seriously in later chapters. But, just as with deconstructions of wilderness tradition and thought, attempts to dismiss rather than reconceive environmental crisis meant throwing a very important baby out with the bathwater. Doing this was particularly odd, given the fact that the baby was thriving; almost all of the many problems that constituted environmental crisis—the problems that, taken together, seemed to create a significant challenge to human society as a whole—were in fact worsening, not improving. And attempts to craft a new environmentalism without crisis, when looked at closely, too often testified to the success of right-wing rhetoric in making a caricature of 1960s and 1970s–style apocalyptic alarmism stand for all subsequent reflection on and elaboration of crisis by environmentalists. Thus writers such as Harvey showed no awareness that environmental crisis discourse had moved well beyond the "apocalyptic ecocide" of the 1960s and 1970s, while writers such as Roszak ignored the possibility that there were different ways of speaking about crisis and only a restricted few resembled puritanical doomsterism. Neither, in short, considered that environmental crisis discourse was never as unitary as the conservative parody asserted. Even more, neither acknowledged that environmental crisis discourse had never stood still but had been changing, diversifying, and critically refining itself since its inception—and that even as they wrote their dismissals of it, it was continuing to do so in response to its own much more nuanced critique of the excesses of the 1960s and 1970s.

Just how environmental crisis discourse has in fact changed during the decades since Rachel Carson is one of the primary stories this book has to tell. Even though it may now sound odd to say, environmental crisis discourse has left apocalyptic ecologism and doomsterism behind and moved *beyond* apocalypse into a variety of new conceptual spaces and rhetorics. In the process, environmental crisis has been richly reimagined and made tellingly more relevant than ever to present social and political concerns. Equally, it has had recourse to new scientific findings that indicate that environmental constraints on human society today are, though altered in aspect from those described in the 1960s and 1970s, substantially increasing, not decreasing. Dismissal and forced optimism are thus not the genuine answer to the difficulties 1970s apocalypticism became enmeshed in; a richer and more self-reflective reimagining of environmental crisis is now well under way. As subsequent chapters will show, life *after* apocalypse presents a more, not a less, sobering picture of environmental crisis-in-progress than 1970s end-of-the-world fantasies ever achieved.

Dividing the opposition couldn't have worked if there hadn't already been fault lines within the environmental movement and between it and the other old "new" social movements. My point is that conservatives were sharp-eyed in spotting these, and they worked them for all they were worth. What the right did, then, was to make it substantially harder for the environmental movement to reinvent itself. As Brian Tokar, Mark Dowie, and Robert Gottlieb, historians of contemporary environmentalism, all make clear, the legacy of environmental activism from the 1960s included a much wider spread of issues than the rubric of "nature" could easily cover a much wider array of constituencies than was represented by the national environmental organizations—particularly as they consolidated, aged, and became part of inside-the-Beltway policy-making. As Gottlieb argues, the dominant position in U.S. environmental traditions of wilderness preservation and conservationism (and the debates between them) meant that a variety of equally old urban, working-class, socialist, and feminist sources for contemporary environmental concern were left out. These traditions included workplace safety movements:

> the female-led municipal housekeeping movement, which focused on issues like sanitation, public health, and food and nutrition; the muckraker-inspired urban reform organizations and settlement houses, which led the push for better housing, for new regulatory agencies such as the Food and Drug Administration, and for improving the harsh conditions of industrial labor; and the "sewer" socialists, who helped revolutionize municipal governance over the urban environment.[60]

The conservative movement thus targeted environmentalism at the very time it needed to reinvent and diversify itself. For diversification was a necessity forcefully imposed on it not just by advancing social consciousness and the aging of the environmental movement's postwar wave. Reinvention and diversification of the environmental movement were necessitated equally by a still growing and rapidly diversifying environmental crisis. The logic behind this assertion is elementary. The more complicated and comprehensive that environmental constraints and crisis became, the more environmentalism found it had to work on more and more fronts. As crisis became more inclusive, people came to realize that few or no forms of social practice—from throwing out your garbage to deciding whether or not you factor environmental costs into the Gross National Product or asking whether racism didn't in fact have substantial environmental as well as social consequences—existed without substantial environmental implications. And people came to realize that few or no social groups were without significant environmental interests and commitments. Indeed, as the sun of environmental crisis has sunk lower on the horizon, these new problems and interests, like shadows on a landscape littered with large and small boulders, have leapt into view and grown longer and longer, stretching as far as the eye can see.[61] The right succeeded admirably in making it harder for the environmental movement to accommodate itself to this new landscape of multiple urgencies.

But the story of post-1970s environmental crisis does not stop here. A new chapter for environmental crisis as well as for national environmental politics was written with a new presidency. If the right respun the rhetoric and agenda of the postwar liberal social movements in order to come to power, in 1992 the right shortly found its own rhetoric and some of its social agenda suddenly respun by a still craftier antagonist. As Bill Clinton began reinterpreting the past and reshaping the future in light of a new, globalist paradigm during his 1992 presidential campaign, a new act came into town, bringing with it a new chapter in the complicated interplay of cultural, economic, and environmental agendas in U.S. politics.

CHAPTER 2

Taking Crisis Seriously?

Warning: We the undersigned, senior members of the world's scientific community, hereby warn all humanity of what lies ahead. A great change in our stewardship of the earth and the life on it is required, if vast human misery is to be avoided and our global home on this planet is not to be irretrievably mutilated.
———World Scientists' Warning to Humanity, 1992

We are in an usual predicament as a global civilization. The maximum that is politically feasible, even the maximum that is politically imaginable right now, still falls short of the minimum that is scientifically and ecologically necessary.
———Al Gore, Interview with Bill McKibben, 1992

In his 1992 presidential campaign, Bill Clinton managed to reshape not only the Democratic Party but also discourse about the economy, culture, and (at first) the environment. The essential lever for such change was the fact that he brought the word "global" at last into mainstream conversation in the United States. "Global" meant something very different from "international." It was different from Bush's much more tired-sounding phrase, "the New World Order"—suggesting a realignment of old competing nationalisms, not a transformation of parochial nationalism altogether. With Clinton's first campaign, "global" became a term that signified possibilities, not problems. It came to suggest the end to anxiety about eroding prestige, national crisis, and internal division and the beginning of a new kind of synergistic coherence, one that promised to bring nation and world together to the advantage of all.

Clinton's new story was an extremely positive one; it was a narrative of national recovery that depicted America's new global environment as an exciting challenge, not a howling wilderness. Once this shift had occurred, it seemed clear that the neoconservative nationalist solutions of the Reagan-Bush era were not just wrong, they exacerbated the problems they claimed to remedy. For example, given the *de facto* erosion of national economic borders everywhere, trickle down did not lead to recovery, but trickle out. Economic policies designed to benefit the wealthy in the faith that increasing their incomes would benefit all as excess wealth tricked down proved wrong. The extra money instead trickled out into the increasingly "borderless" global economy. Equally, the monocultural ideal that inspired Reagan-era conservative culture warriors suddenly seemed vastly less suited than bridge-building multiculturalism for creating peoplehood in the United States and for reattaining centrality in an interactive, cosmopolitan, global economy. Most important, with the end of the Evil Empire, that global economy wore a different face. It was no longer a competitive war zone; instead, it was styled as an interactive, interdependent cosmopolitan system and a new frontier for American business and society. The defensive nationalism of the Reagan era focused on external enemies and internal subversives; suddenly, these no longer seemed the problem. Instead, targeting them obsessively was a problem. It meant that one had not thought thoroughly enough about the "newness" of the new global economy, an omission that led to serious mistakes.

New kinds of openness—cultural, political, and economic—were thus crucial. They required a new set of ideas and (perhaps even more) manners that were clearly out of the reach of the aggressive-defensive, programmatically provincial, and rude new Republicans, for whom older, conservative, genteel finishing schools were a thing of the past. Taking advantage of the borderlessness of the new capitalism and rekindling a postmodern-style afterglow of Kennedyesque idealism, the Clinton team propagated the idea that the United States could help create the rising tide that would lift all boats (Adam Smith's phrase), including (especially) its own, achieving a new version of its former prominence. The result was that a "movement" was again countered by at least a sort of "movement"; conservative populism was met with centrist, middle-class, town-meeting, soccer-mom populism. If the populism had a kind of Hollywood-postmodern virtuality to it, well it did; it was far more contemporary than the old black-and-white cowboy flicks that underpinned Reagan. This new shift in discourse took place across pretty much the same heterogenous packet of issues that the right had assembled to create its revolution. Mirroring the right, Clinton yoked economics, culture, and even, for a brief, halcyon moment, the environment together into what seemed an integrated movement for reform.

Culture provides a sharp example of the Clintonian genius. Even as multiculturalism was stigmatized by the right as ethnic separatism by another name, it was reconstructed during the Clinton presidency as a form of national consensus. Thus Nathan Glazer, no friend to the multicultural, entitled a recent book *We Are All Multiculturalists Now*; conservatives moaned that they had lost the culture wars; retrospectives were held to memorialize Allan Bloom and mothball the controversy he started; and the culture wars dropped off the public's radar screen as fatally out of date. Multiculturalism now became the favored new national identity for a global environment. *Time* magazine devoted an issue to describing "The New Face of America"; the cover featured a computer-morphed picture of the racially/ethnically hybrid American of the future. Roger Rouse called this a form of "corporate liberal multiculturalism" and quoted the magazine's nationalist-globalist text:

> there is no going back: diversity breeds diversity. It is the fuel that runs today's America and, in a world being transformed daily by technologies that render distances meaningless, it puts America in the forefront of a new international order.[1]

In this same vein, *Wired* magazine, also no liberal rag, celebrated diversity as the future of the United States and the new global system, predicting that "at the turn of the century, the U.S. [will be] the closest thing the world has to a workable multicultural society" and thus again a light to all nations.[2] Though many—including me—have seen this apparent ascendancy of multiculturalism in the Clinton era as still quite ambiguous, multiculturalism so configured did win the culture wars, something that has had a very visible effect on the conservative movement. Even conservatives have, thanks to the campaign rhetoric of George W. Bush, become compassionate.

As with culture, so with the economy under Clinton. The embrace of deregulation, harsh restructuring, and free-market fundamentalism under Reagan-Bush was overwhelmed in a wave of fascination with the remarkable new features of the global economy. Key features of the global economy made it seem seductively new and genuinely revolutionary. A globalized financial system enabled people to send trillions about the world simply by pushing buttons. Globalization enabled industry to situate factories rapidly virtually anywhere and produce goods that were more cosmopolitan in origin (like orange juice manufactured—simultaneously?—in Brazil, Mexico, and Florida) than all but a handful of people. Marketing also went global, acquiring the ability to reconfigure product lines to meet diverse and changing tastes, and manufacturing's creation of global just-in-time production networks facilitated this process, avoiding backlogs and enhancing product flows. A new global cosmopolitanism that made tourism one of the world's largest businesses grew side by side with a new wave of global migration, one that outdid the great global migrations of the end of the nineteenth and beginning of the twentieth centuries, and both coevolved with the transportation facilities capable of carrying large new streams of people and products around the world. The new media sent information across national boundaries even more exuberantly, penetrating even the most remote areas, such as Inner Mongolia and the Amazon. Borders seemed so porous that entrepreneurial small businesses, communities, and individuals could become, like transnational corporations and states, players on the new global field. In the mainstream rhetoric of the Clinton presidency, a new era of prosperity, freedom, and, above all, mobility seemed to open up as the world went global.

A new paradigm, in short, was in town. Clinton's version of the global economy made it clear from the start that the old mind-set was now the new problem. Success in the global economy was only possible if we avoided the knee-jerk excesses of defensive nationalism. In the newly interactive global economy, trickle down really meant trickle out; even more, protectionism not only did not work but actually undermined economic health. Further, global investment in America increased our prosperity rather than undermined it. The bare fact that the Japanese might buy Rockefeller Center and a good portion of commercial Los Angeles didn't matter; the real key was how successfully a nation managed to integrate itself into the global economy. For while the rising tides lifted all boats, the tide would lift those most who have paid the most intelligent attention to provisioning and positioning of their boat.

Conservative populism quickly attempted to adapt to this new global expansiveness, proclaiming the triumph of capitalism, the end of history, and the unleashing of the Third Wave. Thus by the Gingrich era of the Contract with America, appeals to exuberant free-market libertarianism in lifestyle and deregulated free-market triumphalism in economic policy became vastly more common than appeals to nationalist roots and "common culture." Conservative free-marketeering even struck up an alliance with the avant-gardist, glitzy, and postmodern—a topic to be discussed at length in Chapter 7. This combination helped Newt Gingrich, who shortly thereafter was returned to his former dog status, to have his day.

But these attempts to play the new paradigm game with the new economy finally did not manage to trump the Clinton version—which had trumped Reaganism. The new Republican–libertarian celebration of unregulated individual and corporate entrepreneurialism was countered by Clinton's emphasis on a necessary role for government in the nation's integration with the global economy. Clinton's advocacy of giving people the "tools" they needed for success was broader and more attractive than Gingrich's prescription of laptops for slum kids or Representative Dick Armey's barely articulate calls for unleashing the productive forces of American capitalism. Government needed to set policies that aided, not impaired, national integration into the global economy. To set out on the waters of the global economy, Clinton argued, one had to tend to one's boat: a boat in which occupants were well provisioned with skills and the steersman savvy enough to avoid the reefs of old-style right-wing nationalism and antigovernment sentiment made for advantageous positioning on the waters of the global economy.

Robert Reich, Clinton's secretary of labor, spelled out the implications of this position with exceptional lucidity in his book *The Work of Nations.* Key to successful positioning was not where the capital came from, but who added the most value to a product in the manufacturing process. Who provided the labor to manufacture the goods and who invested the financial capital for the production facilities were not nearly as important as who added the most value during the production process: the pivotal figure thus became the knowledge worker. Rather than lament the loss of U.S. manufacturing oversees, the country should try, Reich argued, to reshape as many American workers as possible into the people who could add this sort of value to the global ecomony. It must turn as many as possible into knowledge workers, whom Reich called "symbolic analysts."[3] America's new identity as home of global symbolic analysts would be the new basis for national unity in a global world. Investment in education was thus crucial; equally crucial was investment in the knowledge economy's essential infrastructures.

The prospect so far was quite fascinating: Clinton used the new mantra of the global economy to respin right-wing respinnings of the older leftist "new" social movements, and the global economy emerged, for a while, as the paradigm of paradigms. True, the market for new paradigms had become increasingly crowded as the millennium drew to a close. In academia, in the corporate world, and in popular culture, many voices (profitably) reached many ears by conveying the message that people lived in the midst of an exceptional period of dynamic, world-historical social transformation—the era of postindustrialism, the service economy, the information age, the post-scarcity economy, the Third Wave, late capitalism, disorganized capitalism, the regime of flexible accumulation, the era of postcoloniality and/or post-modernity, the time of the demise of the nation-state, the time of definitive globalization. For some we were witnessing no less than the end of history, the emergence of posthumanity or, hyperbolically, ultrahumanity. Y2K added, of course, substantial further brio to this mix. Discovering new paradigms for these new eras now seemed a necessity.

But Clinton's embrace of the "global" was successful in cornering a large share of this growth market in stylishly interpreting contemporary changes in mainstream U.S. culture as the change of a paradigm as well as the change of a generation or era. Even in the academic sphere, globalization (available as a term in academic discourse since at least the 1980s), spread well beyond the anglophone sociology that gave it birth. Malcom Waters was prescient in ar-guing that "just as postmodernism was *the* concept of the 1980s, globalization may be *the* concept of the 1990s."[4] It was.

But if globalist discourse was so effective in undergirding Clinton's adminis-tration and changing public debates about culture and the economy, what about its effects on debates about the environment? What happened to environmental politics in the latest round of reinterpretation and policy change? After all, Clin-ton's choice of Al Gore for vice president, the author of *Earth in the Balance*, seemed to put the environment squarely in the mix of issues clothed in the rhetoric of change.[5] For Clinton's administration was prominently (and extraor-dinarily) a two-book administration. Reich's *The Wealth of Nations* and Al Gore's *Earth in the Balance* were not just two serious and informed books on important topics; more strikingly, they both prominently featured the term "global." Fur-ther, both argued that this new term signaled a major, world-historical change for humanity, one that had to be understood for the United States to free itself from past mistakes and ensure itself a viable future. And, further still, both ar-gued that recognizing the novelty of our now-globalized world was crucial to the formation of a variety of different specific policies towards those ends.

Prospects were thus favorable for the environment joining the economy as part of Clinton's new discourse of the global, thereby coming up with a full package of cultural, economic, and environmental positions to counter conser-vative Republicans' extremely successful assemblage. True, Clinton's famous campaign slogan—"it's the economy, stupid"—indicated that not all global concerns would be treated equally, but some sort of partnership did seem a lively possibility. Enhancing that possibility considerably was the fact that, for at least a decade before Clinton and Gore took office, a wide variety of global environmental concerns had been brought together in calls for reshaping the world's economy, all in service of an extremely optimistic vision of a new global human future. The deep sense of well-nigh irreconcilable antagonism between corporate-led economic growth and environmental health—an antagonism fundamental to the post-Carson environmental movement and one that found its most eloquent expression in the Club of Rome's significantly titled book, *Limits to Growth*—seemed on the verge of being set aside when both economic and environmental issues were thought about, at last, in a truly global context. Rethought in a global context and ingeniously intertwined, a new form of eco-economics seemed to promise no less than a future of world peace, prosperity, cooperation, *and* sustainability.

The growth of this new ecoeconomic discourse—dubbed "ecological modernization"—has been charted by Maarten Hajer in *The Politics of Environmental Discourse*. It was elaborated during the 1980s by a number of national U.S. environmental organizations but it had previously and more forcefully been worked out in Europe and in a variety of international fora (like the Organization for Economic Cooperation and Development [OECD] and UN commissions on development, safety, and the environment). Late to surface in U.S. popular discourse (one wonders why), it was premised, Hajer makes clear, on an awareness that "both in government and in industry a simple denial of environmental risks has ceased to be an option."[6] In short, confronting crisis in public discourse became necessary, both because of the growth of the problems themselves and because of the need for people in charge to maintain their legitimacy in the eyes (and hearts and minds) of their citizens. If Reagan-Bush set the United States back a decade in this respect, subsequently a substantial change seemed imminent thanks to events like the terrible summer of 1988 (the year of the sweltering summer, appearance of medical wastes on New Jersey beaches, runaway wildfires and droughts, all leading *Time* magazine to wonder whether environmental meltdown had just begun), the public glare created the environmental summit in Rio in 1992 and Clinton's choice of Al Gore, author of *Earth in the Balance*, for vice president.[7]

Earth in the Balance called for a new global environmental Marshall Plan for the post–Cold War era: it tacked environmental crisis directly onto a global vision of possibility. In the new post–Cold War era, humankind faced comprehensive environmental crisis rather than war; it needed to join together in solving not just a common problem, but *the* common problem for mankind.

Henceforth, environmental (and not military) scenarios would provide all humanity (and not just opposed superpowers) with its most exemplary case of a truly "strategic" crisis. In going on to outline how to respond to crisis, Gore elaborated for the United States much of the rhetoric and agenda of "ecological modernization."

Ecological modernization, first and foremost, did not try to deny crisis; Gore's version was typical in foregrounding scary descriptions of a multifaceted environmental crisis deeply rooted in the practices and structures of modern environmentalism. In thus taking crisis seriously, ecological modernization called, in tones of real urgency, for a social transformation to meet it. The ecological crisis was "evidence of a fundamental omission in the workings of the institutions of modern society," Maarten Hajer wrote. However, when Hajer continued, the other shoe dropped: "unlike the radical environmental movements of the 1970s, [ecological modernization] suggests that environmental problems can be solved in accordance with the workings of the main institutional arrangements of society."[8] As Hajer's first sentence suggests, the project was conceptually vast. The second sentence, though, applied a choke chain of centrist politics and practicality to the visionary philosophy.

The vision was expansive. Modern society omitted environmental concerns from its calculus; it saw the natural world, in effect, as a vast reservoir of natural resources, enduring beyond and outside human effects upon it. In the current phase of modernism, however, this old optimism was gone; pursuing freedom from want by means of the production of goods was an activity that had become increasingly overshadowed by a second concern. This was the perception that nature was limited and that the human production of bad results—the production of environmental risks and deterioration of all sorts—had grown beyond the ability of both nature and society to absorb them. Modernity must as a result restructure itself to cope with this challenge.

In publicizing the expansiveness of this vision, rhetoric was indeed enthusiastic. As reported by Mark Hertsgaard (an environmental essayist much taken with ecomodernization) in 1989:

> even as mainstream a figure as William Ruckelshaus . . . felt there was no time to lose. The shift from business as usual to an environmentally sustainable civilization would be as basic a transformation as the Agricultural and Industrial Revolutions, Ruckelshaus had said. Tinkering around the edges would not suffice; agriculture, industry, transportation, energy, housing and many other spheres of human activity had to be reconfigured from the ground up.[9]

Or, as an executive from AT&T put it: "We are talking about restructuring the technological basis of our economy . . . integrating environmental considerations into all technology and economic behavior."[10] The Green businessman Paul Hawken and Amory and L. Hunter Lovins, CEOs of the Rocky Mountain Institute and prominent experts in ecoefficiency, called this integration "natural capitalism," arguing that "there is no longer any serious scientific dispute that the decline in every living system in the world is reaching such levels that an increasing number of them are starting to lose." Contemporary civilization was poised at "an extraordinary threshold":

> Recognition of this shadow side of the success of industrial production has triggered the second of the two great intellectual shifts of the late twentieth century. The end of the Cold War and the fall of communism was the first such shift; the second, now quietly emerging, is the end of the war against life on earth, and the eventual ascendance of what we call natural capitalism.[11]

Al Gore depicted the present moment similarly as a "civilizational" crisis. His book looked back to the decade of work culminating in the 1992 United Nations Conference on Environment and Development (UNCED) in Rio de Janiero, even as it was centrally located in mainstream U.S. environmental discourse; *Earth in the Balance* grafted U.S. environmentalist concerns onto global geopolitical discourse. More indebted to newer Third Wave visions of a new economy, Ruckelshaus and the AT&T executive spoke of ecological modernization in different terms and tones, as changes to the fundamental institutions and practices of modernity; Hawken and the Lovinses, fascinated with the nuts and bolts of industrial systems and new technologies, wrote in still another kind of voice—that of the Green technologist and social engineer. In a still different voice—that of the academic calling for the greening of the university curriculum—ecological modernization promised a final unification of culture and nature as nature became a concern taken account of by virtually every university discipline and every human cultural, social, and economic activity. Ecological modernization's insistence on internalizing ecological concerns and producing thereby societal transformation cropped up everywhere. True, Maarten Hajer asserted—in a somewhat over-fastidious manner—that ecological modernization "should not be compared to a paradigm shift."[12] But, in public rhetoric like this, it dressed itself up as a paradigm shift, from its hat all the way down to the soles of its boots. In that vein, it began the astonishing work of alchemizing an environmental crisis at last so severe as to be undeniable into something that felt strangely like unlimited possibility.

The full program of ecological modernization was fleshed out gradually. The key feature of ecological modernization (to combine phrases from the first two quotes above) remained "integrating environmental concerns" into all "spheres of human society." This made for a wide variety of possible consequences in different areas. First, it made for substantial change on a governmental level. It shifted policy-making from a "predominantly 'react-and-cure' formula for regulation"—beloved of all those dreary old Second Wave environmentalists but sadly ineffective, ecomodernists maintained—to the "more innovative 'anticipate-and-prevent' variety."[13] In setting economic policy, this meant "incorporating the environmental considerations at an early stage of decision-making and a plea for the use of economic and fiscal instruments [to induce desired changes in practice] instead of concentrating on legal regulatory instruments [to compel them]."[14] Just for starters, for example, the customary way to calculate the standard measure of economic health, the Gross National Product (GNP), had to be modified to include environmental considerations. Presently, expense-generating environmental calamities are added to the GNP, not subtracted from it. That means, for mainstream economists, that catastrophes like the *Exxon Valdez* oil spill are economic pluses, not minuses. Everything spent on cleanup and remediation only raises the GNP. By that logic, the more befouled the world, the more prosperous its people.

Emphasis on upstream management rather than downstream regulation thus quickly led to advocacy of a variety of specific policy proposals. These included (along with revising GNP calculations), the following: risk assessments and risk management instead of outright prohibitions; cash valuations of environmental damage (again instead of outright, ethics-based prohibition) and, more positively, cash accounting of "ecosystem services"; tradeable pollution bonds; energy and environmental taxes; full-cost pricing based on the inclusion of environmental with other costs in the prices of goods and services; and the greening of now often outrageously brown government subsidies.

In the private sector, ecological modernization tried to bring environmental concerns inside the system of economic production, making them a regular part of economic production rather than treating them as antagonistic to it. As Paul Hawken and the Lovinses remark: "it is easier, as the saying goes, to ride a horse in the direction it is going," so working with rather than against market structures and money valuations is a better way to go.[15] The new upstream restructuring of society also appealed to Green consumerism; in its strong form, this meant providing the citizen with the information and choices necessary for Green consumption, which then, in turn, would alter the agendas of producers. The overall result would be to induce business to use its creativity to solve environmental problems; using incentives, not rigid bureaucratic regulation, it would encourage corporate innovation, not foot-dragging.

Technological development and industrial strategy were another prominent area for ecological modernization in the private sector. Here, many argued for a "win-win" application of ecological knowledge to industrial production. Corporations could learn from rather than fight against environmentalists by adopting technologies that would turn out to be more profitable because they fit economic and ecological needs simultaneously. Developing and implementing more efficient and less polluting new technologies thus became crucial activities; corporations needed to enlist environmentalists to help develop these technologies. In the process, the argument went, the culture of antagonism between corporations and environmentalists would dissipate, something that would help further spread change throughout society.

Whole new ecological industries would spring up and open new areas for entrepreneurship.[16] This would enhance the global economic power of the nations wise enough to pursue this course; even as Reich called for turning U.S. workers into symbolic analysts, Gore and ecological modernization called for turning the U.S. into an environmental innovator and entrepreneur. Doing this would create jobs rather than sacrifice them to environmental considerations; so much for Wise Use and the antagonism it attempted to foment between labor and environmentalism. "Resolving environmental crisis," Hajer wrote, would help not only "in the fight against inflation but also help to create jobs," and environmental remediation would thus be "a positive-sum game, [in] that the environment and development [could] go hand in hand, or with the idea that environmental investment creates jobs."[17] Private-sector job creation and environmental protection would be further enhanced by governmental policy changes by shifting from taxing people to levying environmental taxes on resource use and the production of wastes. As Robert Ayres wrote: "the underlying basic idea of the change would be to reduce the tax burden on labor, so as to reduce its market price—relative to capital and resources—and thus encourage more employment of labor vis-à-vis capital and especially fossil fuels and other resources."[18]

As the above clearly suggests, ecological modernization had a third key feature. It formed the basis for a new kind of culture of civility and creative cooperation, not adversarialism. Even as all were swept up into environmental crisis—and as they had also been involved in creating it (or so ecomodernist depictions of civilizational crisis endangering "our common future" made people feel)—all needed to work together to remedy it. Mark Hertsgaard took this perception as reason for hope: "first, most people want to do right by the environment and, if given the chance, they will—as long as they are not penalized economically for it," he wrote. "Second," he continued, "far from being enemies, economic and environmental health can reinforce each other."[19] Even politicians (alas, mostly in Europe) could be heard saying, Maarten Hajer reported: "We are all Greens now. . . . Talking green no longer connotes a radical social critique. . . . [I]t functions as a symbolic umbrella, as an inclusionary device, that constitutes actors as joint members of a new and all inclusive 'risk community.'"[20]

Clearly this community has never been as well established in the United States as in Europe. Still, for proponents of ecological modernization, the environment was humanity's common problem and made people look toward their common future. Win-win ecomodernization patched together corporations and environmentalists. Likewise, Green marketing put consumers together with corporations, and ecoentrepreneurialism patched together business and labor. Reinforcing this win-win philosophy of ecological modernization on the national level was the even more prominent elaboration on the international level of sustainable development—a program that, moreover, had a wider mandate as it sought to yoke not just economic development with environmental protection, but the two with international development, social justice, and environmental justice as well. Sustainable development patched together Northern ecomodernist industrialism with Southern developmentalism as it opened up a common future globally.

In theory and even practice, the actual coalitions could be quite wonderful. Maarten Hajer's description of the possibilities for ecologically modern rain forest activist coalitions exemplified how interesting they could be:

> The systems-ecologist might insist on the importance of the rainforests as an essential element in his or her mathematical equations that model the world as a biosphere, as an integrated and self-reproducing eco-system; the World Wildlife Fund is more concerned about the moral problem of forest destruction; while the singer Sting connects the fate of the rainforest to that of the culture of the indigenous people, thus stretching the idea of habitat protection to its limits. NASA may add to the credibility of the story-line through the publication of satellite photography showing the change of the forest cover over time.[21]

If one added an international sustainable-development perspective to this, coalition-building only expanded. Indigenous communities, local industries such as rubber tapping, global industries such as ecotourism, and government supporters of debt-for-nature swaps and regulated bioprospecting all became potential partners.

The possibilities ecomodernization advanced sounded enormously, excitingly progressive. The system did not need to be dismantled; it could be transformed. We could still have development; we just needed to make it sustainable. There were also important achievements; Hajer cited as "paradigmatic examples of ecological modernization . . . Japan's response to its notorious air pollution problem in the 1970s, the 'pollution prevention pays' schemes introduced by the American company 3M, and the U-turn made by the German government after the discovery of acid rain or *Waldsterben* in the early 1980s."[22] Equally important, ecomodernization provided environmentalists with a new ideal, one that could spring resurgent from the ashes of the ecology movement that had been "neutralized" (Samuel Hays's phrase) by the 1980s. That movement's ideal of opposing large centralized technological and economic systems with small-scale, diversity-enhancing, distributed, and democratic systems, and its emphasis on living lightly on the earth harkened back, Hays wrote, not just to hippie alternative culture but even more to "the do-it-yourself style that ran from Yankee ingenuity of the early nineteenth century to the home-repair-craftworkers of the twentieth."[23] Ecomodernization, by contrast, yoked that Yankee ingenuity to the age of global environmental crisis and global interconnectedness, huge transnational corporations, and new megatechnologies, a time when no one (and especially wired-up Americans) could hope any longer (or so the new common sense had it) to step off the global-social grid.

But evaluating what ecological modernization and sustainable development have in fact achieved—as opposed to promised in theory and rhetoric—presents a very different problem. It is crucial for an era in which new environmental paradigms have been elaborated with such fanfare to assess not just how people talk the talk but also how they walk the walk. And even the most positive assessment would have to conclude that there is still, alas, a wide gap between actual achievement and the fact that "ecological modernization has produced a real change in *thinking* about nature and society and in the *conceptualisation* of environmental problems in the circles of government and industry."[24]

Green technology and industrial reform have indeed made some progress. Corporations have made strides with ecoefficiency and ecorestructuring. "[D]oing more with less," Mark Hertsgaard reports, has indeed done wonders. "Germany and Japan use half as much energy per dollar of GNP as the United

States, not because their citizens suffer lower standards of living but because their economies use energy more efficiently. Even in the wasteful United States, GNP grew by an average of 2.5 percent a year from 1973 to 1986 while energy use grew not at all."[25] But even with results like these, problems remain; energy efficiency and pollution-control technologies have their limits, and many of these have been swallowed up by growth: "If, for example, automobile tailpipe emissions have declined since 1970, "the number of vehicles . . . grew a whopping 62 percent . . . [and] since 1980, the number of miles driven annually per vehicle has risen by about 20 percent."[26] Further, possibilities for win-win efficiency diminish as time goes on: "capturing the last 5 percent of emissions of a pollutant from stacks or tailpipes may cost as much as removing the first 50 percent."[27] And would all this activity have been commenced in the first place without environmental regulation in the form of nasty old Second Wave restrictive laws? The corporate community replies, usually, with a resonant yes, but for the most part the realities are different. Bad old Second Wave laws and sustained political opposition were extremely necessary.

What about the possibility of still more systemic industrial and technological reform? Mark Hertsgaard is bullish on the Lovinses' proposals in *Factor Four: Doubling Wealth, Halving Resource Use.* The book describes "super-refrigerators" that use 86 percent less energy and "equally impressive gains for construction, office equipment, lighting, irrigation, railways, agriculture, and a host of other products and activities"—all things that the Lovinses claim are possible within existing technologies.[28] *Natural Capitalism* collects a wide variety of other items into its list, items familiar to those who have followed Green technolgies. These include water-saving ultrasonic dishwashers, Swedish waterless toilets, subsurface drip irrigation, management-intensive rotational grazing, and heat-saving superinsulation. Still more dramatic and more visionary technologies abound, *Natural Capitalism* suggests, on the frontiers of biomimicry and nanotechnology.[29] But the ratio of realization to vision seems, for the most part, all too small. What happens with the new generation of hybrid "hypercars" reaching the showrooms in the United States in the new millennium is an interesting test case: Will they catch on at all, and, if they do, will they prove revolutionary or (as roads and other infrastructure continue to multiply globally) merely accommodationist, an ingenious way to continue (and enmesh people more deeply in) an unsustainable system? And if the off-the-shelf improvements are slow to be deployed and potentially ambiguous in their results, how can we rely on the more visionary ones?

Still other industrial innovations, however, promise even more. The goal, for example, of "'industrial ecology,' an engineering discipline that goes beyond pollution prevention to design 'industrial infrastructures as if they were a series of interlocking man-made ecosystems interfacing with the natural global ecosystem'" has a marvelously comprehensive ring to it.[30] Hawkins and the Lovinses add a host of further corporate movements to the mix; all promise fundamental restructurings, not just single inventions. These include Walter Stahel's advocacy of "cradle to cradle" reuse and remanufacturing, an idea already enjoined on some manufacturers in Europe by "takeback" laws for goods such as cars and packaging; Michael Braungart's concept of the service economy, "where consumers obtain services by leasing goods rather than buying them outright"—something that incentivizes increasing not productivity but savings on resources, energy, and wastes; Sensei Taiichi Ohno's training of "changemasters" to help corporations eliminate *muda* or wastes; and the attempt by the Interface Company to become "the world's first truly sustainable enterprise," remanufacturing and renewing all the carpeting it leases rather than sells, thus putting "zero scrap . . . into landfills and zero emissions into the ecosystem."[31] While no one in his or her right mind would disdain advances on these fronts or dampen enthusiasm for making them, it is also important to keep clearly grounded in a demand for the actual spread of such practices in fact as well as an embrace of them in vision.

Another area for ecological modernization has been, as we have seen, government policy. In this area, it is particularly sobering to contemplate what has been done. Proposals noted above for handling problems upstream rather than regulating them downstream have concentrated on what is most acceptable to industry: strategies such as risk assessment and tradable pollution bonds. But policies like risk assessment and tradable pollution bonds supplant potentially stricter regulation, replace ethical and legal prohibition with market logic and zero-tolerance policies with the tolerance of supposedly acceptable risks. Further, risk assessment has been roundly attacked as a practice that legitimizes environmental risks more than preventing them and thus as "an applied science of mortality management," not a guarantor of safety.[32] The long list of criticisms of it includes the fact that it assesses individual pollutants' effects separately while never considering the cumulative effects of "cocktails" of pollutants and sets standards of proof so high when it comes to evaluating risk (i.e., 95 percent certain) that cancer rates (for example) "must reach extraordinary high levels" for studies to be conclusive.[33] The elaboration of a much more restrictive—and effective—method of vetting new chemicals and practices, the precautionary principle, by contrast requires that "when an activity raises threats of harm to human health or the environment, precautionary measures should be taken even if some cause and effect relationships are not fully established scientifically" and that "the proponent of the activity, rather than the public, should bear the burden of proof."[34] That would be an upstream-oriented way of doing more, not less; yet unsurprisingly, there is little support for such a move from industry. Indeed, as Ulrich Beck comments: "a liberalization of the causality of proof would be like a bursting dam and this would imply a flood of risks and dangers to be recognized that would rock the entire social and political structure through its broader effects."[35]

Or take the question of subsidies. Tom Athanasiou and others have criticized the persistence of crazy government subsidies—under which, according to a 1994 UN study, more than a trillion dollars a year go to subsidizing environmentally destructive industries; Paul Hawken and the Lovinses claim that the total for these subsidies is 1.5 trillion a year.[36] Changing them has supposedly been a part of the ecomodernist package, but the reality has different; for the most part, the trillion dollars are still in place; vested interests are powerful still. Depressingly enough, win-win rhetoric is not working here. The same goes for the imposition of an energy tax in the United States. Floated by Clinton shortly after he took office, it was dropped quickly in the face of strong opposition. The internalization of ecological costs in consumer pricing that a truly strong program of ecological modernization calls for also looks very far away indeed. If shifting subsidies and modest environmental taxes are not forthcoming, who indeed could hope for full-cost pricing, pricing that incorporated all environmental costs into the sums consumers paid for goods and services?

What would a gallon of U.S. gasoline cost if all the environmental costs to present and future generations were included, even as subsidies were withdrawn? What would it mean for the world economy to incorporate the full costs of the ecosystem services it uses? These latter were recently estimated at $36 trillion a year for an economy of $39 trillion.[37] Worse, even this figure omits an important consideration: most of the "services" living systems provide cannot be duplicated by people and thus in effect cannot be monetarized. They are irreplaceable necessities; money cannot remedy damage to them. Even Hawken and the Lovinses, enthusiastic proponents of ecological modernization, warn that:

> A pesticide may sell for thirty-five dollars a gallon, but what does it cost society as it makes its way into wells, rivers, and bloodstreams? Just because markets do not address value, goodness, justice, and morals does not mean that such concerns can be safely ignored.[38]

But to go on—Green consumerism has had some effect; Hawken and the Lovinses report how, after Nigeria's hanging of Ken Saro-Wiwa and seven of his colleagues for "protests against environmental deregulation in Ogoniland caused by multinational petroleum companies, Shell stations in Germany were burned to the ground, boycotts in Holland slashed sales, and employees in London were chastised by family and friends" and Shell began "to reexamine all its racial, economic, and environmental policies."[39] But boycotts this passionate have been few indeed, and the record of Green consumerism has been much more ambiguous.

Some have blamed an absence of adequate information for consumers to act upon as a reason why ecoefficiency has come so slowly or not at all. Advertising has not been known for revealing effectively the environmental risks of products; the example of a Canadian legislator proposing the addition of pictures of diseased lungs to the prim little warning tags on cigarettes U.S. consumers are familiar with gives one an idea of just what advertising could do if it wished. But for some reason, ecological modernization seems to have taken a different turn so far. Green consumerism means, for the most part, something rather different from what it should. Thus Tom Athanasiou reports that "Antienvironmental and 'green' PR [i.e., PR that merely greenwashes still brown industries] are a billion-dollar-a-year industry, and the largest PR firms in the world are self-consciously involved in what they sometimes call a 'new environmentalism,' one that, as *Fortune* magazine put it, will be 'more cooperative than confrontational—and with business at the center.'"[40]

Recently Jared Diamond proclaimed the greening of corporate America because: "given a choice between buying equally priced products from a clean company or a dirty company, of course they would buy the clean product." The problem, though, is that "consumers are barraged with manufacturers' claims of environmentally sound practices. How can we distinguish the valid claims from the deceptive ones?"[41] Revealingly, the problem that Diamond describes indicates that so far Green consumerism has meant, for the most part, greenwash. His solution involves an interesting ecomodernist collaboration between the World Wildlife Fund (WWF) and industry. The WWF would certify a company's practices and products as environmentally sound, and consumers would have that information to guide their choices. A good idea, indeed, but it does have a number of pitfalls. For some, who have already been incensed about the ways in which the WWF has already cooperated with corporations, these certifications will be a highly uncertain and thoroughly double-edged. They could produce a still more convincing greenwash as easily as they effect the opposite.

And are we truly all on the same side at last—are we all Greens now? If so, one might too quickly answer, the right doesn't know it yet. Win-win alliances have extended only so far. Further, along with the persistence of opposition by the right, win-win rhetoric has another limitation: it all too frequently excludes radical and populist environmentalists and disallows radical and populist positions, something that has helped disunify the environmental movement. Side by side with ecomodernist collaborations, the environmental movement, as noted in the previous chapter, has been riven by a painful set of internal divisions, the most profound of which, perhaps, is a division between radical grassroots activists and the mainstream, national, Washington-based, large environmental organizations. Gloomily, Maarten Hajer sees this splitting of the movement not as accidental but as something the now-hegemonic philosophy of ecomodernization has helped produce. For ecological modernization is, he argues, a strategy dedicated in part to taking "the sting out of the tail of radical environmentalism in order to secure various social and institutional commitments," and those with more radical and populist views thus often become ecological modernization's opponents.[42] By making people feel that crisis has gone too far and society has become too interdependent for anything but systemwide change to be effective, ecological modernization seems to put the power to avert crisis into the hands of elites, the only ones with power enough to effect change and the position necessary for coordinating activities on so many fronts. To critics, this ironically means turning to the very people who got society into its problems in the first place.

It is thus not surprising that radical-grassroots environmentalism has come back onto the national scene of late, specifically in Green Party support of Ralph Nader and antiglobalization protests. Radical-grassroots environmentalism seeks, generally speaking, more disruptive, democratic, socially just, decentralizing, and anticorporate forms of alternatives to existing social structures. It emphasizes, as ecological modernization does not, societal, not just technocratic, change. It doesn't just try to ride the camel in the direction it is going; it talks back to the camel or lies down in its path. Mark Dowie and Philip Shabecoff have given vivid portrayals of the possible radical or transformative potential for these movements should their scattered efforts be recognized, advanced, and collected into what they call the "Fourth Wave" of American environmentalism.[43]

Taken together, however, radical and grassroots groups work to the same end as ecological modernization—toward a widespread internalization of environmental concerns in the workings of U.S. society. They start from an urgent, often highly personal, and local version of ecological modernization's central assumption, namely that environmental crisis cannot any longer be denied—and that we live in a system in which it is increasingly endemic, affecting not just our opportunity for occasional "nature" experiences but our everyday lives at home and in our workplaces, our economic, social and cultural experiences, and our personal and psychological health. They then try to build novel alliances between formerly adverse parties (for example, business, labor, and Greens for ecomodernization and, for the Fourth Wave, labor, Greens, and civil rights activists) to effect change. Perhaps the growth and persistence of both will set the stage for transformative environmental politics in the future. For now, that future is too far away to read—indeed, further away than it was in 1992.

Whatever its limitations, it was ecological modernization that seemed fully to enter mainstream U.S. national politics with Al Gore's election as vice president and Clinton's tentative adoption of global environmental crisis as part of his agenda for bringing the United States into the new global era. It didn't, however, stay there for long. Emphasizing the economy over the environment, Clinton created an environmental record that quickly became an extremely sore point to Green critics.[44] Perhaps, given the decade-long conservative assault on environmentalism and America's position as the world's leading producer of greenhouse gases and the world's most unconstrained consumer of resources, it should be remarkable that a U.S. attempt to take crisis seriously seemed at first so possible. But, remarkable or not, the political realities of office quickly caused environmental crisis to fall off Clinton's rhetorical and practical agendas. Environmental crisis as a new paradigm was no longer foregrounded even when, toward the end of Clinton's second term of office, he took a wide variety of concrete actions that have made some call him the "greatest environmental president in American history."[45] Protecting the Arctic National Wildlife Refuge, setting aside land as off-limits to development, and even issuing an eleventh-hour executive order to protect millions of acres of federal forests did not invoke, as ecological modernization does, a vision of comprehensive environmental crisis as part of a project of fundamentally restructuring society. Clinton's most celebrated acts followed the much more traditional logic of preserving nature. Even his and Gore's other actions such as defending the Clean Air Act and setting up a program to raise automobile fuel efficiency seemed more attempts to hold onto and extend the legislative legacy of the past rather than to inaugurate a whole new paradigm.

Probably the most fundamental reason why the Clinton administration dropped ecological modernization from its rhetoric and much of its policy was its embrace of the global economy—its attempt to ride that tiger in a way that economically benefited the United States. That choice involved espousing an economic and social reorganization of nation and world that did not seek to internalize environmental conditions at all. It meant, in fact, not greening the economy in an ecomodernizing style, but creating a new and much more high-profile phase of the old brown economy, one that for a period simply pushed environmental considerations, ecological modernization, and even environmental debate to the side. Though globalization theoretically *can* proceed in different ways—and though some have argued that it does offer significant environmental benefits—globalization of the economy and likewise globalization of society and culture have in practice created a set of new problems for ecological modernization to deal with—even before it had a chance to work through old ones.[46]

Most notable, publicly, has been controversy about the environmental implications of free trade, as embodied in NAFTA (North American Free Trade Agreement), GATT (General Agreement on Tariffs and Trade), and the WTO (World Trade Organization), and in further trade proposals such as the failed MAI (Multilateral Agreement on Investment) and the in-negotiation FTAA (Free Trade Area of the Americas) and GAIS (General Agreement on Trade in Services). What is feared is that these agreements and organizations are taking environmental regulation out of the hands of democratically elected governments around the world and putting it into the hands of unelected corporate-friendly decision-makers. These agreements prohibit restraints of trade, a category that threatens local environmental legislation; worse, they set up legal mechanisms whereby transnational business can sue governments for damages when governments seek to prevent companies from exploiting and exporting scarce resources; when they resist transnationals' attempts to privatize and provide basic services like water, sanitation, and education; and when they seek to pass protective environmental and social welfare laws. Measures to protect the environment and ensure social welfare then can be—and are being—challenged as restraints on trade, and nations may be held liable for huge sums representing the loss of profits—profits past, present, and even future.[47]

But while these immediate political stresses have received the most attention, globalization in a variety of forms—economic, social, and cultural—has been creating more serious, fundamental, and structural problems for the environment. Accordingly, globalization in a wide variety of forms has become increasingly the object of intense critical scrutiny.[48]

The global economy as people in the United States have come to know it has been fixated on renewed and intensified rates of economic growth. Growth was always important, but the arrival of the global economy has made growth for all still more of a fetish in the United States than it ever was. Domestically, embracing globalization was what promised to end the U.S. economic slide and economic recession; internationally, growth prompted by globalization promised to enrich and transform the entire world. And once the economy did indeed take off under Clinton, growth seemed magically to become hypergrowth: new, speeded-up rates of growth seemed to many to be regular features of a qualitatively new economy, not the temporary result of an expansion of the old one. Now deeply tarnished in the wake of the dot.com decline, the installation of an old-paradigm president, the revelation of corporate mismanagement and deception during the boom years, and the realization, via terrorism, of globalization's darker potentials, this new fetishism of growth looks rather different. It is easier to see that, from the start, recent celebrations of growth were far less innocent than the celebration of progress that accompanied consumerism and developmentalism after World War II. Unlike earlier enthusiasms, contemporary celebrations were shadowed by the prospect of a number of downsides, especially environmental ones. Not only was the anxiety about violated natural limits, (raised by environmentalists during the 1960s and 1970s) never thoroughly dispelled, but conscious and unconscious awareness of the risks of growth were kept alive in a number of quarters during the 1990s, even as growth was fetishized. Thanks to the Rio conference, the debate about sustainability, the excesses of antienvironmentalists, and the assertion by a number of influential observers that development for all was not possible within the limits of the earth's ecosystems, global growth's environmental shadow grew steadily longer.[49]

Accordingly, as economic globalization took off, it provoked strong environmental critiques. Concern was raised by the way that, in times of rapid expansion, an increasingly global economy incorporates all as it grows. It reaches out spatially to include all places on the earth and reaches inside natural processes to control, rework, and even possess by patenting them. Writing about today's increasingly rapid conquest of space, the essayist Tony Hiss reports how detailed satellite photos taken several years apart can make a sobering animation of forest and field yielding to mall, junkyard, development, and industrial sites.[50] Deforestation in the Amazon has increased substantially, not declined, since the UNCED conference in Rio embraced sustainable development. Hitherto remote, supposedly still premodern places in the world have been rapidly reshaped and hooked up to urbanized global (post)modernity.[51] In a recent advertisement, the Nature Conservancy announced—with painful forced cheer in the midst of disaster—its "Third Great Party to Save the Last Great Places." The ease with which post-Fordist manufacturing facilities can be rapidly assembled and spread about the world and the globalization of extractive industries and the development of megatechnologies for resource

extraction and production have combined to hasten environmental degradation. These same factors have helped prevent prompt recognition of the damage. Exported to remote places, social and environmental injustice and damage
stay hidden longer from the affluent communities of the world, the beneficia-
ries of this process—something that dulls awareness by the affluent of sharply
rising environmental and social risks.

Even as the global economy has absorbed space, it has set about penetrating
and reworking nature radically on the microscopic level. New bioengineering
enterprises have come up with such innovations as cloned sheep, genetically
modified plants and organisms, modified agriculture and food production,
genetically engineered animals for scientific and medical research, and genetic
therapies and stem-cell-grown organs for transplantation. Some have even
quipped that market selection is replacing natural selection as the motor for
evolution. With this transformation, some feel not just that nature is more thoroughly exploited than ever before; equally, society is increasingly jeopardized by
new, potentially high-impact risks and instabilities.

In its attempt to incorporate global space—to make the new global system
into one that has no alternative spaces left, one in which everything is at last "inside"—the global economy has instituted a variety of novel manufacturing and
marketing technologies and techniques. These help ensure that American-style
consumerism, long seen as environmentally unsustainable, becomes the global
norm. The new system of globally disaggregated production—whereby the orange juice I drink in the morning is manufactured in both Florida and Brazil—
is coupled with a new global marketing strategy, which the chairman of Sony
has described as "glocalization," guaranteeing that consumer goods appeal to
polycultural tastes and consumerism spreads all over the world. Together these
two developments mean that raw material, partly assembled products, and finished goods are sent hurtling about the earth as never before.

The greatly expanded global transportation system that spreads these goods
far and wide is also environmentally damaging.[52] Barry Lopez writes mordantly
about the thousand 747 cargo jets continuously now aloft hauling cargoes of
"drill pipe, pistol targets, frozen ostrich meat, lace teddies, dog food, digital tape
machines, pythons and ball caps," and even a "yacht headed for the America's
Cup race [and] a tropical hardwood bowling alley from Bangkok" and flying, in
the process, over the "rocket fire and streams of tracer ammunition" from
the earth's many small wars.[53] Lopez's juxtaposition of the goods above to the
conflict below provides a haunting image for global consumerism's social and
economic impacts. The "rocket fire" below hints at the balkanization of the

world that some feel has accompanied globalization. As important, though, is the fact that these problems stay *below*—so far below the agents of the new consumerism that they appear anything but real. A global economy that can separate consumption ever more widely from production creates a class of affluent consumers disconnected from the environmental destruction and nasty social conflicts that spread as the world system becomes more unequal and more unsustainable. The planes ride silently and even beautifully over the colorful rocket fire and the ruined ecosystems. If Lopez shows the systemic grotesqueness of the new global transportation system that facilitates these concealments, others point out its energy wastefulness; still others indict global trade as a major cause of the biodiversity loss. Hitching rides on this transport are invasive species that wipe out local flora and fauna at rates so alarming that the conservation biologist Michael Soulé has said their damage "may soon surpass habitat loss and fragmentation as the major cause of ecological disintegration."[54]

Finally, the new global economy has revolutionized finance, and negative environmental consequences are again the result. In the global economy, capital is even more mobile than Lopez's consumer goods or industry's modularly constructed products. It can, at the push of a button or two, either flee any place that lays environmental restrictions upon it or take over any business, like the Pacific Lumber Corporation, that manages itself with such long-term ecological and social conscientiousness that it becomes attractive to those who would strip it for short-term gains.[55] Further, today, much of the enormous sum of money that sloshes daily about the globe—97.5 percent of it according to one calculation—represents transactions in the money system rather than the real economy. This only increases pressure upon corporations to live for short-term profits. Corporations have to compete against "the often more lucrative games of the world of pure finance" for their investment funds, even as they suffer from the boom-and-bust instabilities created by so much money searching for a place to turn a profit.[56] Much more than before, corporations cannot afford to let environmental or social considerations stand in the way of their realizing short-term profits, even as they have larger and larger war chests to invest in their pursuit of them.

Globalization of the economy has caused environmentalists the greatest concern. But political-social globalization and cultural globalization also have extremely threatening sides. Moving beyond a world of nations means, on the most overt level, a weakening of nations' abilities to institute and enforce social regulations—including environmental ones. This is especially worrisome because there is no transnational regulatory body now in place able to stand up to the power of the transnational corporations (TNCs), which have swollen to the economic size of nations. Of the top fifty economic units in the world, the majority are TNCs. Further, meaningful nation-based environmental regulation is being directly challenged, as noted above, by global trade agreements. Even more, TNCs' power to relocate to where labor and environmental regulations are the most favorable—that is, the least strong—works toward a socially and environmentally degrading globalization that represents, according to Tom Athanasiou, "harmonization down."[57]

In more subtle ways, globalization's undoing of national and local communities is ominous. The transnationalization of public and private institutions, along with the transnationalization of many ordinary lives, means that both place-based community and ecologically related place sense are put at risk. If a sense of community is important for acting on behalf of a social movement like environmentalism, an environmentally or ecologically grounded place sense is often what motivates people to join the cause in the first place. A measure of the threat on both these fronts is that both contemporary students of culture such as Stuart Hall and contemporary geographers such as Doreen Massey who have tried to think through the consequences of recent globalization have begun to argue that place sense must now be conceived in terms of "routes" not "roots." Our idea of place is altering rapidly and coming unstuck from local community, geography, and thus from ecology as well. Today, they argue, place is best retheorized as an "intersection," "a site," or a "meeting place."[58] Such terminology invokes a world of malls and airports, not landscapes or ecosystems. Particularly at a time when many have come to value indigenous and peasant communities for their environmental knowledge, traditions of environmental stewardship, and environmentally sensitive cultures, globalization's destruction of local culture and place awareness is particularly regrettable. Even cosmopolitan multiculturalism, while breaking down racism and cultural exclusiveness, similarly tends to detach cultural identity from place and especially from legacies of alternative (usually nonmodern) environmental practices; it highlights instead transnational mobility and its relationships with a new global capitalist system.[59] Local places quickly lose all their particularities and become, to use Edward Casey's term, "sites" rather than places—locations stripped of inherent qualities and made easily fungible thanks to the technologically enhanced power of global capital.[60]

Transnationalized culture also presents dim environmental possibilities. Wiring up the earth with the new communications media means hastening the export of the environmentally unfriendly U.S. lifestyle. The new global manufacturing and marketing apparatus mentioned above exacerbates this problem by cultivating a new, postmodern kind of consumerism. In this new era, a veritable sea of designer or taste-culture products, shorter-lived in usefulness than ever before, reach a wider variety of global-polycultural consumers. Further, the new consumerism marketizes more areas of human activity (from travel to therapy) and reaches a far greater age range of people (from infants to the edge of the grave). Also, in selling a wide new range of symbols—ones oriented to whole ecologies of cultural identities and lifestyles as well as to class and status—the new consumerism colonizes individual psyches all over the world more deeply than ever before. And since this "symbolic economy" is in fact not as detached from material production as its proponents claim, it also expands environmental impacts along with marketable products.

A closely related phenomenon is the urbanization of global culture, something that likewise results in loss of concern for, knowledge of, and even experience of the natural environment. Physical experience has changed. If in the United States, urban populations grew to exceed rural ones after World War II, the same tipping of the balance is now happening globally.[61] Tony Hiss writes that during the past forty-five years: "about everyone in the Western world has moved for the first time [fully] indoors."[62] This condition is spreading globally, and environmental knowledge and experience can be lost in the process.

Even more than urban growth, the urbanization of U.S. and world culture has altered social environments for people, even those far from urban centers. Accordingly, much of U.S. culture is now hyperurban. As Burton Pike has argued, the contemporary media have helped urbanize audiences far from cities; in much of the material broadcast, we have even, Pike continues, "lost the conventions that opposed urban to non-urban cultures."[63] For while modern urban culture historically has made space for a number of Green cultural forms and practices, from pastoral poetry to wilderness activism, contemporary postmodern hyperurbanism has sponsored cultural movements that seek not just to marginalize but to erase all these, either by excluding them altogether or by turning them from reality into consumable image or even simulation. One example is the way that more and more people have been brought—as Chapter 7 shows—fearfully to confront or even accept with interest the startling proposition that "nature" is now in some sense ending and to imagine, without ecological realism, that their lives can continue (and even improve) in explicitly "postnatural" environments.

Much more broadly, though, the new "global" culture has donned a less extreme but still environmentally challenging form of hyperurban dress. Cel-

ebrating a newly interactive world of permeable (not defensive) borders, it
has valorized speed, openness, mobility, hybridity, interactivity, and cosmopolitanism, even as it has detached human economies, cultures, and poli-
ties from territorial and also ecological roots. Reinforcing this hyperurbanity,
contemporary technoculture has emphasized even forms of transgenic (not
just transnational and transcultural) mobility. These new emphases often
constitute something much more radical than a simple increase in mobility;
they don't just accelerate people across geographies but jettison situatedness
in geography, place, ecosystem, and even bodies altogether.

As promising as it seemed at the start of the Clinton-Gore administration, the
political use of the new global paradigm has proved unkind to environmentalism. Successful in helping to reshape cultural consensus and economic life
in the United States, globalization has departed from its original environmental promise. As it first appeared on the mainstream U.S. new-paradigm scene,
it seemed to offer a kind of grand unified theory of a better future. At the
start, economic globalization promised to expand and globalize prosperity;
social globalization sought an end to bitter nationalisms and the possibility of
world-destroying international conflict; cultural globalization offered a way
out of the legacy of colonialism, racism, and ethnocentrism; and global ecological modernization theorized ways of creating a sustainable world. But the fact
that the environmentalist discourse, like gravity in physics, could not be made
to harmonize with the other three soon became clear as not just ecological
modernization but environmental perspectives generally were erased by enthusiasm over globalization in other areas.

The likelihood of this erasure should probably have been clear from the
start. For while the economy, society, and culture all prepared for the new millennium by dressing up as new "global" possibilities, the environment's global
outfit was far less prepossessing. The environment came, for all its new-paradigm designs and filigrees, not as possibility but as crisis. The "global" environment appeared as the global environmental *crisis*—a crisis grown to the
point that it now included everything. While globalization in other areas
seemed to open up new visions of humanity's future in a time of increasing
contention and cynicism, the best environmentalism could do was to promise
hope for averting what otherwise would be appalling.

For a while, then, globalization discourse—in both the popular arena and in
academic theory—was able to ignore or at least hive off environmental
concerns for separate consideration. The Seattle protests in 1999 at the WTO

ministerial meeting helped change matters somewhat, prompting Clinton to call for incorporating environmental concerns in world trade negotiations. Thought along these lines has also produced a list of the environmental advantages globalization could confer and sensible recommendations for greening.[64] Now that the collapse of the "new economy" into recession has punctured dreams of endless growth and, even more, the events of September 11 have exposed, for many, some of the darker possibilities of globalization, such ignoring and hiving off is no longer possible. The discursive field has changed again. In an address at Yale after September 11, Bill Clinton forthrightly commented on the need to grapple with globalization's problems. Arguing that optimists would say that the "dominant trait of the world in the twenty-first century" was "the globalization of the economy and culture that has lifted more people out of poverty in the last twenty years than any time in all history," Clinton also asserted that pessimists would point out that "the environmental crisis facing us is so great that it threatens to engulf all the progress" and that "half the world's people aren't a part" of the new prosperity. Both of these pessimistic viewpoints, Clinton went on to say, now need attention.[65]

The arrival of contemporary globalization thus further complicated what was an already extremely complicated and conflicted field: American environmental politics at the end of the twentieth century. Effective discourses of denial of crisis coexisted with calls for internalizing environmental concerns everywhere, thanks to crisis; but these calls themselves proved anything but clear. They could mask environmental depredation as well as held out positive hope, and though they might establish win-win alliances, they did not silence the deniers or unite even environmentalists. Worse, just at the moment when all this was happening, a whole new array of environmental problems began to open up as the result of globalization of the economy, society, and culture, a globalization that decidedly did not internalize environmental concerns.

With the inauguration of George W. Bush, the retreat from effective environmental advances seemed to continue. Environmental politics seemed to return to a period of successful doubt, if not outright denial, that crisis existed. Though in his first year of office Bush moved the conservative agenda forward on many fronts, he took environmental politics backwards. Admirably, Bush sought to erase the last rhetorical traces of the divisive culture wars his party once sponsored and effectively papered over the right-moderate split in the Republican Party with his compassionate conservativism. Bush's environmental actions and statements throughout 2001, however, were very different. By the end of 2001—the date at which my survey of U.S. environmental politics stops—it seemed clear that Bush was unchanged in his commitment to rolling back environmental protections and that the Republican Party was still, in that area, firmly under the influence of the right.[66]

Few today remember that, in national politics, Republican environmentalism was once not an oxymoron. As William Cronon has pointed out, it included the legacy of Theodore Roosevelt but it was also strengthened by presidents such as Herbert Hoover, Dwight Eisenhower, and even (despite his personal lack of sympathy for the environmental movement) Richard M. Nixon (signer of the Clean Air and Water Acts, the National Environmental Policy Act, and the Endangered Species Act).[67] Robert Proctor has added that "President Richard Nixon has the distinguished honor of having signed into law the most potent environmental legislation of the century."[68] At the beginning of the second millennium, however, after decades of Republican antienvironmentalism, Republican environmentalism seems almost never to have existed. True, Republican moderates on the national level do exist; for example, where I live, a number of state and local Republicans have real and admirable environmental commitments. But the takeover of the national party by the right has put their positions and actions in a deep shadow.

The losses charted in these chapters are profound. More than anything else possible in the political arena today, I believe, an end to the organized denial of environmental crisis and a recommitment by both parties to seeking out alternatives to it would reenliven faith in the future in the United States. For despite decades of rhetorical denial and political dispute, environmental crisis has not disappeared. Indeed, even as the politics of mentioning, discussing, and perhaps even acting on environmental crisis has become more Byzantine—more and more entangled and complex—the scope, complexity, and volatility of environmental crisis have grown substantially. As elaborated by environmental scientists, social scientists, popular science writers, environmental writers in the nature tradition, and environmentally conscious journalists, the crisis has developed and diversified at an alarming rate. The next chapters will attempt to face that fact. Whatever may or may not be happening with our struggles to cope with environmental crisis, crisis itself has not stood still.

Part II

Elaborating Crisis

An Introductory Caution

The chapters in this section need to be prefaced with several cautionary re-marks. It is unlikely that the scientific and, even more, popular-scientific elab-orations of environmental crisis reviewed below will remain unchanged over time. It is very possible that some elements of these elaborations will prove wrong. Given the extreme complexity of ecological processes, strict scientific certainty about always incomplete data is difficult to come by. Equally, the politicizing of science that is inevitable when scientists and others track envi-ronmental danger, damage, and risk in a context of social conflict leads to as-sertions that in hindsight may seem biased as well as prove untrue. All too easily, even serious projections and prophecies turn into quaint curiosities or even repugnant attitudes when viewed from the standpoint of a later time.

The history of crisis is indeed littered with a number of odd, dated fan-tasies and even objectionable assertions. The alarm about global cooling that preceded the hue and cry about global warming today seems strange indeed. And Paul Ehrlich's 1968 predictions of worldwide food and water crises of apocalyptic dimensions to occur in the 1980s not only did not come true but led a number of believers to make policy recommendations that seem today inhumanly draconian and reprehensibly biased against non-Western peoples and the poor.

But it is important also to remember that the history of crisis is also lit-tered with understatements. Perhaps few will remember Fairfield Osborn's concern, in his 1948 book, *Our Plundered Planet,* that the present world popula-tion would double in about seventy years. He turned out to be the optimist, not the pessimist; only fifty-three years have passed and the world's popula-tion is close to tripling.[1] Even more pointed are other instances where pes-simists were proven correct despite high-profile attempts to debunk their concerns as hysterical. Thus alarm about the ozone hole survived much propa-ganda and much professional-sounding counterscience analysis, and concern about global warming is now turning out to have a similar trajectory. That the pessimists prevailed in these contests resulted, in the case of ozone depletion, in action that may have been enough to save the world from a major global catastrophe just in the nick of time. Doomsters, apparently, can turn out to be absolutely correct and vital to humanity's safey.[2]

One further caution is also necessary. Environmental warnings can, thank goodness, also err thanks to successful remedial action—action that comes in large part because of environmentalists' warnings. Environmental doomsters' warnings are, after all, alarms sounded in the hope of action, not pronouncements of inevitable fate; it is good, then, that some of these calls to action work and some possible futures are avoided. Recalling some "solved" problems—like leaded gas and unregulated tailpipe emissions as a crucial part of a First World air pollution crisis—can be quite instructive. It is alienating, today, to read old fiction about air-quality issues—for example, Philip Wylie's *The End of the Dream*, which I discussed in the Preface. Its depiction of millions dropping dead on New York City pavements as a killer toxic cloud of air pollution sweeps up the streets seems indistinguishable today from the old Japanese horror movies about radioactive mutations; both seem part and parcel of the vast, musty storehouse of humankind's odd old apocalyptic tales. But Wylie's fiction becomes far less strange if one recalls that a 1952 London smog event—a catastrophic "inversion" of the sort that New Yorkers and weather forecasters made so much of in those days—actually did strike down three to four thousand people with quasi-apocalyptic suddenness and that Merril Eisenbud, Mayor Lindsay's environmental director for New York City, warned that pollution could destroy the city.[3] Perceptions of Wylie's "excesses" are thus mitigated if one realizes that current amnesia about particulate air pollution comes from the fact that a real problem was dealt with thanks to strong expression of public concern like Wylie's; current amnesia does *not* come from the fact that the problem wasn't real in the first place.

Most important, though, is the fact that even "solved" problems do not completely go away but linger on in less visible ways and/or threaten to return with growth. For a "solved" environmental problem represents for the most part not a crisis dispelled but one temporarily coped with. Despite the apparent victory in the United States, the global future of air pollution by particulate matter remains an open question. Whether Mexico City will get its horrendous air pollution under control is uncertain; a huge cloud is now resident over the Indian Ocean; and the appalling conditions of many Chinese cities could well spread far beyond China if the developing world industrial-

izes with soft coal. And in the developed world less visible forms of air pollution continue; SO_2 emissions have shrunk significantly, but emissions of fine
and ultrafine pariticles are up, causing "significant effects on health in urban
areas." Pollution by motor vehicle exhaust has been identified as a cause of
"21,000 premature deaths annually" in Austria, France, and Switzerland, and,
in the U.S., diesel exhaust has been shown to be a significant cause of cancer
in metropolitan areas.[4]

That apocalyptic prophecies do not come true thus does *not* mean that the
problems they highlight have completely disappeared and that environmental
concern can simply be dismissed. For far more important than the present
status of any particular environmental problem in an era of accelerating
human-caused environmental change is the momentum of the underlying
forces that cause that change. Even according to an organization committed
to growth, the OECD (an organization of industrialized market-economy
countries), the developed world still displays "environmental degradation
[that] has increased at [only] a slightly lower rate than economic growth."[5]
Though ecological modernization and sustainable development have been
struggling to delink economic growth from environmental impact for some
time now, not enough progress has been made to show that the goal is even
possible, let alone reachable.[6] The often-dismissed and much-maligned
doomsters of the 1970s, the authors of *The Limits to Growth*, who asserted
that continuing population and economic growth would lead inevitably to
environmental crisis have not been, in sober fact, disproven yet. Though some
of their specific findings have been rebutted by critics, their most fundamental assumption has not.

In the developing world, the picture is even more grave. Continued economic and population growth still means an unrestrained expansion of
human environmental impacts—something that brings with it worsening environmental conditions, the continuation of old problems, coupled with the
appearance of new ones. Environmental issues promise, therefore, to grow in
importance as humanity moves into its twenty-first-century future. Stresses
promise to rise and perhaps overwhelm the dikes people ingeniously build to
contain them; crisis promises to cast a longer and longer shadow across all
human activity.

CHAPTER 3

Natures in Crisis, Part 1:
An Inventory of the External World

Based on available scientific evidence we are certain that:

- *Ecosystem services are essential to civilization.*
- *Ecosystem services operate on such a grand scale and in such intricate and little-explored ways that most could not be replaced by technology.*
- *Human activities are already impairing the flow of ecosystem services on a large scale.*
- *If current trends continue, humanity will dramatically alter or destroy virtually all of Earth's remaining natural ecosystems within a few decades.*

———*Issues in Ecology*, Spring 1997

The litany of ecological complaints plaguing the world today . . . include: overpopulation, destruction of the ozone layer, global warming, extinction of species, loss of genetic diversity, acid rain, nuclear contamination, tropical deforestation, the elimination of climax forests, wetland destruction, soil erosion, desertification, floods, famine, the despoliation of lakes, streams and rivers, the drawing down and contamination of ground water, the pollution of coastal waters and estuaries, the destruction of coral reefs, oil spills, overfishing, expanding landfills, toxic wastes, the poisonous effects of insecticides and herbicides, exposure to hazards on the job, urban congestion, and the depletion of renewable resources.

———John Bellamy Foster, *The Vulnerable Planet*

W. B. Yeats, writing about the 1916 Easter Uprising in Ireland, once proclaimed that "a terrible beauty is born." A similar phrase can describe how elaborations of environmental crisis have expanded over the last several decades, despite the concerted attempts chronicled above to deny and discredit them. A terrible heterogeneity has appeared. Environmental crisis, already seen as diversified and multiform by many in the 1970s, has steadily assumed a striking new variety and multiplicity.

Even a short list of current environmental crises is of necessity quite long. At the least it must include an energy (and also other resources) crisis; a multifactoral waste crisis; an open space crisis; a wetlands crisis; a food production crisis; a crop diversity crisis; a forest crisis; a soils crisis; an ocean crisis; a freshwater crisis; a biodiversity crisis; an acid rain crisis; an ozone hole crisis; a global warming crisis; an environmental toxification crisis; a global disease crisis; a population crisis; and a growth or development crisis. Many of these individual crises themselves are plural. Problems with wastes, for example, include garbage, sewage, and toxic wastes—and the latter of these problems breaks down further into wastes from agricultural chemicals and fertilizers, industrial chemicals, and nuclear energy and weapons, items often treated as separate crises; soil crisis includes loss of arable soil, runaway development, factory farming, salinization and desertification, radically different problems requiring radically different action; and ocean crisis includes overfishing, warming temperatures, dieback of coral reefs, and massive eutrophication and pollution, again very different problems requiring different forms of action.

To these more and less familiar crises, less conventional ones need to be added—crises that are simultaneously crises of society and of the environment. These include intrasocietal conflicts over environmental injustice; potential regional and international conflicts over environmental security; the unforeseen effects of new, revolutionary, and megatechnologies added to the effects caused by the expanded use of old ones; and a variety of social-structural crises—crises caused by a system structurally committed to environmental damage and unsustainability, thanks to commitments such as capitalism's need to grow or die and its practice of relentlessly externalizing environmental costs. If these crises seem unmappably plentiful, this abundance becomes greater when one considers that each area has accumulated its own collection of activists, experts, science, regulatory law, regulatory structures, interests, and patterns of controversy; the intellectual and social variety surrounding each crisis further blurs the clear eyes that would grasp the whole.

Most of these different crises have recently become global. Far more than 1970s visions of crisis, a wide variety of environmental crises now enfold the earth and all mankind. This claustrophobic globalization of crisis has occurred in several ways. Thanks to growth and the industrialization of more and more of the world, human interventions have the power to transform large-scale global environmental systems like the atmosphere and oceans. Equally, they impact global inventories of local systems such as soils, forests, rivers, lakes, and species—inventories of things that are of the same type but that don't function so clearly as part of a single, global, ecological system. Thanks to both processes, no unaffected space is left on earth.

As human-made environmental crisis has grown more enveloping, a watershed in global history seems to have been passed. Daniel Botkin has written that the discovery that "we people can affect the entire earth . . . is a relatively new idea" and that "as recently as 1967, such human influence seemed preposterous even to most of those who had thought deeply about nature." Now, a few short decades later, most of those who have thought deeply about nature accept that notion, realizing that even as peoples' health depends on nature's, nature's health depends, often quite sensitively, on people.[1] Indeed, human-induced biospherewide changes such as ozone depletion, global warming, and the chemicalization of the global environment have been not only comprehensive but also terrifyingly rapid—the work of only a few blind human generations.

These new demonstrations of human power have been sadly constraining, not liberating. People see themselves increasingly determined by what has been done in the past to nature—as living at the effect of various kinds of damage already done. Past environmental actions have become a large part of nature's present fate, as more and more environmental problems are created by people, not "nature" or forces altogether beyond human control. Society has gone so far along this path that once-popular dramas of facing nature as a worthy opponent—dramas once featured in great epics—have become today more matters for nostalgia or quotation than present recounting. Sebastian Junger's popular book, *A Perfect Storm*, for example, looks back to the age when the Grand Banks still had fish. Now these once-fabled waters are fished out. Human-made environmental problems loom increasingly large nowadays in the list of human challenges, constraints, and also woes.

In an environment so changed in both fact and social perception, the logic of the environmental-catastrophe scenarios of the decade of crisis has been seriously disrupted. Old scenarios of environmental meltdown today seem naïve in their apocalyptic dress. People have become too sophisticated—and also habituated to crisis—to respond simplistically to end-of-the-world alarm-sounding. This increase in crisis sophistication does not, of course, mean that crisis itself has gone away. Instead, it indicates that more and more, crisis has become part of the milieu in which people, even in the crisis-denying United States, actually dwell. At the heart of the collection of data and analyses in this and the following chapters lies this one essential assertion. Environmental crisis is no longer an apocalypse rushing toward a herd of sheep that a few prophets are trying to rouse. It is not a matter of the imminent future but a feature of the present. Environmental crisis is, in short, a process within which individual and society today dwell; it has become part of the repertoire of normalities in reference to which people construct their daily lives.

To map a field as heterogenous and diversified as environmental crisis today is difficult. It is almost impossible thanks to not just the sheer multitude of crises but also the even larger multitude of possible connections between them. Given all the interrelationships between the many kinds of environmental problems there are today, it is almost impossible to predict what specific pathway future environmental deterioration will take. The problem is not insufficient knowledge to construct a scenario; it is that adequate knowledge exists to construct too many of them to be readily numerable, let alone illuminating. Rather than write a narrative or scenario, then, the best that anyone trying to gain a comprehensive view of environmental crisis today can do is to flesh out an inventory—an inventory of accumulating forms of damage and areas of concern. In this spirit, I'll focus in this chapter on ecosystem damage, moving on to other types of environmental problems in the next two.

Surveying damage to ecosystems alone means a sizeable inventory. I'll start arbitrarily with the forest crisis. Between 1950 and 1990, about half of the earth's tropical forests were destroyed.[2] Further, and this is a deeply sobering figure, at current rates, this means the world's remaining primary tropical forests will be gone in less than forty-five years. According to John Terborgh, a professor of environmental science and botany at Duke University, "the last tree is predicted to fall in 2045." In its 2001 report, the Food and Agriculture Organization (FAO) of the UN calculated that 13.9 million hectares (or 34.35 million acres) of natural tropical forest were lost *each year* during the 1990s—a mind-numbing figure that translates to the more easily visualized, but more mind-boggling loss of 66 acres *a minute*. True, the FAO's estimates for tropical forest remaining are larger than Terborgh's and subsequent estimates of forest loss hold that the rate is less than previously thought. Still, the death knell for tropical forests is perhaps only postponed, not necessarily eliminated.[3] Though the FAO also reports that reforestation is occuring in the North at the rate of 1.5 million hectares per year, this doesn't even approach offsetting what is happening in tropical forests in terms of number of acres lost or ecological significance.

Loss of the earth's tropical forests is a grave prospect, but looking behind the forests themselves, the sense of world-historical gravity increases. Driving these developments are a variety of factors not likely to go away and not easy to mitigate. Deforestation comes from carrying out present business as usual—from a rapid scything of forests for paper, wood, wood pulp, and short-lived cattle plantations, rain forest ranches soon to become bare scars as the soil is destroyed. Wood products are woven intimately into our economies and daily lives. The OECD predicts that: "globally, forest sector production will increase by 87% from 1995–2020, with the highest growth in non-OECD regions."[4] Forest loss is further hastened by the by-products of today's fundamental industrial processes, such as acid rain, a global problem due to worsen as the developing world industrializes. Concerning the developed world, meanwhile, where natural forests are slowly increasing, the United Nations Environmental Program's report, *Geo-2000: Global Environmental Outlook*, holds that: "60% of the forests in West and Central Europe are seriously or moderately degraded, mainly as a result of pollution."[5] Forest loss and forest degradation thus become only a symptom of deeper and more unstoppable forces. Thinking it out this way, one could feel that, absent significant action to stop present trends, the earth's remaining forests have even now lost their independence from humankind. Today, that independence is an illusion: like other limited resources, the global economy has transformed them into what Heidegger called "standing reserves"—on-the-shelf resources for human production, to be used when the need arises. By exploiters and protectors alike, they have already been inventoried; their days as well as their quantities may well be numbered, for their continued existence is dependent on changing human choices and trends.

New technologies have, of course, added to the speed of the process—not just global transport for forest raw materials and products but new extractive technologies as well. It is stunning to see feller-bunchers operating. A brief cut in Carlos Diegues' 1980 movie *Bye Bye Brazil* shows an uncannily agile machine rush up to a rain forest tree and clamp its scythelike mandibles about its trunk, then extrude quickly a horizontally aligned circular saw below into the live wood. A second or two and the tree is severed with one lick of the machine's metal tongue, and the tree is flung to the side; the manic machine scoots then quickly to the next, the next, the next, and so on, destructive energy seemingly limited no longer by any social or material constraint. This is a physical and local image that embodies in small-scale form something that Alan Durning has caught in larger form by imagining a time-lapse film presenting global deforestation from space. If each millennium became a second, the third of our planet's surface that was forest would begin to change only in the last three seconds and vanish only really in the last fractions of a second (i.e., the decades since 1950). Developments like these moved John Terborgh to give his book on the loss of forest preserves the title *Requiem for Nature.*

With such an analysis and description, crisis conceptualization shifts—something that will prompt me to interrupt my inventory of specific forms of damage here and there with comments about these larger changes. It is important to recognize just how much labeling forest loss the depletion of a resource trivializes it. The possibility of an approaching end to the world's primary tropical forests pushes the significance of the event beyond what the word "resource" or "depletion" can express. A qualitatively new kind of gravity is added to our present moment; and forest loss is just one of a lengthening list of globally significant losses. This list runs from finally confronting the end of the fabled marine abundance of the Grand Banks off Newfoundland to the imminent end for much if not all of the world's population of free, available freshwater, to the ends of species that are occurring nowadays not just one every month or year but every ten minutes or so.

Equally important, however, is a second recognition. The prospect of these "ends" does not mean that people confront an onrushing apocalypse, the end of humanity. These foreseeable "ends" are something that people are in the process of *living through.* Apocalypse, by contrast, almost seems too easy; with a big bang—with prophecy, revelation, climax, and extermination—it and we are over and done with. Living on through loss seems by contrast as bad or even worse; it means experiencing environmental deterioration, steady decline in human well-being, and increasing constraint on future human action consciously and slowly while realizing that they are likely to continue for generations after one is gone. People alive now are living within a time when significant biospheric legacies that have been part of human beings' practical, psychological, and spiritual lives since their beginning as a species are disappearing.

Side by side with the sense of gravity that losses like these entail is another emotion—a feeling of claustrophobia and struggle. For the earth produced as a result of all this activity will not be a depleted planet but rather a hyperactively ravaged and hyperabundantly problematic one. It will be an earth on which runaway development, consumer overabundance, and a continual increase in the tempo and extent of human interventions create not depletion and exhaustion but a proliferation of injury and problems. Forest loss, like other major ecological changes, sets off a cascade of problems—it involves economic and social disruption, it sacrifices a carbon sink, it entails the loss of numerous species of plants and animals, it alters the hydrologic cycle, it plunges local populations into misery, and it degrades life for global populations through large-scale economic and environmental change. What once was described as a "running out" gradually shifts, in the perspectives of those living through the change, into the need to deal with rapidly multiplying natural *and* consequently human problems.[6]

Crisis so depicted mobilizes responses that come as strongly from urban as from rural traditions—ones associated with urban proliferation rather than rural depletion, with overcrowded cities, not emptied dust bowls. Even more, it calls up cultural associations that come more often from life down, not up, the social scale. These traditions invoke the pain and problems of immersion in unpleasant and dangerously unhealthy conditions and in the social conflicts that go along with them—pains and problems that come from urban slum experience rather than rural experience of scarcity and depletion. Lawrence Buell demonstrated this when he showed how the rhetoric of the urban sanitarian movement of the nineteenth century resurfaced, with a significant twist, in today's toxic discourse, particularly in the responses people have had to finding that the environment they were raising their children in is damagingly polluted. The sanitarian reformers' descent into urban slum conditions—a Virgilian tour of the "underworld" undertaken by the elite—is transformed today by the recognition that the underworld is now a place where potentially everyone lives including the observer-commentator.[7]

Dwelling in contemporary Love Canals, for example, leaves little space for the stern prophecy, apocalypticism, irony, or contemplative melancholy of Victorian and modern reflections on the fall of civilizations and the end of societies.[8] Prior to the days of hyperactive environmental problems, literary and philosophical elites could contemplate the rise and exhaustion of civilizations much more comfortably. As environmental problems have grown more and more into nightmares of hyperactivity and hyperabundance, and as all, even the literarily and philosophically inclined, can readily imagine themselves affected by them, large-scale prophetic views of the process have become harder and harder to maintain. Claustrophobia and immersion in conflict replaces detachment, irony, prophecy, reflective melancholy, and apocalypticism; the multiplicity of doctors, lawyers, scientists, action groups, grief work groups, child psychologists, and pediatric surgeons, and the snarl of insurance or Medicare claims, debt woes, marriage stresses, uncertainty, information gathering, meetings, and strategizing that people need to deal with in order to cope with such conditions allow little space for detached views of the whole.

If the earth's forests are at risk, so also are its oceans. Human beings now take "a quarter to a third of the ocean's production," something that, the ecologist Stuart Pimm adds: "may not seem like much, but may already be too much. Even at current levels of exploitation, let alone levels that will accompany a doubling of the human population, we are already harming our natural resources."[9] Indeed, "overwhelming evidence," Pimm contends, "shows we are destroying the ocean's ability to supply even what we take now."[10] Once-rich fishing grounds have already been exhausted; oceans have been filled with sewage and Styrofoam; globally, their coral reefs are dying. And diminishing in these ways, the oceans are in the process of being subjected to the grave global logic of inventory, both as finite resource and finite sink. The effect is to counter age-old associations that oceans have had for the human imagination: as illimitable, as the cradle of life, as the source of the "oceanic feeling" of wholeness and totality. In this vein, Stuart Pimm has quite pointedly asked: "How big are the oceans?" From "a human-centered view"—from the perspective of their productivity—his answer is that they are "very small."[11] Ninety percent of the ocean surface—the "blue" ocean—is not very productive. Again, the melancholy accompanying the prospect of the oceans' present degradation and diminishment and the "death" of their age-old significance to the human imagination is impossible to calculate in instrumental-rational terms.

Paul Hawken and the Lovinses predict: "we will lose 70 percent of the world's coral reefs in our lifetime, host to 25 percent of marine life"; the United Nations Environmental Program (UNEP) projects that: "more than half the world's reefs are potentially threatened by human activities, with up to 80 per cent at risk in the most populated areas."[12] Gary Gardner reports that 27 percent are already gone.[13] The Worldwatch Institute's vice president for research, Hilary French, reports that: "the world's fisheries are under siege as a result of habitat destruction, pollution, and over-exploitation, with 11 of the 15 world's major fishing grounds and 70 percent of the primary fish species either fully or overexploited."[14] In 1990, the world's commercial fish catch declined by over 4 million tons, and even a *Wall Street Journal* reporter noted that "the fleets are so big and the technology so good that fish no longer have anywhere to hide."[15] In July 1992, the government finally closed the Grand Banks off Newfoundland to fishing—much too late to hope to restore fish populations, Colin Woodard argues.

A significant part of the reasons for the crash of fish populations in the first place was the development of megatechnology in the form of factory-freezer trawlers, which made their first appearance in 1951. Woodard describes the *Fairtry*, the first of these, which featured below decks:

> an on-board processing plant with automated filleting machines, a fish meal rendering factory, and an enormous bank of freezers. She could fish around the clock, seven days a week, for weeks on end, hauling up nets during fierce winter gales that could easily swallow the Statue of Liberty. With radar, sonar, fish finders, and echograms, she could pinpoint and capture whole schools of fish with chilling effectiveness.[16]

In the course of time, trawlers like the *Fairtry* nearly quadrupled in size and their numbers grew to seven hundred or more. Problematic then was the sheer size of the take—including the "bycatch," fish but also mammals, turtles, birds, and invertebrates unwanted by people but necessary to the marine ecology. (Simply thrown away, this bycatch reaches 27 million tons annually, a significant percentage of a total catch that, in 1994 to 1995, was about 75 million tons.)[17] Also destructive, however, were the huge nets that tore up essential seafloor habitats for fish "like gigantic ploughs." Woodard describes this gear:

> Dragging the bottom for cod or flounder, nets are spread open by a pair of metal "doors" or "boards" weighing tens to thousands of pounds. The bottom of the trawl mouth is a thick cable bearing the weight of 50- to 700-pound steel weights that keep the trawl on the seabed. Many drag tickler chains along the bottom to scare shrimp or fish off the bottom and into the net. Scallop, oyster, and crab dredges consist of steel frames and chain-mesh bags that plow through the seabed to sift out target species. With each pass, trawls . . . sweep away boulders and cobbles; crush . . . bottom plants and structure-building animals; and kill . . . animals in the sediment.[18]

To compensate for the loss of wild fish, the aquaculture industry sprang up—something which has not been a genuine compensation but a troubling new form of pollution. The uneaten food and feces of fish and shrimp crowded into pens takes a severe toll on ecosystems. Further, establishing the pens themselves destroys environments. In particular, shrimp aquaculture has destroyed large tracts of mangrove forests which "are now recognized," Hilary French writes, "as playing a central role in protecting coastlines and serving as spawning grounds for oceanic fisheries." "In Thailand alone," she continues, "some 253,000 hectares of the country's 380,000 hectares of mangrove forests have already been destroyed by shrimp farms, according to the country's National Economic and Social Development Board"; globally, half the world's mangroves are gone.[19] And the sustainability and even rationality of the whole enterprise becomes even more questionable when one realizes that the farmed fish and shrimp do not take the stress off wild fish but add to it. "Higher-value farmed species, such as shrimp and salmon," French writes: "are themselves carnivores, which means that large numbers of lower-value fish are sacrificed to feed them. For each kilogram of farmed salmon and shrimp, 5 kilograms of wild oceanic fish are harvested and ground into high-protein pellets."[20]

As a canary in the cave, we can look at the fact that a large freshwater sea like the Aral is dead. As Tom Athanasiou describes it, its "feeder rivers were diverted—sometimes by *nuclear* explosives—to support a massive cotton monoculture that, once in place, generated chemical runoff in such profusion that the region's mothers could not safely breast-feed their children."[21] The sea's revenge, Athanasiou goes on to report, was that, as its level dropped: "it lost its moderating influence on the local microclimate, even as its waters receded to expose vast sterile, saline plains. The storms of chemically laden dust and salt were first noticed by the cosmonauts in 1975, and by the 1980s were poisoning farmlands as far as 1,200 miles away."[22] A larger-scale, saltwater example comes in Tania Aebi's *Maiden Voyage,* her account of circumnavigating the globe in a small sailboat. Leaving Malta, she was startled to find her boat "was dogged by numerous logs, barrels and other hazardous flotsam, highlighted by thousands of plastics in every imaginable form." Aebi had "read that the Mediterranean was a sea dying slowly of pollution, but had never dreamed that I would encounter a solid pavement of rubbish."[23]

More painfully still, Colin Woodard calls the Black Sea dead, largely thanks to massive pollution. "In the 1970s," Woodard writes:

> when Sorin Strutinsky was a boy, the waters of the Black Sea were still clean and clear. . . . One summer, when Sorin was still in high school, the sea began to change. The water had a sticky, slimy feel. It smelled bad— like rotting eggs—and there were lots of dead fish in it. After a swim in the Black Sea, bathers found their bodies covered in a strange coating. Afterwards, some became sick, and others stopped swimming in the sea altogether.[24]

Tourism failed; "fecal contamination and toxic algae blooms forced regular beach closures at the height of the short summer tourist season. There were outbreaks of cholera and hepatitis. The wind carried blankets of decomposing fish onto shore."[25] An invasion of *Mnempiopsis leidyi*, a "bell-shaped comb jelly," was the finishing touch: "it reproduced rapidly, sweeping the sea of zooplankton, the larvae of surviving fish, crabs, and mollusks, the only creatures that were keeping the monstrous algae blooms in check."[26] By the late 1980s, it "had reached a total biomass of nearly one billion tons, more than ten times the weight of all the creatures landed by all the world's fishermen in a year."[27] While the UNEP is more reticent than Woodard—maintaining that "semi-enclosed seas such as the Mediterranean, the Black Sea and the Baltic are highly polluted," not "dead"—the upgrade is not all that comforting.[28]

Woodard goes on to describe other ocean catastrophes fulfilled or in the making, including the formation of the huge dead zone in the Gulf of Mexico (a "7,000 square mile swath of oxygen-less water in which few creatures can survive . . . [that's] been likened to stretching Saran Wrap over an area the size of New Jersey and suffocating anything that cannot escape").[29] The dead zone was created thanks to agricultural runoff from the U.S. heartlands and toxic waste from "Cancer Alley," the ninety-mile stretch of the Mississippi between Baton Rouge and New Orleans, "home to 136 petrochemical plants and seven oil refineries, as well as paper mills and power plants."[30] Still, to jump from these limited catastrophes to the thought that a similar fate might befall the world's largest oceans is dizzying. The thought, however, has been entertained by some. According to Jan Post, a marine biologist at the World Bank, the first steps have been taken: "the ocean today has become an overexploited resource and mankind's ultimate cesspool, the last destination for all pollution."[31]

If the "degradation" of the oceans is, in the eyes of science, increasingly plausible and apparent these days, freshwater limits are as or more measurable. Paul Ehrlich claims that we now use more than half the earth's available freshwater runoff; further, people now pollute half the water they handle.[32] More than 4 million hectares of U.S. cropland are irrigated by drawing down aquifers, and "buildings in Bangkok and Mexico City are sinking because the groundwater beneath them is being drawn away," while levels in wells are falling "in Manila at the rate of 4 to 10 meters per year . . . and 25 to 30 meters per year" in the Indian state of Tamil Nada.[33] And this is happening in a world in which clean water is already at a premium. Approximately 1.12 billion people don't have access to potable water and 2.4 billion are without proper sanitation; roughly "one-third of the world's population lives in countries classified as experiencing moderate to severe water stress or scarcity"; and "if present consumption continues [not increases, as is expected], 2 of 3 persons on earth will live in water-stressed conditions by 2020."[34]

But it is the analysis by Maude Barlow of the International Forum on Globalization (IFG) of global water supplies that truly concentrates the mind. Barlow factors in continuing growth in global consumption of water rather than calculating according to a continuation of present consumption rates. Water consumption is now doubling every twenty years at twice the rate of population growth; by 2025, she calculates, the global demand will be 50 percent more than currently available. By 2025 then, "as much as two-thirds of the world's population will be living in serious conditions of water shortage [while] one third will be living in conditions of absolute scarcity."[35] Barlow's figures are, to be sure, considerably higher than the OECD's projections, which see a 10 percent increase in OECD countries and a 30 percent or more increase in non-OECD countries by 2020; as an extrapolation of recent growth rates, however, they represent a plausible estimate and are deeply sobering.[36]

But whatever future trends are, what has already happened is serious. Already the United States has lost half its wetlands (a figure that also holds true for wetland loss globally), and only 2 percent of its rivers remain free flowing; 37 percent of its freshwater fish are threatened with extinction. Further, in the United States, the UNEP adds: "more than 40 million people obtain their drinking water . . . from a system in which there were violations of health-based standards."[37] In China, Barlow adds, already 80 percent of the rivers are "so degraded they no longer support fish," and the Yellow River, which failed to reach the sea for the first time in history in 1972, failed to reach it for 226· days in 1997.[38] In Poland, three quarters of the rivers are "so contaminated by chemicals, sewage, and agricultural run-off that their water is unfit for even industrial use."[39] In Taiwan, the industrial "miracle" has had a number of side effects: "in some parts of the country, only 1 percent of wastewater and sewage is treated—as a result, the lower reaches of virtually all rivers are biologically dead. Three million metric tons of hazardous wastes are dumped [into them] each year."[40] Worldwide, according to the more conservative OECD, "it is expected there may be a four-fold increase of industrial pollution to water courses by 2025."[41]

Barlow extrapolates from grim present-day conditions like these into a grimmer future. Right now: "in the *maquiladora* zones of Mexico, for example, clean water is so scarce that babies and children drink Coca-Cola and

Pepsi instead," and in India, "some households spend a staggering 25% of their income on water."[42] In the future, conditions like these, she argues, will spread globally as, the IFG argues, today's preliminary moves by companies such as the two French transnationals, Vivendi SA and Suez Lyonnaise des Eaux (called the "General Motors and Ford Company of the water world by the Canadian Union of Public Employees") spearhead the privatization of the earth's water supplies.[43] This privatization, abetted by the deregulation of trade now pursued actively by global agreements and agencies such as NAFTA and the WTO, will mean that disparities of wealth will soon have a much sharper edge to them, both globally and locally, than ever before. Yet another of the earth's commons will be taken over and sold back to those who can pay; those who can't will—as indeed well over a billion people now must—drink potent cocktails indeed. Even now: "modified tanker deliveries already take place in certain regions that are . . . willing to pay top dollar for water on an emergency basis . . . barges carry loads of freshwater to islands in the Bahamas and tankers deliver water to Japan, Taiwan, and Korea."[44] Even better, several public-spirited companies are now "developing technology whereby large quantities of fresh water would be loaded into huge sealed bags and towed across the ocean for sale."[45] As Global Water Corp. says: "Water has moved from being an endless commodity that may be taken for granted to a rationed necessity that may be taken by force."[46] In the city of Cochabamba in Bolivia, the privatization of public water supplies put them into the hands of Aguas Del Tunari, a local subsidiary of the San Francisco–based Bechtel Corporation: "In a country where the minimum wage is $60 per month, many users record water bills of and above $20 per month, and water was shut off completely for others."[47] A successful revolt ended this situation, but a future of global social conflict and painfully heightened disparities thanks to water shortages is a serious prospect today.

A significant addition, then, to the grave list of "ends" faced by people in the present era is the end of something that is as much a social as a biospheric creation. The end of the commons has not stopped with the enclosure movement and the privatization of land. No—in an era of increasing environmental constraints, privatization has found not just one but a number of other new frontiers to conquer. In the new millennium, a number of "commons" are under grave pressure. Water provides just one example. Energy has been deregulated. Air has also been privatized to a degree, as companies have won, under government regulations, the ability to purchase the right to pollute. The U.S. decision to issue tradeable pollution bonds and the Kyoto accord's plan to set up carbon dioxide trading internationally have arguably established a quasi-property right in air. Even nature's power of reproduction is now patentable: the progeny of genetically engineered seeds, bacteria, and animals are now able to be privately owned.

These "commons," more properly speaking, were social creations, not just simple natural inheritances. Though some people may still feel that the water they drink and air they breathe were always simply there for them or that the seeds of their plants and progeny of their animals are theirs, this is not in fact true. Samuel Hays points out that in the United States: "the early conservation movement had generated the first stages in shaping a 'commons,' a public domain of public ownership for public use . . . not subject to private appropriation."[48] Then, with the environmental legislation of the 1960s and 1970s, air, water, and biodiversity became much more strictly protected as public commons, while customary practice and legal decisions continued to protect natural reproduction from human ownership.[49] Conflicts over rights to these resources, conflicts between people and between nations, are old. But both incentives and abilities to privatize these commons have spiked sharply upward in the last decades, even as human stresses on these global commons have further and further eroded and endangered them. Easy as it is to imagine grotesque possibilities resulting from the commercialization of water, it is even easier to imagine the gothic social consequences that could result from the privatization of air.

Still another "global" environmental system—arable soil—is potentially in crisis, and this situation in turn creates the prospect of a food crisis for humanity. First, the earth's stock of available arable land is diminishing. From 1970 to 1990, deserts expanded by "some 120 million hectares, claiming more land than is currently planted to crops in China" and "the world's farmers lost an estimated 480 billion tons of topsoil, roughly equivalent to the amount on India's cropland."[50] Along with desertification, salinization and waterlogging (thanks to irrigation techniques) further deplete the world's storehouse of usable soil, so that "in the past half century the world has lost $1/4$ of its topsoil" and the United States a third to nearly half of its topsoil, soil that it takes five hundred to a thousand years to create.[51] As of 1996: "40% of the earth's vegetated land surface 'has diminished capacity to supply benefits to humanity, because of recent, direct impacts of land use,'"[52] and "soil loss currently exceeds rates of soil reformation 10 to 1."[53] The UN estimates that as a whole: "the twentieth century experienced topsoil loss equal to that of the previous 1000 years."[54] In Iowa, the old prairie soil that is left is, according to Evan Eisenberg: "half dead, the roiling crawling life burned out of it by pesticides, and relentless monocropping. Petrochemicals feed its zombie productivity. Iowans assure their guests that the coffee is made from 'reverse osmosis' water, since agricultural runoff has made the tap water undrinkable."[55] Just since 1945, according to the "World Scientists' Warning to Humanity," 11 percent of the earth's vegetated surface (an area larger than India and China) has been degraded.[56] In China, meanwhile, economic development, claiming farmland, adds dramatically to the rate of loss of arable soil: "estimates of loss range from 50 million to 100 million acres since the 1950s, out of a total of 272 million to 346 million acres."[57]

The practice of monoculture factory farming is also a matter for intense scrutiny—a practice that once seemed to be our solution to food crisis but which may be leading us into it yet again. On the one hand, monoculture factory farming of plants and animals stresses soils and ecosystems. Dependant on fertilizers and pesticides, monocropping produces wastes that degrade soils and toxify ecosystems. An advertisement placed in the *New York Times* by the Turning Point Project, describes the problem in as nightmarish a way as possible:

> factory farming of hogs, chickens and beef brings another big problem: *1.3 billion tons of manure each year*. Infested with chemicals and antibiotics (used as a growth stimulant in factory farm production) the manure is put into open lagoons or sprayed onto fields where it can leach into the watertable and rivers. In North Carolina (1995), a hog waste spill of 35 million gallons killed 10 million fish and closed 364,000 acres of coastal wetland. And in 1998, runoff from chicken factory farms found its way to Chesapeake Bay, causing an outbreak of a deadly bacteria, *Pfisteria*. Hundreds of people became ill; millions of fish were killed.[58]

In a more somberly restrained fashion, the OECD warns that the "more intensive use and increasing risks of agrocultural chemicals" in OECD countries contributes to "pollution of ground and surface water."[59]

At the same time, the OECD warns that the same practices contribute to "increasing resistance of pests to chemical control"—which is just one of a litany of concerns that scientists and environmentalists have about big agribusiness today, concerns that criticize monocrop factory farming for degrading the soil and perching the world's food supply on a terribly risky prop.[60] Soils crisis thus blends inescapably into a return of anxiety about the future adequacy of global food production.

Though global food supplies shot up as a result of the "Green Revolution" and are still rising, and though many consider this one of a handful of notable environmental success stories, others have begun to worry about problems returning in the future. Critics of the "greenness" of the Green Revolution argue that the large-scale agricultural practices it disseminated globally present a number of potential problems. Standardization of food crops on a restricted genetic pool of mass-produced seeds which are then planted on huge tracts of land increases the need for fertilizers and pesticides, because large expanses of single crops are more vulnerable to pests than small diversified farming is; also, overstressed soils' productivity has to be maintained by chemical means. Pollution and soil degradation are one result. A second concern is a new, extremely risky vulnerability to pests. Increased use of pesticides hastens pests' abilities to adapt to the poisons even as it wipes out the pests' predators and thus undercuts the ecological constraints that help keep pest species in balance. Factory farming's standardization of seeds further aggravates the problem; "the FAO," Hilary French writes: "estimates that 75 of crop genetic diversity has been lost over this century" and "in the United States, more than 70 percent of all cornfields are now planted in just six varieties of corn."[61] With so much of the same crop in the same place and with so few predator species left to eat the pests, monocropping is, as Janine Benyus puts it: "like equipping a burglar with the keys to every home in the neighborhood . . . [or making] an all-you-can-eat restaurant" for the pest species that manage to adapt to the pesticides.[62]

If arable land continues to be lost, soils continue to degrade, and agricultural techniques seem to be subjecting the world's food supply to growing risks, food anxieties are heightened thanks to still further problems. One is ongoing ocean depletion as: "nearly 1 billion people world-wide, most of them in Asia, rely on fish as their primary source of animal protein."[63] A second is uncertainty whether technological innovation will continue to allow food supplies to keep up with continuing human population growth. Once technology provided the magic bullet; predicted to arrive imminently, food crisis was staved off by the Green Revolution, giving the lie, apparently, to environmental prophets of doom. Bill McKibben, however, points out that while, with the Green Revolution and subsequent developments in seed hybridization, food production grew faster than population after World War II, "the world reaped its largest harvest of grain per capita in 1984." Worse, population since then has kept on rising, and there is a growing feeling that "we're running into walls" with food production and that we're "getting to the point where gains will be small and hard to come by."[64] The OECD is more optimistic about continuing growth in food supplies (projecting a continuing increase by 10 percent to 2020); the UN's Department of Economic and Social Affairs, however, warns that: "the increasing scarcity and degradation of agricultural and other environmental resources cast serious doubts as to how long food production can surpass population growth."[65] Agricultural agronomist Vernon Ruttan comments that in the early 1960s: "it was fairly easy to tell myself a story about where future yield increases were going to come from." Today, "I can't tell myself a convincing story about where the growth will come from in the next half century." Thomas A. Sinclair of the United States Department of Agriculture (USDA) Agricultural Research Service at the University of Florida is similarly pessimistic about raising the ceiling of production for cereal crops: "It's hard to see where improvements in that would come from."[66]

To such oncoming problems, genetic engineering is one high-profile response these days. But, as Chapter 5 shows, its visionary claims to be a magic solution to a wide variety of problems, including food production, are persistently overstated, making it doubtful it will inaugurate a second Green Revolution. As bad is that genetic technology is also felt to involve a variety of risks that expand in size and gravity in direct proportion to the technology's promises of dramatic results. A vivid example of this process comes when *Science* reports that many scientists feel that altering photosynthesis is: "'the great white hope' of the future of agriculture. . . . All the relatively obvious steps have been taken. Photosynthesis is what is left."[67] The choice of words evokes a most unfortunate history; great white hopes have had (to put it mildly) bad track records. But perhaps the association *is* appropriate: reengineering one of the most basic and essential biological processes of plants, one on which our species is acutely dependent in a number of different ways, may achieve the worst track record yet.

The large-scale shift, in discussing problems, from nightmares of depletion to nightmares of hyperactivity and hyperabundance parallels a still more fundamental change: an alteration in the vision of what our most intractable environmental limits are. More important these days than concern with the earth's limited resources is concern with the limitations of its sinks. Forests, oceans, freshwater, and soils have been increasingly physically stressed in their role as sinks as well as through extraction and exploitation. Acid rain destroys forests; effluent kills rivers and bays, making the ocean "mankind's ultimate cesspool." The energy crisis signals the shift from depletion to overflowing sinks in an even more pointed way. As the environmental scientist and policy expert John

Holdren points out, these days: "what environmentalists mainly say on this topic is not that we are running out of energy, but that we are running out of environment—that is, running out of the capacity of air, water, soil, and biota to absorb" our effluents. Today, startlingly, worse than having too little fossil fuels is the fact that we have *too much* of them. Fossil fuel emissions threaten to wreck global ecosystems; overflowing sinks present a greater environmental problem than shrinking resources. When antienvironmental heckling from the right focuses, as it most loudly does, on debunking fears of resource depletion, it (conveniently) targets, Holdren makes clear, an anachronism.

People are also, Holdren sagely adds, running out of: "the ability to manage other risks of energy supply, such as the political and economic dangers of overdependance on Middle Eastern oil and the risk that nuclear energy systems will leak materials and expertise into the hands of proliferation-prone nations or terrorists."[68] In saying this, Holdren implies that not all sinks today are physical sinks and not all "pollution" today is just material effluent. Society's ability to deal with hazards and absorb risk is an overstressed sink every bit as much as polluted rivers and oceans are.

With these considerations in mind, it is time to interrupt consideration of a series of crises in different ecosystems (forests, oceans, freshwater, and soils) and focus on a multifactoral problem that impact them all: the pollution crisis. When overflowing sinks become an issue, production is no longer simply production of goods; consumption is not simply the using up of that good; and growth is no longer an uncomplicated blessing. Production yields a hyperabundance of bads as much as (or, indeed, sometimes more than) an abundance of goods; consumption is also the production of wastes; and growth is the growth of stresses on sinks as well as wealth for people. For as nature metamorphoses into human culture, it metamorphoses thence into waste.

The statistics are sobering. As of the early 1990s, the average American generated, directly and indirectly, over twice his or her weight in garbage daily.[69] Further, according to the rule of thumb advanced by Donella Meadows and her colleagues, every ton of garbage consumers discard means 5 tons of waste at the manufacturing stage and 20 tons at the site of resource extraction.[70] And the tonnage is increasing: municipal waste, the OECD maintains, is projected to grow in OECD countries by 43 percent between 1995 and 2020; in non-OECD countries the rate will be higher, doubling by 2020.[71]

Disposing of wastes without side effects is also a thing of the past. Wastes pollute rivers and oceans; in the early 1990s, U.S. cities pumped 2.3 billion

gallons of municipal effluent into the coastal waters along with 4.9 billion gallons of industrial wastewater.[72] Incinerators raise fears about the release of airborne toxins, and even septic tanks in some areas, leak human wastes. The *New
York Times* reports on such a problem in Florida: "new studies show that vast
colonies of human viruses migrate regularly into coastal waters . . . from the 1.6
million septic tanks in the state, making 20 percent to 24 percent of those who
come in contact with them ill, 1% chronically so." This only mildly hints at the
potential for problems here.[73] Toxic chemical wastes, a particularly nasty category of waste, were produced in the early 1990s at the rate of 400 million tons a
year, 300 of which were made in OECD countries—a rate that is still rising.[74]

Disposal of chemicals and other industrial wastes has produced sensational and tragic results. In July 1989, Al Gore reports: "a farmworker in the
Ukraine named Vasili Primka was walking by the side of the River Noren
picking mushrooms [and] tossed his cigarette butt into the water. The river
exploded and burned for five hours."[75] Previously, closer to home, the Cuyahoga river in Cleveland became so polluted it caught fire. Incidents like
Bhopal, Chernobyl, and the *Exxon Valdez* have kept fears of such calamities
alive (the estimated losses caused by Chernobyl are $300 billion and 40,000
people), and on more intimate levels, scandals like Love Canal have brought
poisons deep into middle- and lower-class American domestic settings. At
Love Canal, "citizens complained . . . about the ooze, skin irritations, and the
fact that rocks dug up in the neighborhood exploded when dropped on a hard
surface. Some mentioned that dogs and cats had been losing their fur."[76] Most
painfully, cancer rates, birth defects, and miscarriages went up, and the area's
children suffered from a variety of painful disorders. All this was not enough
to prickle consciences deeply or galvanize Argus-eyed government regulators
into action. Only two years later, when Lois Gibbs and other residents held two
EPA inspectors hostage for several hours, demanding action, was Love Canal
declared a national disaster area and residents relocated.

Though Love Canal may have been dealt with, other places (some with
shockingly visible stigmata) have not. Thus the biologist Joe Thornton writes of
"toxic sacrifice zones" in the United States. These include "the Mississippi
River's chemical corridor—called Cancer Alley by the area's environmental activists, where over 100 large chemical plants line the river's banks between
Baton Rouge and New Orleans," and northeastern New Jersey, "where middle-
and working-class neighborhoods are nestled among hazardous waste landfills,
incinerators and dozens of chemical factories."[77] To this list Hilary French adds
the new free-trade zones such as the "actively polluted border between northern

Mexico and the United States." Here, "chemicals known to cause cancer, birth defects, and brain damage were being emptied into open ditches that ran through the shantytowns around the factories."[78] By 1993, only 150 of 30,000 Superfund sites had been cleaned up. And despite the efforts of many like Lois Gibbs, one in every six Americans now has the misfortune to live within 4 miles of a Superfund site and one in every sixty "lives within one mile."[79]

The next chapter will discuss in depth the much-debated effects environmental toxification has had on the human body. Here it will suffice to describe the overflowing of sinks—to chart what is being put into the environment. The chemical industry targeted by Rachel Carson is still a major source of environmental risk. Mark Hertsgaard maintains that, as of 1992, 65,000 chemicals were in regular economic use; that only on 1 percent of these were toxicology data available; that 80 percent were not even tested for toxicity; that every day one million tons of hazardous wastes are generated in the world, 90 percent of them in the industrial nations; and that between 1990 and 1994, industry "dumped more than a billion pounds of toxic chemicals in [U.S.] waterways" and 40 percent of them "remained unsafe for fishing, swimming or basic recreation in 1996."[80] Slightly differently, Sandra Steingraber notes that current estimates of chemicals in common use vary between 45,000 and 100,000, with 75,000 as the most commonly cited figure (the official EPA estimates are in that range, but estimates can run as high as 600,000). As bad is that only 1.5 percent to 3 percent of these have been tested for carcinogenicity, something that prompts Steingraber to add that: "as one critic has noted, it is as if the bureau of motor vehicles issued everyone a driver's license but did not get around to giving a road test until decades later."[81] Of the chemicals positively found to be carcinogenic, forty are found in drinking water, sixty are released into the air by industry, and 66 are "routinely sprayed on food crops as pesticides."[82]

Reviewing figures like these makes it painfully clear just how limited the success has been of Rachel Carson and the antitoxics movement she began. Most environmentalists today are caustic in describing not just the gaps in testing but the risk assessment procedures themselves.[83] As Theo Colborn, Dianne Dumanoski, and John Peterson Myers argue in *Our Stolen Future:* "the tool of risk assessment is now used to keep questionable compounds on the market until they are proved guilty."[84] And the production and use of chemicals has skyrocketed. Whereas in 1950, before Rachel Carson wrote *Silent Spring*, 10 percent of our cornfields were sprayed with pesticides, in 1993, the figure had climbed, not diminished, to 99 percent.[85] Or, as Shirley Briggs, executive director of the Rachel Carson Council, summed up the situation as of 1990 for merely the chemicals Carson targeted:

Silent Spring recorded a rise in the production of pesticide active ingredients in the United States from 124,259,000 pounds in 1947 to 637,666,000 pounds in 1960. By 1986, according to Environmental Protection Agency (EPA) figures, production had risen to 1.5 billion . . . pounds for the range of products cited by Rachel Carson, and U.S. use was about 1.09 billion pounds. . . . If wood preservatives (fungicides), disinfectants and sulphur are taken into account, the figure for U.S. pesticide production (not including the latter three categories) is about one-quarter of the world total, so the annual burden on the earth must be about 6 billion pounds of these products.[86]

It is easy to look back on the 1950s with dismay as a strange (and alienating) period in American culture. A single photo of Jones Beach in 1945 speaks volumes.[87] In it, effluent from a large sprayer driven by two men shrouds a happy male bather in a mist of DDT; the sprayer bears a sign reading "DDT Powerful Pesticide Harmless to Humans," while the person—hopefully a man, not a child, but quite possibly a child—standing in a jaunty, ready-for-anything position, looks (as the cloud obscures his bathing suit as well as his age) wholly naked and exposed in the fog erasing him. The picture evokes the long, grotesque history of corporate disclaimers of danger and (thereafter) liability and the conviction of so many that society after World War II was poised to win yet another war, that against pests and pestiferous microbes. The specter of the media-slaphappy adult or duped, oblivious child in the mist, so proud to assert the triumph of his species over the insect world and so thrilled to have his photo taken for the newspapers, is just one of many of these images. Sandra Steingraber records others:

> in one short, children splash in a swimming pool while DDT is sprayed above the water. In another, a picnicking family eats sandwiches, their heads engulfed in clouds of DDT fog. Old magazine ads are even more surreal: an aproned housewife in stiletto heels and a pith helmet aims a spray gun at two giant cockroaches standing on her kitchen counter. . . . In another ad, the aproned woman appears in a chorus line of dancing farm animals who sing, "DDT is good for me!" . . . Some . . . even describe childhood games that involved chasing [DDT] trucks. "Whoever could stay in the fog the longest was the winner," remembers one friend. "You had to drop back when you got too dizzy. I was good at it. I was always the winner."[88]

Easy as it is to consider such events part of the nation's benighted past, it is more realistic to wonder if things aren't in some respects even worse today. Today, Joe Thornton writes: "a cocktail of hundreds or thousands of man-made chemicals can now be found absolutely anywhere on the planet, from the deep oceans to the North Pole, from the Mississippi River to our bloodstreams."[89] Indeed, people have chemically reworked these apparently most pristine places the most intensely. The poles serve, Thornton points out, as "the ultimate global sinks for persistent organochlorines," chemicals that, dissolving at warm and condensing at cold temperatures, are brought there to stay by atmospheric currents, a process called "the global distillation effect."[90] Bioaccumulating up the food chain, these same chemicals concentrate in the higher animals; seals from Lake Baikal carry PCBs and DDT in their tissues at levels of up to 160 parts per million, and a blue-white dolphin stranded on the Mediterranean coast of France had PCB levels of over 800 parts per million—more than ten times the level that would make its body legally hazardous waste in the U.S."[91] Chemical pollution is, in short, now everywhere in nature—and also everywhere in human bodies; in the United States and Canada, "at least 190 organochlorines have been identified in the tissues and fluids of the general populations."[92]

If visions of Carsonesque apocalypse have faded somewhat—if the earth has not yet been eerily silenced by mysterious drifts of white powder—perceptions of a slower process of risky chemicalization have increased. With the discovery of a new class of problems caused by environmental chemicals, Carson's more apocalyptic concern with toxic poisoning and cancer has been supplemented by explorations of more subtly deleterious effects that some chemicals have had on wildlife and people. These will be explored more fully in the next chapter; for now, Sheldon Krimsky's list of effects gives a vivid impression of both their variety and strangeness: "intersex characteristics (reproductive organs with combined male and female features) found in marine snails, fish, alligators, fish-eating birds, marine mammals, and bears; declines in human sperm count of as much as 50 percent; increased risk of breast cancer; small phalluses in Florida alligators resulting from pollution; penises found on female mammals; undeveloped testes in Florida panthers; masculinized female wildlife with a propensity to mate with normal females; and cognitive deficiencies in children."[93] With this contemporary form of chemicalization, the world does not abruptly end and ecosystems are not suddenly silenced. But living on into this time means living into deeper and deeper deformity.

Civilian production of sewage, garbage, industrial wastes, and chemical pollution does not exhaust the list of wastes (more and less toxic) presently stressing the earth's sinks. A serious but much less often cited source for the degradation of ecosystems and biota is the military. Military wastes have a dramatic recent history; the nuclear legacy in particular is imprinted on many minds and bodies. The United States has grappled with the problem of disposal of radioactive wastes; lying to nearby residents about its actions, the Hanford Nuclear Reservation in eastern Washington State poured liquid nuclear waste into the Columbia River. Russia has a much worse track record—in Chelyabinsk, until 1956 nuclear wastes were poured directly into the Techa River; in 1957 a nuclear waste dump exploded; and in 1967, officials, unable to store wastes or get rid of them in the rivers, poured them into Lake Karachay, a lake with no outlets. Instead of isolating the waste, however, the lake spread it; "in 1967," as Mark Hertsgaard describes, a cyclone: "swept across the drought-exposed shores of Lake Karachay and whirled its deadly silt high into the air and across the surrounding landscape. Five million curies of radioactivity were dispersed over fifteen thousand miles; nearly half a million people were affected."[94]

Back at home, though, Hertsgaard goes on: "an internal report by the U.S. Energy Department's nuclear safety director warned in 1993 that there was a 'high' likelihood of disaster at U.S. nuclear weapons plants because of deteriorating equipment, poor management, and worker sabotage. Government experts first admitted in 1985 that tanks containing fifty-seven million gallons of nuclear waste at the Hanford complex were not only leaking but could well explode."[95] The accumulation of civilian nuclear wastes adds to the problem, of course, and the worst part of it, as noted above, is that nobody has created a way to dispose of them that is convincingly safe.[96]

Perhaps the actual weaponry produced, even more than the conditions created by their production, represents a still greater potential environmental and social nightmare—one much more discussed today. There are forty thousand nuclear warheads still in existence in the world, and the prospect of terrorist acquisition of nuclear material has been greatly enhanced by the triumph of the free market over communism and the breakup of the evil empire. As bad is that "it takes," Hertsgaard reports, "about fifteen pounds of plutonium to make a Hiroshima-strength bomb. There were four hundred thousand pounds of plutonium lying around in the former Soviet Union in 1991, plus 2.4 million pounds of enriched uranium. Often this material was poorly guarded."[97] Now that, with the September 2001 attacks on the World Trade Center, global terrorism has ratcheted itself up to a new level, the possibility of nuclear devastation—or the use of a conventional bomb to spread radioactive material over a wide area—is part of the possible future for the United States and humankind.

Clearly, however, few people would categorize war and terrorism as "environmental" problems. But few would deny that development of chemical, nuclear, and now biological technologies raise environmental as well as social risks in a number of ways: they increase the possibility of pollution through manufacturing accidents, manufacturing processes, unwanted side effects of applications and products, disposal of wastes, and, lately, raising a nation's vulnerability to terrorist interventions. Recently, environmentalists were criticized for dramatizing the danger that U.S. chemical plants pose to civilians thanks to their vulnerability to terrorism; after posting color maps on the Internet showing the location of plants and the possible effects of a terrorist attack upon them, Greenpeace was accused by the chemical industry of helping terrorists find new targets. Though this criticism is more than a disingenuous (since September 11, the media has been filled with more or less detailed speculative scenarios for new terrorist acts) the concern environmentalists have raised about new environmental-health risks posed by chemical plants in an era of terrorism is genuine. Once again, society's capacity to control hazards and absorb risks seems to be as stressed a "sink" as physical ecosystems are today. All this means that "environmental" and "social" considerations are now locked together in a tighter embrace than ever before as environmental risk is augmented by societal conflict in an important new way.

Overflowing sinks threaten yet another of the earth's ecosystems, and it is time to return from a more general consideration of pollution to the specific inventory of damage to the earth's environmental systems. If forests, oceans, freshwater, and soils are globally stressed these days, so is the atmosphere. Pollution affects the earth's atmosphere as well as its lands and oceans, and once again a postapocalyptic era of growing degradation, steady decline in human well-being, increasing constraint on human action, and rising risk seems to be the result. Increasingly air-pollution apocalypses like Philip Wylie's seem out of date, even as people are living on into and through times when the atmosphere as an overstressed global sink is degrading ecosystems and human health in subtler but ultimately even more scary ways.

To be sure, outside the United States the stuff of Wylie's fantasy has not completely gone away. Al Gore vividly evokes conditions in Poland, where, in some areas: "children are regularly taken underground into deep mines to gain some respite from the buildup of gases and pollution of all sorts in the air"; in Romania, where, in the "'black town' of Copsa Mica [one visitor] noted that 'the trees and grass are so stained by soot that they look as if they had been soaked in ink.'" In the north of the former Czechoslovakia, "the air is so badly polluted that the government actually pays a bonus to anyone who will live there for more than ten years; those who take it call it burial money";

while in the Ukraine, "eight times as many particulates [are put] into the air each year as [in] the entire United States of America."[98] Though the post-Soviet world leads in sensational imagery of this sort, there are indications that an industrializing Asia is perhaps catching up. Along with massive air pollution around industrializing cities in China and from fires in exploited tropical forests, a "haze of air pollution about the size of the United States" has been found to cover the Indian ocean in the wintertime. The "brownish haze is composed of several kinds of minute byproducts from the burning of fossil fuels for industry and transportation," and it may have serious implications for both global and regional climates.[99]

In the United States, large-particle air pollution seems to be a thing of the past, even though subtler problems with particulates remain.[100] But what has emerged in the wake of this "solution" is a series of invisible but in some ways graver problems for the atmosphere and for humanity. These are recent environmental problems scientifically; they promise gradual (but in one case at least, accelerating) degradation more than apocalypse. Though the new, invisible atmospheric pollution includes acid rain, it is pollution by ozone-depleting chemicals and greenhouse gases that has been the basis for the most robust discourses of continuing atmospheric crisis.

A much-noticed feature of these problems is that they are truly global. They represent damage to the biosphere as a whole, not just to a local ecosystem. Less commonly noted, however, is a second characteristic. Ozone depletion and global warming in particular are problems that people can perceive now at best only through their instruments, not their senses—yet these are problems that can have sweeping and terrible impacts. Hidden from people's sight but perceptible to their instruments, these problems strip the familiar of its capacity to reassure and raise anxiety about possibly catastrophic damage where no visible stigmata yet exist. Right now the risks are rising, but the whirlwind has not been reaped save in phenomena such as forest diebacks, increases in skin cancers and melanomas, and global shifts in infectious disease patterns.

At the same time, however, the invisibility of the new air-pollution problems makes them particularly dangerous. They raise the possibility that decisive indications will not come in time for remedial action. Processes are already at work; by the time things are widely noticeable to the senses, society will have gone too far. And, even if people acknowledge trouble at the first onset of publicly alarming visible symptoms, they still may not be able to halt the damage any faster than, say, a pilot can stop a fully laden oil tanker (a process which takes many miles to accomplish). Stopping these forms of pollution is necessarily a slow process, thanks to both the nature of the pollution (ozone-depleting chemicals, for example, have long destructive lives in the atmosphere) and the inflexibilities of our society (greenhouse gases, for example, come from its most fundamental industrial processes and are not easily stoppable now or in the near future without severe social and economic consequences).

The first and most traditionally visible and local of these global and virtual atmospheric problems is acid rain, the change in the pH, or measured acidity, of rain caused by the emission of sulfur dioxide and nitrogen oxides from burning coal, by auto exhausts, and by the burning of grasslands, savannas, and forests; pH is measured on a scale on which 6.5 is neutral, but the scale is logarithmic, so 5.5 means ten times the acidity of the neutral figure. As Clive Ponting remarks: "a pH of 6.0 is the critical level; below this animal life begins to be affected. . . . In water with a pH of 5.5, salmon are affected and molluscs are rare. Between 5.5 and 5.0 there is severe damage to eggs and larvae and snails can not survive below a pH of 5.2. Fish can not live much below a pH of 5.0 and at a level of 4.5 even the flora is badly affected."[101] Acid rain has killed lakes in Europe and the United States; it was responsible for raising the specter of *Waldsterben* (or "forest death") in Germany. A deterioration of the forests then becomes part of the worsening of other problems, such as the release of toxic heavy metals usually sequestered in soils, released when the soils become acidic. Acid rain has gone: "often as low as a pH of 3.1 (vinegar is 2.4) and once at Wheeling, West Virginia, in the heart of one of the most polluted areas in the United States, a pH of 1.5 (battery acid is 1) occurred."[102]

Acid rain as an apocalyptic problem, rapidly wiping out whole forests, has not seemed to be true, in part because forests have deteriorated rather than simply died and in part because great strides have been made in lowering the emission of sulfur dioxide and other air pollutants in developed countries. But if the developing world continues to expand its reliance on coal, the problem will remain globally significant; even short of that, acid rain continues to be an extremely important issue. "Current acid deposition levels in Northern Europe and parts of North America are at least twice high as critical levels," the OECD asserts.[103]

The second of this triad, ozone depletion, is a substantially worse problem, one that succeeded in shocking and then scaring the international community into action. As Bill McKibben reports, chlorofluorocarbons (CFCs) were developed in 1928 by a chemist at General Motors (Thomas Midgely, the same scientist who suggested tetraethyl lead as a gasoline additive).[104] CFCs were considered nearly ideal; useful, nontoxic, and stable, they didn't burn or react with other substances or oxidize metals. They thus seemed to have no environmental impacts. Further, they proved to be excellent in a variety of applications, such as coolants, solvents for cleaning metals, and insulators. They enhanced human comfort and promoted industrial progress; they could also be discarded safely.

But when Sherwood Rowland, a scientist then at the University of California at Irvine, discovered their propensity to destroy the earth's ozone layer, Bill McKibben reports, he was appalled: "I just came home and told my wife, 'The work is going very well, but it looks like the end of the world.'"[105] Once the short-wavelength ultraviolet light (the light that the ozone layer filters out) breaks up a CFC molecule risen into the upper atmosphere, a free chlorine atom is released; this atom is capable of destroying, in a series of reactions, about 100,000 ozone molecules before it is finally removed. The result, as is widely known now, is a threat to the ozone layer that has significant consequences for terrestrial life.

As more and more of the formerly excluded UV-B radiation strikes the earth, it causes a variety of kinds of damage. It causes skin cancer—a 1 percent reduction in ozone means a 3 percent to 6 percent increase in skin cancer, a figure that suggests the 1980s, in which ozone was reduced by 3 percent, should have witnessed 9 percent to 19 percent increases in skin cancer rates.[106] It also causes immune system suppression, snow blindness, retinal damage, and cataracts in people. And it particularly endangers single-celled and very small organisms, such as the microorganisms in the top few meters of the ocean—the floating plants and animals that are the base of most ocean food chains: "Antarctic ozone depletion has already receded photosynthetic production among phytoplankton," Joe Thorton reports, "by 6 to 12 percent."[107] Exposure to UV-B light also reduces leaf area, plant height, and photosynthesis in green plants and affects cultivated plants more than weeds.[108]

Ozone depletion has thus made sunlight far more toxic to humans than before, degraded health in a variety of further ways, and threatened the health of the world's ecosystems. Much worse however is the chilling fact that, had it gone unnoticed, it could have meant apocalypse. And worse still, it did this damage and raised this risk worldwide in an astonishingly short space of time. It did so, moreover, as an utterly unintended and unanticipated effect of one apparently innocent and even ecofriendly human invention/intervention. It signaled, in short, both the unprecedented new power people had over the entire biosphere and the terrible potential that even well-intentioned human interventions could have. One person's miracle intervention could have brought down the biosphere.

Perhaps now that significant international action has been taken, the worst possibilities of ozone depletion have been avoided. As the authors of *Beyond the Limits* write, "governments and corporations at first acted as doubters and foot-draggers, but then some of them emerged as true leaders," and the ozone hole became the premier case of a coordinated attempt by the world's societies to pull back from a condition of environmental overshoot.[109] The Montreal Protocol was signed in 1987; DuPont announced it would phase out its manufacture of CFCs completely; and a still stricter phaseout treaty was signed by more countries in 1990. Yet the startling recognition that human beings were able so to threaten the planet's environmental systems quickly and with such globewide efficacy needs to remain clear.

Two important footnotes to the drama of ozone depletion need to be made before moving on to the third of the new atmospheric pollution problems. Even if the (invisible) problem of ozone depletion has been alleviated, it is nonetheless critical to remember the role that denial played in delaying action. For if the early enthusiasm over CFCs is understandable, the conservative and corporate attempts to deny the problem once the cat was out of the bag not just were infamous but could have led to horrific results. Reagan's second Secretary of the Interior Donald Hodel earned himself "international ridicule" when he was quoted as saying "that the ozone layer would be no problem, if people would just wear broad-brimmed hats and sunglasses when they went outside." Similarly inspired, the conservative scientist-governor, Dixy Lee Ray, wrote, in 1990, five years after the existence of a huge ozone hole in the southern latitudes had been demonstrated, that "measurements" showed ozone was increasing, not decreasing, and, anyway: "the form of skin cancer caused by ultraviolet radiation is relatively harmless, though irritating and unsightly, and 99 percent of the cases can be cured if treated in time."[110] Grotesque untruth was thereby added to untruth, for deadly melanoma as well as manageable skin cancer is the result of increasing UV-B exposures.

The second footnote is equally serious. Apocalypse (probably) averted by a rare instance of rapid international action does not mean problems gone away. Ozone depletion represents a continuing process of ecological deterioration and decline in human welfare. It remains a source of future risk as well. The damage that has been done to the atmosphere is still going on, as the CFCs originally deposited in the atmosphere continue (as they will for a generation) to destroy ozone. As of the early 1990s, more than 75 percent of the population of Queensland, northeastern Australia, who have reached the age of 65 have some form of skin cancer, and the authors of *Beyond the Limits* end their happy tale of international action on a cruel note: "this is the story of overshoot. Everybody hopes it will not be a story of collapse. Whether it will be or not depends on how erodable or self-repairable the ozone layer is, on whether future atmospheric surprises appear, and on whether humanity has acted, and will continue to act, in time."[111] For even if people stop producing ozone-depleting chemicals alto-gether (which they haven't), the world is still in an ozone crisis. The EPA "esti-mates that atmosphere levels of CFCs will increase threefold over the next hundred years, even if *all* CFC production is stopped by the year 2000, because of continued leakage . . . from old refrigerators, air conditioners, plastic foam furniture, and styrofoam cups."[112]

But as terrible as ozone depletion is, global warming is the most serious problem of the triad. A virtual problem now, what is being done presently to the atmosphere promises to produce quite palpable effects during the life-times of today's children. This delayed response, coupled with the invisibility of the problem, has raised serious questions about the world's ability to deal with it as *immediate* self-interest is not yet clearly involved. A worse disincen-tive to act is that its primary cause—the emission of carbon dioxide—is hard-wired into the fossil-fuel economy and cannot be reduced by a device like a catalytic converter. As Jeremy Leggett does the numbers, future prospects for carbon dioxide emissions are almost limitless. Arguing that "we were cur-rently adding 6 billion tonnes of carbon as carbon dioxide each year" from the burning of fossil fuels, Leggett then adds that "ecologists were warning, mean-while, that producing even 200 billion tonnes more carbon from the burning of fossil fuels risked ecological catastrophe." (A metric tonne is slightly heav-ier than a U.S. ton, equaling 2,240.6 pounds). Leggett then goes on to explain the significance of passing that limit:

> Beyond that point, the atmospheric concentration of carbon dioxide would be such that not only would the absolute temperature rise itself be a prob-lem, but the prospect of natural amplifications of global warming would rise rapidly. Beyond the 300 billion tonne level, the risk would certainly become intolerable. Yet the total amount of carbon in fossil fuel deposits below ground was fully 10,000 billion tonnes, according to the best estimates at the time. . . . Burning just a few per cent of this buried fossil fuel would amount to a flirtation with ecological catastrophe.[113]

Forget fears of depletion; running out of fossil fuels would be a blessing com-pared to *not* running out of them.

Though meaningful awareness of the dangers of global warming has been successfully postponed by disinformation campaigns in the United States and meaningful international action is not now very likely, the scientific consensus is now firm that global warming is indeed happening and involves enormous risks for the earth's ecosystems and human society. In 1990, the Intergovernmental Panel on Climate Change concluded that "even an immediate reduction in global man-made carbon dioxide emissions by 60 to 80%" could leave us with a global temperature increase of 3 to 7 degrees Fahrenheit by 2075. And this judgment comes at a time when developing countries—including 1.2-billion-strong China—are seeking to industrialize rapidly, promising to increase global carbon dioxide sharply. During the 2000 presidential campaign, scientists leaked further information updating these warnings—information that made global warming even more of a scientific certainty and that raised predictions of temperature increases by several degrees. But George W. Bush was still able to prevent global warming from becoming a significant campaign issue by asserting it wasn't yet scientifically established. And the best the world has managed to do by way of crafting an international agreement is inadequate: the OECD concludes that stronger policies than even those agreed to at Kyoto—policies that the Bush presidency has, moreover, torpedoed—are urgently necessary "if the worst effects of climate change are to be averted."[114]

Burning a gallon of gas produces $5^1/_2$ pounds of carbon dioxide, and no filter prevents it.[115] And "global car registrations are growing more than twice as fast as the population—50 million cars in 1954, 350 million in 1989, 500 million in 1997."[116] Worse, the OECD predicts that: "motor vehicle kilometers traveled in OECD countries are expected to increase by 40% from 1997 to 2020, and passenger air miles to triple."[117] But vehicle exhausts are only part of what is a staggeringly large problem.[118] According to the UNEP, total global carbon emissions from fossil-fuel burning, cement manufacturing, and gas flaring put 6,500,000,000 tonnes of carbon *per year* in the atmosphere during the 1990s. Burning biomass—from sources such as clearance of fields and forests and runaway forest fires—poured another 3,940,000,000 tonnes per year into the global atmospheric sink.

The potential dangers of climate change do not come just from an increase in human production of greenhouse gases. Many of the worst risks come from the possibility that human actions will trigger vicious positive-feedback loops in environmental systems, thereby accelerating global warming and the damage it causes. Rising temperatures threaten to increase the amount of water vapor in the atmosphere; water vapor is another potent greenhouse gas. Warmer oceans "kill coral reefs (which when healthy metabolize and thus sequester CO_2) [and] the warmed ocean can actually release more CO_2, just as happens when you open a soda warmed by the sun."[119] Further, in heated arctic oceans, convection may slow, thereby reducing "the amount of carbon dioxide that could be taken down into deep water—normally 25 per cent of the global total [is] sequestered this way."[120] Also, the reduction of phytoplankton and algae, thanks to the ocean warming and the admission of UV radiation through the ozone hole, would reduce a huge global carbon sink. The destruction of forests—by warming temperatures, windstorms, fire, and decay, along with releasing carbon dioxide into the environment—reduces yet another an important carbon sink. Forest fires may also increase in a warmed world, releasing still more carbon into the atmosphere as forests become drier and as they come "under attack in some areas as a result of furious windstorms"; already, on the Kenai peninsula in Alaska, where a four-million-acre tract of forest has been killed by recent rises in temperature, people are trying to clear a "'defensible space' around houses for fire protection" and agents have ceased writing fire insurance.[121] And where global warming causes better-adapted types of forest to replace existing ones, "those dead forests could release truly staggering amounts of carbon into the atmosphere."[122]

As McKibben also reports, another feedback loop supposedly ready to cut in is methane, a gas more potent than carbon dioxide in its greenhouse effect. It is added to the atmosphere by the decomposition of wastes, by the production of gas, oil, and coal, and by emissions from the bottoms of rice paddies, the bellies of livestock (the number of cattle, sheep, and goats now stands at more than two billion and is increasing), and the stomachs of termites (which proliferate in cleared forest areas; a single termite mound emits 5 liters of methane a day). As the world warms, there is the possibility of vast releases of methane as the permafrost melts and methane is released from the mud of the continental shelves—some estimates of which "run as high as .6 billion tons [of methane] a year, an amount that could more than double the present atmospheric concentration" and thus prove to be "a nasty example of a feedback loop."[123] Once feedback loops like the above cut in, global warming can suddenly and catastrophically increase; indeed, incidents of sudden, runaway global warming have happened before in the earth's history.[124] Though the Cato Institute suggests that all people need to do is to move a few miles north or change into a lighter shirt, most ecosystems are incapable of picking up and leaving or putting on jackets, and even for mobile humans, the possibility of millions of environmental refugees in a rapidly warming, ecologically deteriorated world (such as is anticipated when low-lying populous countries such as Bangladesh are submerged) is sobering to consider.

As temperatures rise, global warming may produce a wide variety of significant, potentially very severe ecological changes. The list is hotly debated and speculative; accordingly, many of its components can be best seen as indicators of rising risk rather than certain entailments. First on the list are disastrous changes in global climate patterns resulting from the fact that the poles will heat more rapidly than the tropics, reducing the temperature differential between the two that drives the earth's weather. Most agree that violent and frequent storms and more droughts will occur—and will bring with them more floods and fires. Research scientists from Swiss Re, an insurance firm worried about liability exposures to come from global warming, anticipate: "an increasing risk of flooding from torrential rains, increased danger from storm surges, increasing draught, more bush fires and forest fires, more thunderstorms, hailstorms, and tornadoes."[125] Clearly associated with climate change are other losses: the World Wide Fund for Nature predicts significant biodiversity and habitat loss—the loss of up to half the habitat in places such as Sweden, Finland, Estonia, Latvia, and Iceland and up to a third of the habitat within the United States.[126]

Global warming also threatens to deplete and stratify nutrient supplies in the oceans; with global warming of just one to two degrees centigrade and increasing global stratification, "the biological impact could be devastating."[127] Phytoplankton, the basis of the entire marine food chain and a significant carbon sink, would be dramatically reduced. Further, global warming and rising temperatures have already been implicated in the worldwide die-off of coral reefs.[128] Subtropical glaciers will disappear—and along with them an important water source for water-poor tropical countries; and a rise in sea levels—$1\frac{1}{2}$ feet in the next hundred years—will result in the flooding of coastlines and indeed whole nations, something that will not simply relieve the world's wealthy of some prime beachfront property but will also create literally millions of environmental refugees. Further, the melting of arctic permafrost and ice will occur—and is arguably by now well under way. Leggett reports on the 1995 breakage of 500 cubic kilometers off the Larsen Ice Shelf in Antarctica and scientists' shocked responses to the event; in January, 2002, a still larger section, an area larger than Rhode Island, broke off.[129] Further, data "the Pentagon had been sitting on for years . . . showed that over the last forty years ice depth in all regions of the Arctic ocean had declined by some 40 per cent," while "fully a quarter of the ice in the Southern oceans has disappeared."[130] Still more startling is the recent discovery of open water at the North Pole and reduced ice around it. Global warming even raises the possibility of weakening or shutting off ocean currents such as the Gulf Stream altogether—something that has happened in the past and that resulted in major global climatic changes.[131]

To this list still more needs to be added, especially the possibility of an increase in the level of pathogens in the world's oceans and the substantial probability of the emergence of new infectious diseases and a wider spread of old ones, such as malaria, dengue fever, and yellow fever.[132] But the significance of projections like these runs beyond its indication of specific pathways and scenarios for change. Like many critical environmental problems today, global warming makes people realize that they dwell in a steadily increasing condition of risk, uncertainty, and unpredictability. Nature is no longer slow to change, an enduring foundation, a vast, serene background to rapid and ephemeral human actions; it is becoming as tightly strung and volatile as people. Wallace Broecker has been widely quoted as saying: "Climate is an angry beast, and we are poking it with sticks."[133] One prod too many, and perhaps a sudden, irreversible change in state will be the result. And the prods are increasing, not decreasing: the United States was scheduled to produce 15 percent more carbon dioxide in 2000 than it did in 1990. And if China keeps growing as expected, by 2025 its increasing emissions will raise global emissions by 17 percent.[134]

Global warming thus does not just embody newer sorts of crisis problems— virtual, global, and hyperabundant forms of environmental deterioration. It is also a crucial part of the shift in the conceptualization of environmental crisis from apocalypse ahead to the prospect of growing environmental and social deterioration coupled with an increased risk of large-scale catastrophe. So far, this chapter has emphasized ecosystem degradation, decline in human health and well-being, and increasing social stress and constraint on future actions as the result of hyperabundance; as important as these features, however, is yet another—the specter of rising risk. Including risk with the others puts "postapocalyptic" conditions in their most realistic light. Rather than dispelling apocalypse altogether, living in "postapocalypse" is closer to experiencing a very *slow* apocalyse. Experience of this sort does not involve a terrible and conclusive moment ahead when people breach nature's limits and disrupt nature's fundamental equilibrium; it means that one has already entered (or perhaps is already well into) a time when limits have been breached and the risks from disequilibrium are rising. It also means not only that damage is occurring—as it has been doing for some time—but that its deepening is hard to reverse. Before one hits a wall one can stop, but once one has polluted an aquifer or desertified an area of land, stopping further damage and repairing takes time—indeed, a long, long stretch of it.

But living amid rising risk and growing degradation raises a further possibility—that future change could come suddenly and seemingly out of the blue. It suggests the possibility of sudden systemic change, change that cannot be predicted because it results from processes that are fundamentally nonequilibrial and chaotic. One further alteration to a complex, self-regulating system—even a small one—may produce a cascade of changes that result in a phase change of the whole system; a slight increase in water flow from a faucet turns a coherent stream into turbulence; one car more on a freeway can turn smoothly moving traffic into a snarl; one further intervention into an ecosystem, and it can crash. Perhaps unsurprisingly, popular culture has recently made much of chaos theory. Chaos theorists love to point to an imaginary butterfly in Beijing whose wing motions are capable of rapidly and exceptionally amplifying to produce a thunderstorm over Manhattan three days later. Popular culture, as Chapter 7 explores, typically finds excitement in such changes, dreaming of systemic change that produces a higher level of order, a new kind of society. But a more realistic view of sudden systemic change (one that seriously factors in environmental stresses and imbalances) foregrounds collapse as or more prominently than emergence, devolution as well as a sudden leap to a new plane. And anxiety about this likelihood survives even the most exciting respinnings of risk, chaos, and emergence that popular culture generates. Persisting nonetheless, it becomes part of the present state of uncertainty in which people already live, a society that has already shed the comforts of faith in nature's or its own integrity and equilibrium.

Space demands that I conclude now with one other environmental crisis that has been publicly depicted as every bit as urgent and every bit as "global" as the warming of the earth's atmosphere.[135] More properly a "biotic" crisis than an ecosystem crisis or a crisis in a global environmental system, it is a crisis of the entire biological legacy of time, even as global warming and disruption of the nitrogen cycle are crises of space, of the entire biosphere. The biodiversity crisis focuses on the greatest wave of extinctions of fauna and flora that has taken place in 65,000,000 years—the contemporary threat to the world's biodiversity. This onrushing round of species extinction (most often estimated, according to the Harvard biologist E.O. Wilson, to be proceeding at a thousand times the normal background rate) has been brought on by human growth and development and threatens to rival the five great episodes of biodiversity loss in geologic history, the Ordovician, Devonian, Permian, Triassic, and Cretaceous extinctions.[136] From such episodes, estimates suggest, it has taken approximately 5 to 10 million years for the earth to recover. But the new round of extinction is very different from the older ones in one crucial way—people are causing it. And what human society, at present, is extinguishing at so unprecedentedly dizzying a rate can be repaired only in time frames at least several times longer than the evolutionary span of the human species. Ends of this sort are grave indeed.

Biodiversity loss is proceeding at rapid rates. Edward O. Wilson estimates that 27,000 species cease to exist each year—a figure that works out to three species every hour; a few commercial messages, a sip of Corona, and they're gone. Robert May, Stuart Pimm, and other biologists forecast losses of up to one third or one half of all species within this century.[137] Though these figures are speculative calculations, not measurements, a 1998 survey of biologists found: "70 per cent said they believed that a mass extinction is in progress."[138] The prospect of such massive loss has affected many today with a sense of terrible gravity as they live through losses of such profound significance; it has had particular effect on those who have studied the species now vanishing or endangered, those who have had environmental-ethical, aesthetic, and spiritual commitments to them, and those who believe that sympathetic connection with other species is hardwired into our psyches thanks to coevolution.

Equally, however, people have been concerned about the same events from a different perspective; that of the danger that biodiversity loss represents to humankind. The most memorable evocation of the gravity of current biodiversity loss from this perspective comes from Paul Ehrlich, who elaborated a metaphor that has galled readers on the right so much that they have singled it out for particular attack.[139] A passenger on "Growthmania Intercontinental" airlines is appalled to see a worker popping rivets out of the airplane wing and finds out that the man is doing so because they can be sold for $2 apiece. The man is assured that there's no danger; lots of rivets have been lost already, and the plane still flies. The man—unlike us, on the earth to which the plane is the analogy—switches quickly to another airline. Ehrlich interprets the substance of the analogy in this way:

> Ecosystems, like well-made airlines, tend to have redundant subsystems and other "design" features that permit them to continue functioning after absorbing a certain amount of abuse. A dozen rivets, or a dozen species, might never be missed. On the other hand, a thirteenth rivet popped from a wing flap, or the extinction of a key species involved in the cycling of nitrogen, could lead to a serious accident.[140]

Listing a number of invasive species past and present, David Quammen envisions the world this type of biodiversity loss will produce, providing yet another unhappy vision of a future in which the earth's ecosystems become more and more slummified. He argues that in the wake of biodiversity loss, the world will be populated increasingly by "*weedy* species, in the sense that animals as well as plants can be weedy." These are ones that "reproduce quickly, disperse widely when given a chance, tolerate a fairly broad range of habitat conditions, take hold in strange places, succeed especially in disturbed ecosystems, and resist eradication once they're established." Quammen then fleshes out the "near-term future" he foresees. It is one:

> in which Earth's landscape is threadbare, leached of diversity, heavy with humans, and "enriched" in weedy species. That's an ugly vision, but I find it vivid. Wildlife will consist of the pigeons and the coyotes and the white-tails, the black rats (*Rattus rattus*) and the brown rats (*Rattus norvegicus*) and a few other species of worldly rodent, the crab-eating macaques and the cockroaches . . . and the mongooses, the house sparrows and the house geckos and the houseflies and the barn cats and the skinny brown feral dogs and a short list of additional species that play by our rules. Forests will be tiny insular patches existing on bare sufferance, much of their biological diversity . . . long since decayed away.[141]

To put it another way, the world will be, according to Quammen, more completely us and our pets and our pests. Summarizing the views of the paleontologist, David Jablonski, Quammen argues that along with the loss of spiritual and aesthetic values, the decay of fundamental environmental infrastructures will occur. The world will not be able to carry out its usual functions as well as before; there will be a significant decline in its services. These include basic, daily services such as "cleaning and recirculating air and water, mitigating droughts and floods, decomposing wastes, controlling erosion, creating new soil, pollinating crops, capturing and transporting nutrients" and larger-scale functions such as "shielding Earth's surface from the full brunt of ultra-violet radiation."[142] In 1997, a group of ecologists and economists at the National Center for Ecological Analysis and Synthesis in Santa Barbara attempted to estimate the total economic value added yearly by ecosystem services like these performed by the earth's biosphere; the figure for their value to people is higher than "the global sum of gross national products."[143]

Quammen's depiction of the consequences of biodiversity loss is more contemporary in feel that Ehrlich's, which, though arresting, owes much to the old rhetoric of apocalypse. Quammen evokes a world with decaying infra-structure, one in which people live on in unraveling ecosystems that increas-ingly afflict people with urban-style deterioration and loss of services, not a crash that kills. Yet as Quammen's vision of global slummification makes clear, dispensing with sudden apocalypse is no cause for celebration. With rapid species loss, people may expect, Quammen suggests, progressive ecosys-tem and social deteriortation. Robert May concedes that: "it may be that a grievously simplified world—the world of the cult movie *Blade Runner*—can be so run that we can survive in it."[144] But the prospects of survival like that, May makes clear, are a vision less of comfort than of unhappiness.

Discussions of biodiversity loss, like all of the post-1970s tallyings of damage to ecosystems surveyed in this chapter, thus have a final important feature. Even as they emphasize ongoing ecosystem degradation, decline in human well-being, increasing constraint on human action, and rising risk, they evoke two distinct and sometimes contending strains of representation and response. On the one hand, they stretch nature-based environmental sentiments out to a new extreme of world-historical gravity as one contemplates the magnitude of losses occurring now and certain to come in the near future. Nature sentiments are deeply wounded by these losses; people discover themselves experiencing the loss of species and landscapes they have coevolved with over vast stretches of time and are deeply spiritually, psychologically, and aesthetically attached to. A more sobering grief at actually living through death and degradation re-places a horrified sense of rushing toward a wall just ahead, and environmental rage and especially mourning become more and more central components of contemporary nature feeling, ethics, aesthetics, and spirituality. They become important as ways of living in nature as it is now.

On the other hand, as crisis depictions tip toward the vision of urban-style degredation in nature, environmental mourning seems to yield to another complex of feeling. To this second sort of awareness of crisis, nature has ceased utterly to exist as an "other" to humankind; pristine first nature seems to be completely eroded by a degraded, urbanized version of second nature. And nature like this exists as deteriorating human infrastructure, everywhere stressed and modified by people, everywhere inspiring them with a sense of disturbing uncertainty, everywhere threatening to cause conflict between them. This process includes all; no privileged outsiders seem to be left to con-template it in splendid isolation. Rapidly approaching seems to be a time in which only money can hope to place a contested and fragile glass wall between the wealthy (immured still in a degraded world, but protected from its decay by artificial environments) and the many doomed to experience the full consequences of infrastructure breakdown; even this wall, however, will be porous and fragile.

In representing the forms of ecosystem deterioration inventoried above, then, people draw on two different kinds of language and economies of feeling. Both strains remain vital to any attempt to tally up and psychologically confront ecological crisis today. A many-stranded nature tradition keeps people valuing, defending, experiencing, and scientifically investigating ecosystems and biota that, however degraded, still are the necessary and the only planetary kin and companions human beings have. Critical visions of urbanized, in-crisis second nature, by contrast, present a much fuller picture of how human society is intertwined with environmental degradation-in-progress; a focus on second nature instructs people not just about ecological decline, but also the social deformation, human conflict, and injustice that are integral parts of environmental crisis. The former perspective leans toward ecological, ecoethical, spiritual, and psychological solutions, the latter prompts forms of social activism, ranging from ecomodern social reform to Green radical-democratic insurgency.

According to both perspectives, the new human ability to modify the world signals that global human and environmental history has definitively turned a crucial corner. People have entered a world in which the robust (and even, at times, cautious) exercise of their power to modify nature has made their past actions increasingly into their present fate—or, better, not just their present fate, but the fate of all life-forms on the planet. Having lived for several generations with environmental crisis, human and nonhuman creatures now dwell in a world into which it is woven, intimately and everywhere.

CHAPTER 4

Natures in Crisis, Part 2: Deepening Intimacy

According to one chemical industry estimate, chlorinated synthetic chemicals and the products made from them constitute forty-five percent of the world's GNP.

——Theo Colburn, Dianne Dumanowski, and
John Peterson Myers, *Our Stolen Future*

Ronald Reagan may have been the most potent new carcinogen of the 1980s.

——Robert Proctor, *Cancer Wars*

Nowadays, a mosquito infested with the malaria parasite can be buzzing in Ghana at dawn and dining on an airport employee in Boston by cocktail hour.

——Natalie Angier, *"Case Study: Globalization,"*
New York Times, May 6, 2001

Something particularly anxiety-producing happens when one shifts attention from humanly caused damage to nature to environmentally caused danger to human health. Peoples' responses to the effects of environmental crisis become much sharper and more urgent, when they, not ecosystems or biota, are the victims. More important, perhaps, environmental damage of this sort expresses itself in the most fearfully intimate manner; it induces destructive change *inside* and not just around human beings. Exploring environmental health risks makes for a sense of crisis far more claustrophobic than what even severe ecological deterioration produces. Expansive feeling for nature seems no consolation at all when the body's basic well-being is attacked.

When one considers environmental impacts on human health, one quickly feels that, though apocalyptic visions of the imminent end of nature are out of date, people today dwell more deeply and disturbingly than ever before within a form of environmental crisis. As Theo Colborn, Dianne Dumanoski, and John Peterson Myers point out, for example, no human being anywhere today remains free of residues of human-made toxic chemicals in his or her body. Researchers wishing to do epidemiological studies confront the lack of "an uncontaminated population for comparison. No young person alive today has been born without some in utero exposure to synthetic chemicals that can disrupt development."[1] Everywhere today, human bodies come into the world bearing the marks of environmental deformation already in place, not anticipated.

To be sure, this very awareness of involvement and hapless exposure can lead positively to new, potent recognition of human interdependence and oneness with nature. Ulrich Beck describes this awareness vividly:

> people have the experience that they breathe like plants, and live *from* water as fish live *in* water. The toxic threat makes them sense that they participate with their bodies in things—"a metabolic process with consciousness and morality"—and consequently, that they can be eroded like the stones and the trees in the acid rain. A community among Earth, plant, animal and human beings becomes visible, a *solidarity of living things,* that affects everyone and everything equally in the threat.[2]

Yet the nightmare side of this heightened perception of physical connectedness can also lead to a much deeper level of fear and more desperate solipsism than before. Peoples' capacity to feel vulnerable through their bodies, their tightest couplings with the physical world, runs high. No longer can they resort to the Cartesian mousehole, the supposedly fundamental separation of self from world, that Western philosophy hollowed out of an all-too-physical world and that helped give people in the modern era a sense of autonomy and identity. An environmentally altered world that threatens disease—and thereby mocks the assumption of human autonomy that had helped alter it— seems to close in on human thoughts, feelings, and identities as well as bodies, making expansive identification with nature impossible.

As the last chapter argued, people have exercised their relatively new power to modify nature everywhere rapidly and convincingly; contrary to age-old faith in nature's separateness from people—an assumption rooted in classical Greek tradition but with a vigorous five-hundred-or-so-year modern history—nature's health now seems to depend on human actions and modifications. But also becoming true today is the next rotation of this now viciously closed circle. Human social and personal health increasingly depend on nature's health, which increasingly depends, in turn, on past human modifications and present human practices. Nothing drives home this awareness so much as warnings about and examples of tightening reciprocity between degraded environmental systems and degraded human health. Public health, which had been conventionally understood as societal, not environmental, reform, turns out nowadays to be every bit as environmental in emphasis as public health advocates, from the Civil War on, well knew.[3]

Steadily deepening human-made damage to macroecosystems of a variety of kinds has been increasing stress on human bodies. As the itinerary of ecosystem damage given in Chapter 3 repeatedly noted, environmental deterioration impacts human health as well as nature. Thus, for example, Paul Epstein, associate director of Harvard Medical School's Center for Health and the Global Environment, has written that: "there are strong indications that a disturbing change in disease patterns has begun and that global warming is contributing to them"; others have estimated that the Kyoto Accords alone could, if implemented, save as many as eight million lives.[4] Water problems caused by depletion, pollution, and environmental destruction also produce widespread health effects. Environmental pollution by heavy metals and synthetic chemicals now affects everyone in the world, causing a wide spectrum of human damage, from extensive neurological damage (mercury and lead) and cancer (dioxins, furans, and other synthetic chemicals) to a grotesque and frightening array of developmental disorders (endocrine-disrupting chemicals). And all around the world, the erosion of the ozone layer has afflicted people with cancer and weakened immune systems, as well as deteriorated ecosystems in a variety of ways.

As stresses on the environment rise, then, so do stresses on human health. The magnitude of the overall problem stands out sharply in attempts to estimate the global disease burden that results from environmental deterioration and decline. Hilary French reports that the World Health Organization estimates that an astonishing one quarter of the global burden is so caused. "A recent analysis by Cornell University ecologist, David Pimentel and his colleagues," she adds, "reached an even starker conclusion—that some 40 percent of all deaths worldwide are attributable to environmental decline."[5]

For some observers, the category of environmentally caused health damage expands even further. In an increasingly restructured second nature, an ever-widening number of human-made social practices and environments as well as human-restructured natural ones need to be considered part of environmental health agendas. The industrialization of agriculture and industrialized food processing have, for example, raised new concerns about the safety of the U.S. foodstream as well as threatening people with serious health risks from environmental pollution. Workplace hazards have also been added by many to the "environmental" list—something that causes a significant rise in environmental health statistics. According to a study published in the *Archives of Internal Medicine* and cited by *Rachel's Environmental and Health News*: "occupational illness killed an estimated 60,300 workers and made 862,000 workers sick in the U.S. in 1992."[6] Urban conditions have also been considered a source for environmental concerns about human health from the nineteenth-century sanitarian movement to the present. Today, developing-world urbanization in particular is seen as raising prospects for the spread of both feared old and even more fearsome new diseases globally as well as locally. Recently, some have even made the argument that inequality and rapid social change need to be included among environmental health problems. If so, inequality and change would be among the largest causes of environmental health problems.[7]

A full study of these unhappy environmental inscriptions on people's bodies caused by human-made environmental problems is beyond the scope of this chapter. Instead, I shall confine its focus to two specific high-profile areas that are crucial to understanding environmental health concerns. First, I shall focus on the contentious topic of health risks caused by the production, use, and disposal of a wide variety of synthetic chemicals. A specific subset of the larger issue of industrially produced toxins, it is a problem that has confronted First World populations with the prospect of chronic disease *caused* by modernization. Second, I shall consider health risks caused by rising First World vulnerability to infectious and epidemic diseases, a concern connected to a broad spectrum of environmental problems and one that confronts First World populations with the prospect of the rollback of one of the most celebrated achievements of modernization, the control of infectious disease. The first issue burst into mainstream awareness thanks to Rachel Carson's *Silent Spring* and helped create and define the postwar environmental movement in the United States. It has, however, had a complex and tangled subsequent history. The second is as yet, for the most part, a deepening shadow on the horizon—one put there by a number of recent incidents and a variety of ongoing social and environmental changes.

Pollution of the environment by synthetic chemicals gives rise to one of the most contentious environmental issues today. It quickly creates implacable adversaries. In pursuit of profits, chemical manufacturers and the industries dependent on them off-load their risks onto and injure their workers, the people near their facilities and waste sites, and the public at large. When industry-produced risks cause disease, the disease feels unlike natural illnesses; it doesn't come from bad luck or fate. "Germs, after all," Robert Proctor writes, "were almost never the direct and intentional product of industry."[8] But dangerous, industrially produced chemicals are. Worse, industry's rationale is to make and continue making profits—something that gives it powerful incentives to fight off any attempt to stop production of these chemicals even when health problems are discovered. And since "ordinary" people are the victims and the corporate establishment commits the injury, rage at this disparity of influence and power makes rage at victimization burn even brighter. Going through trials in which hired experts summon up uncertain science to contend with each other may well intensify the anger rather than bring catharsis.

The result is that environmental health issues surrounding the production, use, and disposal of chemicals persist as hot-button controversies. They helped ignite the postwar environmental movement in the first place and they have subsequently created a strong populist movement specifically focused on toxic pollution. Indeed, antitoxics controversies are so much a feature of the U.S. political landscape today that it is strange indeed to learn, as Andrew Szasz points out, that as late as 1973 an "EPA public opinion poll showed positive attitudes toward the concept of living near 'national disposal sites.'"[9]

Sandra Steingraber's *Living Downstream* positions itself right in the middle of these controversies. It is a contemporary *Silent Spring;* it combines passion and science in a strongly adversarial indictment of the modern industrial and agricultural chemical industry for its practices, products, and effluents. *Living Downstream* reverses, however, the emphasis of Carson's book. Unlike Carson, it focuses more on toxification and human health than it does on the toxification of the environment. This change in emphasis indicates Steingraber's perception of how much worse things have become since Carson's classic. Part memoir of a survivor of environmentally caused cancer, part survey of the multiple forms of chemical poisoning that bodies are nowadays exposed to, Steingraber's book abounds with disturbing statistics that point to one central conclusion: peoples' bodies, increasingly, are toxic environments.

Cancer rates are up dramatically. Women born in the United States between 1957 and 1958 have three times the rate of breast cancer of their grandmothers. At mid-century, cancer was the fate of 25 percent of Americans—a statistic that profoundly shocked Rachel Carson. Now it is the fate of 40 percent—38.3 percent of American women and 43.5 percent of American men contract it. "All types combined, the incidence of cancer rose 49.3% between 1951 and 1991."[10] In 1992, 1.2 million people in the United States received diagnoses of cancer— a figure that works out to 3,400 a day. Lung cancer, breast cancer, prostate cancer, testicular cancer, colon cancer, melanoma of the skin, non-Hodgkin's lymphoma, and multiple mylenoma all increased. The rate of increase has affected all age levels and has become especially steep in the last twenty years. "Cancer diagnosis has become as significant a generational marker as patchouli oil," Stengraber writes. And the usual objections to these figures—that they are the artifact of an aging population and improved detection methods—do not apply. Steingraber makes it clear that the numbers she uses are based on age-adjusted tables, and the cancer researcher John Bailar argues that the continued high level of cancer death rates (which have risen 6 percent between 1970 and 1994, despite a decline of 1 percent between 1991 and 1994) do not suffer from bias caused by improved detection, as incidence rates would.[11]

Figures like these are truly shocking—a 40 percent cancer incidence rate for Americans is almost overwhelming. Equally shocking, however, is that, though well known to cancer researchers, these figures have not become part of the wider public's store of common knowledge. Steingraber best expresses their overall significance in a pointed revision of terminology common in cultural and social theory today. The notion that bodies are not natural givens but socially inscribed has received wide play in cultural studies and social theory; social inscription of the body is seen as a key part of the social construction of identity. But most analysts pursuing this track stop with discussions of how bodies are constructed by racial, gender, and class codes, something that leads to a surprising omission. They omit the ways in which human bodies are also "constructed"—often in a quite fearful manner—by socially created environmental deterioration and pollution. As the ecofeminist Mary Mellor argues, it is necessary to see social construction of the body as an issue that involves concerns such as the availability of food, fuel, and shelter, health care, sanitation, education, maturation, and dying as well as gender and race, concerns that are "not a focus in many contemporary feminisms."[12] While many contemporary feminisms (and, even more, contemporary theories such as poststructuralism and postmodernism) indict a wide variety of contemporary cultural, social, and economic practices, they mostly ignore a problem that is at least as large: the disastrous inscription of the body caused by environmental pollution and degradation. The result is an elite blindness as startling as the popular ignorance of cancer rates. Steingraber fills that gap. "Our bodies too," she writes, are inscribed. They "are living scrolls of sorts" and "what is written there—inside the fibers of our cells and chromosomes—is a record of our exposure to environmental contaminants."[13]

This record is called the "body burden," the total of all the environmental contaminants that people have stored up in their bodies. It encompasses "all routes of entry (inhalation, ingestion, and skin absorption) and all sources (food, air, water, workplace, home, and so forth)."[14] The total is alarming. The average American body contains detectable levels of DDT and dioxin; 177 different organochlorine residues; and all 209 of the chemical varieties of PCBs, with different varieties sequestered in different organs.[15] Rachel Carson raised the issue of insecticides in breast milk in 1962; "a dozen years later, 99 per cent of breast milk sampled in the United States was also shown to contain PCBs."[16] The level was so high in one out of every four samples that it exceeded the legal limit: "by 1976, roughly 25 percent of all U.S. breast milk was too contaminated to be bottled and sold as a food commodity."[17]

Tracking the sources of these body burdens, Steingraber comes up with a long list. People breathe air that, in cities and industrial areas, has been found to contain "100 different chemicals known to cause cancer or genetic mutation in experimental animals"; people eat foods produced in a "strange" age where "carcinogens [are] a basic element of . . . food production"; people drink and wash in water toxified with pesticides and industrial chemicals.[18] "According to the most recent tally, forty possible carcinogens appear in drinking water, sixty are released by industry into ambient air, and sixty-six are sprayed on food crops as pesticides."[19] The sources of these inscriptions increasingly are peoples' environments, interior and outdoors, far and near, as they are exposed to smog, smoking, winds from toxic waste sites, incinerated vinyl, agricultural pesticides, lawn and gardening chemicals, pet flea collars, gasoline additives, industrial solvents, dry cleaning fluid, and the fumes of paint. What seemed an unnatural perversion of nature and human life in Rachel Carson—poisoning that Carson could compare only to the worst dreams of the Borgias—has now, despite the environmental movement, been normalized as a routine part of the way American society inscribes the bodies of its citizens.

But is Steingraber right? Is her analysis correct? Despite the high impact of many of her statistics, the answer is far from clear. For Steingraber writes today in a tradition that has lost the hold on mainstream science that it once had in the wake of *Silent Spring*. Though antitoxics populism *has* grown in importance as an environmental movement, environmentally produced cancer from industrial chemical poisoning has been moved off the front burner in nonenvironmental circles such as cancer science and medical research. Why this is so is an important story.

At first blush, statistics would seem to argue that the issue today is more important than ever before, not less. As Steingraber reports, the World Health Organization (WHO) found that "80% of all cancer is attributable to environmental influences"—a figure that was derived "by subtracting the rates of countries with the least cancer [the non-industrialized countries] from the rates of countries with the most [the industrialized countries]."[20] Statistics have also shown that, when immigrants come to the United States, "their cancer rates assimilate" no matter how "culturally distinct" they remain.[21] Further, within the United States, the highest cancer mortality occurs in "areas of the most intensive industrial activity."[22]

But as Steingraber herself immediately adds, the WHO figure that 80 percent of developed-world cancers are "environmental" includes considerable ambiguity about what "environmental" means. The term, Steingraber writes, "does not mean what ecologists use the word to mean," and that fact makes all the difference.[23] For what gets designated "environmentally caused" cancer includes cancers attributable to sources other than environmental poisoning by synthetic chemicals. It includes cancers attributable to factors such as diet, lifestyle, and occupation—factors that involve a wide variety of more specific and "optional" risks, from localized workplace exposures to sexual practices, tobacco use, and consumption of fatty foods and alcohol. As causes like these have been investigated, the culpability of industrially produced chemicals has diminished. Also pushing environmental toxification by synthetic chemicals out of the limelight are other recent trends, such as the search for cancer viruses, the subsequent hunt for genetic factors responsible for the disease, and the discovery that cancer is a multistage process, one not mechanistically tied to an exposure to a specific carcinogen. Robert Proctor cites Richard Doll's and Richard Peto's estimates of what causes cancer as being representative of today's mainstream thought. Doll and Peto assign 35 percent of all cancers to diet, 30 percent to tobacco, 7 percent to reproductive and sexual practices, 4 percent to occupation, 3 percent to alcohol, and only 2 percent to pollution and less than 1 percent to food additives, with infection, geophysical factors, and medicines accountable for the rest.[24]

In short, a massive redefinition of the problem has taken place since Carson focused popular and scientific attention on the chemical industry. Though popular concern still runs high, and the fact that sharply rising cancer rates in the postwar period parallel the growth of the chemical industry remains as glaring as ever, cancer research has marginalized industrially produced environmental chemicals as the cause. But whether such a revision is accurate or not remains debatable; Doll's and Peto's findings have been questioned in a variety of ways. The redefinition of "environmental" cancer to separate out environmental toxification from occupational exposures and lifestyle choices is, first of all, suspect. Exposures to synthetic chemicals in the workplace—exposures that are not, for most, optional lifestyle issues—are increasingly seen as environmental concerns.[25] In addition, lifestyle cannot be so easily unpeeled from "environment" when foods present consumers with "limited choices . . . in consequence of the structure of agribusiness" and advertising wields (or used to) enormous influence over people in determining not just what they eat, but their drinking and smoking habits.[26] Most important, though, is the likelihood that the percentages assigned to causes for cancer may "exceed 100 percent by an arbitrarily high amount."[27] This will happen if peoples' cancers have, as is probable, multiple causes; if, for example, environmental pollution should interact with lifestyle choice to produce a cancer, the percentage assigned to each category would increase, and the total of all causes would be more than 100 percent.

And abundant epidemiological evidence remains. Apart from the highly suspicious parallel between the growth of the postwar chemical industry and rising postwar cancer rates, the associations frequently discovered between cancer incidence and residence near toxic waste sites or in industrialized areas suggest that synthetic chemicals may well constitute a very large problem. Similar associations have been discovered between careers in farming, the chemical industry, and the petroleum industry and raised rates of cancer.[28] And as Peter Montague describes them, these associations can be quite vivid:

> on a map showing low cancer rates as a light color and high cancer rates as a dark color, the Mississippi River originates in Minnesota surrounded by light-colored counties, but by the time you make your way down through Missouri, Arkansas, Kentucky, to Tennessee, Mississippi, and Louisiana, counties that touch the river are darker, darker, darkest. This picture *is* worth a thousand words. The Mississippi below St. Louis is a chemical sewer, and people who derive their drinking water from it are twice as likely to get colon and rectal cancer from it, to cite but one statistic.[29]

While the science remains contested, an equally large problem involved in threading one's way through debates about synthetic chemicals is politics. In debates in which science is uncertain, politics are all too likely to play a significant and contentious role. And as one can imagine, this likelihood is especially high when the issue is attribution of responsibility for rising cancer rates to different causes; how this is done is too crucial to too many people for it to remain an academic question. Responding to the vehemence of the controversy, Robert Proctor chose a significant and accurate title for his book on the post-Carson history of cancer research. Though Richard Nixon declared "war on cancer" in 1971, by the 1980s the "war on cancer" had become, Proctor writes, the "cancer wars." Proctor tracks how in the early 1980s conservative-corporate antienvironmentalism made the "cancer wars" a particularly important front in its wider "environmental wars"—the ideological battle discussed in Chapter 1. The result was—and still is—a bloody battle. For in the cancer wars, corporate-conservative antienvironmentalism took the battle deepest into the camp of Carson-inspired environmentalism.

No episode in the cancer wars shows more vividly how science became politicized than one: the attempt to make vegetables seem toxic and synthetic chemicals seem peoples' friends. This transformation began when conservative-corporate antienvironmentalism pounced on Bruce Ames's controversial hypothesis that plants synthesize and expose people to far more toxic chemicals than industry does. The hypothesis was, politically speaking, a blockbuster. "Bruce Ames," Robert Proctor writes, "chairman of Berkeley's biochemistry department, shocked the world in 1983 with his thesis that natural carcinogens are likely to pose a far greater hazard than industrial pollutants."[30] Ames argued that plants manufacture carcinogens as a defense against their enemies—against bacteria, fungi, and insects; he then pointed out that people ingest them in a wide variety of forms. Exposures come, for example, from black pepper, rancid fat, burned meats, browned foods, moulds on foods, some herbal teas and honeys, bruised broccoli and celery, alcohol, alfalfa sprouts, beets, spinach, radishes, and rhubarb. More important, these exposures were significantly greater than the residues of synthetic chemicals on the foods people ate.

Ames thus came to the contrarian conclusion that carcinogens were "natural"—and that (one is not mistaken if one hears an undertone of sneering here) the list of "natural" carcinogens even included some vegetables and health foods held sacrosanct by foolish Green dietetic purists. But Ames's contrarianism did not stop with this point. He then argued that while such foods were carcinogenic, people were tough. Rather than seeing people as vulnerable, as en-

vironmentalists do—rather than, to use Robert Proctor's intentionally politically resonant terms, espousing body victimology—people should realize that
the human body had many methods of defending itself against its continuous
exposure to carcinogens, a position that Proctor, again evoking the cultural-
political context, dubbed body machismo.[31] Human defenses included cellular
repair and the continuous shedding of the surface layers of skin, stomach,
cornea, intestines, and colon. Indeed, there were even some indications that
small exposures to human-made chemical carcinogens were helpful in keeping
these mechanisms in shape. The principal policy conclusion that Ames and
conservative ideologues drew from this hypothesis was clear. Though high-
dosage exposures to synthetic chemicals did cause problems, low-level exposures to them in the air, water, and foodstream did not. A far greater problem
was the one caused by *not* using synthetic chemicals to protect people's foodstream and to ensure people abundant and cheap food supplies.

As startling as they sound to a disciple of Rachel Carson, Ames's assertions
differed from most counterscience in being advocated by a scientist who had a
considerable reputation in his field, who had formerly made significant scientific contributions to environmental regulation, who continued to be highly
respected for work in a number of areas, and who, even in advancing his current, antiregulatory hypothesis, was taken seriously by other scientists. Someone like this gave antienvironmentalism even better material than journalists
like Ronald Bailey or even economists like Julian Simon. Stunningly resonant
with conservative- and industry-favored themes, Ames's views were quickly
picked up by conservative and corporate polemicists such as Edith Efron,
Elizabeth Whelan, and Dixy Lee Ray. Thus amplified, they amounted to what
seems to be a fundamental refutation of nature-based environmentalism and
a science-based affirmation of the slogans of the chemical industry: that
chemicals were "natural" and that people live in a "chemical universe."

In sneering at environmentalism and celebrating a chemically modified nature, Ames's hypothesis asserted exactly what conservatives had argued in
other areas: nature-lovers' notions of the pure and pristine were delusions; the
notion that a pristine first nature existed in opposition to a modernized second
nature or artificial environment was a fiction. Ames's hypothesis added the influential finding that the human body was not the mewling, weak, vulnerable,
environmentally sensitive thing victimology-loving environmentalists said it
was. No, as that hypothesis was amplified (and distorted) by its political and
cultural use, the human body became—to mention just several of the cultural
fantasies that conservative body machismo helped produce—Rambolike or

even Terminatorlike; it was a tough, macho body that was, moreover, capable of artificial improvements to make it tougher. And to these points conservative polemics quickly added yet another as a kind of capstone. The best advice for people to follow in dealing with both nature and the body was just the opposite of the caution and precaution that doomster-victimologist environmentalists continually called for. It was to fly in the face of environmental doomsaying by creating a still more artificial/chemical environment. Risk was "not something to be feared but to be embraced"—an assertion that was made by Paul Johnson of the American Enterprise Institute. "Man," Johnson stated, was "a risk-taking animal" and "not to take risks" was "the biggest risk of all."[32]

While scientists today accept Ames's assertions that there are numerous naturally produced carcinogenic chemicals and that human beings are exposed to them, Ames's hypothesis has done little to stop public regulation of synthetic chemicals. Ames's risk-taking policy conclusions and polemics remain even farther out of the mainstream. Few scientists argue, as Ames has, that DDT shouldn't have been banned, and Ames's challenge that drinking one beer a day was more hazardous than "eating a daily kilogram of dirt containing 1 part per billion of dioxin" has, as far as I know, not yet had any takers.[33]

And objections to Ames's hypothesis abound. First, the effect on people of natural carcinogens is highly uncertain. "No epidemiological data yet support the notion that prevention of exposure to natural carcinogens in fact reduces cancer risk," Lorenzo Tomatis and colleagues write, and, as William Lijisky points out, vegetarians have a much lower cancer risk than others, something that would be impossible if natural carcinogens in vegetables were a major cause of cancer.[34] Also, natural carcinogens do not build up in the environment; "nature has ways of reassimilating them."[35] Second, the possibility that interactions between chemicals in the environment considerably heightens risk hasn't been investigated. Both Ames's assays and conventional regulatory risk assessment procedures do not consider the added risks caused by simultaneous exposure to a variety of chemicals, something people actually experience in daily life. They test only for each chemical separately, despite evidence that exposure to several chemicals simultaneously sharply increases the likelihood of adverse health effects and suspicion that simultaneous exposure "to these new compounds may enhance the toxicity of the older kinds of exposures."[36] And Ames's comparisons of levels of natural and synthetic chemicals in foods omit exposures to synthetics that occur from other sources than food—from the manufacture, application, and disposal of synthetic chemicals and the products made from them.

Ames's natural carcinogens hypothesis is not the only argument raised against current practices for regulating synthetic chemicals. An equally strong challenge has been made to the use of high-dosage animal tests to determine the chemicals' carcinogenicity. Though at extremely high doses, the argument runs, chemicals can produce cancer, at low dosages they may be safe; high dosage tests thus may not replicate the long-term exposures to low dosages of synthetic chemicals that most people experience. To this, and still other forms of conservative fault-finding with regulatory risk assessments, environmentalists respond by outlining the defects that slant contemporary risk assessment in the opposite direction: for example, the failure to test the majority of manufactured chemicals, the extremely high burden of proof required to ban a chemical, and the testing only of individual chemicals, not the mixtures of them that people actually encounter in the world. Whatever truths emerge from battles like these, the heat of the political struggle over cancer and synthetic chemicals has been considerable and will continue to remain high. That battle became white-hot during the Reagan years; many environmentalists considered the Reagan administration was more virulent in its antiregulatory assault on environmental health than it was in its attack on nature preservation.[37] The attack was so intense that a congressional study group was moved at the time to assert that the administration itself was "a public health hazard."[38] And Robert Proctor subsequently attempted to tally up the number of Americans who died as a direct result of the Reagan administration's actions. Proctor writes, summarizing a study by Patricia Buffler, dean of the University of California at Berkeley's School of Public Health, that just one of its acts, its "five-year delay in requiring warning labels on aspirin, led to the needless deaths of 1,470 children from Reye's syndrome, a fatal complication suffered by children treated with aspirin for chicken pox or flu."[39]

On the other side, conservatives have no less vigorously condemned environmentalists for unscientific claims of danger and unreal notions of the "purity" and healthfulness of unaltered nature. And some new findings that apparently support this position, such as the recent Long Island breast cancer study that found no correlation between breast cancer and exposure to certain environmental "carcinogens."[40] Despite what might seem at best a conceptual stalemate, however, concern about the cancer risks of synthetic chemicals will likely continue to run extremely high. The use of old and development of new chemicals is expanding dramatically; were mistakes to be made, the consequences would be extremely painful and difficult to correct; and there remains enormous pressure from industry to deny problems and forge ahead at all costs, pressure that is likely to stimulate popular outrage.

For example, having been told by their consulting toxicologist that they had the highest levels of PCBs in their blood he had ever encountered, residents of the small Alabama town of Anniston sued Monsanto and its chemical division Solutia Inc., achieving their day in court in January 2002. There, Kevin Sack reports in the *New York Times*, they heard opposing counsel tell them, in his opening statement, the following bit of Amesean wisdom. "We would all rather live in a pristine world," the counsel said, acknowledging how people really feel. But, he continued, "we are all going to be exposed to things on a daily basis. Our bodies can deal with it."[41] In contexts like these, corporate use of Ames's theories come off rather badly. When a corporation (staffed with people, one suspects, who would do anything *not* to live with such exposures) tells people carrying extremely high levels of chemicals regulated as carcinogens in their bodies—chemicals that the corporations produced and exposed them to—that "*we*" are all exposed to such things and that "*our* bodies can deal with it," it is hard not to regard the entire industry, its assertions, and the theory behind them with equal distaste.

Whatever the truth value of Ames's hypothesis, there is no question about its interest as a cultural artifact. Its conversion of environmental pollution and its most intimate consequences for the body into the celebration of chemicals, risk-taking, and the machismo of the human body was a revealing and high-profile symbol in U.S. culture in the last two decades of the century. The apocalyptic metaphor Rachel Carson so powerfully cited as a warning, that people were living in "a sea of carcinogens," became in Sandra Steingraber's depiction of deeper, postapocalyptic immersion in crisis still more disturbing. For even as Carson attributed her metaphor to "a scientist," Steingraber revised it by quoting an epidemiologist. People were, Robert Millikan wrote, nowadays living "in a toxic soup without breasts or prostates, et cetera."[42] Carson's sea of carcinogens thus became an environment in which people could and did dwell, not drown; they could only do so, however, in a maimed and deformed fashion.

But before Steingraber sought to extend and perhaps even intensify Carson's nightmare, life in a sea of carcinogens was magically changed into something positive by the corporate-conservative amplificaton of Ames's hypothesis. According to that amplification, people lived in a chemical universe, with body machismo and a new kind of risk-loving adventurousness—and this was an attitude that, as later chapters explore, had an enormous impact on popular culture, literature, and film in the last two decades of the twentieth century.[43] This remarkable embrace of the toxic and advocacy of hypermale body machismo and risk-taking (an attitude vigorously espoused by conservative women such as Edith Efron and Dixy Lee Ray, as well as men) emerged in not just scientific controversy but even more in a wider cultural contest with recent but deeply ingrained environmental perceptions of nature's fragility and humans' body vulnerability.

Whatever one thinks of the debate over chemicalization of the environment and cancer, conservatives' attempts to checkmate environmental concerns about the health effects of industrial chemicals were forceful and, to a degree, effective. But whatever victories were won were enjoyed only briefly. Corporate-conservative antienvironmentalism's offensive in the cancer wars was countered in an unexpected new way. A new class of health effects attributable to industry's chemicalization of the environment was discovered. Not so clearly apocalyptic as the plague of cancer Carson described, the new health effects showed up in what Theo Colborn called "more subtle health decrements."[44]

This appearance of new problems brought with it, according to Sheldon Krimsky, a whole new paradigm for chemically produced environmental disease. Krimsky narrates how this happened: "with cancer understood as a multistage process, environmental carcinogens [were] . . . viewed as one of many factors that might contribute to cancer risk" and a "new generation of journalists and environmental risk specialists . . . [began] to view synthetic chemicals as friends not enemies and the plaintiffs against 'chemical crimes' as the purveyors of junk science." But just then, "a new theory of chemical-induced diseases" arose "to weaken public confidence." This was a theory with a "unifying theme" that did not center around "abnormal cell types, cell proliferation, and cell metastasis" but focused on "the scrambling of messages during and after fetal development."[45]

When a British Broadcasting Corporation (BBC) TV documentary (*Assault on the Male*) sensationalized one of the symptoms of this new poisoning—a startling, apparently worldwide decline in male sperm counts—the phrase it used to characterize the underlying problem was culturally resonant: "we live, in effect, in a sea of estrogens."[46] The old metaphor cited by Rachel Carson, countered by Ames, and further elaborated by Steingraber and Millikan thus resurfaced in yet another new form. But a fuller description of the problem than the one advanced in the BBC documentary characterized the new toxic sea in much broader terms. It was not just a sea of estrogens; it was a sea of endocrine-disrupting chemicals. And people swam in this sea, shockingly, not just without their breasts or prostates. They also swam with deformed reproductive tracts; with reduced sperm counts; with increased testicular cancer, endometriosis, and vaginal cancer; with abnormally short penises; with impaired immune systems; with a variety of further reproductory and developmental abnormalities; with behavioral abnormalities such as attention deficit hyperactivity disorder (ADHD); and with diminished cognitive functions—to name just some of the more than two dozen postulated outcomes.[47] In an astonishingly short space of time, the Ramboesque world of Ames metamorphosed into a scene that seemed to come instead from Hieronymous Bosch.

The new kind of pollution of the global environment came from an ill-defined class of chemicals. Called endocrine disrupters, they were quickly renamed by industry (one wonders why) "endocrine modulators" or "endocrine-active substances."[48] Endocrine disrupters do not necessarily cause cancer, cell death, or DNA changes in the person exposed to them; since they disrupt the endocrine system that regulates the complex process of human development, however, they may strongly afflict that person's children with a host of developmental disorders. If this is an effect that confounds traditional expectations based on experience with both toxic and carcinogenic chemicals, there are also many other effects that are equally counterintuitive. Endocrine disrupters confound conventional "dose-makes-the-poison" toxicology in a variety of ways. They are dangerous in extremely tiny exposures, and that danger depends not on the amount of the exposure so much as when an embryo or a child experiences it. They do not necessarily become more dangerous with increased dosage but are sometimes less dangerous in large quantities, as an excess of the chemical triggers mechanisms that block its effects. They grow disproportionately more threatening when combined with other, similar chemicals. And they yield, as noted above, an astonishingly wide variety of effects not just on human bodies but on human behavior as well.

"Currently," Krimsky writes, "more than 70 chemicals (including chemical groups like PCBs, phthlates, and phenols) used substantially as pesticides and plasticizers have been implicated as being actual, probable, or potential endocrine disrupters." The pesticides include, Krimsky continues, "220 million pounds of pesticides known or suspected to be endocrine disrupters [which] were applied to 68 different crops in recent years," while the plasticizers include materials for food processing and packaging.[49] Still other products containing endocrine-disrupting chemicals include some contraceptive spermicides, personal care products, and industrial detergents. Added to plastics (such as bottled drinks, packaged foods, and even cans lined with a thin layer of plastic), they were discovered not to remain part of that apparently benign and inert substance but to leach out of it. Thus, for example, Theo Colborn and colleagues report that researchers investigating bisphenol-A found "stunningly high concentrations in such canned products as corn, artichokes, and peas."[50]

One of the most studied and most feared of the endocrine disrupters, PCBs, has been found: "virtually everywhere imaginable: in the sperm of a man tested at a fertility clinic in upstate New York, in the finest caviar, in the fat of a newborn baby in Michigan, in penguins in Antarctica, in the bluefin tuna served at a sushi bar in Tokyo, in the monsoon rains falling on Calcutta, in the milk of a nursing mother in France, in the blubber of a sperm whale cruising the South Pacific. . . . Like most persistent synthetic chemicals, PCBs are world travelers."[51] Worse, PCBs, like a number of other such chemicals, are concentrated by the food chain, and may become more and more dangerously concentrated as they travel far away from where they were released. This happens because the chemicals themselves are unnaturally stable even as they show a terrible affinity for fat. While "the members of the PCB family that contain fewer chlorine atoms do have a few enemies, including two bacteria from the *Achromobacter* genus," Colborn and colleagues write, "chlorine heavies like PCB-153 are impervious to almost everything save ultraviolet B radiation from the sun."[52]

The arctic food chain is particularly good at storing PCBs, which have reached their highest level in human beings in the Broughton Islanders in the Canadian Arctic—a group that since the announcement of this fact has been shunned by other Inuit communities as the "PCB" people. With fish and game being the mainstay of their diet, the Broughton Islanders eat the animals at the top of the food chain, the animals in which PCBs are especially concentrated; indeed, they are unable to do otherwise, for they cannot afford expensive imported food or, to spare their children, imported milk (which costs $4 a bottle).[53]

These chemicals do damage to animals and people alike by disrupting the body's hormone system—a communication system essential to normal development. Hormonal communications control many different aspects of human and animal development, ranging from sexual differentiation to neurological structures in the brain, and the effects of PCBs and other hormone-disrupting chemicals on that process are now under investigation. The "evidence shows that humans and animals respond in generally the same way to hormone-disrupting chemicals."[54] Affected animals have exhibited problems such as a wasting syndrome in young birds; feminization of males, deformed reproductive tracts, and diminished reproductive capabilities in a variety of species; immune-system problems in a number of species; parental inattentiveness and unusual parenting arrangements such as two-female nests in birds; hyperresponsiveness to stress in rats; and hyperactive behavior in monkeys.

In humans the most publicized and, for some, shocking statistic came from research into male sperm counts. Worldwide, "human male sperm counts dropped almost 50% between 1938 and 1990," Danish investigators reported in 1992—findings that have subsequently been disputed but have also been confirmed by other studies.[55] The Danish investigators also found raised incidence of genital abnormality in boys, such as undescended testicles and shortened urinary tracts. Further concern has been raised about the relationship of homone-disrupting chemicals to testicular cancer and prostate disorders in men and abnormal development of the reproductive tract in both sexes.

But a number of studies have pointed to a variety of other severe problems, changes in mental and emotional capacities as well as bodily structures. Children born to mothers who "had eaten 2 to 3 meals a month of fish" from the Great Lakes, waters rich in PCBs, "were born sooner, weighed less, and had smaller heads than those whose mothers did not eat the fish." They also scored "poorly on tests assessing neurological development, lagging behind in various measures, such as short-term memory, that tend to predict later IQ."[56] Tested at eleven years old, children who were exposed to higher levels of PCBs showed, according to a paper in the *New England Journal of Medicine,* "deficits in general intellectual ability, short-term and long-term memory, and focused and sustained attention."[57] For the most highly exposed, there was a loss of 6.2 points in IQ.

The endocrine disrupter hypothesis is, to be sure, still a hypothesis: recently, the *New York Times* criticized the Science and Environmental Health's Network's advocacy of it as a problem, asserting that the hypothesis lay "outside the mainstream of science."[58] Peter Montague, president of the board of S.E.H.N. and publisher of the environmental report *Rachel's Environmental & Health News,* quickly responded that it had had substantial impact. But whatever the status of the hypothesis, once again a combination of scientific uncertainty, concern about possibly devastating health effects, and the interests of a powerful chemical industry has produced a hot-button issue, one that promises to keep synthetic chemical pollution prominent among environmental concerns for years to come. For chemicals labeled as carcinogenic and as endocrine-disruptering chemicals have effectively restructured the place where everyone dwells. Exposures to carcinogens and endocrine disrupters occur regularly (and even especially) in the womb and among nursing infants. There is "no young person alive today," Theo Colborn and her colleagues write: "born without some in utero exposure to synthetic chemicals that can disrupt development."[59] Joe Thornton reports that: "a nursing child's dioxin dose exceeds by a factor of 6 to 10,000 the standard of every government in the world for adults' acceptable daily intake"—a figure made much more terrible by the fact that infants' lower body weight means even greater toxicity in these doses.[60]

And this risky environmental deformation will be around for a very long time even if society were to change its current practices. A group of twelve toxic chemicals has been singled out by the UN for such regulation worldwide because of their tendency to persist and bioaccumulate in the environment; these have been significantly labeled persistent organic pollutants (POPs). Still other chemicals, Joe Thornton reports, have half-lives that rival those of nuclear wastes."[61] Coupling pollution by heavy metals like lead and mercury with pollution by synthetic chemicals, Anne Platt McGinn writes that despite the new POP regulation: "the present toxic waste challenge could take on the dimensions of a crisis during the next two decades." If risks exist in the continuing production and use of many chemicals and heavy metals, danger also exists from the disposal of those already produced. Anne Platt McGinn estimates that in Africa alone today: "more than 200,000 tons of abandoned pesticides" are stockpiled.[62] Further, the anticipated "waste pile" just from synthetic chemicals embodied in plastics utilized globally is huge, as we near "the end of the useful life span of 'long-lived' (20–30 years) PVC materials such as pipes, siding, and other construction materials."[63]

A still newer environmental health concern—one that is now a potential crisis more than an actual one—involves the possible spread of new emerging and the resurgence of old infectious diseases both globally and in the United States. It differs significantly, however, from concern about synthetic chemicals in a number of ways. First, the problem arises not as a result of the actions of one particular industry but as the feared outcome of a host of large and small, global and local, environmental changes. Raising the likelihood of a substantial increase in serious infectious disease are trends like climate change, development, habitat destruction, pollution, overpopulation, urban slummification, the industrialization of agriculture, and the rise of global transport and mobility. A host of decisive human modifications of natural and social environments—rapidly expanding modifications that lead not just to the destruction of macroecosystems but also to deeply problematic alterations in microbiological environments—are thus responsible for the rise of infectious disease, not a decisive intervention in one area. Not only does anthropogenic environmental change become yet again global in scope; it also reaches down to disturbing new depths, destabilizing humanity's ancient and haplessly intimate environmental connection, its link to microbiological ecosystems.

Second, the possible effects of these changes do not evoke the same associations in people as the effects of synthetic chemical pollution. Destructive chemical pollution incites both irony and rage. A particular set of interested parties seems to have utilized modern technology to enrich themselves while accomplishing the horrible goal of making nature unnatural, toxic, not sustaining. By contrast, the prospect of rising global disease is not so clearly attributable to a self-interested group; responsibility for it ranges all over the world, from First World greenhouse gas emissions to Third World slummification, from agribusiness misusing antibiotics to Third World populations destroying forests and habitats. Clearly, few corporations have invested money in spreading global diseases, as opposed to marketing chemicals. Nor have environmental groups launched themselves directly at corporate throats over the issue of emerging disease.[64] As nobody's specific responsibility, then, the prospect of global disease further suggests that modernity is failing, not ironically defeating itself. It thus raises fears that perhaps run deeper than those raised by synthetic chemical poisoning—it suggests that, rather than being a malign misuse of modern technology, global disease problems show that modern science and technology are on the verge of breaking down, that the fragile protective walls they have erected between people and forces beyond their control are gradually crumbling.

The prospect of increased infectious disease worldwide has not yet become a divisive environmental issue in the United States. Its worst political potential seems to be the possibility that it could lend support to a new round of First World stigmatization of poor, marginalized, and Third World peoples from whom new and reemerging old infectious diseases all too easily seem, to the better off, to come. For the most part, however, fears of global disease have so far united, not divided people: they have brought together even hitherto conflicting parties, making it seem important that government officials, scientists, and environmentalists all pull together to prevent new outbreaks of disease. In public concern over the new threats, a number of professions have been romanticized and new potential heroes have emerged. Popular writers such as Richard Preston and more serious students of global disease such as the journalist Laurie Garrett have indeed sounded this new heroic note in the context of global disease. Garrett has romanticized the adventures of Centers for Disease Control and Prevention (CDC) researchers out in the dangerous (Third World) bush, calling them "disease cowboys," and Preston makes a CDC researcher the heroine of a novel about bioterror. In the same vein, the journalist Madeline Drexler quotes Hans Zinsser, who wrote during the depression that "infectious disease is one of the few genuine adventures left in the world." "Modern adventurers," Drexler continues, "like to up the ante, but even the most extreme sports wouldn't produce the adrenaline of a race against pandemic influenza or a cloud of anthrax at the Super Bowl."[65]

This new celebration of the risk-running adventurousness of disease workers is not, however, clearly part of any specific political agenda, as it was for conservatives fighting the cancer wars. It is part of an attempt to gear society up to face and deal with what seems to be no less than the possible return of ghastly, premodern horrors in terrifyingly new, postcontemporary, and global dress. What is significantly lacking in preparations like these, however, is a sense that doing something about the underlying environmental changes responsible for the new disease threats is at all possible. This lack of faith in being able to do anything about the roots of the problem, as opposed to dealing with its symptoms, is, in many ways, one of the direst aspects of today's fears of the emergence of new and reemergence of old infectious diseases.

The reason why a significant rise in infectious disease represents, for people in the First World at least, a return to premodern terrors is easy to see. Growing environmental exposure and vulnerability to disease brutally dispels the comforting amnesia modern populations have developed about both their past and their microbiological environment. Undoing amnesia about past history means, Madeline Drexler reminds us, recovering the memory of the damage disease-bearing microbes have done—a memory that leads back to the beginnings of civilization yet one that subsequent world history has kept vividly alive. For just the Christian era, this would mean recalling "the plague of Antoninus (A.D. 166–180), probably smallpox, [that] killed between one-fourth and one-third of Italy's population"; the plague of Justinian (bubonic plague) that killed "10,000 people daily in Constantinople and eventually spread . . . as far north as Denmark"; the Black Death of Europe, in which "between 1346 and 1350, one-third of Europe's population died"; and the introduction of a variety of diseases into the New World by Europeans, diseases that "killed an estimated 95 percent of the pre-Columbian Native American population."[66]

Undoing amnesia becomes even more unsettling when it requires people in the developed world to remember just how exposed and vulnerable to microbes they really are. Microbes are minute; viruses, Drexler points out, "are tiny, ranging in size from about 20 to 400 nanometers in diameter—millions can fit into the period at the end of this sentence."[67] Microbes are incredibly lively; while "humans crank out a generation every 20 years or so, bacteria do it every 20 to 30 minutes, and viruses even faster."[68] And they are also ineradicably everywhere; they inhabit people every bit as much as people dwell among them. They make digestion and elimination possible; they are drawn into lungs with every breath. Indeed, bacteria constitute a large part of us; Lynn Margulis and Dorian Sagan point out that: "fully ten percent of our own dry body weight consists of bacteria, some of which, although they are not a congenital part of our bodies, we can't live without."[69]

Microbes begin colonizing human bodies, Madeline Drexler reports: "during passage through the birth canal. Immediately after delivery more organisms swarm in, some becoming permanently established in or on the baby's body." As unsettling as this may seem: "in most cases, that's lucky for us. The bowel alone contains hundreds of microbial species, some of which break down food into absorbable nutrients and may disarm carcinogens in the diet." Further, they "synthesize vitamins" and "stave off colonization by more virulent bacteria and stimulate the immune system," for inside people they control each other.[70] Even potentially dangerous antibiotic-resistant microbes can be held in check by other intestinal flora—a protection that might possibly be removed if a person with them takes a broad-spectrum antibiotic that kills the nonresistant flora, thereby creating ecological space for the dangerous, antibiotic-resistant bacteria to multiply.[71] Undoing amnesia about microbes, in short, reveals to humans that human beings are not just themselves, not autonomous individuals, but instead are, in even the inner sanctums of their bodies, integrated with and indeed wholly dependent on other forms of life—worse, dependent on ones that often do not mean them well.

Characterizing microbes in this manner—as not necessarily good in their "intentions" toward people—doubtless goes over the line, but a real temptation to speak this way comes from a further trait of microbes. Microbes repeatedly amaze their human students by how incredibly resourceful they are. In descriptions of what microbes can do, scientists repeatedly depict microbes as having what seems uncannily almost like agency. Through an astonishing variety of mechanisms, microbes are able to share and swap genetic information, mutate, and evolve to get around defenses that both human immune systems and human ingenuity design to neutralize them when they prove dangerous.[72] Representative examples of what such resources can mean abound. For example, Jaap Goudsmit theorizes that: "the decline in chimpanzee populations resulting from human invasion might have created a biological imperative for the simian immunodeficiency virus (SIV) to seek out new hosts—humans."[73] Goudsmit's language uncomfortably evokes microbial agency: the tricky virus circumvents a setback by finding its way into people. Nature is a "witty agent," a coyote trickster, writes Donna Haraway.[74] And the collective nature of microbial ecosystems makes this "wittiness" far more frightening. Lynn Margulis and Dorian Sagan argue that, thanks to bacterial ability to transfer genes with each other: "all the world's bacteria have access to a single gene pool and hence to the adaptive mechanisms of the entire bacterial kingdom."[75] Further, microbes have practiced their arts for a very long time. "Never underestimate an adversary that has had a three-point-five-billion-year head start," Drexler quotes the microbiologist Abigail Salyers as saying.[76]

Why people in the developed world have not been forced to remember history or contemplate microbial agency is simple: it is thanks to the victories of modern science. For years, popular concern about dangerous microbes has been allayed because of the victories of public health science. For years, public health scientists and practitioners have successfully battled microbes of the threatening sort in a variety of ways, including vaccination, public health education, food safety measures, and urban sanitation as well as through the development of antibiotic drugs. Their victories in this battle have formed one of the great success stories of modernity. Thanks to these victories, societies go through a "health transition," or "epidemiological transition," as they develop—life expectancy lengthens and epidemic infections decline. To societies that have passed through this transition, relative freedom from epidemic and pestilential infectious disease has been accepted by most as simply a regular feature of the environment in which they live.

Recently, however, renewed concerns in the First World about the strength of the walls people have erected between themselves and microbial disease have sprung up. Just yesterday, it seemed, the thought was impossible. As Laurie Garrett writes: "the 1950s and 1960s were a time of tremendous optimism. Nearly every week the medical establishment declared another 'miracle breakthrough' in humanity's war with infectious disease."[77] Extremely dangerous diseases such as staphylococcus and tuberculosis were reduced suddenly to "easily managed minor infections"; other diseases, such as smallpox, polio, and malaria, were soon, people felt, to be eliminated from the planet. In 1944, penicillin was introduced into general clinical practice; by 1965 "more than 25,000 different antibiotic products had been developed."[78] In 1955, the World Health Organization "decided to eliminate all malaria on the planet"; in 1977, when Ali Maow Maalin was cured in Merka, Somalia, smallpox was (officially) eradicated. Globally, prospects seemed higher than ever: "as nations moved out of poverty and the basic food and housing needs . . . were met, scientists could use pharmaceutical and chemical tools at hand to wipe out parasites, bacteria, and viruses."[79]

But by the 1980s, the situation seemed to be changing. Thanks to a variety of global environmental and social changes, a significant challenge by adapting, mutating, and newly emerging microbes seemed to be threatening to undo the health transition and diminish the efficacy of antibiotics. Garrett reports how the world historian and expert in global disease history, William McNeill, told scientists in 1989 that disease-causing microbes on the planet, far from having been defeated, were ready to pose a greater-than-ever threat to humanity. McNeill argued that: "the more we win, the more we drive infections to the margins of human experience, the more we clear a path for possible catastrophic infection. We'll never escape the limits of the ecosystem. We are caught in the food chain, whether we like it or not, eating and being eaten."[80] Garrett tots up the evidence presented at the conference where McNeill spoke:

> viruses were mutating at rapid rates; seals were dying in great plagues as the researchers convened; more than 90 per cent of the rabbits in Australia died in a single year following the introduction of a new virus to the land; great influenza pandemics were sweeping the animal world; the Andromeda strain nearly surfaced in Africa in the form of Ebola virus; megacities were arising in the developing world, creating niches from which "virtually anything might arise"; rain forests were being destroyed, forcing disease-carrying animals and insects into areas of human habitation and raising the very real possibility that lethal, mysterious microbes would, for the first time, infect humanity on a large scale and imperil the survival of the human race.[81]

Garrett's language is intentionally sensationalizing; nonetheless the stage seemed to be set for some sort of microbial revenge.

If bacteria can thus seem so much like people's enemies, bent on revenge, Madeline Drexler may seem correct in calling Mother Nature the "most menacing bioterrorist" out there.[82] But McNeill's comments indicate another perspective. Thanks to having gone through the health transition, the developed world has created an imbalance in its millennia-long negotiations with microbes, even as it opened up large new environmental space for its own growth—something that is a unique new step in a history of touchy relationships that is older than civilization. As human population and environmental impact have risen, the relationships between people and microbes have been repeatedly destabilized. From the time of the domestication of animals (when, as Jared Diamond argues, a larger number of zoonoses, or diseases that move from animals to people, began afflicting humankind) to the rise of cities (when, as McNeill argues, the "diseases of civilization took hold") and in various subsequent phases of globalization (such as the medieval world network that helped transmit the medieval plagues from China to Europe, and the disease transfers effected by Eurocolonialism), human development and expansion has evoked microbial responses.[83] New emphasis on sanitation, provision of clean water, pasteurization of milk and other improvements in food safety, and the development of vaccines all helped mitigate those responses during the past century and a half. To this arsenal, people then added antibiotics. But that latest—and apparently most decisive—addition, along with a host of other ongoing ecological and social changes wrought by human development and growth, has perhaps put humanity again in a terribly risky position.

First of all, the walls constructed by antibiotics may be about to crumble. Madeline Drexler evokes how different from today the time before antibiotics was: "not long before antibiotics entered our lives," she writes, "staph in the bloodstream killed 90 percent of its victims. A man who nicked himself shaving could die from erysipelas, or strep infection. Children lost their playmates to scarlet fever, meningitis, osteomyelitis. Bacterial pneumonia, the leading cause of death, killed a third of its victims."[84] Antibiotics virtually ended this terrifying level of risk just a few decades later, pushing such problems out to the margins of First World human experience.

Since as early as 1945, however, scientists have issued warnings about microbes' ingenious ability to adapt and become resistant to antibiotics. The more heedlessly and excessively antibiotics were used, the more difficult this problem became. But antibiotic usage was not restrained; it burgeoned until, as Drexler puts it, "all the earth's bacteria became bathed in antibiotics—millions of tons over the past half century."[85] Excesses such as continuing human overuse of antibiotics and the introduction of antibiotics into large-volume farming gradually transformed both hospitals and factory farms into petri dishes for growing antibiotic-resistant bacteria. Today, industrialized agriculture soaks a great portion of peoples' food in antibiotics; animals and even fish are fed antibiotics in bulk, and even more startling, thanks to the use of antibiotic pesticides on fruit, a "1993 study found higher levels of multi-drug-resistant bacteria in the intestines of vegetarians than in meat eaters."[86]

The result of these excesses, Drexler argues, is an increasing risk of infectious microbes learning to defeat every antibiotic thrown at them, even the drugs of last resort. A few such infections have occurred and, worse, Drexler believes, the world is now one step away from finding that its "most widespread hospital infection" is untreatable.[87] Even now, with antibiotics still functioning, drug-resistant infections contribute to 14,000 deaths in U.S. hospitals yearly. The prospect of those defenses ceasing to work has led epidemiologist J. Glenn Morris, Jr., to state that antibiotic resistance is "probably the biggest health threat in the U.S."[88] Misuse of antibiotics and misunderstanding of the ecological rather than simply antagonistic relationships between microbes and people has caused society, as the physician Imre J. P. Loefler sadly puts it, to: "waste resources that, if husbanded, would have helped us treat infections perhaps for hundreds of years. We squandered because of ignorance, consumerism, mercantilism, cynicism and carelessness."[89] And can society count on the development of new antibiotics to replace the ones thus wasted? Concern is growing that efforts to do so are no longer adequate, as the development of new drugs has slowed dramatically. This has happened thanks to the reluctance of drug companies to invest in new products that *won't* be heedlessly (and therefore profitably) prescribed and thanks to the possibility that "most of the easy drug targets"—the "chinks in bacterial armor"—have already been discovered.[90]

Perhaps some of society's misuse of antibiotics was preventable, and some not. It is hard to condemn doctors from intervening rapidly with broad-spectrum antibiotics when patients are at risk (the young, elderly, or health-impaired) and where lab analyses for more precise treatment are either too slow to chance waiting for or unavailable. It is easier to condemn industrial agriculture for practices that raise productivity while also increasing the suffering of animals—practices such as feeding antibiotics to livestock to make them grow and to control disease brought on by the inhumane crowding of animals in factory farms. But whether preventable or not, the prospect of a postantibiotic era is extremely serious. It is almost staggering to imagine life without effective antibiotics.

Still more serious, however, is the fact that the possible failure of antibiotics is just one of a number of possibly drastic disease futures now on the horizon. Thanks to many of the environmental changes inventoried in the last chapter, old diseases are threatening to spread, and some truly awful new ones have been emerging. For example, Hilary French reports that: "over the past two decades, more than 30 infectious diseases have been identified in humans for the first time, including AIDS, ebola, hantavirus, and hepatitis C and E."[91] And Gary Gardner adds: "20 familiar infectious diseases—including tuberculosis, . . . malaria, and cholera—re-emerged or spread" in the last twenty-five years.[92] The reason for these trends is clear. According to the WHO, "environmental changes have contributed in one way or other to the appearance of most if not all of the emerging diseases," and the same goes for reemerging old ones.[93]

The first of these disease-heightening environmental changes is a factor important to both the emergence of new infections and the increasing virulence of old ones; it is the result of ongoing global development. Human-caused habitat destruction and biodiversity loss—a loss which Paul Ehrlich, as noted above, likened to taking rivets out of an airplane one is flying in—disturbs the stability of the balance achieved between hosts and bacteria, which ordinarily do not wish to kill all their hosts. The clear-cutting of biodiversity (as in forest loss or monocropping) may cause dangerous microbes emerge to affect people. On a graphically small-scale level, "Tom Monath had seen it happen several times in West Africa, where such simple actions as chopping down a stand of trees and leaving the stumps in place could spawn a yellow fever outbreak."[94] More generally, Hilary French writes that: "90 percent of the 1.5–2.7 million deaths caused by malaria annually are linked with underlying environmental disruptions such as the colonization of rainforests and the construction of open-water irrigation schemes, both of which increase human exposure to disease-carrying mosquitoes."[95]

Serious global consequences have also come from the leap that human immunodeficiency virus (HIV) 1 and 2 made when they jumped the species barrier between chimpanzees, sooty mangabeys, and humans; scientists now worry, Madeline Drexler notes, about further leaps from at least "twenty-four other African primate species . . . affected with similar retroviruses" as a result of the pressures human beings are placing on these animals and their environments.[96] If HIV did indeed, as many scientists now think, jump from animals to humans thanks to the enormous expansion of the rapidly-growing African bushmeat trade, the potential for further harm is great. "By mid 2001," Drexler writes, "AIDS had killed more than 450,000 Americans and infected more than a million"; globally the results have been still more horrific.[97] Were other simian retroviruses to follow the path of HIV1 and 2, the results could be even worse.

Rising pollution also increases risk of infectious disease. The dolphins that washed up in 1990 along the shores of North Africa, Spain, and France in respiratory distress were shown to have suffered from "startling brain damage and acute immunodeficiencies."[98] Behind these was the deadly morbillivirus, but the reasons why it so affected the dolphins included immune deficiencies created by swimming in polluted waters and by a decline in fish populations, which caused the dolphins to live off stored up fat—a deadly strategy, however, because body fat was where PCBs had accumulated. "Massive colonies of algae" caused in part by the discharge of "high levels of nitrogen-rich human and livestock fecal matter" also create marine illness—as well as expanding the "habitat available to microbes that cause cholera."[99] Colonies of the species *Ptychodiscus brevis* secrete a powerful neurotoxin; worse, the algae is a concentrate of viruses and bacteria. Thus in Chesapeake Bay, Rita Colwell found "veritable stews of viruses, plasmids, transposons, and bacteria intermingling" as "human and animal waste washed into the bay, carrying with it a variety of pathogens."[100]

Erosion of the atmosphere also alters and deforms microbial environments. Along with damaging animal and human immune systems and raising human skin cancer rates sharply, depletion of the ozone layer, evidence suggested, "was driving a higher mutation rate in sea surface organisms, possibly allowing for more rapid rates of adaptive [microbial] evolution."[101] But the real damage will probably come from global climate change—which, experts feel, is even now increasing global disease substantially. To pick a few examples, global warming has been linked to increasing disease, such as diarrhea in children, which now involves 2.5 million deaths per year and has been shown to rise "by millions of cases worldwide per degree of increase in ambient temperature above normal."[102] "Already," Hilary French observes, "dengue fever and malaria both appear to be expanding their reach northward into cooler climates—locally occurring cases of malaria have been reported in recent years in Florida, Georgia, Texas, Virginia, New York, New Jersey, Michigan, and even Ontario."[103] Global warming also threatens to increase ocean-borne pathogens. One theory for the 1991 outbreak of cholera in South America— an outbreak that started in Peru and contaminated "the water supply of every country on the continent but Paraguay and Uruguay before it gradually wound down two years later"—was that El Niño-warmed oceans encouraged the growth of "large blooms of plankton that can harbor the organism."[104] If El Niño warming can have such effects, the results of global warming can be much worse. "The oceans have become nothing but giant cesspools," Garrett quotes oceanographer Patricia Tester as saying: "And you know what happens when you heat up a cesspool."[105]

Ongoing urbanization and population growth in the developing world have also dramatically affected conditions for the emergence and spread of global disease. Laurie Garrett argues that poverty plays an enormous role in amplifying disease and providing fertile ground for the emergence of new diseases. Starvation and stress foster disease, both by lowering individuals' disease resistance and by forcing people to take greater health risks in order to survive. Though these problems are as old as humankind, today they yield new dangers because they take place in a more populous and more globalized world: overcrowding and population increases worsen conditions like these that produce disease, while globalization guarantees that diseases so produced will spread rapidly throughout the world.

Thus, on the one hand, Madeline Drexler sees as ominous projections that by 2025, 65 percent of people in developing countries will live in cities: "Overwhelmed by unsafe water, poor sanitation, and widespread poverty," she writes, these cities will become "magnets for infections from isolated rural areas and launch pads that allow pathogens to reach other fast-growing populations."[106] Factors like these combine to create the advantageous situation for microbes Garrett calls Thirdworldization—a process that occurs in places within the developed as well as the developing world. And recent global economic restructuring has not helped stop this process. Former CDC director William Foege has argued that: "structural adjustments ordered by the World Bank and the International Monetary Fund, coupled with a genuine capital crisis following the fall of the Berlin Wall, had severely worsened the human condition and improved odds for the microbes."[107]

On the other hand, globalization threatens to rob developed-world populations of at least some portion of their present privileged status with regard to infectious disease. Current estimates of the global disease burden caused by environmental change (which run—as noted above—from 20 percent to 40 percent) break down very differently when sorted out geographically. In the developed world the figure for the burden of environmentally caused disease is presently only 5 percent, with the lion's share of the problem occurring in developing countries.[108] But such comfort is precarious thanks to contemporary globalization, which has made microbes as cosmopolitan as people. "After 60 years of near continuous decline in deaths from infectious disease in the United States," Gary Gardner notes, "the trend turned upward again in 1980, and deaths have nearly doubled." Even in the days before bioterrorist incidents in the United States, the Central Intelligence Agency (CIA) was concerned. Gardner adds that the CIA has identified infectious disease brought in from the rest of the world as a "new security threat."[109]

Laurie Garrett produces a fascinating itinerary for some of these new global cosmopolitans. All methicillin-resistant *Staphylococcus aureus* bacteria "descended from a strain that first emerged in Cairo, Egypt, in 1961"; its descendents had spread by the end of the decade to "New York, New Jersey, Dublin, Geneva, Copenhagen, London, Kampala, Nairobi, Ontario, Halifax, Winnipeg, and Saskatoon. A decade later they were seen planet-wide."[110] Virulent, highly antibiotic-resistant strains of *Streptococcus pneumoniae* turned up all over the world in the 1990s, "some able to withstand exposure to six different classes of antibiotics simultaneously."[111] Strain 23F "appeared in Spain in 1978 in a hospital setting, bearing all its resistance capabilities save invulnerability to erythromycin" which, however: "was acquired when the organism, carried by an infected human, made its way to Ohio. Subsequent improvements in the bacterium's ability to withstand hostile drug-laden human ecologies came as the organism's descendants made their way to South Africa, Hungary, the U.K., back to Spain, and then again to the American Midwest."[112] The 19A strain appeared in Durban but: "matched one that surfaced ten years earlier in a little boy living in a remote village in Papua New Guinea. . . . [T]he bizarre bacterium made its way to South Africa a decade later, and from there to Spain, Hungary, England, the United States, and eventually all over the world."[113]

Mosquitoes or mosquito-infected people brought West Nile virus to New York; a shipment of African green monkeys carried the Marburg virus, one of the world's dreaded new hemorrhagic diseases, to Germany. Cargo ships, as well as El Niño waming, have been suspected of being responsible for the 1991 outbreak of cholera in South America. The globalization of the world's foodstream has also served as a vehicle for migrating pathogens. Madeline Drexler charts the fascinating and fearful odyssey of *Shigella* from a production site in Mexico to Minnesota and she vividly notes the possibilities for other transmissions in the fact that, for example: "a single patty may mingle the meat of a hundred different animals from four different countries."[114] Summarizing the effect of these changes, William Foege asserts that: "international and domestic American health were so thoroughly integrated by the 1990s due to globalization of the microbes that it was impossible to ensure a disease-free existence for people in North America and Western Europe without providing similar assurances for residents of Azerbaijan, Côte d'Ivoire, and Bangladesh."[115] Though many debate the virtues and vices of globalization, few indeed have imagined it is easy or even possible to stop; solutions to the exposures it causes thus focus almost exclusively on improving the global public health system.

Will new global "plagues"—as the title of Garrett's books suggests—be the result? Most probably, should today's worries be borne out in fact, increases in infectious disease would most likely be more complexly patterned than the term "global plague" suggests. It is unlikely that rising infectious disease would lead to a simple succession of plagues scything through the world's populations. Despite the extreme vulnerability contemporary global connectedness entails, the threat of infectious disease today couples a low-probability risk of a succession of large-scale, global catastrophes with a much more likely scenario of increasing deterioration, disease, medicalization, and environmental constraint produced by less sensational ills. And regardless of which— plagues or lower-level immiseration—occurs, the effect on the world would doubtless be uneven. The developing world would likely suffer much sharper increases in misery than the developed world; First World health care systems would still make a difference. At the same time, though, the first-world would not be out of the soup. If infectious disease were to widen still further the gap that already yawns between the developed and developing worlds, the latter would appear steadily more threatening to the former. It would become a still more potent source of microbes dangerous to both societies. And the increasing gap in welfare between the two areas would mean deteriorating relationships between the increasingly populous and the increasingly well-off regions of the world, a development that would seriously threaten global stability.

Both the pairing of low-probability risk of megacatastrophes with a substantially higher probability of gradual immiseration and the anticipation of problems created by widening environmental gulfs between the First and Third Worlds are not confined to concern about disease. As the next chapter shows, they emerge in other areas as well. Each represents, in fact, yet another new look that global environmental risks have donned of late, as peoples' impacts on their ever more sensitively dependent environment have increased.

The prospect of environmental and environmental-social changes causing rising levels of infectious disease is a dark cloud on the horizon. If it stays there, well and good; but if it were to advance just a few steps toward the United States, the results could be large. The immiseration that AIDS (a disease researchers believe emerged thanks to human encroachment on primates' habitats) has caused is already vast. Should one First World–centered problem discussed above become true—should bacterial innovation finally outpace human ability to develop new strains of antibiotics—the results would be fearful. And should

even the familiar old woes like malaria (a woe that nowadays includes one untreatable variant) continue to move North thanks to global climate change, the
resulting reduction in the quality of life in the United States would be very hard
for most to accept.

If one couples the findings of the previous chapter with the concerns of this
one, damage to global ecosystems—to the physical environment that surrounds people—is combined with rising risks to human health—the physical
environment within people. The result is a depiction of environmental crisis
as something both all-encompassing and fearfully intimate. As crisis like this
has been elaborated in greater and greater detail, it is not surprising that the
past several decades have produced a variety of bizarre fantasies of escape
both from earthly ecosystems and from human flesh. As we shall see in subsequent chapters, fantasies like these range from some of the hype surrounding
the building of Biosphere 2 (a vanguard technological experiment with considerable scientific interest, but one that has multiple and conflicting symbolic implications), to more science-fiction-based dreams of terraforming
and inhabiting artificial off-world environments and the seriously elaborated
cyberrobotic dream of transferring human consciousness from meat to silicon. For the people who elaborate these and other fantasies of escape from
embodiment in ecosystems and even flesh, terran nature and human bodies
are no longer adequate. Chapter 7 and 8 will explore these interesting attitudes at greater length. Here it is worth noting that while, among enthusiasts,
these attitudes may come from a latter-day gnostic spirituality and/or a desire
for perfection, more and more, these days, they come in fact as a response to
dwelling within environmental crisis—as a response to a growing suspicion
that nature and the natural human body are a lost cause.

CHAPTER 5

Environmental Crisis as a Social Crisis

A global economy allows ecologically unsustainable forms of life to not only endure but flourish. In the last few centuries we have changed from ecosphere people to biosphere people, to use Raymond Dasmann's terms. Ecosphere people derive their livelihood from the ecosystems within which they exist. . . . They are attuned to feedback from their ecosystems which allow them to effectively coexist with them. . . . By contrast, biosphere peoples collect portions of their livelihood from distant ecosystems. . . . By greatly enlarging feedback loops, they can easily fail to notice their ecological mistakes, avoid the consequences for a long time, and displace their errors onto other societies.
———Andrew McLaughlin, *Regarding Nature*

Invention is the mother of necessity.
———Thorstein Veblen

By definition, human society is at the root of the heterogeneity of problems described in the last two chapters. Human-caused, or "anthropogenic," environmental crisis is, after all, humanly caused. Society, more than nature, is thus environmentalism's most important problem. Ecological modernization highlighted this fact; Al Gore, William Ruckelshaus, Paul Hawken, and Amory and L. Hunter Lovins saw environmental crisis as a civilizational or social-structural problem.[1] Others, more radical than these, have also agreed with ecological modernization on this point. Thus, for example, the eco-Marxist John Bellamy

143

Foster commences a book on environmental crisis by arguing that: "we must begin by recognizing that the crisis of the earth is not a crisis of *nature*, but a crisis of *society*. The chief causes of the environmental deterioration that faces us today . . . are social and historical, rooted in the productive relations, technological imperatives, and historically conditioned demographic trends that characterize the dominant social system."[2] Richard Hofrichter argues that even the term "environmental problem" is "already a capitulation," ignoring "an underlying historical narrative that links health and ecology to the social order."[3] Kicking off this widespread shift to the social-systemic analysis of environmental crisis was the controversial 1972 book, *The Limits to Growth*. In it, Donella Meadows and her colleagues depicted global crisis as a social-systemic problem, one that resulted from economic and population growth. Recently, Meadows and her colleagues held, this problem had become so severe (and measurable) that it was leading demonstrably toward a near-term global environmental meltdown. To meet this challenge, *Limits to Growth* called for fundamental societal change and a "Copernican revolution of the mind."[4]

Limits to Growth forcefully elaborated a stripped-down version of environmental crisis as a social crisis. In focusing on human economic and population growth as the two crucial trends propelling people into environmental crisis, Meadows and her colleagues singled out forces that seemed to them, structurally speaking, the most basic. Driving the acceleration of damage in all the areas surveyed above in Chapter 3 were, thus, human population growth and world economic growth; each of these factors ratcheted up the stresses in all the other areas. Quickly, however, controversy surrounded Meadows's apparent findings; even more important, opponents argued that for a variety of reasons, growth in population and economic output was not necessarily linked to environmental destruction. Concern about population and economic growth as social-structural causes of environmental crisis has not gone away, however, and I will begin this chapter with a short survey of contemporary wisdom in this area.

Attempts to delink economic and population growth from environmental impact have not succeeded in dispelling thoughtful concern about those issues; responsible recent attempts to calculate the degree to which factors like human ingenuity and expanded knowledge have diminished them as ecological constraints have found that they still represent serious problems. The formula that *Limits to Growth* used to calculate environmental impacts—I = PAT (environmental impact = population × affluence × technology)—still obtains. Despite several decades of ecomodernization, the OECD has held that within the developed world, "environmental degradation has increased at [only] a slightly lower rate than economic growth"—and this has happened despite the fact that with recent globalization, more and more of the negative impacts of First World affluence have been shifted off onto the Third World.[5] And though in its latest report on world population the UN found "overall trends with sustainable development [have] . . . become worse compared with five years earlier" and looked to population to present a happier picture, its report nonetheless concluded that it still represented a major problem.[6] After considering a number of possible refinements in the I = PAT formula's inflexible linkage of population growth to rising environmental impact, the UN report concluded that while "environmental problems vary in the extent to which they can be linked directly to population size, growth or distribution," even the problems apparently least linked to population growth are affected by it, and population concerns remain "necessary and vital components" of any attempt "to safeguard the environment during the twenty-first century and beyond."[7] It appears, in short, that thoughtful attempts to revise the findings of *Limits to Growth* today, though they have complexified its calculations (and set aside some specific predictions generated by them), have only reaffirmed the book's fundamental logic.

Turning to the issue of population growth specifically, it is necessary at the start to recognize that the subject is now highly vexed, to say the least. It is difficult to write about overpopulation now without engaging a number of different criticisms that come from a startlingly dissonant variety of different ethical-political and pragmatic-ideological commitments. Advocates of a right to life, of reproductive rights, of free-market capitalism, and of Marxist and anarchist ideas of social justice have all targeted environmentalism's concern with overpopulation. Partisans of all of these positions have sought to make the subject of environmental crisis as a result of population growth a taboo subject, ethically condemning calls for population control while pragmatically denying that fixed limits in nature or natural scarcity constrain future population growth.[8]

Neither the ethical-political condemnation of population control nor the pragmatic-ideological denial of natural limits and scarcity have really succeeded in erasing population issues as a public concern. Environmental fears of overpopulation in the 1960s and 1970s were indeed vulnerable to ethical criticism for their sometimes inhumanist attitudes—which accused the world's too-fecund poor of pushing the earth past its limits—and draconian policy recommendations—which included mandatory sterilization and denial of humanitarian aid to the poor. Since then, however, environmentalists have cleaned up their act. They have internalized the most significant ethical critiques and corrected their past excesses. For example, they have embraced the idea that empowerment and support of poor women through education and child health care are more ethical *and* effective means for reducing population growth rates than draconian political controls.[9] They have also clearly understood that environmental impacts come from population and affluence together and that by those standards, the people of the rich North have greater environmental impacts than those of the poor South.[10] As for the more pragmatic-ideological denials of natural limits and scarcity, few environmentalists now believe that the earth's carrying capacity is an easily determined, inflexible, external limit, as their critics still regularly claim they do. Indeed, environmentalists are well aware that limits and scarcity are not simply givens of nature, but highly socially mediated, and that appeals to them may often be disingenuous forms of social control, designed to keep the poor poor or justify a wide variety of other socially dubious projects.[11]

But having said that, I need to add something still more important. Recognizing that environmentalists' concern about population growth has been problematic in its most simplistic forms does not mean that a more thoughtful form of concern about population growth is not an ethical, as well as environmental, imperative. For recognizing that inflexible limits in external nature don't exist most emphatically does *not* mean that nature is totally unlimited. It doesn't for a second imply that that there are no real ecological constraints on human activity at all. Though population control has often involved ethically repugnant attitudes, ethical problems do not go away if one simply drops the issue. No, as population rises and stresses increase, ethical concerns about both peoples' progressive immiseration and their treatment of each other do not disappear but increase sharply.

The only way to assess the importance of these ethical and environmental concerns is to take a close look at recent trends in population growth. The good news is that the rate of global population increase seems to be declining. But anxiety about human numbers has not gone away; though rates of increase have declined, global population itself is still increasing. Since the 1965-to-1970 period, the 2001 UN world population report holds, "the world total fertility rate has declined by 45 per cent from 4.9 births per woman to 2.7 births per woman."[12] But "world population is expected to continue growing," and three projections have been made for the future. The "medium-level" variant is based on the assumption that the fertility rate will continue to decline to 2.1 children per woman.[13] This rate projects a world population of 9.3 billion by 2050—which means over 3 billion more on the planet than today. A low variant, assuming 0.5 of a child less, results in 7.9 billion by 2050, while a high variant (0.5 of a child more), results in 10.9 billion.[14] Which variant will describe the human future—or will population size surpass even the highest of these three estimates? As or more important, will population growth level off before ecological and social systems have irreversibly deteriorated? The low variant has leveling off occurring between 2040 and 2050; in the medium-level scenario, it happens roughly by 2050; the high-level variant has population levels still rising sharply at 2050.

Scenarios like these suggest that current population trends are like a wager with acute environmental risk, and that this wager entails at best huge potential population increases still to come and at worst, disaster. Though rates have indeed fallen to 2.7 births per woman, what certainty is there that they will drop to 2.1 in the immediate or even distant future? Isn't 2.1—the figure for "replacement-level fertility"—a wished-for choice for the middle-level estimate as much as it is the most likely projection of overall historical trends? And what would any of the UN's projected increases mean? Right now, estimates about how many people the earth can sustainably support vary widely. The demographer Joel Cohen has devoted a book to the extreme, nearly impossible complexity of making informed guesses on this point. His conclusion is that we are nearing our limits: "the human population of the Earth now travels in the zone where a substantial fraction of scholars have estimated the upper limits of human population size."[15]

A number of further observations concentrate the mind on the magnitudes involved in the enormous wager that population growth represents. Concentrating on anticipated ecosystem stresses alone, a number of observers have calculated that at present, humankind already uses 38.8 percent of the net photosynthetic product (NPP) of the earth's land surface—that is, of all that the world's land plants do not require in order to keep life on the planet alive.[16] (This is up from an estimated 12.5 percent used by humankind in the 1970s).[17] Another doubling of the earth's population would mean that humans consumed 80 percent of the earth's NPP, leaving only 20 percent left over for all other forms of nonplant life. Stuart Pimm does a fuller audit—he puts the human use of plant production at 42 percent of the global total; human use of accessible freshwater runoff at 40 percent; human use of the oceans' production at 35 percent; and future human-caused extinction of the earth's biodiversity at one third to one half of all plant and animal species.[18]

And figures like these do not even begin to factor in remedying existing patterns of social inequality; for all in the world in the next century to consume at First World rates would require numerous additional earths.

If potential ecosystem stresses are great, potential human immiseration also is severe. Bill McKibben points out that the loss of life involved in the horrors in Rwanda was something the planet made up for in two days; Paul Ehrlich, Gretchen Daily, Scott Daily, Norman Myers, and James Salzman calculate that people are adding 10,000,000 souls to the planet every six weeks. Given figures like these, possibilities for runaway genocides and rapid deterioration of social and environmental infrastructure blossom in a still more populous future.[19] And the geographic distribution of contemporary population increases further suggests that potential conflicts may be global ones. The UN projects that while in 1950, 68 percent of world population lived in less-developed countries and presently 80 percent does, by 2050 the figure will stand at 87 percent—a pattern that suggests trouble ahead, as the developed world continues to try to appropriate the lion's share of the earth's resources and sinks and the even more crowded developing world increasingly resents this.[20] As population expert John Bongaarts points out, young developing-world population bulges create severe social stresses. Children need housing, food, clothing, and education, and young adults require jobs but depress wages, thereby heightening poverty and social unrest. Rapidly growing populations thus mean a powder keg of suffering in a world where peoples free of those problems live hours (or a few cable channels) away, thanks to globalization.

The second engine pitting society against nature is material growth. If the worst woes of overpopulation are concentrated mostly in the developing world, the developed world creates more than its share of woe through the broadening footprint left by its economic machine. First World growth brings with it increases in not only resource and energy use but also pollution. As of now, Bill McKibben writes, his daughter, at four years old: "has used more stuff and added more waste to the environment than most of the world's residents do in a lifetime. In my thirty-seven years I have probably outdone small Indian villages."[21] Similarly, he notes, the "57.5 million Northerners added to our population during this decade will add more greenhouse gases to the atmosphere than the roughly 900 million added Southerners," and the figures for resource use and energy are similar.[22] Equally striking are figures for energy and material wasted in the process of consumption:

> A recent report of the US National Academy of Engineering indicates 93 percent of all the material which enters into commerce becomes waste before

the product reaches the consumer. Paul Hawken estimates that 80 percent of the remaining 7 percent which is embedded in the products goes to waste within 6 weeks of use. For example, only 3 percent of the energy produced by a nuclear or coal-fired plant to power an incandescent light bulb actually results in light![23]

What is most sobering is to realize that growth rates of present magnitudes have been a feature of very recent history—the postwar era—and have been accelerating still further as we have entered the era of the global economy. Barry Commoner argued in 1971 that "*most pollution problems made their first appearance, or became very much worse, in the years following World War II*" (his emphasis), and he yoked this to the postwar boom in technology.[24] McKibben points out that, when the U.S. economy grew fiftyfold in the twentieth century, four fifths of that growth came after 1950, and Clive Ponting remarks that: "it has been estimated that the *extra* industrial output produced in the world *each* decade after 1950 is equal to the whole industrial output of the world before 1950."[25] Between 1970 and 1990, total industrial output doubled.[26] In 1998, the UN reported that the costs of public and private consumption would exceed $24 trillion, a figure that was over twice the level of 1975 and six times that of 1950. As James Gustave Speth summarily puts it, "The scale of human activity—economic production—is doubling every 20–25 years."[27]

Equally important is that during this time, income gaps between the First and Third Worlds have widened: in 1750, the ratio was 1 to 1; in 1930, it was 4 to 1; and in 1980, 7 to 1.[28] Further, the UN reports that, while GDP expanded about eightfold between 1950 and 2000, compared to a population increase of slightly less than 2.4 times, this added wealth was nonetheless accompanied by further increases in inequality.[29] World economic growth has thus stressed the planet not only through absolute increases, but also through increasing disparities between rich and poor, a condition usually associated with augmented environmental depredation and stress, thanks to the continuing excesses of the wealthy and the acceleration of the struggle of the less-well-off to catch up to them. Moreover, the pool of absolute poor, those who need what others have and who often degrade the environment to survive, is exactly the same size as before. There is no sign of stresses like these abating—not just for developing nations, like China, newly industrializing with coal, but also for the world leader in energy and resource consumption and greenhouse gas emissions, the United States. As George Bush declared at Rio, "the American way of life is not negotiable."[30]

Considering human population and economic growth as structurally fundamental factors driving a host of different specific environmental crises is thus extremely sobering. Equilibrium, from this perspective, is definitely a thing of the past. Systemic growth like this makes it clear that, in the absence of genuinely sustainable development (a goal no one thinks society has reached and many believe is not even being taken seriously), every problem noted in the previous chapters will proceed in one way only: it will get worse.

Systematized in a computer model in *Limits to Growth* and in the I = PAT formula, perceptions like these lie at the heart of subsequent attempts to style environmentalists dismissively as gloomy, neo-Malthusian doomsters. But even if one sets aside contemporary evidence and accepts debunkers' arguments about human abilities to delink growth from environmental impact by exercising ingenuity, a risky situation remains—one far riskier than what past societies faced. One is forced to buy into a vision of ever-rising environmental disequilibrium, instability, and risk. Even if human innovation manages to reduce the environmental impacts of continued growth, this "progress" is not the old-fashioned kind—a movement forward on an open road—but is increasingly a desperate struggle to keep one step ahead of an accelerating nemesis. More growth means more environmental problems to solve; even if qualitatively more ingenuity rises up to solve them, that only sets the stage for still vaster environmental problems for the next generation. To several far more subtly inflected elaborations of this dire logic I now turn.

Population and economic growth are relatively crude indices of rising environmental disequilibrium. Today, thought about the societal forces driving us into environmental crisis has developed far beyond stark emphasis on these two factors. Thanks to the pressure of environmental crisis, environmental perspectives have been recently incorporated into many areas of thought, and people have begun to consider from widely different viewpoints just how many of the social, economic, cultural, and ideological structures that they inhabit (and that inhabit them) help propel society deeper into environmental crisis. Society is caught up in a larger momentum, the argument goes. People are not simply free to choose to stop affecting their environments as they do. Even as they try to act, they are shaped by a wide variety of societal, ecomomic, cultural, and/or ideological structures larger than themselves. Out of perceptions like these, a whole new class of social-environmental crises has been explored that differ according to the different analytic frameworks chosen.

The list of the more or less systematic environmental critiques of modern world society's entrapment in its own momentum has grown quite long. These critiques are most powerful when dealing not just with specific social practices (for example, clear-cutting versus other forms of logging, or how the public health system is funded and structured), but with beliefs and practices deemed basic to the overall social system. By now these systematic critiques of social-environmental problems include the following: Green structural critiques of capitalism; of industrialization; of consumerism; of ideologies such as anthropocentrism, mastery, and progress; of private property and privatization; of science and technology; of inequitable development, neocolonialism and racism; of patriarchal culture; of modernization and postmodernization; and of globalization. These all focus on ways that social structures and practices control people as much as people do them. As important, they all show that society's environmentally destructive momentum is not something that began recently. And worst of all, they all unhappily reveal that this momentum is no longer just propelling society toward environmental-social crisis but is now increasingly accelerating society *within* it.

In the limited space I have here, I shall discuss just two examples of the many more or less sophisticated theories of environmental-social crisis now in circulation. I choose them as representative examples of ways that systemic logic leads all too easily to the conclusion that society's entrapment in an environmentally destructive momentum not only has deepened but is now accompanied by a new kind of present awareness—the realization that crisis no longer lies somewhere down the road but is already very much in progress in the present. Not every one, doubtless, would agree that the two analytic frameworks I am singling out to discuss at length—let alone all the analytic frameworks listed above—present equally important or credible versions of systemic environmental crisis. Also, there may be those who remain unconvinced by any exposition of systemic logic, any sense that social structures can cohere in a monolithic, totalizing, and determinative fashion. But even skeptics might well take pause at the recent proliferation of analyses like these; it is itself a sign that people are responding to new, heightened perceptions of environmental deterioration and constraint.

The first of these environmental-social crises I shall consider is one that is brought on by what, adopting frequently used terms, I will call accelerating hyper- and postmodernization. It offers a crisis scenario for those focused on the developed world. My second concerns environmental crisis brought on by a dysfunctional pattern of international relationships, a crisis for people who think about the relationships between the developed and un- (or, better, under) developed worlds. Both forms of analysis embody the awareness that people are already well out beyond the limits, dwelling not in a movement toward environmental crisis, but firmly within that crisis, entrapped in momentum already achieved in the past. Both also recognize that society today is no longer innocent or naíve about what it is doing environmentally.

The environmental crisis created by hyper- and postmodernization is a crisis of intensified development, a crisis of the First World heading more and more rapidly where no society has gone before. In hyper- and postmodernization, developed-world society has entered into a condition of deeper environmental risk than before, even as its naíveté about such risk has disappeared. I use the terms "hyper-" and "post-" modernization advisedly to describe two ideal types of cultural-social-industrial-technological complexes; these are caricatures, really, for the two types are neither as pure nor as separate as the terminology would imply. But though the terms refer to assemblages that are each messily complex and complexly woven together, the terms are recognizable enough, thanks to several decades of social analysis, to be useful as starting points.

Hypermodernization is an intensification of modern development that continues to rely on reductionist, objectivist science, technologically expressed through the engineering mentality, brokered by government-funded research, and put in the service of large, hierarchically organized, monopoly industries producing mass-standardized goods. Ideologically, it aims at increasingly domination or conquest of nature and it typically relies on accelerated or megatechnologies (like the fearfully effective tree-felling and fish-harvesting technologies mentioned in the previous chapter) to achieve its ends.

Postmodernization updates this science-technology-institutional-ideological complex like a revised software release. It relies on science and complexity theory to create a hipper, more "ecological" engineering mentality that serves the interests of hipper, more "ecological," weblike transnational corporations— which are, in turn, aggressively funding and seeking to privatize what is clearly a far less "objective" and socially neutral kind of science. Ideologically, postmodernization embraces risk and calls for dynamic social and evolutionary change, and it seeks to realize these goals through glitzy new signature technologies that are varying mixtures of the actual and the visionary, such as genetics, robotics, nanotechnology, and computing. It often styles these new technologies as qualitatively new ones that operate according to nature's principles, or "bio-logic," not mechanistic logic; as distributed, not centralizing; as chaos-driven, not bureaucratically hierarchical; as post-scarcity information industries, not scarcity-era bricks-and-mortar factories. Further, many such industries also claim to be "Green" and ecofriendly in their effects as well as in their underlying logic.

In fact, however, while making claims like these, postmodern industries often speed up rather than alter many of the ecologically and socially troubling effects of hypermodernization. They open up dramatic new areas for human engineering of the physical world; they turn nature more and more into a factory; make organisms and microbes into machines; distance people further than ever before from appreciation and experience of nature; erase rurality and urbanize both the agrarian and the micro-worlds; and reduce biodiversity. As well, they dismantle nature's last barriers to human intervention, such as the integrity of species, the slowness of evolution, and the "otherness" of "life"; turn more and more of the commons into the products and property of individuals; open vast new areas of the environment (globally and microscopically) to capitalist exploitation and commodification; and consolidate social power and wealth into fewer hands.

Together, as Sun Microsystems head Bill Joy has pointed out, hyper- and postmodernization aim at completing the rapid and drastic manipulation of nature achieved by late-twentieth-century nuclear, biological, and chemical (NBC) technologies and seek to extend it into new, futuristic realms by means of genetics, nanotechnology, and robotics (GNR) technologies.[31] (I must quickly amend Joy's acronym to GNRC, for Joy's own computer industry is clearly part of this new technological wave; it provides GNR industries with many of the tools they need in order to develop and it reorganizes global society for new growth and thus new environmental impacts.) With this development, a whole new plateau of environmental concerns has been reached.

I will start with the new technologies. GNRC technologies have raised intense enthusiasm among partisans and intense concern among critics. They have been hyped and damned as unique in their achievements and effects by both groups; a hyperbolic, sometimes lurid, discourse about their inherent risks and benefits has sprung up. This discourse is usually popularizing and techno-deterministic, advertising broadly the assertion that the new technologies will automatically yield vast benefits or unprecedented disasters regardless of what human beings do with them. At the same time, a richer and more scholarly analysis of their risks and benefits has been derived by focusing on society's ways of absorbing and deploying the new technologies rather than on the supposedly inherent qualities of the technology itself. Without seeking to resolve at the start the considerable theoretical and attitudinal conflicts between these two discourses, I would like to consider each in succession.

If celebrations of the new technologies reached a high point in the 1980s and 1990s, so did condemnations. On the one hand, the new technologies were celebrated as forces making the end of the twentieth century into a postmodern equivalent of the Western Renaissance. On the other, they were damned as leading humanity closer to the end of the world. The often eloquent and frightening damnations included two components: they styled the new technologies as both ethically repugnant and potentially species-destroying.

From its beginnings as a research enterprise in the 1970s and its emergence as an industry in the 1980s, genetic engineering was singled out for especially sharp criticism. According to ethical criticisms of it, genetic engineering threatened the sanctity of life. It raised a host of troubling issues: Should "life" be patented and privately owned? Should people be cloned? Should people have the power (if wealthy enough) to have designer babies? Should genetic screening results be communicated to peoples' health insurance carriers, imperiling their coverage? Is the creation of chimeras— creatures that result from the mixtures of two species and that, like the mouse bioengineered to grow a human ear on its back, are sometimes extremely strange—be considered ethical?[32] Should animals be engineered to become factories for production—like cows remade to produce huge amounts of milk from enlarged udders? Wouldn't that inhumanly increase their suffering as producers for people and jeopardize their identities as cows-*an-sich*, and wouldn't it also confine them even more irrevocably to factory farms, places in which their quality of life has already taken a nosedive? And if cows should not be turned into factories, what about bacteria? And what will be the effect on people and human society generally of usurping those powers formerly reserved to God or evolution? These ethical questions vary widely in import and style; they range from those that would suggest imposing absolute barriers to developing genetic engineering to those that would operationally guide it as it develops.

Along with ethical complaints, genetic research and engineering also prompted environmental condemnations that were often sensationalizing and apocalyptic in their description of new, large risks to both the environment and human health. Bill Joy considered genetic engineering uniquely dangerous because it creates organisms that replicate themselves—and that could, unlike chemical spills, continue to grow after their release. The fear, then, is that even if these organisms were intended only for a specific ecological niche, they could spread indefinitely and uncontrollably throughout the environment, something particularly dangerous if they were pathogenic in the first place or, if initially thought safe, they mutated or proved to have dangerous unintended side effects on ecological and/or human health. In addition, the historian of biotechnology Sheldon Krimsky remarks, not only could one not recall such a creation once it was released, one could not adequately test in advance for the risks it might raise: "the range of unexpected outcomes for inert chemicals is probably much narrower since the biological entities mutate."[33] Still further high-stakes concerns about the safety of biotechnology came from the fact that it allowed people to set aside the "natural barriers" between species. What evolution had organized over millennia, human beings could rework in a minute; the possibilities for unintended consequences seemed staggeringly large. These concerns led the biologist Robert Sinsheimer to suggest, Krimsky reports, that: "some *kinds of knowledge* may prove too dangerous for society to have in its possession" and the biochemist Erwin Chargoff to warn: "no genius will be able to undo what one cretin has perpetrated."[34]

To those hearing about self-replication and its theoretical possibilities from both biotechnology enthusiasts and critics, there seemed to be no limit to the possible environmental destruction and human health damage that could come from mistakes, workplace accidents, unintended side effects, and even terrorist interventions that would surely accompany the new technology. A food crop engineered to resist herbicides or plants engineered to kill their own seeds could initiate damage if the engineered genes spread to other valuable species; a bacterium engineered to protect plants against frost might perhaps change weather patterns. Human organs grown in engineered animals and transplanted to humans could open broad new disease pathways, exposing people to new rounds of epidemic diseases; microbes genetically engineered to be pathogenic or carcinogenic might, if mistakenly flushed down laboratory drains, scythe through human populations, giving workplace accidents a dramatic new kind of impact.

And genetic engineering, thus sensationalized, was far from being the only new technology that seemed capable of producing what was no less than a potentially substantial risk to the entire biosphere. Other, more visionary technologies seemed similarly ultra-high-risk. While many of these technologies themselves, let alone the risks they entailed, seemed far-fetched compared to today's actual capabilities, they vividly illustrated the risk-running—and risk-fearing—aura that has recently surrounded cutting-edge technology. One relatively obscure—and fundamentally hypermodern, rather than postmodern—source of such technologies was the new "discipline" of geoengineering. Global warming could be contained in a cost-effective way, Lowell Wood, a physicist at the Lawrence Livermore National Laboratory, argued, by releasing microballoons into the earth's atmosphere to reflect sunlight away from the earth or (more ambitiously) by placing a giant sheet of superfine reflective wire mesh a million miles out in space between us and the sun. Edward Teller, architect of the hydrogen bomb and advocate of Star Wars technologies, said that: "it is a big problem, but it may be realistic if it is handled with care and if the consequences are predicted and understood."[35] Remediation like this sounded enormously risky, given all the possible unforeseen and unwanted effects it could have on the earth's complex ecosystems; even worse, deploying it would simply allow people to go ahead and increase carbon dioxide further. One might worry indeed about any who became its advocates.

A much more widely publicized visionary technology that entailed almost unimaginably high-risk downsides was nanotechnology. Nanotech, a postmodern rather than hypermodern technology, fired up the popular imagination with its claims that it would use self-replicating "molecular assemblers" to make everything from neobiota to buildings. When Eric Drexler began to popularize these features of it, nanotechnology's cultural stock shot up; for some enthusiasts, it promised to revolutionize industrial society, replacing the dark satanic mills of nineteenth- and twentieth-century manufacturing with miniaturized molecular assemblers. At the same time, though, these very same powers raised the possibility of biospheric catastrophe, thanks to the fact that molecular-level nanotechnological "assemblers," like genetically modified organisms, would be designed to self-replicate—like life. Thus, as Eric Drexler wrote: "'plants' with 'leaves' no more efficient than today's solar cells could out-compete real plants, crowding the biosphere with inedible foliage. Tough omniverous 'bacteria' could out-compete real bacteria. They could spread like blowing pollen, replicate swiftly, and reduce the biosphere to dust in a matter of days. . . . We cannot afford certain kinds of accidents with replicating assemblers."[36] A workplace accident could do in the entire earth.

Writing on the downsides of postmodern technology, Bill Joy also took seriously the threat that self-replicating robots might someday replace humans. Unwilling at first to admit that this hoary old science-fiction fantasy might become fact, Joy changed his mind, thanks to continued expansions of computing power. And robotics scientists like Hans Moravec added to the brio of enthusiasm and apocalypse by pointing to the possibility that human consciousness could some day be transferred from meat to silicon and embracing the notion that the human species' progeny might some day be artificial "mind children," not the children of our bodies.[37] With notions like these in the air, it wasn't surprising that robotics scientists received widespread attention when they recently announced that they had at last succeeded in designing a largely self-replicating robot, one capable of evolving itself.[38]

The megarisks of all these hypermodern and postmodern technologies suggest that a single technological intervention could destroy all humanity. This notion has one famous historical precursor. It dates back to the decision whether to conduct the first atomic test, Trinity. A calculation by Edward Teller revealed that an atomic explosion might: "set fire to the atmosphere. A revised calculation reduced the danger of destroying the world to a three-in-a-million chance."[39] The military went ahead with the test.

As awful as this exposition of risk sounds, it will appear less convincing and less sobering to some than it does to others. For even in its horrors, postmodern technological sensationalism is still, to some degree, high on pop-culture futurism, even if that high has a bitter, dystopian taste to it. It relies, in short, as much or more on science fiction than scientific fact; and, indeed, simply to embrace Joy's analysis—which embraces in turn the claims of people like Eric Drexler on nanotechnology and Hans Moravec on robotics—is to tread on scientifically shaky ground. Thus, in a recent edition of *Scientific American*, Gary Stix reported that: "scientists with tenured faculty positions and NSF grants ridiculed [Drexler's] visions, noting that their fundamental improbability made them an absurd projection of what the future holds." Even more damningly, Stix added, scientists seeking to establish themselves found that "the visionary scent that has surrounded nanotechnology" helped them get funding and advance their careers, for "labeling a research project 'nanotechnology'" gave it additional allure.[40] The sensational benefits and sensational risks of postmodern technology thus provided material for effective hypes but were not sober truths.

In recounting the history of early recombinant DNA research, Sheldon Krimsky recorded a similarly large gulf between scientific insiders' detailed and serious dialogue about risk and a public discourse that could easily seem cartoonish by comparison. Commenting on the growth of genetic engineering, he also mordantly echoed Stix's observation about the business value of popular sensationalism: "ironically, attention over the risks of genetic engineering brought additional media and investor interest in rDNA products."[41] Reflecting on these issues, one could begin to suspect that futurist enthusiasm *and* catastrophism might well function as a diversion—even a convenient diversion—from much messier and far sadder kinds of social and environmental problems. Both activities might conveniently obscure a much more confusing, realistic, and messy drama of technological development and absorption.

Observers and critics of the new technologies who distrust popular discourse and its sensationalizing technodeterminism have indeed not been relieved of worry. Instead, they have focused in greater detail on two areas. Though many of the more sensational risks raised by early publicity surrounding the new GNRC technologies seem less and less plausible to insiders today, scientific debate and several decades of risk assessment have not ruled out uncertainty; indeed, they have in some ways multiplied it. Part of the reason for this is a new and admirable sense of caution, something learned from the mistakes of the past.

A look at the example of biotechnology should illustrate the situation well. As Sheldon Krimsky argues, biotechnology today takes place in an "age of anxiety"; biology's "age of innocence" has been left behind by the powerful new effects that biological research now provides. What is true of biology is true of heroic new technologies generally. "Industrialized nations," Krimsky writes: "have had decades to reflect upon the adverse consequences of synthetic chemicals and nuclear radiation. We have watched the internal combustion engine and fossil fuel power plants transform our precious natural resources into generators of illness and ecological damage. The mistakes of our technological history are apparent before our eyes."[42] As a result, Krimsky and Roger Wrubel write: "the public's scrutiny" comes now "at the early steps of innovation, before the technologies are on-line and before products are marketed."[43]

At the same time, however, this intensified commitment to testing for risk has not meant that the risks can be dispelled or even controlled. For, as Krimsky also argues, risk assessment itself is problematic in a number of ways. The history of microbiologists' often well-intentioned and scrupulous risk assessment of specific research programs and technological applications pointedly exposes many gaps—areas in which risk assessment has not eliminated potential dangers. As tests for specific dangers look in increasingly fine-grained detail at possible hazards, they tend to engender a need for still further testing by discovering new uncertainties as they eliminate old ones. Even more important is the fact that, however scrupulous concern at the start may have been, risk assessment cannot begin to keep up with the rapidly increasing number of specific cases researchers and industry generate as they proceed. The multiplication of new processes and products that is under way races far ahead of what specific assessments (which require considerable time to discover all the potential problems, design practicable tests for them, and then carry out the tests) can manage. And as financial investment in and reward from biotechnological innovation grow, the likelihood of politics interfering with cautious risk assessment increases.

A still more fundamental reason for persisting uncertainty comes from what Krimsky calls the unavoidable clash of two scientific paradigms. Molecular genetics, like physics, is: "predictive and deterministic (strongly at the macro level, and statistically at the micro level). As a science, it has come to symbolize the quintessance of the Baconian doctrine of power emanating from knowledge." In ecology, by contrast: "explanations rather than predictions dominate. The emphasis is on systems (communities, ecosystems, nutrient cycles) rather than elements, interactions rather than reactions, and change rather than stability. . . . There is an aversion to any mechanistic view of causality in biological systems."[44] Thus, for example: "ecologists have no illusion about predicting the behavior of GEOs [genetically engineered organisms] released into the environment."[45]

Barry Commoner has recently shown just how wide is this conceptual rift between molecular genetics and ecology. Commoner focuses on the "central dogma" of molecular genetics: Francis Crick's assertion that "Once [sequential] information has passed into protein it can't get out again." This dogma, Commoner goes on, holds "that genetic information originates in the DNA nucleotide sequence and terminates, unchanged, in the protein amino acid sequence."[46] What this means is that specific genes control specific traits; modification of them therefore will yield controllable results, something that ensures that biotechnological intervention, conducted carefully, can be safe. But a significant "surprise" came, Commoner writes, with the recent completion of the sequencing of human DNA: "Instead of the 100,000 or more genes predicted by the estimated number of human proteins, the gene count was only about 30,000"—which made people "only about as gene-rich as a mustardlike weed (which has 26,000 genes)."[47]

Why this shortfall? Commoner argues that it was no surprise because biologists had known for some time that there were a number of cellular processes that contradicted the propositions of the "central dogma." One, named "alternative splicing," meant that a single gene could produce variant protein molecules: "the current record for the number of different proteins produced from a single gene by alternative splicing is held by the fruit fly, in which one gene generates up to 38,016 variant protein molecules."[48] Specific genetic traits thus do not arise from specific genes. Rather, a number of different processes in the whole cell collaborate to produce them. Commoner then strongly faults molecular geneticists for suppressing the most important implication of this knowledge: the existence of cell processes contradicting the central dogma means that genetic engineering is not safe. For, when genetic technology adds a foreign gene to an organism, it doesn't just make a single change; it alters a complex system. And since the results of alterations to complex systems are often multiple and unpredictable, genetic technology entails a massive risk of "unintended, potentially disastrous, consequences."[49] Thus where molecular geneticists argue that risks can be tested for and controlled, ecologists, recognizing the fundamental unpredictability of complex systems, advocate the precautionary principle.

Risk thus remains a significant issue for biotechnology. And with the entrance of biological scientists into commercial ventures, temptation to celebrate risk-taking and satirize precaution once again runs extremely high. It is thus troubling when Theo Colburn and her colleagues report in *Our Stolen Future* that: "when questioned about the risks of releasing genetically engineered organisms into the environment, one of the world's prominent biologists saw no reason for hesitating. He told a group of journalists that our society has to 'be brave' and forge ahead with new technologies despite uncertainties."[50] His concealment of self-interest and his dubious extension of "bravery" from his and his colleagues' enterprise to people at large—people who neither assent to nor even know of the hazards involved—echo the libertarian-conservative discourse of risk described in the last chapter. An even uglier cat seemed to emerge from an all-too-familiar bag when Don Westfall, the vice president of Promar International, observed that: "the hope of the industry is that over time the market is so flooded [with genetically modified products] that there's nothing you can do about it. You just sort of surrender."[51] The result would be a confirmation of Commoner's worst fears: society would be committing itself to yet another "massive uncontrolled experiment whose outcome is inherently unpredictable."[52] The politics of risk discourse and the many uncertainties of risk assessment would then do exactly what environmentalists have accused risk assessment of doing: they would provide a cover for continuing to develop, not restrict, dangerous technology. As such, they would represent a fascinating adaptation of old ways to the new age of anxiety. A society that had lost the environmental naíveté it had when the postwar chemical industry first geared up would, thanks to risk assessment, be able to repeat what it did then because it could tell itself it was proceeding differently.

But if precise determination and effective social control of the risks raised by the new technologies are an area of great concern, a still more serious problem comes when one considers the ways in which society absorbs and deploys technology. A look at how the new technologies articulate with older ones and how the combination of the two further articulates with societal growth presents the most realistic and serious version of hyper/postmodern social-environmental crisis today.

Years ago, Jacques Ellul, one of the most famous and most controversial students of the evolution of technology and social techniques, wrote that two processes, amplification and accommodation, powered the expansion of technology and of technique, the mentality that accompanies it.[53] The fundamentally heroic process of amplification extends technology and technique into more and more places in peoples' lives, even as it vastly increases their impact upon nature. The preceding chapters have included a number of examples of technological amplification, such as the new hyper- and megatechnologies associated with the accelerating, globalizing economy.

But once the expansion of technology has done its work—and, in the process created environmental problems and disasters—growing perceptions of technology's darker side give greater and greater prominence to the second process, accommodationism. As Ellul argues, "technique, in its development, poses primarily technical problems that can be resolved only by technique," for people can never foresee all the consequences of a given technological action.[54] The unintended consequences and disasters that result from technology must be dealt with, and the diagnosis is usually that they are resolvable only by further applications of technology and technique. This fundamentally hair-of-the-dog logic Ellul calls accommodationism. It comes into play when new technologies seek social acceptance and adoption by promising to repair the excesses and damage wrought by the old. Accommodationism is, in short, a social process that follows closely on the heels of amplification and that drives society much more sneakily, but also ineluctably, into environmental difficulties.

Unsurprisingly, with the advent of a second wave of postwar technological innovation in the United States, accommodationism has become as much of a growth area as amplification. The first wave galvanized Rachel Carson and the postwar environmental movement into action. The second wave of technological innovation sprang up in the wake of raised environmental damage done by the first and deepening concern about the diversification and globalization of environmental crisis. Developed in this context of rising environmental concern—in an "age of anxiety" to use Krimsky's terms—the second wave of postwar technological innovation has not just assumed, as its predecessor did, the mantle of "progress" and the "new"; though it has not shied away from being more brazen than postwar industry and calling itself a new "renaissance," it hasn't spoken in only these terms. Much more, it has been welcomed and also styled itself as a means of remediation of the environmental problems created by earlier technological interventions into nature. It has presented itself, in short, as a nick-of-time, hair-of-the-dog technology for people who already perceived themselves to be living in environmental crisis.

Accommodationist ecological-social crisis is created by a society that burrows deeper into environmental and social crisis by following messy intervention with even messier remedial adaptation. Tom Athanasiou describes adaptation as: "a weapon in the arsenal of denial . . . [that] helps conservatives to force prevention from the agenda. It is far easier to breed drought-resistant crops (the Israelis are doing so), or to ensure against worsening oceanic storms by raising the height of off-shore drilling platforms (Shell Oil is doing so) than it is to turn society as a whole, with all its complexity, onto a postgreenhouse path."[55] Thanks to such accommodationism, hyper-/postmodern technologies continue to operate and even find new opportunities within environmental crisis. New technologies are summoned up to remedy the problems created by old ones; these efforts, however, allow people to continue using the old ones. The result is not a genuine solution but a sad process of nesting more and more messily within and progressively adapting to a wrecked nature.

Energy politics provides a variety of examples of this effort. Despite generations of environmental screeds, the possibility of energy scarcity has recently stimulated not fundamental social change but a variety of remedial measures. It has spurred the development of new technologies for extraction in more difficult places; in doing this, it has even attempted to adapt to environmental opposition through the development of new (supposedly) environmentally friendly extraction techniques.

So far, this sort of adaptation has been successful; known global fossil-fuel reserves have expanded greatly. In response to this success, however, Jeremy Leggett pursued a still more ingenious tack. Presently known reserves are so vast, he argued, that continuing use of only a small portion of them would drive the world into massive and irreversible ecological catastrophe from global warming.[56] Attempting to prevent the system from continuing its accommodationist spiral into global warming—and thus into a flowering of new crises to manage and adapt to—Leggett met with executives in two other industries, banking and insurance, to warn them about how global warming could wreck their businesses and to advise them to use the power of their massive investment portfolios to help accelerate the world's transition to renewable energy. Withdrawing their huge investments from the fossil-fuel industries would do more than send a message. Such an act was necessary because these industries have, via investment and insurance, trillions of dollars at stake, investments now threatened by the potentially catastrophic effects of global warming; coastline flooding alone puts $2 trillion worth of insured assets at risk.

The strategy was ingeniously ecomodernist in that it worked with the system, not against it. At the same time, it was significantly more aggressive and subversive than ecomodernism usually is. It did not try to be relentlessly win-win; instead, it assumed that capitalism was not as monolithic as its critics often felt. But even here, the question remains whether Leggett will turn out to have been an optimist. Tom Athanasiou has reported on sophisticated challenges facing Leggett's attempt to set capitalism against itself in this way in advance of meltdown:

> Far from heeding Greenpeace's urgings to champion a solar transition, the insurance industry's post-Andrew innovations have focused on "shorelining," an actuarial device by which construction codes are strengthened and coastal zones declared uninsurable, and on the development of "Act of God" bonds and "catastrophe futures" that will actually allow investors to *speculate* on natural disasters. According to George Lloyd-Roberts of Lloyds of London, such adaptations, in combination with government bailouts for insurers hit by "super cats" ("cat" is industry lingo for "catastrophe") "should be able to secure a stable insurance market even in the age of global warming".[57]

These adaptations represent a display of accommodationist ingenuity at least as inventive as any of Paul Hawken's and Amory and L. Hunter Lovins's proposals for ecological modernization in *Natural Capitalism*. The old wobbling system can indeed be patched up for a while longer.

Given examples like these, it is plausible to consider that the worst consequence of hypermodern/postmodern technological development is not a workplace accident or unintended consequence turned into an apocalypse;

it is rather that the new technologies continue the process of sad accommodationism in a time of deepening environmental crisis rather than enabling
a more fundamental restructuring of social and environmental practices. Replacing a much more "ecological" enthusiasm for solar power—once the
cutting-edge technology of peoples' dreams—with a much more interven-
tionist, risky, and paradigm-breaking set of technological aspirations, GNRC
technologies widen rather than narrow human ecological impact even as
they claim to fix things.

As one would expect if these concerns about the linkage between technological development and increasing environmental impact were true, the
development of GNRC technologies has been accompanied by accommodationist claims that have been almost as insistent and widespread as heroic,
amplification-style claims. Genetic engineering, for example, has proposed to
solve a whole encyclopedia of environmental difficulties. Advocates have
maintained that it will solve increasingly intractable pollution problems, an
assertion buttressed by the fact that the first patented genetic organism was
a bacterium engineered to eat oil spills. Further, in 1980, B.F. Goodrich Co.
"received a patent for a novel plasmid that degrades ethylene dichloride, a
compound found in many waste dumps," Krimsky notes.[58] Along with pollution and toxification problems, genetic engineering, enthusiasts argue, will
provide an antidote to the current biodiversity crisis, allowing scientists to
preserve vanishing species by cloning them. Global warming will also be com-
batted by genetic engineering, by creating specially fast-growing trees to soak
up carbon dioxide—thereby allowing oil companies, of course, to sell more
oil. Polluting chemical fertilizers will be replaced by genetically engineered
microorganisms that "fix their own nitrogen from the vast resevoir available
in the atmosphere"; an unfortunate side effect will be that factory farming
and nitrogen pollution will continue. And declines in human health will, of
course, be countered by genetic therapies and whole warehouses of drugs and
even replacement organs grown in genetically modified "pharm" animals, so
that one can cope with deepening environmental and social stresses on
human health with hearts and livers grown, for example, in swine.

Accommodationist claims thus represent a further step along an already-
moving treadmill on which problems and constraints multiply in sync with
multiplying remedies.[59] And as this treadmill continues, society can go far indeed—and it can go into areas much more ethically and environmentally disturbing than even those raised by postmodern industry today. For the most
painful futures that accommodationism suggests are not the sensational and

apocalyptic meltdowns but futures all too depressingly familiar, plausible, and mundane. A stark version of accommodationism's sad realism is the observation George Wald made on Earth Day in 1970. As Mark Dowie describes it:

> Wald warned that America was perilously close to allowing "anti-pollution to become a new multi-billion dollar business," a huge and very profitable industry that would repair environmental hazards caused by nuclear waste, lead, radon, and asbestos and offer a portion of its profits to the environmental movement. Under Wald's scenario, pollution would "go on merrily in all its present forms," while we "superimpose a new multi-billion dollar anti-pollution industry on top of it. And in these days of conglomerates, it will be the same business. One branch of it will be polluting, the other branch of it anti-polluting."[60]

But no version of realistic accommodationism is more pessimistic than that of Ulrich Beck, who shades the social process of accommodationism into a larger structural critique of capitalism. If accommodationism is fueled by people profiting from keeping things going and making new industries out of ameliorating old problems (both of which create new problems in the process), the system as a whole is increasingly structuring itself to "*profit* from the abuses it produces, and very nicely, thank you."[61] For Beck, a truly gothic capitalist market logic lies behind and reinforces the technological logic we have been describing; far from being the ultimate contradiction of capitalism, environmental crisis offers capitalism its most boundless, if grisly, possibilities. "Through the production of risks," Beck writes: "needs are definitively removed from their residual mooring in natural factors, and hence their finiteness, their satisfiability. Hunger can be assuaged, needs can be satisfied; risks are a 'bottomless barrel of demands,' unsatisfiable, infinite."[62]

Propagating risk and environmental crisis becomes, then, the ultimate extension of consumerist capitalism, the creation of the kind of market that economists and industrialists would (perhaps literally) die for: a market that, in both theory and fact, can never, ever be glutted. Removing breasts and prostates is just an early-generation business in this line. Of course, many Green radicals have argued that if class contradictions did not finish off or hobble capitalism, the ultimate (and apocalyptic) contradiction between a capitalist system devoted to growth and the limits of the ecosystem would. The possibility Beck raises is vastly gloomier. A more and more overtly brown capitalism, Beck suggests, could ride through this contradiction, finding vast and theoretically ungluttable new markets for a new class of Green and/or re-

medial necessities and discovering in a damaged future not its own extinction, but its purest and most Platonically perfect form yet. Environmentally
destructive capitalism would thus accompany and accelerate society all the way
down the resulting spiral to a continually postponed, never-quite-reached bottom—and that slow-motion spiral will be our social-environmental catastrophe, one that we are already decisively in.

This sort of realistic accommodationism is much more a part of our immediate daily experience than the high-tech, catastrophe-producing kind. Once
one looks for them, examples of realistic accommodationism well under way
can be multiplied almost indefinitely. Realistic accommodationism would
shadow the development of new ways to palliate environmentally caused cancer and cling to more visionary claims that cloning could offer the best way to
keep some endangered species from disappearing from the planet (a claim
that, as John Rennie, the editor of *Scientific American*, remarks, would allow a
land-use developer to argue: "that there is no reason to worry about the disappearance of a given species in the wild because we can always ressurect it later
through cryogenics and cloning—whereas we need that ranch land now").[63]

After thinking through an example like this, one begins to realize how difficult genuine solutions, as opposed to ingenious accommodations, are. The
danger is that attempts to cope with an old problem generate new ones although they do not solve the old. At the least, in appraising solutions to environmental crisis that new technologies and techniques propose, one has to
look well past their general claims to the details of their implementation.
What props up the old system, and what actually changes it? Differentiating
between the two is sometimes difficult, but it is essential.

Propping up a dysfunctional system worsens things as it proceeds, and it
can proceed extremely far. "It may be," Ulrich Beck writes, that: "we are situated at the beginning of a historical process of habituation. It may be that
the next generation, or the one after that, will no longer be upset at pictures
of birth defects, like those tumor-covered fish and birds that now circulate
around the world, just as we are no longer upset today by violated values, the
new poverty and a constant high level of mass unemployment. It would not be
the first time that standards disappear as a result of their violation."[64] Living
into crisis in this way could mean moving along a path that no society has ever
taken before, a path littered with the forgotten husks of cast-off standards of
environmental beauty and human health. Such a path could stretch far into
surroundings that people today would consider intolerably grotesque. Incapable of systemic change, the world deteriorating about them, people would

feel forced to jettison their standards instead of acting—which is precisely what corporate-conservative assaults on nature's "pristinity" and "health" and advocacy of risk and chemicalization have been urging U.S. citizens to do.

My second example of a human-made environmental crisis embedded in social structures is equally painful. Rather than looking at the developed world, the planet's vanguard, this example considers the situations of the less "successful," the people on the peripheries of global power. Inspired on the one hand by new First World fears and defensiveness and on the other by a deepened understanding of racism, colonialism, and the problems created by postwar developmentalism, this version of systemic crisis describes an environmental-social crisis-in-progress that comes from the failure of internationalism and globalization to produce social justice and environmental equity as well as environmental health.

On September 13, 1998, in its weekend edition, the *New York Times* ran a half-page headlined: "Kofi Annan's Astonishing Facts!"[65] Introduced thus in carnivalesque style by the *Times*, these facts featured painful data about contemporary global, social, and environmental inequality. Thus we learned that the richest fifth of the world consumes 86 percent of all goods, while the poorest fifth gets just 1.3 percent; the three richest people in the world have assets that exceed the combined gross domestic product of the 48 least developed countries; and the world's 225 richest individuals have a combined wealth equal to the poorest 47 percent of the world's population. Along with these indications of general global inequality came more pointed indictments: Americans spend $8 billion a year on cosmetics, $2 billion more than the estimated total needed to provide basic education for everybody in the world. Of the 4.4 billion people in developing countries, nearly three fifths lack access to safe sewers, a third have no access to clean water, a quarter don't have adequate housing, and a fifth have no access to modern health services of any kind. Europeans spend $11 billion a year on ice cream, $2 billion more than the estimated annual total necessary to provide clean water and safe sewers to the world's population. The summary statistic is perhaps the most pointed: the entire cost of achieving universal access to basic education for all, basic health care for all, reproductive health care for women, adequate food for all, and clean water and safe sewers for all is less than 4 percent of the combined wealth of the 225 richest people in the world.

"Kofi Annan's Astonishing Facts!" jibe perfectly with facts that more or less radical environmentalists have circulated for some time. For example, they reinforce often-cited precepts about how people in the North stress the environment more than people in the South. The "North, with a fourth of the world's people, consumes 70 percent of the world's energy, 85 percent of its wood, and 60% of its food"; similarly, "a baby born in the United States creates thirteen times as much environmental damage over the course of its lifetime as a baby born in Brazil, and thirty-five times as much as an Indian baby."[66] Though, as noted above, the world has in recent years become wealthier and the *percentage* of its population living in poverty has decreased, the gap between the wealthy and the poor has substantially widened even as, in absolute figures not percentages, the same number of people globally are as poor as they always were.

Or poorer. For, as Kofi Annan's facts imply a startling addition to as well as rise in inequality has occurred. To old patterns of social inequality a second layer has been added: rapidly worsening patterns of environmental inequality. Indeed, the union of these two kinds of inequality is more and more inevitable as the environmental crisis deepens. But today it stands out sharply enough—more and more, relative well-being needs to be measured not only in the distribution of produced goods and services but also in the allotment of environmental bads.

Global inequalities of wealth have, of course, an old history. Recently, the innocence that once surrounded this history has been substantially dispelled. Rather than Europe simply pulling ahead of the rest of the world thanks to its scientific, social, and cultural renaissances, something more complicated occurred. As economic historians like André Gunder Frank, Immanuel Wallerstein, and L. S. Stavrianos have long argued, First World successes have come in sync with Third World immiseration. As these economic historians maintain, First and Third World relationships (or, in today's revision, developed and underdeveloped worlds on North and South relationships) have been, since colonialism, driven by a process of inequitable development.[67] Europe entered the colonial and the modern eras simultaneously; its exploitation of its colonies *under*developed them—that is, socially dismantled and economically depressed them—while Europe's development at home—its *over*development—was facilitated by the expropriation of work and wealth from the colonies. Moreover, the process of differential development did not end with colonialism; it continued into postcolonial and then global times.

If differential development has for centuries sponsored social and economic disparities, it has become increasingly clear of late that it also fosters inequitable environmental conditions. When Harry Truman announced U.S.

commitment to helping the "undeveloped" nations of the world modernize, prospects for potential equality seemed high; today, not only are those goals unmet, but new environmental inequalities have been added to old social and economic disparities. And the goal of remedying both sorts of inequality seems, to a number of environmentalists and political scientists today, less reachable than ever before, when global environmental constraints are figured in. Were all to modernize as the developed world now has, these critics maintain, it would bring down the biosphere. As Paul Hawken and the Lovinses put it, if present trends continue: "for all the world to live as an American or Canadian, we would need two more earths to satisfy everyone, three more if population should double and twelve earths if worldwide standards of living should double over the next forty years."[68]

Contemporary environmental inequalities are not, in fact, wholly new. Europeans not only helped free themselves from environmental constraints by exploiting and appropriating the resources of the colonial world; they also exported environmental destruction to it—a phenomenon that Clive Ponting calls, for maximum shock value, "the rape of the world."[69] The fabulous abundances early European colonials discovered were not just abundances of luxury goods like gold; famously, they also included (in the United States in particular) a stunning biotic plenitude, a fabulous wealth of arable soil, wood, game, and fish. This natural inheritance was, however, quickly dismantled by the colonists. The export of much of it back to Europe enabled Europe's freedom from the famines and ecological constraints that haunted medieval times.

Today's environmental stresses, however, add new kinds of environmental deterioration to these old losses. Some of the environmental stresses have, to be sure, pointed to increasing trouble for everyone. First World critics have been quick to see recent globalization as a process of "harmonizing down" or to racing to the bottom.[70] Corporations now easily move where social and environmental protections and costs are low, thereby lowering the whole world's standards. Also, "global" environmental problems such as climate change threaten the world as a whole. Still these apparently common problems may in practice affect rich and poor nations unequally. Even more, still other developments point to a whole new dimension of environmental inequality opening up that is doubly unfair and dysfunctional. Developing-world countries are being forced to absorb a wide variety of the environmental problems created by developed-world economies; at the same time, this very practice allows developed-world countries to continue heedlessly with their excesses as usual.

This new environmental inequality is created in several ways. Developed-world countries continue to appropriate most of the world's resources, accelerating environmental damage in the developing-world countries that supply them. Industrialized countries dominate the forest products trade; they are the world's main consumers of metals; they dominate global consumption, "accounting for more than 80% of all imports by value"; and in scouring the world to locate fossil-fuel reserves, they have discovered "more than 90% of known oil reserves and 60% of natural gas reserves in the developing world."[71] In appropriating this lion's share of resources, industrial countries generate the lion's share of what has to be poured into the earth's (overflowing) sinks. For example, they generate the majority of greenhouse gas pumped into the atmosphere each year (a statistic that, figured on a per-capita basis, is particularly shocking); and while worldwide, "some 300–500 million tons of hazardous wastes are generated each year, according to UNEP estimates," "industrialized countries account . . . for 80–90 percent of the total."[72]

At the same time, industrialized countries, seeking to protect their increasingly vulnerable environments, export more and more of their risky industries, environmental hazards, dangerous products, and difficult-to-absorb pollution. The WHO estimates that "some 25 million agricultural workers in the developing world . . . suffer at least one incident of pesticide poisoning per year, resulting in as many as 20,000 deaths annually."[73] Export of toxic wastes accounts for about 10 percent, the UNEP estimates, of the 440 million tons produced annually.[74] Risky and polluting industries shipped abroad were responsible for the explosion at Bhopal, India which killed 6,000 within a week and to which 16,000 deaths have been attributed overall. "Recent decades," Hilary French says, "have also seen [other] hazardous industries themselves become widely dispersed around the planet"; these include the asbestos industry and, even, the recycling industry: recycling batteries to reclaim lead have poisoned many in the developing world.[75]

To be sure, as the export of hazards like these has grown, many have sought to make its effects clearer; vivid examples of specific abuses have become commonplace. First World children play, as Noam Chomsky has publicized, with baseball bats hand-dipped in toxic chemicals by Haitian women; and First World purchasers of flowers from Colombian flower plantations support, in effect, the exposure of workers to 127 different pesticides, 20 percent of which "are either banned or unregistered in the United Kingdom or the United States" and which cause "headaches, nausea, impaired vision, and other symptoms."[76] Proliferation of knowledge about and condemnations of practices like these has done extremely little to stop them. Though they seem truly outrageous when named, malign dependencies like these are so deeply embedded in developed-world ways of life that they persist even when social critics indignantly expose them, continuing as a general pattern even when awareness is successfully raised about a particular issue. The only thing one cannot do, apparently, is to seem to accept or, worse, approve of them. Lawrence Summers set off a firestorm of criticism when a 1992 memo of his leaked from the World Bank suggested that: "just between you and me, shouldn't the World Bank be encouraging more migrations of the dirty industry to the LDCs [least developed countries]?" He then went on to give a three-part rationale for his proposal, a rationale that was even more provocative.[77] In the subsequent brouhaha, the World Bank said the memo was meant to be ironical. Still, the joke, like Jonathan Swift's modest proposal, exposed truths about the ways in which economic rationality actually works, and some, like the author of an article in *The Economist*, took its proposals quite seriously and supported them.[78]

Developments like these have helped undercut and severely limit the First World fantasy that somewhere on earth "unspoiled" places remain. No longer inspiring serious utopian dreaming or writing, the fantasy survives today only in discourses like tourist marketing, discourses that people participate in only with a degree of cynicism. Much more prominent in serious reflection today is the awareness that the world is filled everywhere with increasingly claustrophobic social-environmental stresses. One important response to these perceptions is the new discipline of environmental security. Fundamentally conservative in its approach and focused strongly on the worries and interests of the developed world, it analyzes what happens when environmental deterioration threatens to worsen social and economic disparities between peoples and nations.

The intellectual framework for environmental security can be traced back, Robert Kaplan argues, to George Kennan's 1947 call for a "firm and vigilant containment" of the Soviet Union. As Kennan articulated the overall challenge more specifically in 1948: "our real task in the coming period is to devise a pattern of relationships which will allow us to maintain this position of disparity [between the United States and others] without positive detriment to our national security."[79] Today, potentially terrible tension between haves and have-nots still exists, Kaplan argues, but it now includes an environmental component. It takes place in an increasingly environmentally degraded, socially disrupted, and ultimately postnational world—a world of social chaos and gangsterism in which national elites have increasingly lost control over their people and in which environmental conditions are an important part of the disruptive inequities. Kaplan cites Thomas Fraser Homer-Dixon's arresting image of the coming social-environmental catastrophe:

> Think of a stretch limo in the potholed streets of New York City, where homeless beggars live. Inside the limo are the air-conditioned postindustrial regions of North America, Europe, the emerging Pacific Rim, and a few other isolated places, with their trade summitry and computer-information highways. Outside is the rest of mankind, going in a completely different direction.[80]

It is clear that this new vision of international catastrophe is very different from Paul Ehrlich's scenario in *The Population Bomb* of environmental scarcity producing world end through nuclear war. This new vision of catastrophe portrays further and further immersion in deteriorated environmental conditions and experience of social chaos, not an abrupt, apocalyptic end ahead. Consonant with both recent perceptions of global environmental decay as slummification and postnationalist visions of a world plagued by ethnic strife, Homer-Dixon and Kaplan depict an elite in increasing danger of being enveloped in a growing miasma of deterioration and small-scale, bitter conflicts associated with this process. Kaplan fleshes the scenario out further, asserting that: "a minority of the human population will be, as Francis Fukuyama would put it, sufficiently sheltered so as to enter a 'post-historical' realm, living in cities and suburbs in which the environment has been mastered and ethnic animosities have been quelled by bourgeois prosperity." By contrast, he continues: "an increasingly large number of people will be stuck in history, living in shantytowns where attempts to rise above poverty, cultural dysfunctions, and ethnic strife will be doomed by a lack of water to drink, soil to till, and space to survive in."[81]

Kaplan, a journalist, not a scholar, immediately proceeds to sensationalize the issue as much as he can. He quotes "my friend"—a "top-ranking African official whose life would be threatened were I to identify him more precisely" who asserts that: "In forty-five years I have never seen things so bad. We did not manage ourselves well after the British departed." Africa emerges from Kaplan's subsequent descriptions as a new version of the old nightmare image of a Third World hell: "children defecate in a stream filled with garbage and pigs, droning with malarial mosquitoes. In this stream women do the washing." In this hell not only disease but also societal decay and population escalate out of control—something that Kaplan documents statistically and also caustically represents, for example, in his description of Damba Tesele, a man who has "four wives and thirty-two children, not one of whom has made it to high school."[82] Traveling to the airport from downtown Conakry, the capital of Guinea, Kaplan observes from his (probably not air-conditioned) cab the state of things:

> The streets were one long puddle of floating garbage. Mosquitoes and flies were everywhere. Children, many of whom had protruding bellies, seemed as numerous as ants. When the tide went out, dead rats and the skeletons of cars were exposed on the mucky beach. In twenty-eight years Guinea's population will double if growth goes on at current rates.[83]

In this new version of an old First World nightmare, "traditional" environmental problems (such as infectious disease and overpopulation) are featured side by side in places like this with "modern" ones (such as urban slummification), an all-too-widespread pairing that other students of developing-world environmental problems, including the World Bank, have noticed.[84]

Kaplan's essay made a splash in the United States when it came out in 1994; it was, however, a description of a new crisis done in an old style, a style I find particularly nasty. Kaplan managed to recycle every vicious and covertly bigoted developed-world stereotype about Third World peoples—something which makes me wonder if the minister remained his "friend" after reading Kaplan's *Heart of Darkness 2.0*. The only differences between Kaplan's and the old racist accounts are that Kaplan gives the familiar clichés a new environmental dimension and a fashionable postmodern, postnational spin. On the one hand, environmental deterioration is sensationalized and exoticized. On the other hand, postnational Africa is presented as a place that has simultaneously slipped back to a time before the nation-state, with its state monopoly of force, and tipped over into a new, lurid kind of postmodern primitivism. For example, he cites, for its shock value, the case of the Liberian "guerilla leader Prince Johnson [who] didn't just cut off the ears of President Samuel Doe before Doe was tortured to death in 1990." Johnson made a video of it, Kaplan reports, one "which has circulated throughout West Africa."[85]

In Kaplan's postmodernized version of the colonial-racist imagination, then, Africa is once again exoticized, this time as a postmodern rather than primitive nightmare. For culturally inclined readers, this portrait represents yet another example of a fundamentally conservative backlash against multiculturalism. For environmentalists, Kaplan's exoticizing portrayal of environmental deterioration hints that advancing global environmental crisis may be accompanied by a new round of First World stigmatization of Third World peoples. Even worse, it shows that stigmatization like this may lead to solutions that are scary because wrong—solutions that would make the problem worse if acted upon.

While Kaplan views the Third World as a vast social and environmental meltdown in process, he sees the First World as "posthistorical," a world in which "the environment has been mastered." Further, following Thomas Homer-Dixon, he imagines that this "mastered" First World can be success-fully walled off from an imploding Third World. To an environmentalist, the assertion that the First World has mastered its environment is at best a painful joke. It hasn't; and with ongoing globalization it has become a more unsus-tainable enterprise than ever. Thus the future of the First World seems more and more to mean anything but its entrance into a posthistorical phase; on the contrary, it entails an increasing immersion in history, materiality, and en-vironmental crisis.[86] Present-day trends have brought water shortage, sanita-tion, food safety, pollution problems, and environmental health and justice issues into prominence in the First World. Further, when one considers that the First World's unsustainable dependence on developing-world countries for resources and sinks is rapidly growing, postmateriality and posthistory are revealed as ideologically charged fantasies, not fact.

Kaplan is equally mistaken in his second point. If the First World has not yet mastered its environment, it has also not been able to wall itself off from developing-world conditions. For to do so means something vastly more dif-ficult from enclosing oneself in an air-conditioned stretch limousine. Many environmental problems don't respect boundaries: global disease is cosmpoli-tan; environmental pollution drifts across boundaries; meltdown outside the global limo will clog the air-conditioning for those seated within. Equally, ris-ing environmental dependence on the rest of the world means that the folk inside the limousine can't remain unaffected by social chaos outside it. What happens, for example, to rich people's cars when they run out of gas and stall in the midst of a slum, let alone a Beirut-style war zone? Something very sim-ilar, one suspects, would happen to Kaplan's global limo if the future turns out to be as he envisions it. For social and environmental circumstances outside the developed world already strongly constrain the folk inside it; these con-straints promise to rise substantially in the future. A group that relies on the rest of the world for its energy resources and sinks—a group that consumes, for example, 70 percent of the world's energy and 85 percent of its wood—is uniquely vulnerable even in its global domination.

Given the increased exposure to problems like these, the United States needs to resist relying on the defensive isolationism that Kaplan's image prescribes. Isolationism is not possible, even if it weren't ethically abhorrent. Indeed, isolationism only worsens matters. Even while perhaps succeeding in the short run, it commits the developed world all the more inflexibly to its present environmental and social path and makes alternatives to contemporary inequitable development even harder to imagine, let alone implement. For the global limo of Homer-Dixon's and Kaplan's devising thus turns out, ironically, for all its scary pessimism, to be another accommodationist image from a disillusioned time, a time in which people already sense they live in crisis. This grim image accepts the fact that the United States is now living in a time of rising risk, but accommodationist nonetheless, it promises too much when it suggests that a few may continue to isolate themselves within an air-conditioned space. Thus it allows the First World to continue living beyond its environmental means and off-loading environmental problems onto the less fortunate, and it holds out First World postmodernity as the only possible image for the world's future, even though that future will be unfortunate for most. The result is to focus peoples' attention on the struggle to get inside the limo, not to explore how society might do something about the deterioration surrounding (and perhaps overwhelming) the limousine.

The discipline of environmental security describes how systemic social problems in international relationships have placed the United States and the world in an advanced stage of a new kind of social-environmental crisis. Proponents view this crisis from their standpoint within the developed world. A deeper, far less accommodationist, and far more painful view of the same problems, however, comes from a developing-world perspective. From its standpoint, this social-environmental crisis is anything but new. It is simply an intensified round of an old historical logic. As a number of First and Third World environmental and social critics such as Wolfgang Sachs, Vandana Shiva, and David Harvey have argued, the global limousine is merely an extension of the old logic of inequitable development—the process of reciprocal underdevelopment of the world's periphery and overdevelopment of the world's core that began with colonialism.[87] Sachs, Harvey, and Shiva, in short, have sought to do for the study of colonialism and neocolonialism what Homer-Dixon did for international security—under the growing pressure of environmental deterioration, they have woven environmental perspectives into analyses that hitherto excluded them.

Seeing social-environmental crisis from the standpoint of developing-world peoples and marginalized peoples within the developed world mounts a far deeper critique of the First World's present position than environmental security wishes to attempt. Ethically condemning inequitable global economic and social development, it also reveals the centuries-long momentum of the environmental unsustainability of the whole enterprise. A systemic feature of human development since at least the medieval period, inequitable development on a global scale has not lessened but dramatically expanded its environmental impacts. There are no further frontiers to colonize, resource-rich places to exploit, or sinks to absorb both pollution and risk. As a result, people find themselves on a rapidly moving and also much narrower treadmill. The situation described eloquently by Mary Mellor is a mirror for First Worlders to hold up to themselves, proffered to them by the Third World: "A minority of the human race is able to live as it were not embodied or embedded [in ecosystems], as if it had no limits, because those limits are borne by others, including the earth itself."[88]

As the process of enhancing inequalities proceeds in a more and more environmentally constrained world, rapidly rising social and environmental problems will result. Some solutions, like environmental security, propose to make the problems worse. Other alternatives—like an alternative to global free-market capitalism, or a multiply-structured world in which Third World agriculture and premodern lifestyles remain important—seem to be less plausible than ever before. Communism has ended; globalization has eliminated the world's remaining alternative spaces; and global environmental crisis reveals a world with stressed ecological systems and overflowing sinks. Whether genuine and fundamental change is possible any longer is an undecided question. Right now the only generally acceptable remedy that has been advanced is sustainable development, and the jury is out on what that phrase will yield in practice. Will it work and begin at last to haul global society back toward sustainability? Will its wise revision of developmentalism turn out to be a prelude to other, more effective interventions? Or is it too little too late; will it prove to be a Band-Aid applied by optimists and pessimists alike to what is in fact a festering wound? Will it finally seem to have been little more than another example of sad accommodationism? Or worse, will it seem to later societies a platform that was a cruel oxymoron from the start?

CHAPTER 6

Crisis History: From Prophecy to Risk, from Apocalypse to Dwelling Place

When people learned I was writing a book about whether the human species was going to survive its environmental problems, the question they invariably asked me was, "Well, will we?" And often, before I could reply, my interrogators would ruefully add words to the effect of, "It doesn't look good, does it?"

———Mark Hertsgaard, *Earth Odyssey*

As the last three chapters have shown, environmental crisis has diversified, deepened, and globalized during the last several decades. Old problems have been explored in new ways; new problems have emerged for the first time. Along with individual problems changing, the way in which they have been made to cohere into a comprehensive picture has also altered substantially. Crisis conceptualization, if I may call it that, also has a history, and how this overall conceptualization of environmental crisis has changed during the post–World War II period is the subject of this chapter. Examining this history will reveal plainly how crisis thought has moved from describing an environmental apocalypse ahead to exploring crisis as a place in which people presently dwell. It will show just how and why society has entered a time in which environmental crisis seems increasingly a feature of present normality, not an imminent, radical rupture of it.

Early postwar versions of environmental crisis, such as Fairfield Osborn's *Our Plundered Planet* and William Vogt's *Road to Survival*, helped establish a recognizable pattern. Osborn and Vogt were vividly aware of themselves as pioneers exploring a subject that was just then becoming one of true global importance. "It is amazing how far one has to travel to find a person, even among those most widely informed, who is aware of the processes of mounting destruction that we are inflicting upon our life sources," Fairfield Osborn wrote.[1] "The few who realize this fatal fact," he continued, "do not as a rule associate it with the vast surges and pressures of increasing population" and thus with the logic of ever-increasing environmental damage that population increases seem to create. At last, in 1948, Osborn argued, an age-old process of population increase threatened human civilization as a whole.

The logic of damage Osborn and also Vogt described foregrounded population increases leading to environmental damage, in particular the destruction of the earth's means of productivity, its soils, forests, and waters. This destruction in turn led toward food crisis—and consequently imperiled human civilization as a whole. The way Osborn and Vogt framed the issue was that population growth destroyed peoples' chance to live in environmental equilibrium and stability. Equilibrium and stability were, for Vogt and Osborn, unquestioned ideals for society, even as they were (equally unquestioned) norms for healthy nature. They celebrated this ideal and norm throughout their books. Vogt entitled a chapter heading "The Books Must Balance" and celebrated nature's equilibrium and stability as a natural version of the democratic ideal: "as in a democratic society, the climax [of an ecological system] survives through a system of checks and balances. If the number of any native species tends to increase disproportionately, some force will arise to control it."[2] With such equilibrium came not only ecosystem "climaxes"—a state in which the ecosystem's diversity, productivity, and stability were maximized and stabilized—but also beauty: "in the stabilized landscape the ecologist and geographer see a beautiful harmony that has much in common with the symphonies. There are dominant and repeated themes, movements that pass naturally from one to another, brilliant or subtle contrasts of phrase and tone."[3]

Vogt developed a "bio-equation" to calculate the carrying capacity of the earth so that we could determine the point where we had at last exceeded our global limits and begun to threaten the overall balance of nature. Our motives to exceed global limits—motives to dominate and multiply—were old components of our human "natures," motives biologically hardwired into us. Only lately, however, had they led society to the point where it actually threatened to destroy the equilibrium of all nature. As Osborn wrote, "humankind is now becoming for the first time a *large-scale geological force*."[4]

As people became such a geological force, they began to do damage. That damage was fundamentally the damage of depletion. Osborn and Vogt both chronicled peoples' depletion of soils in particular, but they also wrote about human depletion of forests and supplies of usable fresh water. Driven by the logic of population growth, these resources would be exhausted in the near future and people would die of hunger and of the scarcity created by depletion.

Both Vogt and Osborn resolutely agreed that the situation was grave— mankind's largest challenge. Presenting themselves as relatively isolated prophets attempting to enlighten an as-yet-unawakened majority, they issued stern warnings. It was a challenge equivalent, Osborn maintained, to war.[5] But both firmly believed that meeting the challenge was possible. Environmental dilemmas and quandaries, Vogt wrote:

> are exerting a gargantuan impact upon the human world of tomorrow. Disregarded, they will almost certainly smash our civilization. . . . There is nothing malificent about these phenomena. If man will find a harmonious adjustment with them, as he surely can, this adjustment should make possible a greater flowering of human happiness and well-being than the human race has ever known.[6]

Announced thus by a few capable of reading present signs and seeing trouble ahead, environmental crisis was ratcheted into a whole new key with the appearance of Rachel Carson—an author who did more than any other to make the problems she saw the concern of the many, not just the prophetic few. Discovering problems that seemed even more frightening than population, Rachel Carson's *Silent Spring* put several aspects of the environmental crisis—toxification of ecosystems and human bodies—in terms so unforgettable that the force of her presentation has never been equaled. Readers came away feeling that they were on the verge of living irrevocably in a poisoned world, one in which the air, waters, and soils were becoming toxic and unnatural to them. Worse, that world seemed increasingly to be a lab the chemical industry used for conducting risky experiments. Even more disturbing, it was a world in which people and their industries seemed to have become suicidal as well as mad; toxifying nature wasn't enough, for people also domesticated the pharmacopeia of the Borgias as part of the normal accoutrements of suburban life by developing countless toxic home and garden products. Carson presented a world, in short, in which people lived in a "sea of carcinogens" and nature was grotesquely "silenced," a world in which death literally rained from the skies.[7]

In depicting environmental crisis in these terms, Carson changed it substantially from the way Vogt and Osborn had presented it. The pace of humanly caused damage quickened substantially—indeed, crisis became fearfully hyperactive. What Carson recorded was not what people had done not since the beginnings of civilization, as was the issue with Vogt and Osborn. She concerned herself only with what people had done since the rise of the chemical industry, in particular since the application of wartime technologies to peacetime uses after World War II—since the time when Vogt and Osborn wrote.

Equally frightening was that the kind of damage people did had changed. What was most fearsome for Osborn and Vogt—depletion—now became pollution; future human suffering from dearth was replaced by future human suffering from a poisonous overabundance. Further, human beings in Carson's rendition were not just a new geological or natural force; unlike geological forces, people moved with shocking swiftness and they were positively unnatural in their actions. And even though Carson's "fable" of a small town's silenced spring still relied on nature imagery and nature feeling to help portray how grotesque the current crisis was, its message was that the nature that emerged from this holocaust would not be just depleted, but eerily dead.

Carson's book thus did not just shift environmental crisis from depletion to hyperactivity, hyperabundance, and pollution; it also commenced a gradual shift in crisis depiction from keening over the values and goods of a lost nature tradition to evoking a world unnaturally deformed by humans. Laments over the lost values (ecological *and* human) of nature continued, but even their tone darkened as futures marred by grotesque forms of denaturalization received more and more attention. Both Osborn and Vogt paid homage to the wonder and beauty of undefaced nature. Osborn commenced his book with an evocation of the immensity of the universe—both its enormous wonders and our incomprehension before "such infinities of space, of time, and matter." Our civilization then became "but an element in the great scheme of nature, boundless and unmeasurable"—something that helped Osborn judge man's defection harshly even as it helped him make the positive ideal of staying within one's limits in that scheme compelling.[8] Carson's most memorable image, by contrast, was of nature eerily silenced; in it, the wonder of a bird-filled spring gave way to sinister amazement at its grotesque transformation.

With Paul Ehrlich's *The Population Bomb*, another defining crisis text of the 1960s, the emphasis shifted further, challenging feelings for nature still more sharply and heightening the impression that the earth was now in an urban-style crisis, one that endangered humans. Ehrlich depicted an earth to come that was slummified and beset with an abundance of urban-style woes, such as overpopulation, disease, and vermin. With increasing population, the "per capita shortage of medical personnel" would increase, and so would "problems of sanitation and . . . populations of disease-harboring organisms such as rats." Epidemic disease would also make a reappearance, with "some of mankind's old enemies, like bubonic plague and cholera, . . . [m]alaria, yellow fever, [and] typhus." Indeed, Ehrlich maintained, "the ancient enemies of *Homo sapiens* are just waiting for the resurgence of mosquitoes, lice, and other vectors to ride high again."[9]

It was thus not surprising that Ehrlich also made his departure from the nature conservation/preservation tradition explicit. Ehrlich wrote as he did, he said, for strategic reasons:

> You will note that my discussion of man's environment has not dwelt on the themes that characterize the pleas of conservationists. . . . I've shed no tears for the passenger pigeons, now extinct, or the California condors, soon to join them. . . . Instead I have concentrated on things that seem to bear most directly on man. The reason is simple. In spite of all the effects of conservationists, all the propaganda, all the eloquent writing, all the beautiful pictures, the conservation battle is presently being lost. . . . Our population consists of two groups; a comparatively small one dedicated to the preservation of beauty and wildlife, and a vastly larger one dedicated to the destruction of both (or at least apathetic toward it). I am assuming that the first group is with me and that the second cannot be moved to action by an appeal to beauty, or a plea for mercy for what may well be our only living companions in a vast universe.[10]

As crisis deepened, Ehrlich considered warnings about an endangered "nature" as inadequate calls to arms. More serious evocations of crisis that accented human vulnerability—evocations of damaged humans and social slummification—were necessary to activate people. As crisis depictions deepened in the wake of Ehrlich's work, the place of the nature tradition in the sounding of environmental alarms became an even more vexed question. Many writers continued to describe environmental crisis as the tragic destruction of ecological systems and crucial human values associated with the nature tradition. But "nature" lost the literal and symbolic lock on considerations of environmental crisis that it had at the time of Vogt and Osborn. "Nature" even came to be, to a growing number of writers, at risk of "ending," thanks to the expansion of human civilization's many powers. Some of these writers also drew on old rifts between environmental and social activists and went beyond considering nature-based activisms simply ineffectual. They argued that older nature-based activisms themselves had been socially insensitive or retrograde.[11]

As awful as Carson's depiction of the poisoning of ecosystems and people was, it left a number of avenues open for its readers. First of all, it did not present the crisis as embedded systematically in our social structures. Crisis was the result of a bad choice between two available mind-sets—between working with nature by thinking and acting ecologically and attempting to conquer and dominate nature. Second, return to a living nature was possible by changing our mind-set. By thinking and acting ecologically, working with ecological, not chemical means, we could return to life in balance with nature—to Vogt and Osborn's old notion of balance and equilibrium. We could establish a harmonious equilibrium that would be as melodiously alive as the silenced landscape of Carson's small town in the heart of America was eerily dead. If crisis assumed an unnatural face in Carson, remedy could still restore nature feeling and nature itself, doing so in the name of restored balance.

In 1971, in *The Closing Circle*, Barry Commoner worked to give Carson's call for ecological thinking a more systematic turn. He elaborated on Carson's appeal to nature and ecological systems by laying out more precisely how these ecological systems worked—which he did by presenting his four laws of ecology ("Everything Is Connected to Everything Else," "Everything Must Go Somewhere," "Nature Knows Best," and "There Is No Such Thing as a Free Lunch").[12] Even more, he went beyond Carson by analyzing our departure from a system of ecological sanity not just as a wrong choice of mind-set, but as the effect of our commitment to a socioeconomic system dedicated to growth and expansion, one that ignored the limits of its ecological base. Most sharply incompatible with ecological sanity was the capitalist private enterprise system, he found. But socialism had also produced distressingly poor results in the U.S.S.R., and "both socialist and capitalist economic theory have apparently developed without taking into account the limited capacity of the biological capital represented by the ecosystem."[13] Implementing the necessary changes—both technological and social—represented, for Commoner, as much an act of social reengineering as it did ecological reform.

In Commoner, though, as in Carson, doing this was still possible. There was an ideal "balance of nature" still available to return to. "Stabilizing cybernetic relations" were "built into an ecological cycle," and these could be the structural underpinnings of a stable society.[14] The whole system could mirror, for example, the ecological cycle of freshwater. In describing this cycle, Commoner wrote how summer growth in algae depletes inorganic nutrients but then increases the ease with which fish feed on the algae, which in turn leads to an increase in nutrients when fish waste decays; thus, Commoner writes: "the levels of algae and nutrients tend to return to their original balanced position."[15] *The Closing Circle*, focusing, like *Silent Spring*, on what happened in the United States after World War II, also indicates strongly that that was the fateful time when limits were breached and the balance was destroyed, the circle stepped out of. "*Most pollution problems made their first appearance, or became very much worse, in the years following World War II*," Commoner writes.[16] It was then that prewar scientific developments were applied in a variety of polluting postwar technologies. To return to life within ecological limits—life within the circle—would be difficult, involving substantial social and economic as well as technological change, but it was possible. Indeed, it was quite possible, Commoner repeatedly emphasized, because a return to ecological sanity would not mean a severe drop in the quality of life, even in a consumer society, thanks to the possibilities of Green technologies.

Clearly, such a return has not occurred since *The Closing Circle*. Indeed, Commoner was fiercely attacked for his suggestion that capitalist dynamics were an important part of the problem. Moreover, since Commoner and Carson, analyses of humanity's systematic commitment to headlong growth and its disregard for ecological limits have intensified considerably. Since Carson and Commoner, then, the return to equilibrium—something that was clearly possible according to the early crisis books by Osborn and Vogt and which remained plausible according to Carson and Commoner— became rapidly less and less believable. Too much environmental damage was done for easy or even moderately painless return; further, as environmental crisis was understood more and more as a problem deriving from the overall social system, the range of possible solutions to crisis shrank dramatically. Changing such a system soon seemed much less possible than it was in Commoner's protrayal.

And at the same time, environmental crisis and the system causing it became global. True, Vogt and Osborn made it clear early on that their perceptions of environmental crisis as a defining challenge for humanity rested on a global vision. As Osborn wrote: "*now*, with isolated and inconsequential exceptions, there are no fresh lands, anywhere. Never before in man's history has this been the case."[17] But these were revelations of early stages of our global reach, perceptible only to the few. The new globalization of crisis located this crisis, even more than Commoner did, in the essential structures of modern civilization, making any retreat from it supremely difficult.

This change to a global, fully systematic, environmental crisis was decisively inaugurated by the Club of Rome's *The Limits to Growth*, written collaboratively by Donella Meadows, Dennis Meadows, Jørgen Randers, and William W. Behrens III. Just a year after Commoner's book, environmental crisis was described in terms vastly more severe. This watershed (and also much-maligned) book brought both systems thought and an encompassing, global perspective irreversibly into the conceptualization of environmental crisis, providing the framework for a wide variety of phenomena to be thought together in dynamic ways. After this crucial turn, there was no going back. The elaboration of a complexly systemic, dynamically expanding, and fully global environmental crisis became as real as specific scientific findings.[18]

The logic went roughly as follows. Return to life within limits was still possible but was excruciatingly difficult, possible only if one effected major, painfully difficult systemic changes within a short period of time. What was driving humanity beyond them was much more serious than people had thought. Yoking Vogt's and Osborn's population concerns to Carson's and Commoner's critiques of modern industrial practice and structure, Meadows and her colleagues isolated exponential human and economic growth as the two fundamental trends that intensified environmental crisis in all other areas. The authors then modeled the effects of these trends in a computer program that chillingly dramatized the certainty of overshoot and collapse if humanity did not change its ways. The addition of a number of homely pieces of uncomfortably vivid folk wisdom also helped concentrate readers' minds on the approaching denouement of the system if not modified. A Persian king, presented with a chessboard by a clever courtier, agreed to pay for it in grains of rice: one for the first chessboard square, two for the second, and so on. By the time he reached the twenty-first square, he owed a million grains; by the fortieth, it was a million million grains. A French riddle had a lily plant doubling in size each day in a pond. Eventually it would, of course, choke the pond; the nasty twist this story adds is that no one was alarmed until it had taken over half the pond. By then, however, it had but one day to go, and the unclogged pond was, as they say, history.[19] Doublings proceed very quickly; at a growth rate of 1 percent a year, a doubling comes in only seventy years; at a rate of 4 percent, it takes just eighteen.

To be sure, others, such as Paul Ehrlich, had written previously about the logic of doublings, but the focus then had been on mainly one factor—population. The Club of Rome showed how the doublings of population and eco-nomic activity initiated a host of secondary changes, both those tending to augment crisis and those attempting to limit it. They then embedded this complexity into a multifactorial, interactive model. This model related eco-nomic growth and population increases to changes in resource needs, persis-tent pollution, agricultural inputs, land yield, and so on. It also incorporated factors that might extend the earth's environmental limits, such as the discov-ery of additional resources, and factors that could extend the life of the sys-tem, such as the possibility of developing cost-effective means of controlling pollution. These relationships were woven into the model in the form of com-plex intertwinings of negative feedback loops that would tend to arrest de-structive activity and vicious positive loops that would accelerate it. But what was most fundamental to the whole model was its underlying system dynam-ics which allowed the authors to generate a potentially infinite number of sce-narios for the future by inputting different values for different variables.

In generating these scenarios, the authors found a consistent pattern. Their realistic "runs" of the model all indicated a world going progressively further and further out of equilibrium, one that constantly found itself in one or an-other sort of crisis—the result of which would be a collapse of social and envi-ronmental systems. It was a world caught in the dynamic logic of doublings. Though the model was quickly and repeatedly criticized as unreliable and though it led the authors to make some inaccurate specific predictions, the sys-tematic logic it embodied remains important. With this model, a systematic description of approaching environmental crisis was given what seemed to be genuine inevitability, global scope, and dynamic force. It also gave people only a short time to act—to bring ourselves back into equilibrium with the environ-ment or suffer the consequences.

In the wake of *Limits to Growth*, small, distributed solutions such as E. F. Schumacher's proposals in *Small Is Beautiful* were gradually overshadowed as possible solutions or even ideals by the vision of a complex, fully global system that had decisively violated the world's environmental limits. Large-scale prob-lems seemed to need large-scale solutions, and work towards assembling ecolog-ical modernization's comprehensive vision began, while the credibility of small, distributed solutions diminished.[20] A number of the values of the U.S. popular counterculture were thus also imperiled, and it was not a total surprise when an influential offshoot of the 1960s and 1970s counterculture that helped advocate the small-is-beautiful concept broke ranks and began transforming itself into the vanguard of a high-tech, ultracapitalist information age. As Queen Mu and

R. U. Sirius put it in an editorial in *Mondo 2000*, "Carly Simon's brother wrote a book called *What to Do until the Apocalypse Comes*. It was about going back to the land, growing tubers and soybeans, reading by oil lamps. Finite possibilities and small is beautiful. It was *boring!*" The new generation, Mu and Sirius claimed, was taking a new direction: it was "a . . . generation of sharpies, mutants, and superbrights," the vanguard of the much more powerfully and excitingly transformative corporate-led information era.[21] Popular countercultural hopes for radical-democratic ecological-social change slid, with surprisingly little resistance, from back-to-the-earth ecological commitments into the embrace of cyberculture and even the new capitalism pioneering it; henceforth, these were what could and would revolutionize consciousness and society in America.

In addition to globalizing crisis, Andrew Ross argues, *Limits to Growth* inaugurated a new emphasis on the "deterioration rather than the annihilation of the future"; it inaugurated the "new, 'slow'" vision of environmental catastrophe.[22] Even as the book seemed to many to provide the most comprehensive portrait of environmental apocalypse yet—it all too easily showed humanity on a collision course with the earth's limits—it subtly suggested that a biblical apocalypse would not be the result. True, the computer model portrayed a rapidly approaching point of no return—the time when people violated environmental limits. But it also portrayed the consequences of that violation as a process that continued and developed over considerable time, a process of eroding and collapsing environmental infrastructure and increasing societal problems, not a sudden apocalypse.

Reinforcing this abandonment of sudden apocalypse in favor of slow crisis was the Club of Rome's refusal to adhere to any particular "scenario" of doom. Paul Ehrlich was very much criticized for the doom scenarios he spelled out in *The Population Bomb*; Barry Commoner distanced himself from generating these "familiar" "horror stories" while describing the damage people did to the "ecosphere."[23] The Club of Rome's computer model obviated the need for scenarios by generating too many of them for any individual one to be central; the truth or falsity of any specific scenario thus became irrelevant compared to the drift of the whole system. Individual scenarios became just possibilities, not scripts for the coming apocalypse; an inevitability became something that emerged from an enormous variety of runs based on an enormous variety of specific inputs—an order that emerged slowly but inevitably from an all-too-lifelike diversity.

The Club of Rome's global-systemic logic and its vision of slowed catastrophe could thus underwrite radical critiques of capitalism and modernism as easily as they could add urgency to calls for reform. But with the rise of ecological modernization, the potential radicalism of the Club of Rome's analysis was blunted and a vision of changes realizable only within the system took its place. Ongoing globalization then added to this momentum by making the world it was bringing about seem a single system. The result was that conceptualizations such as the Brundtland Commission's report, *Our Common Future*, and Al Gore's *Earth in the Balance* became central to the analysis of crisis and development of policy. Meanwhile, provoked equally by *Limits to Growth*, corporate-conservative antienvironmentalism began weighing in. In response to Jimmy Carter's 1977 *Limits to Growth*–influenced *Global 2000 Report:* "incoming President Reagan employed two right-wing futurologists, Herman Kahn and Julian Simon, to rebut its findings in a report entitled *Global 2000 Revised.*"[24]

A kind of *coup de grace* came in the following decades. For by the early 1990s, the situation appeared substantially worse. Even as conservative antienvironmentalism hammered away at *Limits to Growth*'s doomsterism, the unrepentant Meadowses issued a new book. This one was titled *Beyond the Limits*—a title that represented a ratcheting up of rhetoric to go along not just with controversy and inaction but also with what was a much harsher appraisal of the present situation.[25] Human beings had already gone too far and gone beyond their environmental limits; but the consequences of having done so could vary greatly. Different possible consequences would result from different styles of living outside our limits, and these were spelled out in greater detail by a revamped computer model. The new model, World3, again generated a dizzying number of possible scenarios for the future.

Beyond the Limits singled out four possible scenarios as representative possibilities. Based on four different sets of assumptions, these were infinite continuing growth (possible when limits are far off or limits themselves are growing exponentially); sigmoid growth (possible if signals from approaching physical limits are instant, accurate, and responded to immediately, or the population or economy limits itself without the need of such signals); overshoot and oscillation (possible if signals or responses are delayed, limits are surpassed, and ecosystems are either unerodable or able quickly to recover from erosion); and overshoot and collapse (possible if signals or responses are delayed and ecosystems are erodable or irreversibly degraded when limits are exceeded).

The authors ruled out the first two possibilities—the nontraumatic ones—without further ado. The world was already past its limits, and infinite continuing growth was ecologically impossible; sigmoid growth was socially impossible. Humanity's choice lay instead between the latter two scenarios.

Yes, the world was already well into overshoot, but the key question is whether it had eroded its ecosystems irreversibly or whether it had not quite yet done this. An eroded ecosystem cannot repair itself in any (to humans) timely fashion. For an ecosystem that is not yet eroded, such repair is possible. People were now, in short, *beyond* the limits and dwelling *in* crisis, not just being driven towards that point.

Though the authors of *Beyond the Limits* accepted that the world was in overshoot, they considered it still possible for it to pull back in time from the fate of irreversible erosion of our ecosystems. But the situation was most precarious. One example of this was the response to ozone depletion. Global society managed through international treaties to curb its destructively high level of emission of ozone-depleting chemicals. But even here, where concrete action had been taken, the authors hesitated; given our continued emission of some of these chemicals, and given the fact that the ones out there had long lifetimes of ozone destruction still ahead before they would be neutralized, the world might or might not have pulled back from the brink in time. It might, in short, already have gone too far. The collapse might already have started.

But ozone depletion represented the erosion of only one of a number of key environmental systems. In looking at the big picture, the authors concluded that people had a decade or so to act to avoid the worst consequences of overshoot. These conclusions appeared in print in 1992; I write this summary of *Beyond the Limits*'s findings in 2002. *Beyond the Limits*, like the UN Environmental Program, the World Resources Institute, and Earth Island Institute, considered the 1990s to be: "the decisive decade when humanity's environmental decline had to be reversed or it would accelerate beyond our control."[26] Well, the 1990s have passed. As Mark Hertsgaard comments: "it seems clear we have failed the test."[27] Even before this decade had passed, *Beyond the Limits* did not offer any hope for an undamaged, undisrupted world; no "return" to anything was possible. The hope it did offer was for a damaged but restorable world. But now that the book's time limit for remedial action has expired, its analysis would doom the earth to erosion and terrible contraction in the future.

Environmental crisis depiction thus became less apocalyptic and more realistic as it was globalized and systematized. It also became, thanks to inaction, a slow crisis already in process, not an event to come. But there was also at least one packet of positive changes. As environmental crisis thought developed in the wake of *Limits to Growth*, and crisis became a present dwelling place, environmental issues were brought into focus in all areas of human society. In academia, environmental perspectives spread across the disciplines. In public life, a number of different voices began to urge that environmental concerns be internalized into every social practice, from economic policy setting to industrial design—a development ecological modernization helped make into a new paradigm for environmentalism. Environmental perspectives began, as well, to be internalized meaningfully in social justice movements. The deepening environmental crisis had made it clear that the unfair allotment of social and economic "goods" already also entailed an unfair allotment of painful environmental "bads," and both conditions needed correction. The result was the growth of an environmental justice movement and the empowerment of Third World voices in environmental debates. The globalization of environmental crisis seemed at last to be leading to the globalization of environmentalism.

But these positive steps were nonetheless overshadowed by the globalization of crisis itself—and by its ever more intractable and sophisticated picture of society's immersion in it. Matters became substantially more grave when nature-based environmentalism then faced the loss of what had been an important anchoring concept. This concept had helped people anchor their feelings for nature to something seemingly solid, even as it had helped legislators set actual environmental standards. It was also, supposedly, a key principle of scientific ecology. From the early crisis warnings to Barry Commoner's book, the idea of living in equilibrium or balance with nature was a crucial value and standard by which to judge human departures. Equally or more important was the widely accepted idea that nature itself worked by this principle—that ecosystem development tended toward the goal of stable equilibrium in highly diversified climax ecosystems.

The prospect of losing the assurances equilibrium, harmony, and balance provided was thus very significant, but a deepening awareness of crisis as well as antienvironmental sneering at these notions propelled people toward this wisdom. For by the 1990s, the possibility of returning to such a time seemed more and more remote, thanks to analyses like *Beyond the Limits*. Worse, the ideas that such a time *ever* existed or that stability and equilibrium were even discoverable in nature itself became increasingly challenged from within environmental thought as well as from outside it. By 1980, William Catton, Jr., was writing of human society as already in overshoot. Moreover, he pushed the dates for the origin of overshoot much further back than Commoner and Carson had. He argued that the breach came with the era of European discovery and expansion. It came with the discovery of the New World, when available land per European jumped from 24 acres to 120. By 1980, he noted, land per person was down to 11 acres, and we were already living off the earth's "phantom carrying capacity."[28] But much more important was the fact that his models for human-nature relationships had shifted. No longer was homeostasis—a cycle that tended to return to balance—the only norm in town. Instead, Catton pointed to boom-and-bust ecosystemic interactions as models for human behavior. Nature also showed examples of disequilibrium, of runaway growth and crashes, overshoots and diebacks; these were exhibited in such varied creatures as lemmings, Sika deer, lynxes, snowshoe rabbits, and yeast cells put into wine vats. A significant portion of nature, as well as humanity, was thus no longer seen to be governed by the principle of equilibrium.

In 1990, Clive Ponting, in *A Green History of the World*, depicted world history in these terms with magisterial comprehensiveness. He described how human society had evolved through a series of stages (hunting and gathering; agriculture; and industrialism) in a one-way, irreversible, population-driven development toward, perhaps, a global environmental nightmare and ultimate collapse. Looking back, then, people no longer had the comfort of seeing the homeostasis that they had recently, and reversibly, departed from. Ponting pushed the fall from ecological grace back to the invention of agriculture. All human history since the time of the hunter gatherers was boom and bust, and the present moment threatened an ultimate, species-altering, or ending version of it. People had lived for millennia in a state of disequilibrium with nature and had done so from time of the invention of agriculture and the rise of the earliest cities. Now that these imbalances had become global and there was no open environmental space left, modern global society faced the full implications of its history of acute environmental instability and risk. It now dwelt inescapably in the shadow of crisis. Though past history did not absolutely determine future catastrophe, it suggested strongly that contemporary society dwelt in an increasingly grave and pervasive condition of risk.[29]

Daniel Botkin then helped further generalize this condition—this vision of humanity's history of environmental relationships as a one-way, risky passage into deeper and deeper disequilibrium—to the entire biosphere. Instability, disequilibrium, climate change, and risk were not just fundamental to human history and human nature (as they were, according to Catton, to a few odd species in nature). They were fundamental to organisms and ecosystems everywhere: "The biosphere has had a history and what it will be tomorrow depends not only on what it is today, but also on what it was yesterday. Like an organism, the biosphere proceeds through its existence in a one-way direction, passing from stage to stage, each of which cannot be revisited."[30] Chaos, uncertainty, and change, not stability and harmony, became the model for ecosystemic as well as social processes. In perpetual nonequilibrium conditions, on a one-way voyage through difficult seas, including varieties of imminent rocks, human beings and ecosystems had always voyaged and did so now, more vividly than ever. While, for Botkin, an environmentally concerned scientist, this wisdom helped counter helpless nostalgia for a lost golden age and empowered scientists more effectively to manage things as they were, it struck others, like the ecological historian Daniel Worster, as a dire breach in the walls of an already sea-lashed dike.[31]

Heightening the disturbing consequences of this charged appraisal of how ecosystems worked was the popularization of the idea that gradualist change was not a general principle of nature but merely a feature of one particular kind of ecosystem. Gradualism had an old history. Mike Davis writes how in: "temperate and forested lands, energy flows through the environment in a seasonal pattern that varies little from year to year. Geology is generally quiescent, and it's easy to perceive natural powers as orderly and incremental, rarely catastrophic."[32] This predisposition was connected to English and New England landscapes, which were celebrated in terms of equilibrium and balance, and it became "one of the dogmas of Victorian science" in Sir Charles Lyell's principle of "uniformitarianism." This principle held that: "large-scale surface features [of the earth] . . . were the result 'of insensible changes added through vast times' and that the earth was a steady state system without historical directionality."[33] However, Davis, in writing about disaster in Los Angeles, pointed out that circumstances in Southern California hearkened back not to England, New England, and uniformitarianism, but to "conceptions of abrupt 'Earth Revolutions' favored by geologists in barricade-ridden France and Germany"—that Southern California was, as a Mediterranean ecosystem, "a revolutionary, not a reformist landscape."[34] For cultural-social as well as scientific reasons, these landscapes began to seem more and more normative.

Chaos theory and catastrophism thus cut ecosystems loose from what had been an anchor for environmental thought and feeling. They undercut fundamental assumptions about how ecosystems operated and about how human-nature interactions should be governed. As important was that the loss came at a time when deepening environmental crisis was more and more presenting environmental risk and instability as the circumstances in which society now dwelt.

Reinforcing this development was another factor: the rapid spread, to be discussed more fully in the next chapter, of positive interest in chaos as a new intellectual paradigm and as a principle fundamental to a dynamic new human economy. Chaos and catastrophe theory became, in short, sexy and the source of striking new metaphors. Catastrophe theory focused on how the addition of one grain of sand to a growing pile could result in a sudden avalanche, and chaos theory described how a butterfly's wing, agitating the air in Beijing, could produce changes that cascaded up the system to result in thunderstorms in New York City. In elaborating environmental crisis and postmodern/global social theory alike, chaos theory ultimately helped authorize a new risk-taking faith in the unpredictable. Though, as the next chapter will show, the appeal of chaos theory was complex, intriguing environmentalists as well as libertarians and enthusiasts of the new technologies, the battle to appropriate its authority was finally won by antienvironmental celebrants of risk.

Thus chaos theory ultimately raised the price of living in risk and instability to a substantially higher level. To all too many, it justified environmental disregard. And to those who felt they were losing the environmental wars, it displayed its dark side. Catastrophe might not occur at the end of a series of logical steps; even slow crisis might not stay slow. Chaos theory made all too plausible the possibility of sudden collapses triggered by the addition of one obscure grain of sand or the flutter of one tiny intervention far away from the public limelight. Catastrophic change could come at any time in conditions of disequilibrium. And disequilibrium right now was high.

Society thus lived in a new condition of risk. Risk and uncertainty quickly became the premier feature of life in slow environmental crisis and deterioration. Now people lived without foundations; even more, they dwelt in risk and instability. The authors of *Beyond the Limits* noted that: "Twenty years ago few people would have thought ecological collapse on [a global] scale possible. Now it is the topic of scientific meetings and international negotiations."[35] With risk and instability, society was not just beyond the limits; it was immersed in rapidly rising risk. Among the many attempts to describe what it means to dwell in a situation of increasing risk, the premier text is Ulrich Beck's *Risk Society*.[36] No portrait of our rapid domestication in crisis would be complete without it. The term "risk" had the great virtue of encompassing much of the heterogeneity of environmental problems discussed in the preceding chapters. It incorporated the effects of actual deterioration, invisible and still virtual deterioration, long-term consequences from present exposures, and probabilistic disasters, both the low-probability high-impact kind and the high-probability low-impact kind.

Beck begins with the perception that an essential function of modern society is to contain and manage "risk"—but this attempt at management has broken down in a time when accidents have become "undelimitable" (i.e., like Midgely's supposedly benign CFCs, they don't stay relatively confined in their immediate effects and don't respect geographic or sociopolitical boundaries). Formerly, with a much smaller environmental footprint, industrial society was better able to deal with the limited accidents of its own making. The new, "undelimitable" risks are impossible to prevent, hard to accommodate, and difficult to assign blame for. Unable to manage these risks adequately, society thus has to shift more and more of its attention from the production of goods to the management of these dangers and the social controversies they create. No longer does society need to deal only with social conflict resulting from the unequal distribution of goods; it now has to cope also with the tensions and conflicts that come from the inequitable distribution of environmental bads.[37] Thus all are drawn into this new kind of mess as a global risk society is created. Nigel Clark, weaving together several of the analyses presented in Chapter 5, notes that "undelimitability" is very much on the rise nowadays: "The minute scale of human intervention into bio-physical processes—which now includes modifications at genetic, atomic and molecular levels . . . coupled with the grand scale of economic activity . . . raises the possibilities of releases of extremely dangerous matter which defies de-activation or containment."[38]

Risk society thus emerges when modernity, for a host of reasons, proves structurally unable to contain the hazards it produces. This means that its hazards become both uncontrollable and unpunishable. The reasons why risks nowadays have become unpunishable and uncontrollable are legion. More and more, hazards these days cannot be limited in time or place, but are global. Accountability for them is increasingly difficult to assign according to the rules of causality, blame, and liability; the time between the creation of hazards and the manifestation of their effects has now lengthened into not just years but several generations. Further, individual hazards may come from not just one but many causes; the "relation is not one:one but one:many, when we are dealing not with static, isolated phenomena but with interconnected, continuously changing, dynamic situations and parameters." More and more, our potential hazards also include risks that though they entail vanishingly small likelihoods of an accident ever occurring, have the possibility of causing appallingly catastrophic damage—including the extinction of our species.[39] Worse, risks that some people (for example, a factory manager or entrepreneurial genetic engineer) are permitted to take voluntarily become the involuntary hazards for many others, thus allowing risk creators routinely to expose others to a certain fixed percent of "normal" dangers, injuries, accidents, and diseases. All of these "undelimitable" aspects of risk today make for anxiety and social unrest that cannot be controlled by regulation, charmed away by expert opinion, or laid to uneasy rest by punishment.

On the most general level, this state of affairs signals a larger sort of social shift, one that Beck sees as an entrance not into postmodernity but into late or advanced modernity. But whether or not risk society is late-modern or postmodern is not an important question here. What is crucial is that risk society signals a new period in human social history. First, society has built up a considerable volume of ecological karma—a legacy of past problems created and not solved. Second, it has been forced to recognize that fact. And, third, its powers to affect the environment have grown and its remaining ecological space has shrunk. As a result, it can now do fewer and fewer things without producing both severe environmental risk and widespread concern about it; the environmental effects of its past actions and present size increasingly constrain it. It thus becomes a society in which the most significant hazards and threats people face are increasingly those produced by modernization and its effect on nature, not by exceptional human or natural conditions and upheavals. Human-caused environmental threats are, increasingly, an essential part of the "environment" people live in; human-caused environmental woes are peoples' new fatalities.

According to Beck, the chief features of such a society therefore differ from those of early modernity. In early modernity, the problem was scarcity, and the production and distribution of wealth were the chief focus. In advanced or late modernity, "overabundance" and "overweight" are the problems, and the production and distribution of risks become the more salient activities. In risk society, overabundance of development leads to an overabundance of man-made risk. In turn this leads to another sort of overabundance: an almost equally stressful overabundance of information, expertise, disagreement, confusion, and conflict. Perversely, then, the very attempt to deal with risks multiplies their effect, producing further conflict, not resolution. Increased information about them only embroils people further in political-scientific disputes. "The paradigm of these hazards," Beck writes, is: "the gene-altering effects of radioactivity, which, as the reactor accident at Three Mile Island shows, imperceptibly abandon the victims completely to the judgments, mistakes and controversies of experts, while subjecting them to terrible psychological stresses": the political fallout is almost as disturbingly painful as the physical exposures themselves were.[40] Environmental processes "are peculiarly open to social definition and construction." They are thus ripe breeding grounds for "antagonistic definitions and *definitional struggles.*"[41] These conflicts and struggles then threaten to add still further to the over-abundance of man-made environmental threat even as they prevent a society from readily responding to what endangers it.

One concrete example of the contemporary risk problematic would be helpful here. I'll choose something that is, right now, more a "thought experiment," than a real example.[42] It almost happened and it still could; it illustrates vividly how limited science and the political process are when it comes to managing contemporary "undelimitable" risks. Indeed, rather than solving issues, they quickly become part of them.

Recently, the Department of Energy (DOE) proposed disposing of radioactive metal waste—tons of nickel, copper, steel, and aluminum—by recycling it into society's metal stream. In fact, 7,500 tons were recycled by special permit in 1996, and by then thousands of tons of radioactive scrap were already being shipped to China for reprocessing. The proposal was to expand and institutionalize this practice significantly in the United States. In the process, a standard for levels of radioactivity in recycled metal would have to be set. According to a memo from John Hoyle, the Nuclear Regulatory Commission secretary, they "should be based on realistic scenarios of health effects from low doses that still allow quantities of materials to be released."[43] Industry suggested a level of 10 millirem a year.

But that level, a compromise in which economic viability and human safety both played a role, was felt to entail (as so many approved things do) risk. Anne Marie Cusac cites a 1990 NRC study that found that "a radiation dose of 10 millirem a year . . . received continuously over a lifetime corresponds to a risk of about 4 chances in 10,000" of fetal cancer. If people were routinely exposed to this increased level of radiation from birth on, it would mean "92,755 additional cancer deaths in the U.S. alone" each year, Cusac concludes.[44] Calculations of "acceptable risk" frequently work out to significant absolute numbers of potential victims, even when the risk percentage is low; this process can, to understate the issue, make many uneasy, especially when the rate-setting—the setting of figures that determine how many will get sick or die—factors in, as it usually does, corporate profitability and thus economic viability.

From another perspective, then, risk calculations mean that a certain number of individual people are likely to subsidize industry with their lives. Matters get worse when the concerned—those who see themselves as the potential recipients of the process, not the players in it—flesh out statistics like these in domestic, daily, practical detail. Thus Diane D'Arrigo, a staff member at the Nuclear Information and Resource Service, which fought the DOE plan, asks us to: "Think about the metal you come into contact with every day. Your IUD, and your bracelets, your silverware, the zipper on your crotch, the coins in your pocket, frying pans, that chair you're sitting on, the batteries that are in your car and motorbike, the batteries in your computer."[45] Others worry about the frames of their beds and the metal in their teeth: "You certainly don't want people going around with radioactive teeth," says Karl Morgan. Peter Yarnalde, waste coordinator for the DOE Ferrald Project in Ohio, remarks: "when I went in front of the public, I got the crap beat out of me. . . . People asked, 'Are my kids' braces going to be made out of that copper?' . . . [in answering] I went as far as a copper IUD."[46] He tried to assure people that the radioactivity would be so low as not to be dangerous. You can move away from a toxic dump next door—that is, if you learn it is toxic in time. It's harder to move away from your teeth.

And, once set going, this fearfully intimate dread ticks away even as regulators mull over their regulations and the percentages of additional deaths they will possibly cause. It continues ticking at the public meetings in which reasonable bureaucrats show overhead slides and corporate spokespeople speak to the issues with enlightened vigor—people trained (as spokespeople for plans to recycle radioactive metals were) for these presentations by media and public relations specialists who themselves use overheads that read "The Main Point: It All Starts with the Salesman."[47] Worse, the implementation of radioactive metal recycling in real life would doubtless be accompanied by less legitimate techniques of containment—as it was when a program like this was mounted in Taiwan. There, industry and regulators kept secret the use in apartment-building construction, of steel construction rods made from metal exceeding the standards, and the result was sickness for the occupants. Even lawsuits in this area would be programmed to fail because of inability to prove without doubt what the specific source of the hot metal was—as happened with radioactive gold jewelry sold in the 1940s. That jewelry cost individual Americans in the 1980s fingers and even lives. And of course, drastic revisions of estimates of what is tolerable would arise as new studies came up with new data and as more recycled metals entered the environment (producing still more data as people got sick)—and these studies would in turn be loudly contested by industry and its think-tank-funded counterscience. In short, one can expect that problems in this area will breed all of the conflicts, outrages, shabby positionings, and sor-

rows that have accompanied risk creation and management in so many different contexts. Environmental risk thus becomes constant and universal; attempts
to control it may only heighten the sense of pervasive anxiety and vulnerability
as well as stimulating more and more vigorous attempts to cover it over or
greenwash it. The old faith—articulated by Barry Commoner in *The Closing
Circle*—a faith that public revelation of unacceptable risks will yield appropriate
action to solve the underlying problems—is gone.[48]

About this one particular issue: on January 6, 2000, CBS News reported
the government's plan to go allow British Nuclear Fuels, Ltd. (BNFL) to recycle hundreds of thousands of tons of nickel from its Oakridge nuclear facility
into items of daily use like cutlery, bicycles, pots, pans, and zippers. This
would, a BNFL official said, result in less radioactivity than was contained in a
salt substitute he held in his hand. Was it clean? "Nothing can be really
cleaned," he said, citing the assumption, beloved (as this study has repeatedly
shown) to antienviromentalists, that we live in a world of impurity and risk, a
world that is that way, of course, not because of recent decades of pollution,
but because "purity," like "equilibrium" and "stability" was always a myth.
CBS's voice-over, however, revealed that the motivation for the project was
not the laudable goal of countering bad old environmental extremism by
making everyone aware of the fundamental impurity of nature—a goal to be
accomplished, it often seems, by taking on the task of rendering it still more
impure. No, the voice-over revealed that the motivation for the project was in
fact about not philosophical hairsplitting, but money. For industry would
save hundreds of millions of dollars by recycling the metal rather than burying it—a possibility that seemed especially attractive since the arrangement to
recycle radioactive wastes in the nation's metal stream made no provision for
inspections to ensure that concentrations of radioactivity stayed low.

Money, apparently, also stopped the plan from going through. The steel
industry opposed the move out of fear that people would stop buying metal.
Several days later, the *New York Times* reported that the program had been re-
scinded. But the problem remains, growing more urgent with each day's accumulation of new wastes, as no one knows how to get rid of these stocks of
radioactive metal. And for all anyone knows, this rejected solution is still
somewhere on the shelf.

However vexing any specific risk issue is, the real dimensions of the problem
appear when one steps back and views large-scale social trends. Given the social imperatives of growth and technological development today, it is hard

to imagine alternatives to risk assessment, whatever its flaws are. Short of a drastic change in social attitudes and/or the social system, substitutes for risk assessment are unlikely to be found, and battles over how to make it more environmentally responsible will continue. As the contentious process of risk assessment is applied to more and more aspects of daily life, environmental crisis is not charmed away but domesticated. Concerns once represented in the apocalyptic mode become risks and uncertainties, sources of anxiety woven into more and more facets of daily life. Unsurprisingly then, the profession of risk assessment has blossomed of late. Risk has become an important field for academic study and scholarly research. It has become central to environmental sociology and has also been consolidated as an interdisciplinary field of its own.[49] Risk awareness has been widely diffused throughout society by environmentalists and antienvironmentalists alike. And risk assessments have become decisive parts of the regulatory process, crucial to controlling the pressures industrial society places on the environment.

But, as the numerous references to risk discourse and risk analysis above suggest, risk assessment is at best a highly imperfect delimiter of risk. At worst, it is a way that licenses rather than limits a steady increase in risk. Further, the politicization of risk discourse by risk-loving antienvironmentalists and precaution-preferring environmentalists has led to integrating environmental anxieties even more deeply and actively into peoples' daily lives. "Never has the environment been the object of so much knowledge," Scott Lash, Bronislaw Szerszynski, and Brian Wynne write, as they commence analysis: "not from the presupposition of too much silence about the environment, but from that of perhaps an overproduction of expertise on green issues. How," they ask, "amidst the rising clamour, to tell signal from noise?"[50] Commenting on Beck, they underscore that conflict and criticism lie at the heart of this glut of discourse: "as Beck emphasizes, [risk society] is not a critical theory of society, but a theory of critical society—critique is endemic to the risk society, and does not have to be introduced from the outside by the sociologist."[51] Thus, as Beck writes:

> Insurance experts contradict safety engineers. . . . Experts are relativised or dethroned by counterexperts. Politicians encounter the resistance of citizens' initiatives, industrial management that of consumer organisations. Bureaucracies are criticized by self-help groups. . . . Yes, the risk question even divides families and professional groups, from the skilled workers of the chemical industry right up to top management, often even the individual: what the head wants, the mouth says, the hand is unable to carry out.[52]

In such circumstances, even crisis discourse loses whatever transparency it may have had; it becomes part of intense social debate, and analyses of even extreme danger may easily be depoliticized and converted into anxiety and uncertainty.

As the normalization of crisis produces, more and more, a society of criticism, the issue fretted about at the beginning of this book emerges in a new form. Dwelling in crisis means dwelling in a time of crisis debunking, of increased controversy, of politicization of environmental knowledge. Accordingly, it also means dwelling in uncertainty. Further, it means dwelling in a time when dire warnings are accompanied by a sense of lost innocence about such warnings—a clear awareness that adequate action has not been taken in the past as well as concern that it is unlikely to be taken in the present and is perhaps even impossible to take now. In addition to all this, crying crisis in itself begins to seem a dead end; proliferation of crisis warnings becomes tiresomely repetitive and, worse, politically problematic. In a climate like this, is crisis discourse still necessary or even merely useful and helpful at all? Does immersion in risk as a way of life require, in effect, closing one's eyes to attempts to assemble a larger picture?

Clearly, those who have continued to elaborate crisis have testified to rising personal and public stresses. The Ehrlichs' *Betrayal of Science and Reason*, a book devoted to exposing the damage done by right-wing contestation of scientific environmental crisis discourse, betrays clearly a sense of desperate indignation at what the authors see as an illegitimate checkmating of environmental scientists' warnings. Worse, Paul Ehrlich lost his much-publicized bet with Julian Simon—a bet about whether rising shortages of key resources would be reflected in rising prices—and this loss led to an enormous conservative gloating and smacking of lips about the unreliability of doomsters' crisis predictions. In a much more personal vein, Donella Meadows writes of her encounter with considerable opposition to her early presentation of systemic crisis in *Limits to Growth*—something she styles as a moment of surprised loss of innocence. She observes that she and her coauthors:

> had not thought much about the culture into which we were speaking, though we ourselves were part of that culture. But we were at M.I.T.; we had been trained in science. The way we thought about the future was utterly logical: if you tell people there's a disaster ahead, they will change course. If you give them a choice between a good future and a bad one, they will pick the good. They might even be grateful. Naïve weren't we?[53]

In fact her book was enormously influential, but it also became a premier target for the venom and vituperation of the antienvironmental right. In the wake of this firestorm, even ecological modernization sidled away from the Meadows's much starker version of crisis; the Meadows's call for radical systemic change became the ecomodernist prescription of riding the capitalist camel in the direction in which it was going.

In order to survive, elaborating crisis has thus had to become an ethically self-conscious and socially sophisticated social art as well as scientifically scrupulous inquiry. It is hard to do. The waters are littered with cautionary wreckage. Only an extremely absolute and frustrated few would want to sound like Garrett Hardin, who argued that as our environmental ship threatens to sink, we must jettison the prolific—and expendable—poor to save it, or like Christopher Manes, who called AIDS nature's new remedy for overpopulation. Thus advocates of ecological modernization such as like Paul Hawken and the Lovinses labor mightily to pair each revelation of doom with an equal measure of optimism about the exciting win-win remedies to hand. A further group, one that includes Theodore Roszak, acknowledge the pitfalls and challenges of crisis discourse and urge abandonment of talk about crisis as a political liability, no matter what the actual truth about our condition now is. Perhaps the most nuanced embodiment of and response to the frustration and political difficulty incurred in getting people to take crisis seriously came from the economist Herman Daly, when he speculated about a limited-scale, actual catastrophe that might finally concentrate peoples' minds—a catastrophe that might do this without, however, irreversibly destroying them or their environment.[54] His apparently well-tempered catastrophe was one of the few ways of imagining genuine systemic change without, however, calling apocalyptic ruination down on the species. Still, Daly's formulation expressed despair (it's going to require something really bad to get people moving) and wishful thinking (it has to be bad, but let's hope it's not really really bad); and, though kinder and gentler, Daly's well-tempered catastrophe flirted nonetheless with hard-heartedness (it will have to hurt at least some of us, but not, thank god, everyone).

Elaborating crisis is thus not only hard to do but can also perhaps never really be done. Worse, even an actual occurrence of crisis, not just an elaboration of its imminence, is no guarantee that people will fall in line with the analyses and prescriptions of environmentalists. Environmental crisis, as Ulrich Beck has argued, is uniquely susceptible to social construction, and while an actual crisis, like Samuel Johnson's hanging, can indeed concentrate the mind wonderfully, it can concentrate it on the wrong target. Revenge against an outgroup can easily substitute for remedy to ecological crisis—especially given the political machinery devoted to obscuring problems and displacing blame described in Chapter 1.

Looked at critically, then, crisis discourse thus suffers from a number of liabilities. First, it seems to have become a political liability almost as much as an asset. It calls up a fierce and effective opposition with its predictions; worse, its more specific predictions are all too vulnerable to refutation by events. It also exposes environmentalists to being called grim doomsters and antilife Puritan extremists. Further, concern with crisis has all too often tempted people to try to find a "total solution" to the problems involved—a phrase that, as an astute analyst of the limitations of crisis discourse, John Barry, puts it, is all too reminiscent of the Third Reich's infamous "final solution."[55] A total crisis of society—environmental crisis at its gravest—threatens to translate despair into inhumanist authoritarianism; more often, however, it helps keep merely dysfunctional authority in place. It thus leads, Barry suggests, to the belief that only elite- and expert-led solutions are possible.[56] At the same time it depoliticizes people, inducing them to accept their impotence as individuals; this is something that has made many people today feel, ironically and/or passively, that since it makes no difference at all what any individual does on his or her own, one might as well go along with it.

Yet another pitfall for the full and sustained elaboration of environmental crisis is, though least discussed, perhaps the most deeply ironic. A problem with deep cultural and psychological as well as social effects, it is embodied in a startlingly simple proposition: the worse one feels environmental crisis is, the more one is tempted to turn one's back on the environment. This means, preeminently, turning one's back on "nature"—on traditions of nature feeling, traditions of knowledge about nature (ones that range from organic farming techniques to the different departments of ecological science), and traditions of nature-based activism. If nature is thoroughly wrecked these days, people need to delink from nature and live in postnature—a conclusion that, as the next chapter shows, many in U.S. society drew at the end of the millenium. Explorations of how deeply "nature" has been wounded and how intensely vulnerable to and dependent on human actions it is can thus lead, ironically, to further indifference to nature-based environmental issues, not greater concern with them.

But what quickly becomes evident to any reflective consideration of the difficulties of crisis discourse is that all of these liabilities are in fact bound tightly up with one specific notion of environmental crisis—with 1960s- and 1970s-style environmental apocalypticism. Excessive concern about them does not recognize that crisis discourse as a whole has significantly changed since the 1970s. They remain inducements to look away from serious reflection on environmental crisis only if one does not explore how environmental crisis has turned of late from apocalypse to dwelling place.

The apocalyptic mode had a number of prominent features: it was preoccupied with running out and running into walls; with scarcity and with the imminent rupture of limits; with actions that promised and temporally predicted imminent total meltdown; and with (often, though not always) the need for immediate "total solution." Thus doomsterism was its reigning mode; eco-authoritarianism was a grave temptation; and as crisis was elaborated to show more and more severe deformations of nature, temptation increased to refute it, or give up, or even cut off ties to clearly terminal "nature."

But as crisis has become domesticated into daily life, crisis discourse has grown more self-reflective as well as more complexly and subtly encompassing. Circumstances are different; in the United States in particular, people now live threatened by hyperabundance even more than by scarcity; they live not with the fear of imminently transgressing limits (and thus incurring immediate and total punishment) but with the more or less conscious certainty that they have passed beyond the limits—that they live not with sudden apocalypse immediately ahead but in a slow apocalypse, in a slow process of increasing ecological and ecosocial immiseration and rising ecological and ecosocial risk already embarked upon.

In recognizing and responding to an awareness like this, there is as much danger in false optimism as there is in the political liabilities of doomsterism; voices that speak forthrightly to the "age of anxiety" underneath greenwash and ideological disinformation are both psychologically and socially necessary. Where once prophets sought to reveal awful truths to ignorant people and urged immediate action to avoid disaster, now voices need to ask people to acknowledge what they already suspect and what their society, even when denying environmental crisis, is still preoccupied with. If wise enough, such voices will be as self-conscious as possible; they will abandon apocalypse for a sadder realism that looks closely at social and environmental changes in process and recognizes crisis as a place where people dwell, both in their commonalities and in their differences from each other. Seen thus, problems will have both gone beyond and become too intimate to suggest authoritarian solutions or escape— for dwelling in crisis means facing the fact that one dwells in a body and in ecosystems, both of which are already subject to considerable degradation, modification, and pressure. No credible refuge from damage to these is at hand.

A variety of arresting images and anecdotes have been created to express environmentalists' gradually developing awareness of dwelling in such a state. One widely used, characteristic image—employed by the Ehrlichs and Al Gore—invoked a crash, but not a hitting-the-wall-hard sort of crash. It suggested that though we were running into a wall, we were experiencing this collision in slow motion. Because our civilization was in the midst of so slow a smash into its ecosystems and environments, it could not easily see the whole process; it was only aware of a bumper being slowly crushed here, a door caving in there.

Another more complex image of immersion in slow environmental crisis, used by Gregory Bateson and repeated by Gore, was that of a frog in a pot. If you drop a frog into extremely hot water, it will try to jump out. But if it's in the water, and you slowly turn the heat up under it, it weakens gradually, eventually dying before it can act on any realization that it is in mortal danger. This version more convincingly evoked slow crisis as a place of dwelling and it pushed its listeners—struggling people, not struggling frogs—to become conscious of what it means to dwell there. Participation in slow crisis became much more active and conscious in Bateson's than in the crash metaphor. In the automobile accident metaphor, human beings' participation was limited to their initial error; as they crashed, they were unhappily strapped-in witnesses of the inevitable consequences. To be a frog in a gradually heated pot, however, was to have, all throughout the process, the option of jumping out but not to exercise it. In thinking about the frog, then, people would be brought to consider more fully their own reactions—to think how a slow environmental crisis might well be similarly deceiving them and to question their own propensity to stay where they are.

The frog image thus became more and more haunting as one fleshed out as fully as possible the logic of the frog-human's blindness to a deteriorating environment. Were people, like the frog, blind because of individual psychological reasons? Or were they blind on account of systemic social pressures? The answer, clearly, was both. Individuals were all too easily led astray by rationalizations and accommodations. And systemic social forces were equally powerful. How could a good capitalist, for example, even when provided with an acutely aching ecological conscience, get out of the pot? Even if that conscientious capitalist were the CEO of a transnational corporation, how could he or she take decisive steps toward an ecologically sustainable economy when corporations were subject at every turn to market discipline and the compulsion to seek short-term profits, not long-term social good? Even corporate CEOs would not have the power to go against market forces; the system would constrain them too. On both the individual and the social levels, then, environmental crisis was not simply a set of external problems; like the frog in the pot, people stayed inside it thanks to an utterly believable and banal psychological and social logic at work inside themselves.

Still further images for contemporary crisis have been developed to focus on peoples' growing immersion in nonlinear forms of environmental risk rather than visible environmental deterioration. These also emphasize another new feature of contemporary crisis: the fact that people are increasingly not ignorant about environmental crisis, but conscious of it. Wallace Broecker, one of the early investigators of global warming, has written that: "the inhabitants of planet earth are quietly conducting a gigantic experiment. . . . So vast and sweeping will be the consequences that, were it brought before any responsible council for approval, it would be firmly rejected."[57] Imagining humankind as engaged in a dangerous, illegitimate, one-time experiment vividly expresses today's pervasive anxiety about and knowing assumption of risk.[58]

All of these elaborations of anxiety have the flavor of voices that reveal to their listeners the full extent of something already in process; they depict people as already fully involved in environmental crisis, not startled by its approach. "We are now," Ulrich Beck writes: "living in the hazardous age of creeping catastrophe. What generations before us discovered despite resistance, and had to shout out loud at the world, we have come to take for granted: the impending 'suicide of the species.'"[59] And what it means to live with such assumptions is neither simple nor self-evident. Indeed, one can readily understand Beck's comment as opening up two new fields of inquiry, in one of which he is a notable pioneer: the sociological and psychological exploration of the intricacies of life *inside* environmental crisis. Environmentally conscious people, Beck makes clear, need therapeutically to excavate new psychological and sociological landscapes as well as scientifically track damage to the old ecological one.

By now it should be clear that throughout this book, I am advancing my own crisis metaphor. I've done this again and again by proposing that people today dwell in rising environmental and environmental-social risk and that they are pressed to try to domesticate themselves within this condition. My metaphor intends to express the problematic nature of that state in several ways. First, it would make it clear that people today dwell within and increasingly *feel* they dwell within an environment and environmentally constraining/constrained society that are "beyond the limits." Second, in doing so it would suggest that, along with perhaps resisting these changes, they also try to adapt to these circumstances the best they can. Third, in seeking to so adapt, people have been trying to look out for their own interests, getting their own expert information, remedying their own problems. In fact, they have been encouraged— even forced—to do this. In a time of staged and unstaged environmental controversies, they suffer from an absence of collectively pursued and (even more fundamentally) collectively supported solutions. "Dwelling in crisis" is thus all too often augmented by "domestication within crisis."

Much more positively, my metaphor of dwelling in crisis rules out sets of responses while ruling others in. What it tends to rule out is easy to say. Giving way to disinformation, turning over responsibility to distant authority, and deciding that one's environment is terminal and therefore to be abandoned are all hard to do if one internalizes the metaphor. One knows one's dwelling too well to be disinformed; one is too locally and intimately touched to hand all responsibility to an outside authority; and one knows that no other credible refuge exists. What the metaphor rules in—what tasks it sets before people, what possibilities it opens up for people—is perhaps initially far less clear but in fact far more interesting.

Over a century ago, Thoreau, in his essay "Walking," noticed how easy it was to "walk a mile into the woods bodily, without getting there in spirit." He continued: "the thought of some work will run in my head and I am not where my body is—I am out of my senses. In my walks, I would fain be in my senses."[60] What Thoreau wittily sought was a readjustment of consciousness that represented, finally, an expansion and refreshment of it. Living in one's senses while one dwells within environmental crisis is much more difficult; it becomes a challenge and a project, not just a regret and a necessity. Like Thoreau, who sought to "know" the beans he cultivated at Walden, one needs to study environmental crisis in order to *know* it; doing that, one needs to be able to come to one's senses within what one has learned.

Accordingly, it is not surprising to find that coming to one's senses in a damaged world has inspired a number of environmental-theoretical and practical programs. The ecopsychologist James Hillman has emphasized how peoples' anesthetization to their environments accompanies and perhaps even helps cause further environmental deterioration and he has argued eloquently for the cultivation of aesthetic awareness of the world as a crucial response. David Abram has urged a new phenomenology that internalizes the wisdom of premodern cultures—the animistic, preliterate experience of the environment as human beings' conversation partner, not as realm silenced by the invention of literacy and print, a mute "other" there only to be exploited and reshaped. Applying such wisdom today means opening oneself to conversations with a reanimated world as it is now under many forms of siege, not seeking a vanished New-Age/premodern arcadia. Still others, such as Phyllis Windle and Joanna Macy, have emphasized the need for a new form of environmental experience and practice—that of environmental mourning. Environmental mourning is a means of both absorbing, internalizing, emotionally surviving, and remembering the species, landscapes, and other environmental goods that have been irrevocably lost and of continuing on to love and be engaged with what remains.[61] All of these programs advocate ways in which people can seek as actively and positively as possible to dwell in their senses and within crisis; all suggest that doing so will help reverse society's environmentally destructive momentum. A further approach, one that comes from ecofeminism, joins elements of these predominantly individual-psychological practices together and weaves them into a collective social project resting on materialist social analysis and sponsoring an activist political program.

Thoroughgoing and persistent awareness of "embodiment" and "embeddedness" in ecosystems—key to a psychologizing and politicizing of environmental crisis—has been clearly elaborated and advocated in ecofeminism for some time. It is, to translate it into my terms, a way of dwelling actively within rather than accommodating oneself to environmental crisis. It brings with it a number of benefits, but most important here is that it helps people to live in their senses even when to do so is hard. Highlighting just how vulnerable people are to environmental damage because they are all embedded in ecosystems and embodied themselves, this awareness makes people experience in their senses the full impact of dwelling in environmental and ecosocial deterioration and rising risk.

Further, emphasizing embodiment and embeddedness makes people pay particular attention in their lives to what ecofeminists and Marxists call the work of reproduction as opposed to the work of production, of producing goods. This labor focuses attention on the environments one actually dwells in (environments that are local, regional, national, and global) rather than what one might produce from them. One focuses therefore on ecological and social health—on concerns such as safe food and water, nurturing children, nursing the elderly, and tending bodies, and on education, sanitation, nutrition, and community creation. Doing so serves to correct old environmental as well gender biases. Further, growth, development, and risk-taking can no longer seem primary and environmental protection secondary. No longer can one use the phrase "sustainable development" (as ecological modernization is tempted to do) as a ploy for proceeding with business as usual; valuation of the work of reproduction puts teeth into the term "sustainable." It guides personal choices, but it also generates public policy—such as calling for internalizing all the costs of reproduction in every economic activity and calculation.

This agenda also urges people to entertain and internalize a new economy of personal and communal environmental feeling today. Formerly, Aldo Leopold helped extend ethics to include species and ecosystems, just as ethics had formerly been extended to include women and "other" peoples.[62] The era of conquest (of people, of nature) was over; an era of citizenship and ethics commenced. People needed to recognize and respect the integrity of species and ecosystems—their integrity and their agency as self-willed, self-organizing, spontaneous, wild entities. With the elaboration and the growing perception that people inhabit an already-damaged world, a more intimate relationship between people and their biotic (and social) environments has become desirable, even as it has been forced upon people as a necessity. A new economy of feeling that accents intimate connections and relational otherness rather than independent coexistence must come into play. People's bodies are vulnerable to ecosystems, as ecosystems are vulnerable to people; environmental and ecosocial deterioration is increasingly an intimate matter; the closed circle has brought people and environment closely together. To achieve sustainability, to dwell in crisis, then, people need to work with a new economy of feeling, one that extends a variety of affects and affective practices to environmental contexts. People need to extend erotic, marital, parental, filial, and other kin feelings to environmental relationships. They also need to consider intimacy, nurturing, education, caring, embeddedness, embodiment, exposure, and vulnerability as crucial aspects of environmental as well as social-human, experience.

If antienvironmental thought could once sneer at wilderness passions as inhumanly purist—as focusing care on wild, pristine, nonhuman places and not giving a damn about the reworked/worked-over human ones—the ecofeminist economy of feeling yields just the opposite response. As humanity's sense of connection with its damaged biosphere and increasingly environmentally stressed societies increases, so does its need to care. Indeed, the worse damage means the more care. A child's sickness intensifies the desire to nurture; something of the same is evoked by wounded environments felt intimately. Equally, a renewed ferocity about the damage they have suffered emerges. If one is reluctant, as McKibben wisely noted, to make friends from among the terminally ill, one is equally fierce about close kin put at risk by what society has done. Perception of deepened environmental crisis thus does not have to lead to political passivity, to calls for inhumanist authoritarian solutions, or to trying to walk away from the damage. Dwelling in crisis that is firmly perceived as such, coupled with the exploration of a new economy of feeling, opens up a very different set of possibilities for care, commitment, and doing all one can.

But environmental problems clearly evoke other possibilities as well. The concluding section of this book focuses on how attempts to explore crisis as a dwelling place have emerged in several distinct ways at the end of the second millennium. In one of these cultural responses, which I shall call the culture of hyperexuberance, the problems of dwelling within crisis have resulted in what is no less than a programmatic yet also exuberantly baroque and shamelessly inventive attempt to escape from embodiment and embeddedness in a difficult time. To the other, which I consider the far more reflective and necessary response, what is most important has been an attempt to continue to come into one's senses as one faces the problems involved in dwelling in deepening environmental and environmental-social crisis.

Part III

Imagining Crisis

CHAPTER 7

The Culture of Hyperexuberance

How high are the extinction risks?
The philosopher John Leslie has studied this question and concluded
that the risk of human extinction is at least 30%. . . . Faced with such
assessments, some serious people are already suggesting that we move
beyond Earth as quickly as possible.
——Bill Joy, "Why the Future Doesn't Need Us," *Wired*, April 2000

To welcome in the millennium, *Wired* magazine published an issue entitled "The Future Gets Fun Again." It included a breathy article on "Newer York" by Michael McDonough [*sic*] (as told to Bruce Sterling).[1] This was a tale of New York City in the new millennium, a story that began right in the midst of environmental meltdown. The environmental crisis (to occur in the imminent future) featured global warming that set "the new whitewash job on the Guggenheim bubbling" and produced blazes that were consuming the "drought-ridden eastern forests three feet down into the topsoil."[2]

In this tricky situation Bill Gates, intervening suddenly like a true *deus ex machina*, called the famous "Green" architect Michael McDonough from a Redmond then suffering from one of its periodic El Niño/La Niña typhoon-floods:

"Listen up, architect," [Gates] continued. "You've designed a lot of stuff: suncatcher houses, recyclable airports, post-consumer newspaper furniture, and all that sort of, uh, thing. But now it's time to get serious! We need another New York. I'm looking for a city I can fund, assemble, and ship ASAP. Downtown, uptown, boroughs . . . the whole nine yards."[3]

Thank god for Bill, one thought immediately; and thank god for all the new-paradigm, just-in-time, visionary plutocrats who might just definitively break, before it was too late, the stranglehold that bricks-and-mortar smoke-stack industries and regulation-happy Second Wave politicians and bureaucrats had on the future. For, thanks to Bill, the new Newer York would be at last a state-of-the art city, a city where:

> software—not the buildings themselves—would be the heart and soul. . . .
> Sure, Newer York would be hard-equipped with, say, tubular tentacles reaching down into the earth's crust, using latent-heat transfer for air conditioning, but it would be Microsoft product that would track and maintain that system in cybersymbiosis with all other building networks and their regional infrastructure.
>   "This is a truly modern architecture, as an intelligent, cognizant entity, rooted to the earth at its base, with CO_2/oxygen exchange throughout the assembly—just like an organism," he said.

But the authors did not stop with these revelations; they immediately made another feature of their ultranew-tech solution perfectly clear. This proposed new cyberpostmodern ecodesign also bid farewell to all the old, boring, Green ideas and concepts of nature people had been mired in for centuries:

> In the past, it had always been the cost of time and attention that was the quiet hell of the wannabe-Green lifestyle. The laudable goal was to live an ecologically sane life, close to the good green earth, reading your Emerson essays on the shore of Walden Pond. But in harsh reality, your daily life meant endless hours of butter to churn, pigs to slop, beans to hoe, trash to sort and recycle.
>   Our primary conceptual breakthrough was realizing, *The Web could manage that.* Can't hire a gardener? Wire the garden and hire a gardening site to maintain it for you![4]

With this decisive intervention, all gross old prepostmodern notions of "nature" and "natural" living were, at long last, as they say, history. A city with wired gardens logged on to gardening sites, with upgradeable skyscrapers of bamboo generating their own energy through piezoelectrics (which turned buildings' swaying into energy)—an engineered city made from clusters of bamboo that produced "35 percent more oxygen than trees" or "as much oxygen as in a Vegas casino"—was the result.[5] It was a city in which nature had become thoroughly technologized and technology had put nature everywhere to work.

The essay then came to the real heart of the matter. A whole new paradigm had arrived, one that would allow people to keep all their old habits without any of their usual consequences:

> We can lead the same bent, weird, trippy, indecent, self-indulgent, consumer-centered, all-American lives we always have. Only we've *progressed*. We've moved into a truly advanced consumer civilization. . . . We are very rich and very smart. We can reach out of our obsolete soot and our flames and our grime and we can create a clean green cyberfuture, and we can keep on getting richer and smarter for as far as the eye can see![6]

Yes, *Wired*'s readers doubtless felt, environmental crisis was truly good for us. It truly was bad, but then it was good too, thanks to Bill. For environmental crisis not only generated urgency and excitement; it was, finally, the breeding ground of out-of-the-box contrarian thinking. Environmental crisis was creative and productive. As people like Bill responded to it, the bad old past disappeared and a future of untrammeled, postscarcity, smart, symbolic-analyst infinitude would be rescued from the squalid outcome of Second Wave old-think, specifically from the environmental mess it had created.

Despite the essay's intensely hyperexcited, mock-breathy, self-parodic tone—a tone typical of *Wired*, one that recruited hip (or, better, smart-ass) sarcasm and parody paradoxically in service of naïve credulity—the message was clear. Crisis like this was cool. And futurist fantasies like these were (if done in the right tone) once again "in." Indeed, they proved enormously popular at the end of the old millennium. Theorists in the academy have been known to consider, when they struggled to understand a tough new piece of cultural theory, its daunting abstraction and extreme obscurity as "good to think with" and therefore valuable. Far more vigorously, cruder aficionados of the "new" did something similar: they valued the licentiousness of prose like *Wired*'s and embraced its probable spuriousness because, regardless of truth, it was "good to dream with." In both fields, attractive new "products" were developed in this way. Much more important than any individual product, however, was the overall atmosphere; a whole new era of utopian-dystopian imagination seemed to have at last arrived in town and begun the task of reshaping the world.

This startling cultural development was accompanied by widespread faith and hype about the end of the millennium. In many quarters—ranging from the mass media to even the academy—people seemed convinced that they were witnessing the emergence of a crucial new era in world history. For the global, the postindustrial, the symbolic economy were all suddenly in existence and in need of analysis and description; a welter of startling new technologies and new cultural movements, from information technology, genetic engineering, and nanotechnology to postmodernism, posthumanism, and postnationalism were emerging onto the scene, each altering world and thought in stimulating, uncertain, possibility-filled new ways. All too seldom has the entire range of this discourse about paradigm-changing, world-historical mutations—one that emerged robustly at the end of the millennium—been analyzed as a discourse rather than as a collection of actual phenomena to be explored; seldom has the whole assemblage been interrogated to see how it perhaps serves the interests of some and is pitted against the interests of others.

Even less noticed, however, is that so much of this new-era discourse was formed in response to environmental crisis. Indeed, I would argue that environmental crisis was foundational to it, that responses to environmental crisis were woven throughout its wide variety of forms that ranged from science fiction and wildly futurist fantasy to serious academic as well as popular theorizing about the new social, cultural, and economic forms supposedly emerging just then in fact. For new-era discourse swallowed the analyses of environmental alarmists even as it alchemized, often exuberantly, those analyses and actually envisioned environmental apocalypse as the dawn of a new age. A short list of the assumptions that new-era discourse took from environmental crisis thought and then virtuosically respun includes the following. Radical natural and social disequilibrium turned into opportunities, not closures; they became the engergizing motor for human innovation and evolution, not the meltdown of the earth. Risk and instability suddenly became exciting and creative, the signs of a renaissance, not a *Weltuntergang*. Going out of control did not mean the degradation of the biosphere but a way to evolve faster. Chaos appeared not as a feature of apocalypse but as something that was good for us.

Respun thus, environmental meltdown appeared no longer as the end of the world; it became the *beginning* of a new world. And with a mere change of dress, the sensationalistic style and imagery that once accompanied 1970s-style alarms about environmental crisis migrated to new-era envisioning of the marvels of the future. In the most hard-core versions, however, the old sensationalism did not even bother to change its dress, for environmental crisis wasn't the beginning of a new world, but *was* the world. Depictions of future societies in the midst of perpetual environmental meltdown multiplied as sexy backgrounds for new kinds of excitement; environmental crisis in full bloom was recruited as an only nominally dystopian background against which thrilling high-tech adventures might unfold. Responding to this bizarre development, Nigel Clark wrote perceptively that postmodernity brought with it: "an element of fascination with our catastrophes, that they are not merely the unintended consequences of producing the things we want, they are themselves events which secretly excite us."[7] Global ecocatastrophe became, in short, weirdly desirable, even fun.

A very disparate and fully articulated discourse about the newness of the supposedly new era thus appeared in American culture during the last two decades of the twentieth century. To highlight the unexplored environmental implications threaded everywhere throughout it, I shall call the movement as a whole "the culture of hyperexuberance." I pick the term in order to show that it was not in fact completely unique but was, troublingly, a reprise of an older phenomenon. It was an explicitly noninnocent edition of the older cultural ideology that William Catton called the culture of exuberance.[8] Catton's culture of exuberance was the artifact of the expansion of the earth's carrying capacity *temporarily* created by the discovery and exploitation of an underpopulated, premodern New World and fossil-fuel energy sources. For Catton, the culture of exuberance lasted throughout American history from discovery times to the 1960s; it was a fundamental part of Western modernity. Its exuberance depended on the opening up to European modernity of the vast new environmental spaces provided by first, the "discovery" of the "new" world and second, fossil fuels.

The newer edition of this culture, the culture of hyperexuberance, in contrast, was born in the 1980s. It appeared across a wide swath of American popular culture, marked corporate styles, and left its imprint on popular social analysis and theory. It has had an especially vigorous life in film and literature. It helped birth a whole new postmodern school of futurist fantasizing; bring a new emphasis on visioneering to corporate culture, product design, and advertising; make mainstream versions of postmodern and cyborg culture vastly popular; and sponsor new movements in science fiction and blockbuster film. It loudly *claimed* to be exploring vast new environmental "spaces." These included cyberspace; microworlds; space gained through visionary technology and social reorganization; and space gained by a "postmaterial" and "postscarcity" economy that had supposedly detached itself from the material realm—the world that the old industrial economy had exploited and degraded—and become symbolic.

Too few seriously examined the claim to have opened up new environmental spaces within a (sometimes terminally) degraded world. It didn't matter, apparently, that these spaces were fictional (like cyberspace) or were ones (like microworlds) that, when engineered in sober fact, threatened new, more than they relieved old, environmental stresses and hazards. Nor did it matter that they were in fact still very much connected with the socially retrograde and environmentally polluting infrastructure of the soon-to-be-notorious era of bricks-and-mortar institutions and smokestack industries.

But implications and connections unexamined did not mean implications and connections dispelled. The truth was that underneath the celebrations and analyses of new technologies and the new economy lay exacerbations of old contradictions, unresolved like a guilty conscience. Most secretly knew that this new hyperexuberance was at bottom anything but innocent—that it was, to put it plainly, a crock—that its bold-faced assertions of an era beyond scarcity were not just suspicious but false. Most secretly knew they were contradicted, at the least, by both a deepening environmental crisis and a widening gulf between the superwealthy and the poor. More concretely, most, if forced to think about the issue, would have admitted that the exploration of cyberspace, microworlds, and new social forms relied every bit as much as the old culture of exuberance had on a fossil-fuel economy and limited natural resources in a world increasingly exploited both humanly and environmentally.

The major difference, then, between the new culture of hyperexuberance and the old culture of exuberance lay in the strained and at times almost bullying brazenness of its claims; these were signs of the exaggeration necessary to overcome not just public resistance to the new but persisting suspicions that the new was in fact both a worse and less naïve version of the old. Hyperexuberance had little or none of the innocence of the culture of exuberance— a culture that didn't realize or admit that it had filled its limits and gone out of balance. The culture of hyperexuberance accepted as its foundation exactly what environmental crisis elaboration held: that people were already beyond their limits, out of balance and in disequilibrium with nature. It accepted these premises and sought to alchemize them into possibilities, not horrors, yet a sense of catastrophe persisted nonetheless, not despite that alchemy so much as *within* and *through* it.

Elaborating this culture meant a process of imagining and crafting new technological, social, cultural, and economic possibilities out of the concepts and findings of environmental crisis. Looking at mainstream versions first, we see that to create the desired illusion (to turn doom into total liberation), hyperexuberance employed a cultural version of the politics of respinning discussed in Chapters 1 and 2. Respinnings took two persistent forms. First, they revealed, astonishingly, that the very environmental and social crises that had appalled environmentalists were good, not bad. Violated limits, disequilibrium, risk, chaos—these were all to be sought and courted, not eschewed. Do this, and scarcity could be metamorphosed into the astonishing consumer abundance provided by a new post-scarcity economy. Second, a wide variety of the features of old "ecological" utopias—environmentalists' versions of the good life—were appropriated by the new corporate-driven culture of hyperexuberance. They were lifted from environmental discourse and plunked down into the party for the information economy. Cornucopian abundance, bio-logic, neoevolution, and even wildness all suddenly became what corporations, not nature, gave society.

If one didn't notice these two processes at work, the effect seemed almost magical. Sometimes it seemed as if Glinda the Good Witch had touched all the bad old ideas with her wand and made them go away. More often though, the elaborators of the process shed their false innocence and posed as shibboleth-breakers, brave contrarians who highlighted the startling nature of their claims. They assumed this pose even as they enjoyed, unlike the shibboleth-breakers of the past, the status not of unwashed outcasts despised by the powerful but of insiders, elbow-rubbers with the movers and shakers. No mere bohemians, these "contrarians"; no, they *were* (or more realistically were hired by) the powerful. Or at least, they were on the Rolodexes of the powerful. They had arrived.

Popular futurology showed most clearly how the culture of hyperexuberance was able to root itself in the mainstream U.S. public arena. First, it claimed the birth of a whole new era in progress; second, it claimed that it had the key to understanding it. People had to map this emergent world if they were to survive. This was something that left-wing cultural critics, such as Fredric Jameson, advocate of "an aesthetic of cognitive mapping," and mainstream pop futurists agreed on.[9] But the futurists rushed in where Jameson found instead intriguing difficulty: they could provide the map.

One of the key features of this map was that it located new horizons in the midst of social upheaval and environmental crisis. If environmental science once foretold limits and crisis, these were trumped by assertions of human discoveries and social innovation that came from new, limit-breaking paradigms. If the crisis from which this new society was to rise, phoenixlike, was environmental, the name for one of the more popular versions of the new enthusiasm, "cornucopianism," had already been used by environmentalist crisis prophets. William Catton in 1980, in exposing the culture of exuberance and chronicling its supposed end in the oil crisis of the 1970s, thought he had also exposed (and thereby helped finally deflate) the "cornucopian myth" at the root of this era's hopes and assumptions. Little did he realize that very shortly after he penned these words, there would be a startlingly vigorous reanimation of cornucopianism. Thumbing its nose at Catton's doomsterism, this new, widely proclaimed "cornucopianism" promoted itself so blatantly that it seemed to amount to no less than something qualitatively new: a new paradigm.

Nowhere was this dynamic so overt as with the most flamboyant of the celebrants of transformation—someone styled by *Wired* magazine as the "doomslayer" of environmental "doomsayers"—Julian Simon. Presenting himself as shibboleth-destroyer, taboo-breaker, and counterintuitive thinker, he harried, satirized, contradicted, teased, and argued against environmental "doomsters" wherever he could, mustering reams of statistics to refute their claims. Winner of a notorious bet with Paul Ehrlich about resource depletion, senior fellow at the conservative Cato Institute, and author of a *New York Times Magazine* essay proclaiming that the only endangered species in the environmental controversy was truth, Simon asserted that the environmental crisis was a fiction. He labored to prove his point by assembling a thick tissue of facts, data, citations of scholarship, and debunking polemics familiar to brownlash literature.

Simon's apparently most novel revelation in the face of environmental prophets of doom was that "natural resources are not finite. Yes, you read correctly." Scarcity was a myth. Equally important, the possibilities for future development were unbounded; the future depended on the "human mind and heart"—on human creativity and its capacity to reshape its world (under appropriate conditions—you guessed it, those of liberated free enterprise).[10] These precepts were, quite outrageously, an appropriation of the perspective of the radical social environmentalist, Murray Bookchin. Bookchin's anarchist-ecological version of postscarcity environmentally healthy abundance became Simon's corporate-driven, technologically mediated, environmentally limit-breaking cornucopian abundance. Equally, Bookchin's left-wing anarchist liberation became Simon's right-wing liberated free enterprise. Yes, you saw it happen; right there Glinda waved her wand.

Simon's notion of expansion through the liberation of human creativity seemed to many genuinely transformative. Thanks to its alchemical magic, still more of the forces pointing toward environmental crisis were converted from reasons for despair into causes for celebration. First, environmental limits did not mean the end of things; they were beginnings. In fact, breaching them played a positive role. Human creativity was stimulated by them:

> More people, and increased income, cause resources to become more scarce in the short run. Heightened scarcity causes prices to rise. The higher prices present opportunity and prompt inventors and entrepreneurs to search for solutions. Many fail in the search, at cost to themselves. But in a free society, solutions are eventually found. And in the long run *the new developments leave us better off than if the problems had not arisen.*[11]

Environmental "limits" weren't limits once they were breached; they were converted into agents that helped spur mankind to far greater levels of development. Glinda lifted her wand, and suddenly all those pesky old environmental problems were actually good for you. Let them get worse; we'll only get better.

Even more stunningly, population growth—one of the oldest of bugbears of environmental doomsters—was not, for Simon, negative. In fact, Simon famously argued, the more people there were, the better, for the stock of potential human creativity was thereby enriched. Creativity grew exponentially just as population did. In one stroke, environmental crisis disappeared into a future that was now in principle not just alluring but infinite. Even so optimistic a propagandist as Hector St. John de Crevecoeur, writing in the eighteenth century, still linked the potential of the New World to the as-yet-unknown extensiveness of its land—an expanse that, however great, was ultimately, alas, limited. But Simon's "infinite" was not tied to material geography. A far wider vista of open environmental space thus appeared before humankind, a prospect that far outdid Catton's culture of exuberance, tied, like Crevecoeur's optimism, to the earth's limited resources. With this new culture, abundance was unlimited, infinite—a sign of true postscarcity at last. As with cyberspace, so with the environmental space produced by human ingenuity; just add a server or another genius, and there was, once more with the help of Glinda-Simon, more of it. Thus along with respinning population crisis into unlimited futures, Simon detached the millennia-old myth of abundance from its last links to nature and located it wholly in the realm of human invention and production. "Our corunucopia," Simon wrote, "is the human mind and heart" and not a faith "that nature is limitlessly bountiful."[12]

In practice as opposed to principle, Simon's vision of inexhaustibility rested on a number of more specific notions. Resources supposedly became infinite when one considered a number of possibilities—many of which ecological modernization had already explored and advocated, and which Simon repositioned to support not an averting of structural crisis but the opening of doors to infinitude. These included the development of new methods for discovering and exploiting unknown reserves; recycling; substitution, or the invention of ways to use "materials available in limitless quantities"; finding ways to create additional quantities of scarce resources (e.g., "create additional copper the way we grow plants with solar energy"); and imitating the opening of the world inaugurated by the discovery of the New World (*pace* Catton) by exploring the sea, the microworlds of genetic and nanotechnologies, the moon, and beyond:[13]

> Our earthly island of order can grow indefinitely within the universal sea of chaos. Life could even spread from Earth to other planets, other galaxies, and so on, incorporating an increasing portion of the universe's matter and energy. What happens at the end of time is anybody's guess: the universe may or may not be bounded. Who cares?[14]

For his sense of infinitude Simon also appealed, repeatedly, to visionary science. One of his more startling claims was an application to people of the old Baconian assertion about external nature; Simon argued that human beings were infinitely malleable. Freeman Dyson, he noted: "theorizes that even if the world were to get progressively colder forever, it would be possible for human beings to adapt in such fashion as to stay ahead of the cooling; consequently, he writes, 'Boiled down to one sentence, my message is the unboundedness of life and the consequent unboundedness of human destiny.'"[15] If Chinese gasping on pollution claimed, as Mark Hertsgaard reports, that their bodies had adapted to it, Simon took this idea much further; the ethnoevolutionary transformation of human bodies as well as society lay ahead. Reading Simon, one wondered when we would be reengineered, like the first patented bacterium, to eat toxic waste.

In a still more conceptual-theoretical vein, Simon cited physicist Frank Tipler, who argued that: "the ultimate constraint is not energy but rather information. Because we can increase the stock of information without limit, there is no need to consider our existence finite."[16] A sign of this was the assertion that human creativity was increasing, old attitudes were breaking up, and new ones were emerging with what seemed to be an exponential increase in velocity:

> Indeed, a casual reading of lay science magazines shows that the physicists are manufacturing new and competing theories of the cosmos at a very rapid rate. Just a few stray snippets: "For more than a decade now, the nascent field of particle astrophysics has grown like a garden gone wild." Or "Astronomers Go Up Against the Great Wall: The discovery of this huge structure could undermine 'cold dark matter' theory of galaxy formation; but what is the alternative?" And physicist David Layzer "argues that there is an indeterminacy set down in the order of things. . . . Evolution becomes then an open rather than a closed system, offering always the possibility of freedom and surprise. Layzer's conclusion is optimistic: "The new scientific worldview . . . assures us that there are no limits to what we and our descendents can hope to achieve and to become."[17]

It doesn't matter that Simon took these undigested, disparate pronouncements out of "lay science magazines" and wandered all over the map; his goal was awakening enthusiasm, not making sense. And I for one am delighted by the optimism—especially by the touch that the "cold dark matter" theory might *finally* have been put down. That theory (whatever it was) sounded real bad—it must have been the darling of antilife environmentalists who refused to see that "humankind has evolved into a creator rather than a destroyer."[18] And I am delighted by Simon's assertion that there were now no limits—something one of Simon's disciples further confirmed by writing an antidote to the Club of Rome's *Limits to Growth*, a book with the significant title *No Limits to Growth*.

But if Simon was capable of sounding unguardedly silly, his reference to the world as an open system, one in which indeterminacy plays a crucial role, is something I take far more seriously. With this reference—and his previous attempt to relate environmental gloom to an old physics of closed systems—he summoned to his side new ideas about nature that have had an extremely vigorous recent life as ideology as well as science. Lifted from their specific scientific contexts, these ideas became quasimystical faiths and ideologies that stood ready to serve a variety of social ends—one of which was corporate/right-wing/libertarian propaganda about the brand-new era society was supposedly now entering.

To pick the most prominent of these faiths, chaos theory, complexity theory, and post-Darwinian evolutionary theory all had great impact on ways of thought in the social sciences and humanities as well as natural sciences, and they were adopted by a wide variety of corporate strategists, ideologists of new technologies, and social, economic, and cultural theorists. They celebrated "a 'rising flow' of life that seeks increasing complexity, diversity, numbers of individuals, specialization, codependency, and evolvability."[19] At their best, these ideas were eagerly and widely welcomed into environmental discourse as signs of a new science of nature that was no longer reductionist. At their worst, however, they gave the veneer of nature to practices, institutions, and attitudes that were blatantly unsustainable and environmentally damaging. And all too quickly the worst dominated the field. Its scandalous "logic" went as follows: the rising flow of life that expressed itself in a huge reshaping of society, economic growth, and technology was not anything bad, old, or brown; oh no, it incorporated the very logic of nature; it didn't threaten life, it *was* life.[20]

A few examples. Alvin Toffler celebrated, in *The Third Wave*, "the death of industrialism and the rise of a new civilization."[21] In a significant revision of *The Communist Manifesto*, he described how the "human story, far from ending, has only just begun":

> A powerful tide is surging across much of the world today, creating a new, often bizarre, environment in which to work, play, marry, raise children, or retire. In this bewildering context, businessmen swim against highly erratic economic currents; politicians see their ratings bob wildly up and down; universities, hospitals, and other institutions battle against inflation. Value systems splinter and crash, while the lifeboats of family, church, and state are hurled madly about.[22]

In the midst of all this destruction—indeed, dependent upon it—came a "new civilization bursting into being in our midst" with "wholly new ideas and analogies." For us, though we are now in the midst of "destruction and decay," despair is "not only a sin . . . but . . . also unwarranted." This "emergent civilization can be made more sane, sensible, and sustainable, more decent and more democratic, than any we have ever known."[23] Though Toffler was not a brownlasher—he acknowledged that the environment appeared fragile and saw part of the new corporate mission as saving humankind from environmental harm—he, like Simon (and, it seems, thousands of other interested intrepreters of the present's exciting novelties), decisively opposed the doom and gloom of the Club of Rome. Toffler wrote that the "funereal tone" set by *The Limits to Growth* for much of the decade that followed was a sign of the decline of the Second Wave, not a part of true Third Wave vision.[24]

Like Simon, Toffler thus internalized contemporary fear of catastrophe and transformed it into a celebration of risky-chaotic social change that promised to take society into a hyperexuberant new world. Toffler then proceeded to take an important further step: he gave this process the imprimatur of nature. Four years later, Toffler wrote an introduction to *Order out of Chaos: Man's New Dialogue with Nature* by Ilya Prigogine and Isabelle Stengers. Clearly attracted to their ideas, Toffler drew on chaos theory to give a peculiarly interesting kind of support to his vision of onrushing social change. Prigogine and Stengers argued, Toffler held, that "our vision of nature is undergoing radical change toward the multiple, the temporal, and the complex" and that we had "only begun to understand the level of nature on which we live."[25]

This new vision left behind the mechanistic worldview that dominated Western science—a view that emphasized stability, order, uniformity, equilibrium, determinism, and reversibility. It focused instead on randomness, irreversibility, nonequilibrium circumstances, open systems, and evolvability—the fact that order could suddenly be created spontaneously and suddenly out of disorder and chaos through the process of "self-organization." If a preoccupation with entropy and bad old "closed" systems prompted gloomy visions of the cosmological (and, by extension, environmental and social) future, self-organization out of chaos presented a world in which disorder was creative, capable of producing higher and higher levels of order. Self-organization occured when fluctuations within a system amplified to force it "into a far-from-equilibrium condition and threaten its structure."[26] At that point, the "bifurcation point," it could splinter deeper into chaos or leap to a higher level of order, or "dissipative structure."

Of course, for Toffler, wishing to make something out of the new scientific theory, it did the latter. Culling out only the optimistic outcomes of self-organization, Toffler proceeded to argue that Third Wave social changes were the equivalent of Prigogine's and Stengers's new insights into nature. He argued that: "just as the Newtonian model gave rise to analogies in politics, diplomacy, and other spheres seemingly remote from science, so, too, does the Prigoginian model lend itself to analogical extension."[27] It "projects science into today's revolutionary world of instability, disequilibrium, and turbulence." What this projection meant, specifically, for Toffler, was that "Third Wave" society was a nothing less than a "leap to a new 'dissipative structure' on a world scale."[28]

With his and his wife's adoption as mascots by Newt Gingrich and the Republican "Revolution," Toffler's version of social change became one of the most popularly disseminated instances of paradigm change. Crucial to its conceptualization and elaboration was that Tofflerian social change was embedded in nature. Indeed, it was enshrined particularly in biological life, which: "no longer appears to oppose the 'normal' laws of physics, struggling against them to avoid its normal fate—its destruction. On the contrary, life seems to express in a specific way the very conditions in which our biosphere is embedded, incorporating the non-linearities of chemical reactions and the far-from-equilibrium conditions imposed on the biosphere by solar radiation."[29] To the faithful, this meant that life was creative; in open systems, it modified its environment and itself through acts of self-organization. (A more jaundiced observer would wonder if "far-from-equilibrium" conditions didn't also mean a greater likelihood of sudden collapses, even megacollapses—in short, risk as environmentalists such as Ulrich Beck described it). Further, natural systems were shown to evolve most robustly when perched on "the edge of chaos"—in a potential-filled realm between chaos and periodic order. (Here the jaundiced observer would perhaps suspect that unleashing free-market capitalism from even the slightest social constraint, and doing so especially in a time when the environment was already in crisis and "when the lifeboats of family, church, and state [were] . . . hurled wildly about," might well be what "perching on the edge of chaos" *really* meant).[30]

Chaos theory thus appropriated nature to justify theoretically a new regime of potentially higher-stakes environmental disregard than before. There was a deep irony in this process. From one perspective, chaos theory was only the latest manifestation of one of the oldest elements of the nature tradition: wildness. It described a nature that was spontaneous, wild, creative, not able to be subjected to instrumental goal-setting, reductionist scientific method, and linear thought. A.R. Ammons's justly famous poem "Corson's Inlet" (written before the birth and popularization of the scientific theory) elaborated the creative freedom of wildness in virtually the same scientific-philosophic terms that chaos theory later popularized. Similarly, many other nature writers—from Gary Snyder to Gretel Ehrlich—cited chaos theory approvingly once it had spread throughout society. To still other partisans of nature, such as the feminist Starhawk, chaos theory seemed to ground a new, activist ecolocalism as it emphasized the creative power of local complexity, not top-down command-and-control hierarchies.[31] But despite nature partisans' welcome of chaos theory as an end to scientific reductionism and a new support for older notions of wildness and localism, they quickly lost the battle. They lost to the propagandists for the new technologies, the new corporate structure, and the new economy and society.

Once appropriated from nature traditions, the depiction of nature in terms of chaos theory led quickly toward capitalism gone wild in an era in which risk provided the excitement. Who wouldn't prefer embracing a vision of nature as chaotic, disequilibrial, unstable, and simultaneously catastrophic-creative over a vision of environmental (among other sorts of) gloom, and who would hold back from surfing out into the risky unknown with it? Such a world was creatively out of control. It pasted a dazzling veneer of populist empowerment on a global reorganization that undid benefits and social safety nets and created widespread job loss; it distracted from the growing gap between the rich and poor. It helped one forget the miasma of environmental risk by crying "full speed ahead!" and by leaping into the huge new sandbox of corporate and technological enthusiasms.

For the appropriation of nature via chaos theory helped justify an intensification of capitalism that emphasized supercharged growth and a free-market fundamentalist setting-aside of social and environmental regulations even as it helped people forget that ecosystems and nature even existed. The irony was profound. A new philosophy of nature was used to justify a social system that not only intensified its environmental destructiveness but also erased many if not most of the more important rationales for guarding the health of the nature it was supposedly so intimately connected to. Chaos theory exposed the supposed fallacy of former conceptions of nature's health as equilibrial. It deprived environmentalists of appeals to the ideal of stable balance in nature and between nature and society. It also undercut the logic of nature protectionism by asserting that since nature was in continual disequilibrium and change, no form of existing nature ever was "pristine" or "primordial"—something that supposedly well-nigh invalidated all forms of wilderness protection. Most important of all, chaos theory seemed to welcome, not be threatened by, environmental crisis; it made crisis itself seem creative. The chaos propaganda machine became so effective that Donald Worster, alarmed by its implications, felt it necessary to point out that: "the fact ice sheets once scraped their way across Illinois does not provide any kind of justification for a corporation to strip coal from the state."[32]

A further extension of this logic erased nature even more completely. Kevin Kelly, technophilosopher and editor of *Wired*, invoked chaos more aggressively than Toffler. For him, it was the gateway to another striking paradigm shift: humankind's entrance into a neobiological and neoevolutionary era. For Kelly, chaos yielded dramatic changes not only in society, culture, and economics, but also in technology. For, learning from the new sciences, people had started creating a new generation of technologies that weren't distinct from or opposed to nature but merged with nature: "At the same time the logic of Bios [extracted from biology] is being imported into machines, the logic of Technos is being imported into life"; "human-made things are behaving more lifelike, and. . . . Life is becoming more engineered. The apparent veil between the organic and the manufactured has crumpled to reveal that the two really are, and always have been of one being."[33] Expanding on these points in the conclusion to his book, Kelly elaborated the "Nine Laws of God," commenting that:

> These nine principles underpin the awesome workings of prairies, flamingoes, cedar forests, eyeballs, natural selection in geological time, and the unfolding of a baby elephant from a tiny seed of elephant sperm and egg.
>
> These same principles of bio-logic are now being implanted in computer chips, electronic communication networks, robot modules, pharmaceutical searches, software design, and corporate management, in order that these artificial systems may overcome their own complexity.
>
> When the Technos is enlivened by Bios we get artifacts that can adapt, learn, and evolve. When our technology adapts, learns, and evolves then we will have a neo-biological civilization.[34]

In Kelly's neobiological civilization, technology extracted biological processes from physical bodies and ecological systems. Biological principles were now a part of technological systems. Even more decisively, evolution was thereby appropriated from nature—from physical organisms and from ecosystems. The slow, millennium-long process of natural evolution now became technologically assisted neoevolution; natural selection became market selection; and a new feeding frenzy could be released under the mantle of not just growth but an ideology of hypergrowth. *Limits to Growth* thus generated an even more aggressive version of *No Limits to Growth*.

In this spirit, Kelly agreed with Michael Littman that "the problem with Darwinian evolution . . . is that it is great if you have evolutionary time" and adds "but who can wait a million years?" In contrast, today's technology-led change was a form of hyperevolution "that searches for more creative ways to create" and thrived on the "persistent disequilibrium" (read therein risk, restructuring, inequality, crisis) that meant "perpetual dynamism."[35] Risk heightened the thrill of onrushing change, even as chaos theory rationalized it: "give up control, and we'll artificially evolve new worlds and undreamed of riches. Let go, and it will bloom. Have we ever resisted temptation before?"[36]

Kelly's neobiological, neoevolutionary civilization was thus the largest-scale appropriation of nature yet. Nature was now relocated inside machines; and the civilization fully integrated with this lifelike machinery now evolved itself—evolved its bodies and environments. Evolve, in short, became a transitive verb. Even business, integrating this biologic, Kelly argued, needed to change its fundamental identity. Kelly's writing prompted the *Wall Street Journal* to headline: "A New Model for the Nature of Business: It's Alive!"[37] It was also wild. No longer was wildness, as Thoreau wrote, "the Preservation of the World."[38] Now wildness was the patentable instrument of a specific set of new industries, part of their battery of new technologies, and a model for new corporate structure generally.

A small part of Kelly's vision has indeed been put into action. Corporate structures have been redesigned, at least in outward dress, bio-logically as webs, not pyramids. Genetic technology has engineered wildness, instrumentalizing nature's capacity for self-reproduction to produce its products and effects. And instrumentalized "wildness" has already helped produce a variety of specific new software products. It has helped programmers write better software; it has simulated communities of brokers for Suisse First Bank; it has helped International Truck and Engine to iron out snags in production; and it has helped IBM model "the development of specialized markets and cyclical price-war behavior."[39] (One had hoped for something more from wildness than slightly improving the bottom line of International Truck and Engine.) The new economy also instrumentalized the "wild" creativity of its new cadre of symbolic analysts, harnessing it by coupling informal, unstructured, and moveable workplaces to urgent deadlines and telescoping overtime, even as it did away with bad old Second Wave work.

But for Kelly, as for Simon and Toffler, the vision from the top was much more splendid than that. By instrumentalizing evolution as well, people had accessed a new kind of dynamism. With evolution brought on line, progress promised not just to be linear and incremental; it would be exponential. Society would not just continue to evolve; the *rate* of its evolution could be increased. The result would be exponential growth—which was precisely the sort of growth that had formerly appalled the authors of *The Limits to Growth*—it was change that proceeded by a logic of doublings. The same logic that turned a still half-clear pond overnight into an algae-choked, lifeless miasma was now dressed up very differently and pressed into the celebration of the new. Thus reworked as technologically assisted and accelerated neoevolution, it seemed to speed humanity toward a risky but potentially infinite future, not certain disaster.

From such heights it was but a short step to life in perpetual environmental crisis, experiencing all the thrills and ills of having turned life on an earth into a large-scale and risky experiment. In film and fiction, popular culture, just this step was taken. Attuned to the darker side of hyperexuberance, popular fiction and film proceeded to explore a wide variety of high-risk, environmentally degraded futures as sources of excitement, not gloom. A later chapter will explore how miasmic ecocatastrophe became *the* obsessive background for postmodern film and science fiction. For now, though, let's stay with the more upbeat rhetoric of nice marketers speaking to happy and eager masses. As Donna Haraway revealed, the culture of hyperexuberance was capable of turning even the terrible image of the world as a one-time, high-risk global experiment into good, clean fun. Quoting from its User's Guide, Haraway described the Maxis computer game *SimEarth* as:

> one practical training exercise for learning to inhabit the systematically globalized "whole earth." Seldom has subject constitution been so literal, visible, and explicit. The game's promotional material on the box urges *SimEarth* players to "take charge of an entire planet from its birth to its death—10 billion years later. Guide life from its inception as single-celled microbes to a civilization that can reach for the stars." Players can "promote life, create and destroy continents, terraform hostile worlds." Finally, players are urged to "guide your intelligent species through trials of war, pollution, famine, disease, global warming, and the greenhouse effect."[40]

SimEarth was just a game, and one that styled itself as teaching ecological knowledge and principles, at that. But it was also a symptomatic creation of the culture of hyperexuberance, introducing children (and playful adults) to a culture of planetary experimentation and the fascinations of risk.

As much as popular futurology, advertising and corporate public relations were a prime area for elaborating the culture of hyperexuberance. Again, environmental crisis was turned into foundations for a brave new world. Marketing and public relations for the two signature industries of the new economy in the United States today, genetic engineering and computers, were seedbeds of this kind of visionary appropriation of nature. Having commented in a previous chapter on genetic engineering, I'll look briefly here at the computer industry; in its marketing and PR, new-paradigm discourse for an era of actual environmental crisis—discourse that played on the fears associated with it and pretended solutions to it while problems worsened—went into high gear.

Computers clothed themselves, of course, in green. Computers were environmentally friendly: their chips were made from a marvelously abundant substance (silicon); they promised to introduce the paperless society (lightening the load thereby on the earth's forests)—a claim that persisted despite the vast increase in "postindustrial" society's paper consumption. Computers also advanced the study of nature significantly, in new instrumentation and in their ability to simulate ecosystemic interactions, where they were crucial to modeling even global environmental crisis. Further, as they appeared in some advertising, computers seemed to be a postcontemporary version of *The Lackawanna Valley*, the nineteenth-century American painting by George Inness, depicting a train winding peacefully through a pastoral landscape. Though scholars have debated the extent to which Inness's train, when examined closely, really fitted into its bucolic surroundings, with contemporary computer advertisements there was no such question. Computers merged completely with nature. Advertisements featured laptops sitting on sea-splashed rocks in settings that would have delighted the rugged California nature poet Robinson Jeffers or in the lap of some cutting-edge entrepreneur on a grassy hillside overlooking the San Francisco Bay.

But clothing oneself in false green has not been the truest hallmark of the culture of hyperexuberance. Information technology's appropriation of nature became even more overtly hyperexuberant when computers and computer networks were naturalized as ecosystems or even proposed as replacements for them. Computers dealt with information—which was, as *Business Week* put it, not only found in books, but is "stored in our genes and the lush complexity of the rain forest"; further, computers became vessels for growing artificial life in studies that provide conceptual models for biological life, even as, conversely, DNA began to be used experimentally for computing. Even more interesting was that folk like Dr. Bernard Huberman, an "Internet ecologist" at Xerox PARC, gushed that the Web grew "on its own like an ecosystem" and that "the sheer reach and structural complexity of the Web makes it an ecology of knowledge, with relationships, information 'food chains,' and dynamic interactions that could soon become as rich as, if not richer than, many natural ecosystems."[41] Thomas Ray, creator of the Tierra system of artificial life, asserted that the "digital 'naturalists'" who traversed the Net would be like "modern day tropical biologists exploring our organic jungles"; the only difference was, as Nigel Clark pointed out, that "digital ecology promises to expand and evolve into ever more fascinating permutations, while its biophysical counterpart is presently condemned to both physical contractions and perceptual demystification."[42] Perhaps the pinnacle of this fantasizing was reached when the robotics scientist Hans Moravec argued that people would someday upload their consciousnesses to hard disks and that their progeny would be robotic, not biological.[43]

Thus the computer industry clothed itself in a green garb, appropriated biology, and lifted ecosystems out of nature, legitimizing itself as a technology embedded in nature, not opposed to it; more aggressively still, it promised to create a second nature detached from the ailing first. All this helped deflect many potential environmental criticisms that tied the industry to the woes of manufacturing and the material economy, an economy that, when one set the rhetoric aside, the computer industry clearly condescended to utilize.

And use the old material economy it did. In many ways, such as the production of toxic waste in its manufacturing processes, the computer industry added significantly to the environmental stresses of that economy. As Maude Barlow has noted:

> originally thought to be a "clean" industry, high technology has left a staggering pollution legacy in its short history. Silicon Valley has more EPA toxic Superfund sites than any other area in the U.S. plus more than 150 ground water contamination sites, many related to high-tech manufacturing. Close to 30 percent of the groundwater beneath and around Phoenix, Arizona, has been contaminated, well over half by the high-tech sector."[44]

Andrew Ross has commented that:

> according to a study by the Wuppertal Institute, the fabrication of each PC requires the consumption of from 15 to 19 tons of energy and material. The high-grade minerals used for PC components can only be obtained through major mining operations and energy-intensive transformation processes. By contrast, an average automobile requires about 25 tons— not much difference. . . . Moreover the rate of worker illness, including toxic poisoning, in the postindustrial workplace is higher than in industrial sites.[45]

Further, as with other toxic developed-world industries, pollution created by computers has been concealed by being exported to the developing world.

John Markoff writes that, along with "3.2 million tons of 'e-waste' end[ing] up in U.S. landfills" last year, "50 to 80 percent of electronic waste collected for recycling in the United States is placed on container ships and sent to China, India, Pakistan or other countries, where it is reused or recycled under largely unregulated conditions."[46] Recycling operations along the Lianjing River in China, for example, have contaminated water and soil with "alarming levels of heavy metals"; a water sample taken near where "circuit boards were processed and burned, showed levels of toxic materials 190 times the levels for drinking water recommended by the World Health Organization." Dismantling printer toner cartridges, people breathe and absorb the toner through their skin; recyclers also conduct "hazardous operations . . . [such as] open burning of plastics and wires, . . . the melting and burning of soldered circuit boards, and the cracking and dumping of cathode ray tubes laden with lead."[47]

The computing industry has also left a sizeable environmental footprint through its energy use. Roger Anderson, director of the Energy Research Center at the Lamont-Doherty Earth Observatory at Columbia University, has argued that "historically, demand for electricity jumped with each of three technological breakthroughs." These were "lights and electric motors in the early 1900s, air conditioning in the early 1950s, and the rise of personal computers and then the Internet in the 1980s and 1990s." The bulk of the Internet's energy demands comes from infrastructure located "many miles away from the consumer in gigantic, air-conditioned warehouses called server farms," so that "a Web-enabled Palm Pilot uses as much electricity as a heavy-duty refrigerator."[48] In a similar vein, Peter Huber, writing in *Forbes* magazine, has estimated that it takes "'about 1 pound of coal to create, package, store and move 2 megabytes of data' and that computer-related demand already consumes 13 percent of America's electricity."[49]

Perhaps most important was the fact that, along with all of this fantasy and mystification, the computer industry provided society with its central metaphor for the new era of Simonesque exponential infinite growth. The image did great service to the promotion of growth by obscuring all its ecological consequences and even all its ties to a material economy. It focused on the doubling every eighteen months of *processing power*, not the doubling of social institutions, product lines, GNP, buildings, manufacturing plants, marketing concerns, transportation and travel networks, and resource extraction all over the world that these increases in processing power prompted. It also omitted all analysis of the way computing technology helped speed up and globally spread the old industrial economy and U.S. consumerist lifestyle around the world. Restricted thus to processing power, growth might well seem genuinely unlimited—an illusion on a par with cyberspace, the nongeographical space of computer networks. This growth, I want to emphasize once again, was not just ordinary old linear growth; it was exactly what the Club of Rome had dramatized in their parable of the pond and exactly what 1970s environmentalists (vilified for Malthusianism) had pictured population growth as being: it was exponentially dynamic.

As with futurology, as with new-industry marketing and public relations, so with another movement that strongly marked U.S. popular culture over the last several decades: the rapid diffusion of cyberculture from postmodern science fiction, cultural theory, and generational/lifestyle rebellion into mainstream U.S. popular culture. In cyberculture, the new culture of hyperexuberance found perhaps its most sensational expression.

Cyberculture's softer-core claims were designed to help the new technologies fit easily into life in a liberal consumerist democracy. Self-expression was enhanced by a happy infusion of postmodern fragmentation or decentering. In cyberspace, people could experiment with a new freedom from the constraints of their identities—a goal that was simultaneously pursued in academic theory by deconstructionism, poststructuralism, and postmodernism, which held that identities were socially constructed fictions. Cyberspace provided an arena in which the masses could experience this wisdom as playful liberation rather than encounter it in difficult, painstaking analyses of social control and marginalization. In cyberspace, real-world and real-body constraints could be set aside:

> In the ultimate artificial reality, physical appearance will be completely composable. You might choose on one occasion to be tall and beautiful; on another you might wish to be short and plain. It would be instructive to see how changed physical attributes altered your interactions with the people. Not only might people treat you differently, but you might find yourself treating them differently as well.[50]

Along with new psychological experience, in soft-core versions cyberspace promised new fora for social interaction and revitalization of democracy, something necessary for the restoration of community in America and for making a peaceful new global community.

Harder-core claims for the advent of cyberculture extended both these developments well beyond the status of add-ons to ordinary life in consumerist, postmodern America. Deconstructed identities were but a sign of "the possibilities of post-bodied and post-human forms of existence" the new technologies promised; or, as a user's guide to new technological development puts it: "We are *already* cyborgs. My mother, for instance, leads a relatively normal life thanks to a pacemaker. Beyond that, genetic engineering and nanotechnology . . . offer us the possibility of literally being able to change our bodies into new and different forms . . . a form of postbiological humanity can be achieved within the next fifty years."[51] Equally, cyberspace held out the promise of supplanting ecosystems and physical environments. Thus David Tomas argued that there was "reason to believe that these technologies might constitute the central phase in a post-industrial 'rite of passage' between organically human and cyberpsychically digital life-forms as reconfigured through computer software systems."[52]

Claims like Tomas's established a new high-water mark for end-of-the-millennium hyperexuberance. If civilization had broken the hold of the old logic of scarcity, had set aside all limits to growth, had embraced chaos and celebrated disequilibrium, and had appropriated nature's biology as neobiology and evolution as neoevolution, vanguard cyberenthusiasts went still further. People were, in their view, on the edge of a transformation that would mean leaving behind bodies and nature altogether; society was on the verge of the posthuman and the postnatural. As N. Katherine Hayles summarized it (using the term "posthuman" to stand for both conditions):

> the era of the human is about to give way, or has already given way, to the era of the posthuman. . . . Bruce Mazlish has called the posthuman era the fourth discontinuity, arguing that it constitutes the latest of four decisive breaks in human subjectivity. Hans Moravec sees the break more pessimistically, arguing that protein-based life forms are about to be superseded by silicon-based life and that humans will soon become obsolete.[53]

In her subsequent book, *How We Became Posthuman*, Hayles argued that this kind of posthumanism was a defining feature of contemporary cybernetic culture and theory, and she traced its "erasure of embodiment" as it unfolded in cybernetics, literature, and informatics.[54]

Back in the real world, however, as Hayles also clearly saw, the actual effect of these fantasies—fantasies of cyberbodies and cyber-ecosystems—showed in a very different fashion. They helped refortify and thus perpetuate disre-

gard of what was actually happening to ecosystems and bodies. From this perspective, Hayles wrote in very different terms and tones:

> In a world despoiled by overdevelopment, overpopulation, and time-release
> environmental poisons, it is comforting to think that physical forms can re-
> cover their pristine purity by being reconstituted as informational patterns
> in a multidimensional computer space. A cyberspace body, like a cyberspace
> landscape, is immune to blight and corruption.[55]

When popular culture became so preoccupied with issues like postmodern
fragmentation and decentering or the displacement of humanism by posthumanism, it was clear that the old barrier between popular and high culture
had broken down—or at least become more porous than before. For popular
culture was enthusiastically recycling sound bites from new academic theory,
which did not itself attempt to stay as detached from the *hoi polloi* as formerly.
Academic theory was, of course, vastly different in sophistication and also
intelligibility from the language of the masses. And it was committed to a critical assessment, not a naíve embrace of the tendencies of the society it analyzed. Still, its pioneering of theoretical vocabularies to describe what it saw as
historical novelties and even outright paradigm changes abundantly seeded
the terminology, rhetoric, and also preoccupations of popular cyberculture.
In return, alas, academic theory, when it came to environmental concerns,
was seeded by popular hyperexuberance—a reverse fertilization that had
most unfortunate consequences.

The most startling and contrarian-provocative sign of this encounter between academic theory and popular hyperexuberance was the argument advanced by both postmodern and cyborg theory: that "nature" itself had been
superseded. Intensifying environmental crisis had led some nature writers—
most notably Bill McKibben—to proclaim the end not just of individual
species or specific regional ecosystems but of the very concept of "nature" itself—an end McKibben deeply grieved. Cyborg/postmodern theory also proclaimed the end of "nature" as a concept, but it did so manifestly without
grief. More importantly, it was an "end" that came as the result of a very different process. Cyborg/postmodern theory scarcely ever mentioned environmental processes or environmental crisis. Instead, it argued that the *social*
transformations that postmodernity had set in progress made "nature" an
outmoded category of thought.

In the process, advanced developed-world conditions were taken as true all
around the globe, a social erasure as startling as the erasure of environmental

processes it went hand in hand with. To counter this startling combination of esoteric intellectual sophistication with almost Babbitlike provinciality, Katherine Hayles felt obliged to remind readers of her book on posthumanism that: "within a global context, the experience of virtuality [one pathway into the posthuman] becomes more exotic by several orders of magnitude." "It is a useful corrective," she continued, "to remember that 70 percent of the world's people have never made a telephone call."[56] Still, for most U.S. cyberenthusiasts, the furthest they could imagine their way into the condition of the majority of humanity was to call for providing Internet connections to Third World populations. There was no sense that the global majority, not they, might in some way represent the planet's center of gravity. There was little serious scrutinizing of cyborg and postmodern theory from developing-world perspectives, and there was no question about nature's ending. Old concepts of "nature" had been in effect simply superseded thanks to cutting-edge social, cultural, and technological developments in the First World, and their remaining traces needed to be mocked and cast aside conceptually like an embarrassing style from yesteryear. A striking form of critical hyperexuberance, not grief, was the interesting result.[57]

In the best book yet written about postmodernism, Fredric Jameson provocatively argued that postmodernism "is what you have when the modernization process is over and nature is gone for good."[58] What happened, according to Jameson, was "a radical eclipse of Nature itself." With the end of the "final form of the image of Nature in our time"—Heidegger's "organic precapitalist peasant landscape and village society"—our concept of Nature was:

> irredeemably and irrevocably destroyed by late capitalism, the green revolution, by neocolonialism and the megalopolis, which runs its superhighways over the older fields and vacant lots and turns Heidegger's "house of being" into condominiums, if not the most miserable, unheated, rat-infested tenement buildings. The other of our society is in that sense no longer Nature at all.[59]

Putting the same thing somewhat more forcefully, Jameson argued that recently, with late, or global, capitalism, "the purest form of capital yet to have emerged, a prodigious expansion of capital into hitherto uncommodified areas" was achieved. The result was "a new and historically original penetration and colonization of Nature and the Unconscious," a change that was exemplified in the "destruction of precapitalist Third World Agriculture by the Green Revolution, and the rise of the advertising industry."[60] In the process, human culture so expanded and underwent so "immense [a] dilation of its sphere" of commodities that " 'culture' has become a veritable second 'nature.' "[61]

With a different formulation and from a different theoretical perspective, Donna Haraway argued that, in the new era she called the "New World Order, Inc.," "the all-too-full spaces of foundational, unmarked Nature and Culture have been permanently sucked out of the world."[62] Nature and culture had imploded. For Haraway, "nature" was always already a thoroughly cultural construction: nature was always "collectively, materially, and semiotically constructed—that is, put together, made to cohere, worked up for and by us in some ways and not others."[63] With the advent of the "New World Order, Inc.," that constructedness became overtly the norm, not a covert reality suppressed by constructed notions of the "natural." Subsequently, Haraway's perspective became more widespread in environmental debates than Jameson's as a substantial school of thought sprang up dedicated to the notion that nature was socially constructed or socially produced, and sharp exchanges took place between nature-based environmentalists and postmodern social-constructionists.[64]

Both Jameson and Haraway derived their analyses of the present by setting it in opposition to former belief in "nature." Jameson pronounced nature "over" and dismissed environmental politics as bourgeois; for him, the advent of "second nature" ended all consideration of "first nature." Haraway more aggressively sought to hasten "nature's" passing, as "such foundations [of unmarked Nature and Culture] are unlamented by those they marked as nonstandard or branded as resource for the action of the hero."[65] Haraway considered the passing of old concepts of "nature" as a basis for utopian possibility. She welcomed the chance to create new communities based not on kinship but on feminist and nonheterosexual "unnatural" identities. "Queering what counts as nature is my categorical imperative," Haraway once wrote.[66] Her vision of nature's supersession was less dialectical and more contingent than Jameson's; with a new social-economic-cultural-technoscientific complex in place, what counted as nature radically changed, becoming in its most recent shift patently "unnatural"—which meant, most famously for Haraway, "cyborg."

There is much to say for these viewpoints. There has indeed been massive social reworking of both material and semiotic nature in recent decades, something that a strictly nature-based tallying up of ecosystem damage might miss. Jameson's "penetration" and Haraway's "implosion" embodied themselves in a host of commonplace, specific examples. During the past several decades, "nature" seemed to end in a bewildering variety of ways—and to do so through the expansion of culture rather than the developments charted by environmental crisis.

This list—a list that tallies up the ends of many different natures, rather than the end of an essentialized or hypostasized nature—is long. One such "nature" (nature as a space where man is not) seemed to end in development—as when mappings of the United States discovered that there was no place left in it farther away from a road than 30 miles (east of the Mississippi the figure shrank to 10); another (nature as unmanaged, wild, and free) ended in perceptions like Albert Borgman's, that "Nature is now entrusted to us much like medieval cathedrals are to Europeans"—as a valuable example of our past to be carefully maintained and managed.[67] A third (nature as the original or real as opposed to the copy or simulation) ended when, following Baudrillard, people claimed that to those truly aware, all the world was a Disneyland—or a Heritage Village, a Frontier Town, Old Waterfront, a Museum Village—and that this list of museums also included not just lawns and carefully designed and surveilled parks but even wildernesses, where "nature" had been carefully reworked and turned into simulations via roadways, paths, and campsites (requiring advanced booking) and was filled with tagged and electronically tracked wildlife and labeled scenic views. "Nature" as the outdoors ended when nature became another "indoors," planned, organized, and designed. An ad for Peoplesoft was only partially comic in depicting a man working on a laptop on a rock in an ocean bay; he occupied, the ad claimed, an office "designed by Wind and Tides, Ltd., a wholly owned subsidiary of Mother Nature, Inc."[68]

Equally, outdoors experience also lost its outdoors quality when fishing, formerly a practice that connected the small human fisherman with other species and nature's larger presence, took on a very new shape. Dana Phillips wittily describes how bass fishing postmodernized itself as a "sport like golf" and its new model practitioner no longer appeared as a good old boy in a boat, but a "floating avatar of the dispersed urban center, [a] water-borne . . . cruiser . . . piloted by a cyborg dressed in a Goretex jumpsuit covered with the emblems of the new multinational order (Yamaka, Shimano, Mercury, DuPont) . . . monitoring his surveillance equipment, his probes and prostheses."[69]

Further, nature as a fully available commons became nature as commodity, a product offered for sale in stores like Nature Co. Yet another form of nature (nature as the elemental and the exotic, the place adventurers went to get "off the grid") disappeared when tourism (perhaps soon to be the world's largest business) and the media successfully penetrated everywhere (Jack Turner described the trekking route from the airstrip at Lukla to the Everest Sanctuary as "Interstate E——— . . . always crowded with tourists, many of them in shorts and sandals with Pan Am flight bags over their shoulder containing all they need for several weeks in this 'Wilderness'").[70] Even the ultimate adventure became mediatized and put back on the grid when Rob Hall, dying on the South Summit of Everest, communicated with his wife and colleagues via cell phone, an event featured in later books and films about his hapless expedition.

Nature as the premodern disappeared when the electronic media reached even into the Amazon and Inner Mongolia, putting televisions in the homes and video cameras in the hands of indigenous people in tribal dress, and when indigenous people organized to create their own broadcasting networks. Nature as the local and place-based ended when David Bowie, in *The Man Who Fell to Earth*, expressed a key aspect of the new media culture by watching fifty-seven television screens simultaneously, a practice "for which the word *collage* is still only a very feeble name."[71] Nature as life and therefore sacred went when the sheep Dolly was cloned; nature as divine plan or evolutionary design went when genetic engineering completed what Darwin had begun. If Darwin had proved that distinct species were not the result of separate acts of creation but came instead from the always-ongoing, slow process of natural selection, genetic engineering unmasked separate species as merely statistical artifacts that people could and should alter whenever they wished. And nature as the given, as opposed to the artificial, went when the new bioengineered microbes, plants, and animals appeared, and these achievements, combined with the prospect of life-like machines, made some people feel they could do better than nature. These new organisms included the sheep Tracy, "a 'mammalian bioreactor,' so called because, through the introduction of human genes, her mammary glands were engineered to produce a protein, alpha-1-antitryptsin, for the pharmaceutical industry" and, more grotesquely, OncoMouse, engineered so that it "reliably develops neoplasms within months . . . and offers you a shorter path to new answers about cancer. Available only to researchers from DuPont, where better things for better living come to life."[72] Thus died yet another nature, nature as the wild, spontaneous, and free. With human engineering of self-reproduction, people have managed to instrumentalize and even industrialize nature's last inherently "free" and "wild" power. And all of these ends of nature were accompanied by the death of a more general aspect of nature—nature as Other to man. This started going early on, when people realized that they had gained the power to affect and alter the entire biosphere in a brief period of time, and it died again with every new intervention. The new human power scared many who mourned the transition, but it intrigued others, such as, for example, Edward Teller, who became interested in his old age in the possibilities of rapid planetary modification held out by geoengineering.

This list of emergent popularly noticed phenomena is just one of the possible lists one could make of natures' ends. To it I shall add one more—a tallying of large-scale transformations in old patterns of relationship between people and nature, patterns that were established in some cases millennia ago. Here also, many natures found themselves suddenly on their way out; more strikingly, they seemed to be exiting with Rockettelike synchronization just at the end of the millennium. The end of the millennium thus seemed to mark an equally epochal turning point in human and environmental history. As the year 2000 approached, a wide variety of old histories of human incursion into nature seemed to have moved onto a new level (Haraway's perspective) or to have reached their final consummation (Jameson's perspective) all at the same time.

Again, the list is long; again, culture seemed to expand completely to cover nature at the end of the second millennium in a surprising number of different ways. Globalization in effect completed the environmental and social restructuring of colonial history by spelling out the end to alternative spaces and created a world in which there was no longer any "outside-the-system" left. Capitalism in its global phase achieved, as Jameson remarked, a new and original penetration of enclaves that resisted it, marketizing and commodifying the "nature" within people as well as the last shreds of the "nature" without. Contemporary technoscience continued modernity's attempts to disenchant and instrumentalize nature by reshaping it further in a number of ways. It developed the capacity to engineer the formerly mysterious and sacred quality of life, its capacity for self-replication; it also instrumentalized wildness in its development and then applications of chaos theory. As Stephen Kellert has written: "to see chaos theory as a revolutionary new science that is radically discontinuous with the Western tradition of objectifying and controlling nature falsifies both the character of chaos theory and the history of science"; it was in fact a significant extension of science's disenchantment and instrumentalization of nature.[73] And if Renaissance humanism put man at the center of things, reinforced anthropocentrism, and helped subordinate nature to human determination, posthumanism, as N. Katherine Hayles describes it, dematerialized nature as information, erasing its independent status altogether.[74]

These new extensions of capitalism, colonialism, science, and humanism seemed to complete a number of the important narratives of modernity. A variety of older, more ancient narratives of people versus nature also seemed to receive decisive upgrades at the end of the second millennium. A number of ecotheorists, most notably David Abram, have argued that writing and later the development of print had helped silence previously loquacious animals and landscapes, creating artifactual voices that spoke more loudly to people than nature did.[75] The invention of the electronic word took this process still further. The new electronic word was a further step in distancing and derealizing nature. Language as code detached itself still further from actual, physical nature than language as book did—it removed language further from worldly contexts; it undercut its last pretenses of referring to nature rather than constructing its own patterns; it freed itself further from physical constraint by becoming reconfigurable at the push of a button; it helped create a culture of simulations; and it pretended to have absorbed life's code from the biotic realm.

But if the environmental implications of writing are perhaps not widely appreciated, the environmental implications of the rise of cities and the conflict between urban and rural cultures and perspectives are. And the end of the second millennium seemed to introduce something new and perhaps decisively final in this quarter as well. Back at the beginning of history, epics like *Gilgamesh* had recorded human beings' first heroic splendors and also destructive interventions into nature as urbanites newly committed to ecologically unsustainable lifestyles. But by the end of the second millennium there were ways in which almost everyone was an urbanite. The majority of the earth's people lived in cities and conurbations and the vast majority of the earth's people dwelt, thanks to electronic media, with reference to urban culture. Worldwide urbanization was achieved. And even before the rise of cities, another world-historical transformation occurred that had fundamentally altered human relationships with nature. A historically original insertion of human culture into nature, the invention of agriculture reshaped natural ecosystems to human needs and also set the stage for cultural development, ecological destruction, and rapid population growth. Once again, the end of the second millennium signaled a major extension of this insertion of culture into nature. With the Green Revolution, the industrialization of agriculture, the rise of factory farming in agriculture and aquaculture, the development of suites of pesticides and plants, the extension of human manipulation to the genomes of seeds, and the commencement of work on still further forms technological intervention, farming suddenly seemed to have lost its last ties to "natural" ways of life and to have become instead the creation of second nature's thanks to the suppression of the first.

If anything, then, recent material and semiotic reengineerings of nature have been more startling than Jameson and perhaps even Haraway (who themselves were out to startle) have indicated. At the end of the millennium, not just one concept of "nature" but a whole diversified set of cultural and historical meanings of nature was violated and reshaped all at once, as "culture" expanded to cover, transform, and even extinguish (or so it seemed) "first nature" altogether.

But by now one ought to be feeling the shadow of hyperexuberance passing overhead. In academic theory, these ends were too often interpreted and even sometimes hailed as the result of ideological and material progress, not grieved over as a deeper plunge into environmental crisis and constraint. To be sure, postmodern theory and social-constructionism/productionism, like many of the intellectual-theoretical movements of the last several decades, opened genuinely new conceptual spaces; they were indeed "good to think with." But at the same time, the hermeneutic spaces seemed, like cyberspace, virtually infinite; the multiplication of interpretations seemed extendible without limit; and the theory revolution, coming in waves and rippling across the disciplines, seemed able to expand meaning exponentially. All of these features heightened the temptation to ignore the environment, identified as it was with pessimism and limits. All of these features, in short, were ways in which academic theory became a secret sharer of the pattern set by Julian Simon, focusing on human inventiveness; growth fed on growth when human inventiveness made the horizons seem infinite.

To be sure, in many cases this theory growth was genuinely to be welcomed. Opening new theory space was valuable for providing new insights into the way social power operated and thus how the good society might be reconceived. It gave new interpretations to old histories and old texts—something that, for students of culture, was inestimably important, for it reshaped the past as well as the present, kept old texts new, and ensured that old traditions stayed alive and fascinating for new audiences. In activities like these, infinite theory space seemed to be a qualitative good. It also became the way to intellectual prominence, influence, and even material success. As Jean-François Lyotard argued, the most powerful move in the knowledge game became not the extension of old paradigms but the introduction of a new one.[76] This logic operated in the theory boom in cultural studies in the academy. It operated even more in areas with potentially significant technological applications, where paradigm change became, as we have seen, marketing rhetoric as well as a style of innovation.

But the relationship between theory space and environmental space remained deeply troubled; unexamined, it threatened and still threatens to make cultural theory seem as hyperexuberant as contemporary capitalism. Academic cultural and social theory for the most part ignored environmental constraints. It did not attempt to integrate the "ends of natures" through cultural expansion with the rather different sort of "ends of natures" presented in ecological science and ecosocial analysis—ends of natures that showed up in environmental destruction and closely linked social deterioration and constaint. Oriented strongly toward hermeneutic expansion, academic theory was tempted to dismiss uncritically both environmental warnings and the many cultures of nature advocacy and experience that make up environmentalism. Taking environmental crisis seriously seemed all too easy to dispense with in the glow of opening up new knowledge spaces. Environmental crisis was, after all, a depressing matter, something that attached itself to other discourses as constraint, not opening, as indebtedness to, not a break with, the past.

Further complicating matters, many contemporary environmental and social theorists all too often found themselves inscribed in a history of mutual antagonism. The old "new" social movements, as we saw in Chapter 1, were not harmoniously united. Then, as now, ethical obligations to nature have seemed in conflict with ethical obligations to people; nature-love seemed opposed to social justice; protecting nature seemed opposed to protecting jobs. Even worse, civilizationally old biases may have widened these gaps. Antiurban prejudices died hard among nature-identifing folk and antirural prejudices died hard among urban-identifying folk. Even on the level of theory, one's identifications could call up these old attitudes. Finally, as discussed in Chapter 1, attempts to bridge rifts like these were complicated by the constant hectoring of corporate-conservative antienvironmentalism, hectoring that academic theory, alas, often unguardedly fell in step with. The result is that, though genuine blends of Green and postmodern perspectives do exist, they remain relatively rare.[77] Attempts to think nature and culture together are perhaps only now beginning to happen.[78]

Appraising the environmental adequacy of particular social theories has been extremely difficult; the devil is always in the details.[79] But in general, cultural and social theory without environmental crisis has risked involving itself in two forms of hyperexuberance. First, to claim that second nature has terminated first nature risks the error of substituting dismissive "dialectic" for messy confusion and interpenetration. Ecological concerns still apply to simulated environments—even at Disney World, where simulation is everything, huge crowds, flushing toilets, and the profusion of necessary facilities and amenities have stressed sensitive Florida ecosystems into a critical state and have done so regardless of how managed, surveilled, and simulated the park itself is. To pick another example, genetic engineering, despite all the hype, is still merely engineering—an intervention into processes still incarnate in cellular structures, bodies, and ecosystems. And interventions like these, as discussed above, are matters for concern; from an environmental perspective, the more interventions culture makes into nature, the more one looks for the unforeseen consequences those interventions produce.

In this context, it is important to remember that proclamations of a world transformed into second nature do not just come from techno-utopians; they also accompany analyses of environmental crisis, even very early ones. For several centuries, second natures have proved to be as likely disastrous as desirable. George Perkins Marsh told a friend that his 1864 warning about ecological destruction, *Man and Nature*, was "a little volume showing that whereas [others] think that the earth made man, man in fact made the earth."[80] Nineteenth-century urban reformers simultaneously described appalling city-made second natures. And today, the crash of the Grand Banks, the death of the Black Sea, the depletion of the world's soils, the dwindling of potable water supplies, the inscription of bodies by toxic wastes, the intensification of environmental immiseration among the poor and marginalized are all features of a world that has been "socially produced." Contemporary theories of the social production of nature and the dominance of second nature must retain a sense that environmental crisis is one of its consistent productions and one of the ways second nature exhibits itself most prominently today.

The truth is that a thoroughly perfect second nature does not replace an imperfect first nature. An even deeper truth is that all actually existing second natures are, in fact, not "second" natures, but complex mixtures. This perception is both commonsensical and undertheorized; both radically transformed and thoroughly wrecked environments still have ecologies. As Lawrence Buell writes: "even if people were to become as 'posthuman' as the bionic characters of cyberpunk fiction, they would likely remain physically embodied and permeable to the influences of the water cycle, photosynthesis, macroclimate, seismology, bacterial resistance to pharmaceuticals, and the 'natural' advantages and disadvantages of regional habitats."[81] Buell then goes on to uncover a rich and complex history of how nature activism and urban-social activism have been woven interestingly together in U.S. history rather than being solely at each other's throats; theorizing nature today as a mixture of first and second natures allows that collaboration to be recovered and expanded in order to deal with the urgencies of the present.

Second, cultural and social theory without environmental crisis risks becoming a secret sharer in the Baconian fantasy that nature is infinitely malleable. It does so when it asserts or implies that what counts as nature changes simply as society changes. Sir Francis Bacon's early dream of nature's potentially infinite plasticity is one that has resurfaced again and again, as in the work of the Soviet historian M.N. Pokrovskiy, who wrote that in the future: "when science and technology have attained to a perfection we are as yet unable to visualize, nature will become soft wax in [man's] hands which he will be able to cast in whatever form he chooses".[82] It has recently been reinforced in contemporary fantasies of genetic engineering and nanotechnology (which give rise to claims that what was, for Pokrovskiy, still the future has at last arrived, now that science and technology are attaining the necessary perfection). To examine a succession of cultural productions of nature without being haunted all the way by serious concern for environmental crisis is to have hyperexuberant faith in that malleability. A story of increasingly limit-breaking social modifications of nature (and what counts as nature) cannot be separated from society's rich past experience with the problems that such modifications, along with the technologies and techniques that produced them, have created. Equally, chaos and uncertainty cannot suddenly become signs of possibility, utterly detached from their equally important association with risk.

Critical awareness of both considerations—that second nature doesn't simply replace first and that the new "postnature" doesn't in fact realize Bacon's dreams—is necessary to ensure that the ongoing social production of nature is not detached from the ongoing study of environmental stress. Theory space simply cannot sever all its connections with environmental space, however different the two spaces are; hermeneutical infinitude must nonetheless recognize its natural embeddedness, even when that embeddedness constrains its free play.

Of course, saying this is to risk sounding yet again like a doomster, a wet blanket at a good party. And just such a complaint has been raised in supposedly radical-critical social theory as well as right-wing antienvironmental propaganda. In introducing a collection of essays elaborating the social-productionist theory of nature, Noel Castree and Bruce Braun argue that: "deep green environmentalism shuttles between apocalyptics and melancholy, mourning the loss, or desperately seeking to preserve (or at least witness!) the last remnants of a 'pristine' nature."[83] I need first to quibble that environmentalism doesn't need to be "deep green" to lament and worry about losses. For environmentalisms of a wide variety of stripes do not only mourn the loss of "pristine" external nature; they also lament the loss of human health and deplore the social construction of marginally breathable air; they gnash their teeth over undrinkable water and shortening distances from toxic dumps to dwellings; and they fight the defacement of landscapes and the erasure of human places that were not "pristine," but had been culti-vated and cherished over years of human interaction with them. But even setting this rather major objection aside, to reject apocalyptics and lament, as Castree and Braun do, as *bad attitudes*, not happy ones to possess, rather than to ask whether these feelings today are perhaps not real expressions of peoples' engagement with their material worlds, reeks of a very large dose of hyperexuberance. Out with the bad old paradigm; out also with the bad old feelings.

If the "truths" and predictions of hyperexuberance become increasingly sus-pect as one hears them breathlessly repeated, the equally constant barrage of often bullying condemnations of doomsterism, from Simon's jeering to Toffler's characterization of despair as "not only a sin but . . . also unwar-ranted" and Castree's and Braun's aspersions on apocalyptics and melancholy, loses credibility just as quickly. Indeed, the longer one studies the love affair end-of-the-millennium American culture has had with hyperexuberance, the harder it is to conspire with it. Even if the tech stock bubble hadn't existed or hadn't burst, and even if history hadn't returned with vengeance with the United State's new war on terrorism, an overdose of all the brio about the fu-ture and the muscular-moral condemnation of pessimism would have been inevitable. All too quickly, hyperexuberance would have aged and lost both its faux-credibility and diverting novelty. All too rapidly, its consumers would have yearned for the more bracing tonic of realism. People would have yearned for, as most now do, a different treatment of the future.

Today, attempts to imagine the future realistically force one to take envi-ronmental and environmental-social crisis seriously. One has to do this be-cause environmental anxieties have deeply embedded themselves into present consciousness, and there is every indication that they will shadow coming generations even more. One needs to take such crisis seriously from the inside this time, as a context in which one actually dwells, not just anticipates. This very fact is an indication that the constraints that environmental and environmental-social problems have placed on human imaginations have increased. It also means, however, that even small credible environmental hopes have the capacity to evoke enormous energies. Only by confronting constraint *and* creating hope can a future be complexly and compellingly imagined. From this perspective, environmental crisis is not doomsterism; it's just the opposite. It is good to think with. For a society that uneasily frets about dwelling in crisis, it is one of the best things a person can summon up to think with.

CHAPTER 8

Representing Crisis: Environmental Crisis in Popular Fiction and Film

"After the energy crisis of the mid-seventies," Andrew Ross writes, "images of a dark, eco-dystopian future became the official 'look' of the future in popular culture":

> from the mid-seventies through the eighties, such images provided litera-
> ture, television, music videos, advertising, as well as films like *Escape from
> New York*, *Logan's Run*, *A Boy and His Dog*, *Soylent Green*, the *Mad Max*
> trilogy, *Blade Runner*, *The Running Man*, *The Terminator*, *Robocop*, *Aliens*,
> *Cherry 2000*, *Max Headroom*, *Millennium*, *Brazil*, *Hardware*, and a host of
> others. The dark scenarios associated with this look arguably carried
> more cultural power than the nostalgic theme-park constructions of the
> "Reaganite" *Star Wars* genre.[1]

Ross's list of texts could easily be extended to the present. It is a vivid statement of the fact that far from going away under the withering fire of the
antienvironmental rhetoric of the 1980s and 1990s, concern with dark environmental futures has, if anything, proliferated in U.S. popular culture.

Ecodystopianism in fictions about the future dates back earlier than the
energy crisis of the mid-1970s, as the presence of *Soylent Green* in Ross's own
list indicates. It appeared first as Malthusian nightmare and then, under the
influence of Rachel Carson, as ecological poisoning and breakdown.[2] But
what is even more significant is that it quickly went through a number of important changes that had not just literary but also environmental and political
significance. In fact, the history of ecodystopian fictions from the 1960s to the
present has been so vivid and symptomatic of larger social changes that an

examination of it shows the literature to be anything but mere escapist fantasy. Just the opposite: it has not just reflected but influentially intervened in heated contemporary environmental-political disputes from its inception to the present day.

In the following, I describe four important phases of the post-Carson literary, political, and environmental history of ecodystopian science fiction. The 1970s saw the rise and elaboration of the first wave of science fiction about environmental problems—fiction that depicted contemporary society's rush toward environmental apocalypse. This fiction—already referred to in the Preface—variously described the end of nature and human life as people knew it; but contrary to conservatives' incessant satire of "doomster" environmentalism, it did so with wit, inventiveness, and ironic pleasure as well as apocalyptic urgency. Politically, it arose in conscious relationship with the environmental counterculture—a movement inspired equally by Rachel Carson's screed and by utopian idealism. Literarily, it was part of a two-pronged attempt to bring earthly environmental considerations into science fiction, a genre normally preoccupied with technology and off-world experience. On the one hand, fiction such as Frank Herbert's *Dune* (1965) and Ernest Callenbach's *Ecotopia* (1975) incorporated a strain of ecological utopianism into science fiction; on the other, popular literary depictions of eco-apocalypse dramatized post-Carson fears of environmental catastrophe.

With the next generation of ecodystopian science fiction, however, the representation of environmental crisis as well as the impacts this literature had and audiences it spoke to changed considerably. Depictions of environmental crisis became central to the popular-cultural movement I have called the culture of hyperexuberance, the movement described in the previous chapter. In the1980s, a new, "postmodern" style of science fiction emerged and changed how environmental crisis was depicted; most influentially embodied in the cyberpunk movement of the mid-eighties, the new style of crisis representation quickly became an important reference point on the popular literary and cultural landscape. With almost perverse ingenuity, cyberpunk made ecodystopianism in science fiction as antienvironmental as it had previously been environmental. Environmental apocalypse was depicted not as the end of everything but as a milieu people dwelt in as they moved out beyond the limits of nature. More striking still, environmental apocalypse became a source of excitement, not dismay, a stimulus to thrilling new adventures and a path to hitherto undreamt-of new modes of being, not an account of doom and destruction.

At the same time in this second phase, ecodystopianism escaped from its 1970s confines as literature written for a countercultural niche group. It was no longer just a subgenre of a somewhat disreputable adolescent literary form, a form that appealed to only a marginal audience. With cyberpunk, ecodystopian science fiction gained in both audience and importance. Even as fascination with the future spread throughout mainstream American society, science fiction, discovered by an academy increasingly interested in popular culture as well as economic, social, and cultural postmodernization, was promoted in the literary hierarchy and renamed, in a much classier style, as "speculative fiction." Even more pointedly, cyberpunk science/speculative fiction was hailed by academic theorists as a unique index to a new culture- and society-in-formation. No less a critic-theorist than Fredric Jameson called cyberpunk "for many of us, the supreme *literary* expression if not of postmodernism, then of late capitalism itself"; with its arresting and diverse dramatization of the new technologies, new social forms, and new, "posthuman" ways of being, it became an important object of study for literary, cultural, and social theorists alike.[3] With this canonization, moreover, cyberpunk and the "postmodern" began to have considerable impact on mainstream culture. Cyberpunk gave mainstream computer culture its most fetishized concept and term, "cyberspace." Still more broadly, a popularized version of postmodernism helped give a glitzy new futurist and globalized look to U.S. culture, which was then undergoing the shocks of global restructuring and absorption of new technologies. Speculative futures excited the public, inspired corporations, and sold products. In the process, as Ross's list of films makes clear, ecodystopianism became something to conjure with, not run from.

A third step in this history came only very recently, as the postmodern or hyperexuberant phase of science/speculative fiction was transformed from contrarian avant-garde movement into generic norm. No longer so fresh, revolutionary, and provocatively counterintuitive, it now became an important point of reference on an increasingly definite cultural landscape. With this change, it also became a subject of reflection for a new generation of postcyberpunk writers and filmmakers and even, at times, a target for their criticism. Reflecting on the ecodystopian world that cyberpunk writers portrayed, a number of writers brought environmental crisis out of the background and focused on it as an explicit theme. Some writers examined cyberpunk's representation of environmental crisis only to swallow the movement's antienvironmental assumptions whole hog. Others, however, explored these assumptions as a part of a much more critical attempt to revise them. In these different efforts, the crisis anxiety that cyberpunk and postmodern speculative fiction had so dramatically sublimated into narrative excitement returned again to the foreground. Representations of life in radical environmental disequilibrium had to deal explicitly with the challenges that such environmental disequilibrium posed rather than simply (and enthusiastically) charm them away with ideologically charged ideas and action-packed narrative style.

A fourth phase of post-Carson ecodystopian popular fiction may be in formation in U.S popular culture. In the wake of postcyberpunk science fiction, a new kind of popular ecodystopian literature seems to be appearing that goes further in its critique of the environmental practices of contemporary society at the same time that it reaches back to older traditions of environmental feeling and activism. With the aging of the postmodern—and the ebbing of faith in the new economy and rising concern about worsening environmental conditions—popular versions of ecodystopianism seem to be moving out beyond their traditional locus, science fiction, and into a wide variety of popular genres that represent present-day settings in a more realistic fashion. No longer displaced onto the future, ecodystopianism as a central theme in popular literature seems to be appearing in genres like detective fiction, action-adventure fiction, medical thrillers, legal drama, and popular farce. In the process, new kinds of popular fiction and film give environmental anxieties and dilemmas far broader play than did hyperexuberant science fiction, and they represent them as woven more and more intimately into ordinary life than ever before. The reception of films like *Erin Brockovich* and the book/film *A Civil Action* are cases in point; as the wave of crisis sublimation of the 1980s and 1990s recedes, space is being perhaps made for a new wave of environmental populism. Though it looks back in tone and style to the 1960s and 1970s counterculture, this new development is a concern of mass-market, mainstream U.S. culture.

In moving beyond apocalypse, environmental crisis has become more and more a place in which people dwell, a context in reference to which they represent themselves. Ironically, cyberpunk science fiction first made this crucial turn. It represented the excitements of life *in* environmental crisis, as it sublimated vivid evocations of environmental disequilibrium and degradation into narrative thrills and chills and ideologically charged assurances of new sorts of possibilities. Second-generation revisions of postmodern science fiction then took environmental disequilibrium and degradation much more seriously; at their most critical, they represented environmental crisis as a complexly problematic and even painful dwelling place for people. And as crisis concern now spreads beyond science/speculative fiction, anxiety about critical environmental problems that increasingly mark and constrain people in the present is gradually becoming a regular point of reference for a variety of popular-cultural texts, authors, and audiences.

Ecoapocalypse: Encountering the End of Everything

In the first wave of popular post-Carson ecodystopianism, ecocatastrophe as apocalypse established itself as a subset of science fiction.[4] This literature quickly became quite various as it ran out different scenarios of imminent ecological meltdown to their extreme limits. These "extrapolative fantasies" (Brian Stableford's resonant term) presented several kinds of literary pleasure simultaneously.[5] On the one hand, page after page was filled with ingenious invention and satirical wit; depictions of oncoming apocalypse, paradoxically, gave like-minded readers considerable ironic pleasure in the midst of their doomsaying. On the other hand, these pleasures did not undercut the fictions' overall commitment to apocalypse; the stories remained chilling and caustic and achieved moments of ironic agony that made readers feel for a moment the unimaginable magnitude of the losses dramatized.[6] For these losses seemed not just significant but irreversible and absolute; they amounted to the utter destruction of nature and all its symbolic values—something that si-multaneously meant the end of human life as well, as existence without na-ture was felt to be impossible and even inconceivable.

This distinctive blend of wit and apocalypse was created in a number of different ways; apocalyptic "extrapolative fantasies" came in several different literary forms. Perhaps the greatest writer of extrapolative eco-apocalyptic fictions in English is not American, but British. J. G. Ballard's stories, "The Concentration City," "Billennium," and "Deep End" run out three environ-mental extrapolative fantasies that are similar in literary structure but radi-cally different in the problems they target.[7] Space demands I concentrate on just one, but it exemplifies the coolly logical but ultimately startling logic common to all three. "Deep End" runs out to its limit a scenario of heedless human exploitation producing disastrous ecological change. The main char-acter, Holliday, refuses to be taken off a dying Earth on one of the last shuttles to Mars; soon departure will become impossible, as the few remaining space platforms orbiting the earth fall into oceans that have become nearly com-pletely deserts. The origin of this massive ecocatastrophe is human megatechnology in service of off-world settlement. In order to create atmospheres for Mars and presumably other planets as well, people extract water from the oceans, separate the oxygen from the hydrogen, and ship the oxygen off. Soon, the only habitable places left are the former oceans' beds.

Attracted to the smoke of yet another fallen space platform—this time a Russian one—Holliday travels out from his seabed residence to the wreck, which had fallen in Lake Atlantic, the ocean's last remnant. Exploring the crash site, Holliday catches sight of something moving. To his great amazement, he discovers that the water holds one last still-living creature, a dogfish that is miraculously not just still moving but vigorous and healthy. Holliday, a poet and a dreamer, is deeply moved by the fish—so much so that he begins half-consciously to construct on the foundation of this poor creature the possibility of the eventual biological renewal of the planet.

Returning the next day to the fish, he is horrified to discover that two kids, the Merryweather boys, have driven up in their "big stripped-down Buick, slashed with yellow paint and fitted with sirens and pennants" and, discovering the fish, playfully (just like kids) started to torment it. They have breached the dike that Halliday had constructed to make a pool for the dogfish, and are now hurling brick-sized salt lumps at the flailing creature. Before Halliday can intervene, the fish is beyond all salvation: "Down in the center of the basin, in a litter of stones and spattered salt, was the crushed but still wriggling body of the dogfish, twisting itself helplessly in the bare inch of water that remained. Dark red blood poured from wounds in its body, staining the salt."[8]

Holliday drives the kids off, who first apologize ("Sorry, Holliday," the older Merryweather boy said tentatively behind him. "We didn't know it was your fish") and then run off "together across the dunes toward their car, yelling and playing catch with each other, mimicking Holliday's outrage."[9] Holliday's companion, Granger, tries to comfort him: "'Those damn children.' He took Holliday gently by the arm. 'I'm sorry,' he said quietly. 'But it's not the end of the world.'"[10] The irony is monstrous; for Holliday and the reader it *is* the end of the world. "Deep End" thus concludes in agony at the loss of what is, the story makes terribly, mournfully, and almost majestically clear, the last remnant of the earth's nonhuman life. Just at the moment Holliday (and the reader) experience an intense final hope for recovery of the earth's lost biodiversity—a hope that is illuminated, novalike, by a resurgence of all the joy in and feeling for nature humanity ever had—the hope is dashed. And it is dashed by a last, tiny, but momentous act of stupid, "natural," not evil, human brutality, an act that epitomizes the whole human history of thoughtless, even frivolous destruction of nature.

As with "Deep End," so with "The Concentration City" and "Billennium": each story presents an extrapolative fantasy in which some form of nature is brought to the absolute limit of disfigurement and human beings to an agonized experience of this loss. Each story structures its presentation to leave the reader at the end totally *in* catastrophe—in a symbolic space in which all exits have been closed and characters and/or readers have gained a full and achingly clear perception of the magnitude of the impossible situation. This is not just awareness of loss—a phrase that allows for some restful acceptance; it is awareness *as* the end of everything, and it depends on memory as well as loss. For as he closes the trap, Ballard evokes, with painfully affecting absent presence, the ghost of what is now irremediably gone—the emotions and associations of the specific kind of "nature" ended in each story. The result is a reprise of the great scene in the suicide center in *Soylent Green*; the enormous value of nature is evoked at the very moment its loss is shown to be absolute.

Like Philip Wylie's novel discussed in the Preface, John Brunner's *The Sheep Look Up* presents an alternative path to apocalypse. If Ballard is the strict classicist of eco-apocalypse, Brunner and Wylie are its baroque masters. Ballard's stories are ultimately conceptual dramas, cool, compressed, spare but complex thought experiments; their extrapolative structures reveal a relentless and inevitable environmental logic and human psycho-logic at work. Brunner's and (to a lesser extent) Wylie's fictions, by contrast, dramatize a dizzyingly rapid process of proliferation; the effect is not cool inevitability but hysterical loss of control. And the environmental logic behind this process is not the rational logic of inevitability but the ecological nightmare of accelerating positive-feedback loops causing environmental problems to multiply and then suddenly accelerate into meltdown. In dramatizing the hysterical eco-logic of proliferation and acceleration, moreover, Brunner and Wylie add a further quality. Unlike the conceptual artist Ballard, they emphasize the *physical* pressures of environmental meltdown, presenting the sickening degradation of organic life with claustrophobic naturalism.

Wylie and Brunner are both remarkable for their witty and profuse invention of problems to swamp their characters. But Wylie's considerable skill in this regard—discussed in the Preface—cannot match Brunner's larger canvas and more prolific power of invention. Brunner's novel opens in a landscape that is already post-Carsonesque, one in which ecosystems (air, water, soils) are already polluted and birdless. But it does not present just one small town afflicted with one significant symptom (i.e., birdlessness); it presents a nation poisoned and degraded everywhere with sheer excessiveness. Everywhere people grope their way through environmental horrors. Announcers rush to debunk rumors that the sun appeared at Santa Ynez; they do so to avoid mass turmoil created by people struggling to get there before the anomaly ends. The air's also unbreathable. Out in it, people can't speak without coughing: "The acrid air [in L.A.] ate at the back of his throat; he could imagine the tissues becoming horny, dense, impermeable," and Philip Mason (the character we are first introduced to in the novel) resolves to buy a filter mask if he is to stay in the city.[11] Everywhere the water is polluted. Outside, Mason's hands quickly become slimy as well; when he goes to wash them, we discover that the water is not only foul, redolent of sea salt and chlorine, but it is also privatized, a valuable commodity—Mason has to pay for it, dropping a coin in the dispenser for barely enough to rinse his hands. He also scrubs his face, but he regrets the act immediately. There are no towels to remove the dirty soap scum. Paper towels are no longer provided in washrooms, thanks to contamination of the Pacific by cellulose fibers.

And this is just the beginning. In New York, wheezing panhandlers beg for a quarter for oxygen; the continuously falling rain melts stockings and panty hose. In suburbs and on farms, soils are drenched with pesticides (the effective ones are illegal and black-market). Fleas and lice, which have come to infest bodies and homes everywhere, have become resistent—even to the "strong" sprays, which have been banned because of their toxicity but which are still sold widely on the black market because the licensed ones are completely ineffective. The Mediterranean has definitively died, having been poisoned by human and industrial wastes. And off the coast between California and Baja:

> the night stank. The sea moved lazily, its embryo waves aborted before cresting by the layer of oily residues surrounding the hull, impermeable as sheet plastic: a mixture of detergents, sewage, industrial chemicals and the microscopic cellulose fibers due to toilet paper and newsprint. There was no sound of fish breaking surface. There were no fish.[12]

Even more claustrophobically, human as well as ecological health is a thing of the past. Characters suffer from scarily indeterminate infections, patches on their legs that may be an exotic fungus or worse; they endure weeping skin conditions and boils and contract drug-resistant gonorrhea; they wear wigs because of ringworm. A typical well-off family includes children with mental impairments, children with occasional fits, and children whose teeth occasionally crack edge to edge and fall out of their mouths; birth defects are so common and various that people worry about taking out abnormality insurance with pregnancies.

If all of this weren't bad enough, environmental crisis in *The Sheep Look Up* is a social as well as ecological and human health problem. Comprehensive ecosocial crisis shows first in the novel in an all-too-believable depiction of the logic of accommodation (one of the scenarios discussed in Chapter 5). People have, as people will, domesticated themselves as best they can in this growing mess, adapting and coping, exerting their ingenuity at every turn to try to keep living something that they could still convince themselves was a "normal" life. They deal with environmental horrors by taking their vacation elsewhere and by (if they have the money) shopping for health food rather than ordinary fare and drinking filtered and/or bottled water. They deal with environmental problems by using and abusing chemicals to solve their own immediate problems, even though the chemicals (accumulating generally in the environment) contribute to making things much worse later for everyone and therefore for themselves. And above all, they deal with environmental decay by normalizing complaints through linguistic and social routines that do nothing to solve the underlying problems. "Oh nothing to worry about Mrs. Mason," a typical doctor says of really quite appalling ailments: "A very common thing these days, this blepharitis, nothing at all to do with your little girl's strabismus."[13] All of these normalizations, of course, only make problems worse: they lead people to try to fend for themselves within a deteriorating system, not seek collectively to change it.

By the end of the book, all of these strategies have failed. And as ecological problems become more and more critical, a new dimension of social problems emerges. Environmental malfeasance by U.S. corporations and government causes a series of international incidents as well as domestic disasters. And a melodramatic battle between two polarized titans begins; a larger-than-life ecohero, August Train, goes up against a know-nothing, opportunistic, chauvinistic, right-wing, fundamentalist president, the rabble-rousing "Prexy" who succeeds in making Train a sacrificial scapegoat. Environmental crisis thus leads to the social crisis of right-wing demagogery; right-wing demagogery, in turn, eliminates the last hope for ending environmental crisis by eliminating the only person able to bring society back from the brink.

A few final moments remind readers of what is lost. "When," Train implores an audience, "did you last bask in the sun, friends? When did you last dare drink from a creek? When did you last risk picking fruit and eating it straight from the tree?" Like the final realizations in Ballards' stories, like the scene in the suicide center in *Soylent Green*, a moment like this agonizingly evokes the lost goods of nature and nature feeling at the instant of their final disappearance. But unlike some of the far more memorable literature to be discussed later, Brunner, Ballard, and *Soylent Green* do not dwell on and in these experiences of memory in loss; they evoke them only briefly on a one-way trip into ironic judgment, smashup, and then emptiness: a one-way trip, in short, into secular, human-made apocalpyse.

At the end of Brunner's novel, the United States self-destructs. The novel jumps across the Atlantic to Ireland, where smoke blows in from the west. Mrs. Byrne thinks it's a fire and urgently wants to call the brigade; she is told, however, that the brigade would have to go far, as the smoke's from America. The United States is thus history; the novel's judgment on it is final, dismissive, and even triumphantly ironic. The nation's final implosion is ultimately a farce rather than a tragedy or even melodrama. For though there are villains aplenty in the piece, the novel makes clear that ecological and social apocalypse are not their creation but are systemically inevitable. Ultimately, the process whereby problems escalate into inevitable meltdown is a problem of the whole social-ecological system.

Both Ballard's and Brunner's fictions have real literary limitations. Ballard's Poe-esque conceptual melodramas and Brunner's more popular plot-driven action-suspense melodramas seek high-impact conclusions at the expense of deep, long-lasting resonance. Equally, Ballard's and Brunner's fictions are constrained as acts of political imagination. First, their apocalyptic logic tends to invalidate hope for any solutions other than large-scale authoritarian ones; they cry out for a *deus ex machina* to intervene from above into the narratives' terrible extrapolative logics. Second and even more interesting, their intensity of outrage annihilates what it supposedly defends. They dramatize the end of nature even while trying to enlist readers in its defense. Their literary and political strengths are thus Pyrrhic ones; in their greatest triumphs lie their fatal weaknesses—which would indeed return to haunt subsequent literary depictions of environmental crisis.

Getting Off on Catastrophe: Postmodernity and the Cyberpunk Generation

In the 1980s, a new generation of science fiction writers rushed in to enthusiastically embrace what Brunner, Wylie, and Ballard had depicted with dark wit and in so sobering and shocking a manner. If a previous generation of science fiction writers had magnified environmental problems to apocalyptic dimensions, the new generation simply built on this achievement and took it further. Startlingly, the new generation accepted with enthusiasm what had been so problematic for its predecessors: the fact that people now lived utterly beyond environmental limits and in disequilibrium with nature. These writers enthusiastically depicted earth's environmental and social systems as in meltdown and disarray—as, in effect, *in* apocalypse; they then transformed this apocalypse from the end of humanity to the positive and liberating beginning of what they called "posthumanity." And if the previous generation had left no way out save to appeal to authority, the new generation reveled in infatuation with the very sort of authority (free-market capitalism) that was one of its predecessors' prime targets.

The most celebrated early example of how eco-apocalypse could be turned into social normality and source of excitement was Ridley Scott's film *Blade Runner*, a film that was a diminished but elegantly massaged version of Philip K. Dick's novel, *Do Androids Dream of Electric Sheep*. The novel portrays a post-world-war world in which nature has been almost completely finished off. Set in a time when the air is filled with radioactive dust, biodiversity is nearly wiped out, and human bodies and infrastructure are steadily deteriorating, Dick's novel depicts a disturbing world in which nature and human life on earth are diminishing and probably expiring. Not so with Scott's film; it drops the world war and its radioactive legacy, making environmental immiseration part of the general background rather than an overt theme. Even more striking, it gives that background a stylishly haunting and culturally upscale hyperurban global-postmodern atmosphere, thereby romanticizing what in the novel is basically slummification. Underlying this change in atmosphere is a fundamental alteration of theme. The film surgically removes two of the novel's major commitments—its commitment to exploring the residual power of biophilia and natural feeling, and its sad portrayal of the emotional void left by the loss of biota, the dying of nature, and the deterioration of human bodies.

Human beings in Dick's novel need other species, for it is part of their humanness; the ones who can afford to own one of the few animals left are privileged, while the mass of mankind has to make do at best with purchasing cunning electronic copies. People also fear their own radiation-induced physical deterioration into socially outcast "specials" and "chuckleheads." And both of these losses have a further psychological consequence. Painfully aware of something missing, people seek a wide range of substitutes (from electric animals to Penfield mood organs and the simulated religion of empathy, Mercerism) to fill the void. An even worse problem is raised by the androids that Dick's society has built to be its slaves—but which are difficult to distinguish from humans, let alone control when they rebel. For the androids, "flattening of affect" is a hardwired trait, and it means that they are coldly insensitive to the losses humans feel.[14] That people have become so numbed and are so in need of substitutes for what they have lost, the novel presents as disturbing; that androids display a more extreme version of this problem is, the novel implies, deeply problematic.

In *Blade Runner*, by contrast, the loss of other species and the deterioration of human bodies are simply not developed as themes; they remain just part of the atmosphere. And, strikingly, the film's depiction of society's future environment is different; its catastrophically overbuilt, claustrophobically overcrowded, and atmospherically polluted atmosphere is represented as stylish—as the noir but nonetheless hauntingly compelling look of the new, global, high-tech world of U.S. futurist dreams, not a portrait of dreary environmental devolution. Still more remarkably, the painful numbing of affect that the novel depicts is metamorphosed in the film into a strangely attractive and ultimately normative postmodern style. Dick's revelations of his human characters' losses and their search for substitutes is out; in its place is infatuation with a strange, new, intensified, posthuman form of experience expressed in the otherworldly lyricism of the film's dying villain-android and the romantic allure of its heroine-android. For in *Blade Runner*, the androids' emotional difference from humans becomes an actual plus: they are capable of intense new states of feeling.

Over the course of the last several decades, a wide variety of science fiction, from cyberpunk to *Batman*, has spelled out in still greater detail the physical and human environments portrayed in *Blade Runner* (and also the fundamentally antienvironmental messages that come with them). Further, it has presented these catastrophic environments more and more in mainstream, not avant-gardist/cultist, fashion, styling them as exciting new spaces for action and adventure. Of this transformation, the most seminal work remains the fiction that initiated the cyberpunk movement. Breaking onto the literary scene with William Gibson's *Neuromancer* (1984) and Bruce Sterling's *Schismatrix* (1985), cyberpunk's hyperurban atmosphere, its interest in cyborgianism, its fascination with postnature, its flirtations with posthumanism, and its portrait of postmodern/postnatural society made it the fullest exploration of the atmosphere presented in *Blade Runner*. This dazzling array of interests also made its influence extend well beyond what science fiction traditionally commanded; as noted above, it left a decisive mark on both academic and popular culture in the United States. And crucial to cyberpunk's preeminence on both the academic and the popular-postmodern literary scene was one of its most fundamental propositions: the assumption that complex ecosocial crisis is here and is exciting.

In cyberpunk, ecosocial crisis is exciting because key organic limits are violated. First, it is exciting because nature has ended—and ended in a transformation that represents a beginning, not a conclusion. Second, it is exciting because ordinary human embodiment—a more intimate form of "nature"—has also ended; its supersession also promises not an end but a beginning. For in cyberpunk, an electronic environment replaces the old ecological one, cyborg bodies replace the old biological ones, and great new possibilities are thereby opened up.

But ecocrisis in Gibson's and Sterling's novels is even more exciting because it promises two forms of total consummation. First, it leads to total personal transcendence. It labors to provide its protagonists and readers with highs far more intense, cutting-edge, and thrilling than even the most intense moments of the old spiritual legacy of the nature traditions. Designer drugs, genetic modifications, and cyberenhancements are just the beginning; transcendent personal ecstasy brought about by immersion in cyberspace and speeded up evolution is the *summa* to be pursued, a goal that both Gibson and Sterling strive to depict.[15] Second, ecosocial crisis holds out the promise of a great new societal-historical transformation. Cyberpunk promises that crisis is in fact propelling society to transcend all its old history—the history of human beings in nature—and enter a qualitatively new, hitherto unimaginable phase of a disequilibrial, risk-loving society that has bootstrapped itself beyond ecology and evolution.

In Gibson's novel *Neuromancer*, the hero, Case, is a cybercowboy—someone who, as is now well known, jacks himself directly into the "consensual hallucination" of cyberspace, or the matrix. Cyberspace is in turn: "a graphic representation of data abstracted from the banks of every computer in the human system. Unthinkable complexity. Lines of light ranged in the nonspace of the mind, clusters and constelllations of data. Like city lights, receding. . . ."[16] This urban-style postspace houses the new wealth of information possessed by the megacorporations of the era. Though a product of Third Wave technologies situated in rotting Second Wave infrastructure, this new space is not, of course, afflicted with unexciting, downscale forms of pollution or environmental decay. It is clean, beautiful, artificial, pure, and clear, even when at its most violent.[17]

Thus cyberpunk's hyperexciting hallucinatory virtual world, accessed directly through neural interfaces like the jack behind Case's ear, is in fact an exciting new kind of environment for human action. As important is that it is situated in an outer world which is catastrophically environmentally degraded, and both the catastrophic degradation of the outer world and the smooth thrills of the new virtual environment combine to attract the reader's desires and create literary excitement.

Environmental degradation in *Neuromancer* is sketched in in a variety of ways. Untimately, it signifies that "nature" as twentieth-century people knew it has definitively ended. Very much *in* environmental crisis, *Neuromancer*'s outer world is disrupted and toxified by an international war that has left the core of Bonn, for example, still radioactive; equally it is hyperurbanized, as cities have spread everywhere. Home for Case is "BAMA, the Sprawl, the Boston-Atlanta Metropolitan Axis," a world of hyperbuilt, decaying, industrial-era infrastructure. Plainly, no nature is left—all organic nonhuman nature is either paved over or reduced to the weeds that grow in the gaps that open up in the ruins of the rotting Second Wave infrastructure that has taken over the visible world.

Only in simulations do characters encounter undegraded "nature." For example, on Freeside, an orbiting space colony that is also a gigantic mall, a machine called the Lado-Acheson system generates artificial weather. An even more complete simulation is created when Case is swept up into a computer-generated paradise, a shimmering beach complete with long-lost and longed-for girlfriend. This cyber-idyll, created by a powerful computer, is meant to entrap him, but Case breaks out of it just in time to save his life. The message is clear: nostalgia for nature's beauty and for natural feeling (here, for lost first love) is at best fatuous and at worst a deadly trap. The true hero of this future has to put both decisively behind him. The passion that gripped Charlton Heston while watching with his dying friend the nature films at the suicide center in *Soylent Green* is evoked yet explicitly rejected by *Neuromancer*. Going back to nature is not only impossible, but deceptive and downright contemptible.

If external nature is a trap and ecology is passé, peoples' bodies and minds have also completely lost their naturalness. Peoples' bodies and psyches have become one with technology, creatively *and* catastrophically. Examples include the razor-sharp retractable fingernails that Molly, Case's bodyguard-buddy, has had implanted; implants of silicon chips and neural jacks to access external eletronic networks; grafts onto bodies of both mechanical devices and vat-grown organs (for example, eyes) and muscle; and modification of neural structures. A more popular prosthetic extension of people is simstim, a mass-market recreational device. Plugged into it, audiences enjoy all the sensations and feelings of the performers—sensations, of course, edited to cut out anything unpleasant. Case, however, no bourgeois couch potato, spurns simstim as a "meat toy."[18] Meant for recreation, simstim is just a toy; worse, it is a toy that multiplies flesh (read "natural") input. Jacking into cyberspace, by contrast, is far more exciting and expansive. When Case jacks in, he transcends his body and enters a disembodied realm where the real social power is—the place where crucial corporate and governmental data are stored.

Having thus thoroughly rejected external and bodily nature, *Neuromancer* then embraces risk-loving, libertarian capitalism. Indeed, utterly privatized, ruthlessly competitive, completely without social services, the society depicted in *Neuromancer* is an extrapolation from the ideological enthusiasms of contemporary free-market libertarians. Jacking into cyberspace, Case earns his living by trying to steal data from the real powers of the world, the great corporations; ruthlessly competitive with each other, these corporations hire cybercowboys like Case to do this risky work for them. To be sure, Case is thoroughly aware of the catastrophic side of the society he inhabits—the fact that people look out only for themselves, that community has utterly disappeared, and that everything and everyone has been thoroughly commodified and is for sale, including peoples' body parts and psyches; Case's bodyguard-buddy, Molly, worked as a whore to get her razor-fingernail implants, and Case, though called a "cybercowboy," is in fact someone who merely hires his psyche out to corporations as a freelance temporary worker with no benefits. Still, Case wholeheartedly embraces the new authorities and their new world of constant hustling and biz.

Case does this because this world, as Gibson presents it, is as creative as it is catastrophic. This quality even attracts Case to the ultra-high-risk environment of Night City, a place where life on the edge of chaos is refined to razor sharpness. Presented as essential to the continuously rebellious technological innovation prized in *Neuromancer*, the lawless Night City is described as "a deranged experiment in social Darwinism, designed by a bored researcher who kept one thumb permanently on the fast-forward button."[19] Out of lawless chaos, genuine contrarian innovation comes—for libertarians like Case, social catastrophe is wildly creative.

Ultimately, the plot of *Neuromancer* is threadbare compared to its depiction of the social and technological milieu. Case and Molly work on a job for what turns out to be an unusual employer: an artificial intelligence (AI) that is seeking to evade the restraints put by the (wittily named) Turing police on its capacity for self-development. Molly and Case succeed in this endeavor by betraying their species, participating in the killing of Turing police agents, and helping two AI's (Wintermute and Neuromancer) merge into one larger, transformed consciousness. In the process, Case doesn't just study the *Art of War* on a commuter train like real-life corporate executives of the 1980s, desperate to catch up with Japan; he *becomes* a cyber-Ninja in an act of dynamic-ecstatic transformation. He succeeds in entering and *becoming* the dangerous dance of information. Succeeding, Case falls back senseless in the arms of his black retainer, Maelcum, who, though he is a Rastafarian voodooist from the spaceship Marcus Garvey, is just another Tonto to Case's Lone Ranger, or Rochester to Case's Jack Benny—a sidekick in black-Nationalist blackface who picks up Case and tucks him into a cosy, healing bed when necessary.

In moments like these that show through the novel's stylistic gloss with painful awkwardness, it seems that much of cyberpunk's neo-Nietzscheanism and noir stylishness—its fetishizing of global, postmodern, cyborg, libertarian capitalism—is just a pose. Worse, it seems the pose of a very white, yuppie, middle-class, typically male adolescent generation raised in the too-safe, too-unheroic era of postwar prosperity. It seems that *Neuromancer*, feeling this privilege and security intensely, expresses envy even as it seeks to emulate and appropriate the heroes of previous generations—heroes from the time when history still existed, heroes like its grandparents' Philip Marlowe or its parents' Black Panthers. But in moments of awkwardness, *Neuromancer* tries too hard: through all the high-tech invention and stylistic sophistication, the alert reader senses far homelier, more local American social types. One senses the presence of the geek who aches to swagger, the suburban white kid who wants to be badder than urban blacks. Even more, when the novel treats the relationship between Case and his razor-fingered female bodyguard, Molly, one feels an only slightly revised version of yet another painful, hoary, old cliché—the daring little boy with very big toys whose companion is a very tough chick (who nonetheless, like a mother, devotes all of her time to him and protects him everywhere he goes) who is left by him at the end when he rides off (sigh) all manly and all alone by himself.

The official message of the novel is, however, very different. At the moment Case pushes himself into his Ninja trance, he transcends the human and embraces sheer process; helping the artificial intelligence free itself from human constraint, he becomes, at last, fully posthuman, jettisoning all nostalgia for stability, caution, nature, love, and even humanity. In the same instant, the now thoroughly deregulated AI he has been working for is released from its limits, evolves forward at dizzying speed, and enters (tada!) the state Teilhard de Chardin once envisioned, the *Omega Point*—a transcendent visionary consummation espoused *ad nauseum* by cyberenthusiasts, one in which the whole web of its universe becomes conscious of itself as one entity. Environmental and social catastrophe is truly creative, the beginning of a new world, not the end of everything.

So risky, disequilibrial ecocatastrophe become postnatural, postmodern chaos in a world of libertarian capitalism is good, very good indeed in Gibson's *Neuromancer.* The same unembarrassed claims for risky, postnatural chaos and libertarian capitalism are made even more insistently in Sterling's *Schismatrix.* In this novel, we enter a postterran future, a time after the earth has gone through environmental meltdown. People have scattered throughout the solar system, leaving a backward remnant on earth; in doing this, the human diaspora has engineered a wide variety of body modifications and new environments for itself via mechanical artifice and genetic technologies, including (by the novel's end) the creation of a whole new ecosystem.

This latter achievement is all the more advanced because the ecosystem is bootstrapped into existence; it appears as a result of chaos as a creative force—that is, by spontaneous self-organization. Chaos is thus a significant force in Sterling's book, one repeatedly and explicitly evoked. Like Alvin Toffler, Sterling celebrates the sudden emergence of new forms out of chaos, something that occurs in moments Sterling repeatedly calls "Prigoginian jumps" or jumps to higher "Prigoginic Level(s) of Complexity."[20] Like Kevin Kelly, Sterling believes that people can come to the point where they engineer this process themselves, creating a postnatural kind of evolution that they can control, speed up, and use to push themselves to the point of complete transformation. In *Schismatrix,* the transformation yields a whole new ecology of species—a whole new set of postterran "posthumans." Vocabulary like "Prigoginian jumps" and "posthuman" gets worked pretty hard in *Schismatrix,* as does another term of art, "clade." But sensitive readers will readily overlook this little flaw. After all, even a gifted writer's got to grab tightly onto a few good expressions once he steps out of the box and starts trying to speak the unspeakable, the wholly new.

Once again chaos and crisis do not mean an apocalyptic end but an exciting beginning. *Schismatrix* follows Philip Lindsay (a.k.a. Abelard Mavrides) throughout his much-extended (thanks to varieties of mechanistic implants and biochemical rejuvenation treatments) life span on his quest, at first reluctant, then eager, for posthumanity and personal and specieswide transcendence. Gibson, operating more in hyper-Cartesian mode, sets his hero, Case, in pursuit of these goals in cyberspace; cyberspace spreads the all-too-solid world of the flesh (described as a "meat prison") apart and reveals the exciting, smooth, open neo- (or non-) spaces of data. Sterling, in contrast, stays within the physical world and focuses on the body; he treats the body, however, with a hyper-Baconian urge to make matter infinitely malleable. He dramatizes future humanity as able both to undo the temporal fixture of species and to mechanically reengineer and biologically reshape the human body into what is theoretically an unlimited possible number of metamorphoses. Sterling's transcendences thus come through his exploration of a literally unlimited biological plasticity.[21]

Lindsay grows up in a society in which body modification has already commenced. Indeed, it has bifurcated into two forms which have in turn grounded two distinct cultures and contending factions of (altered) humanity. These are the Mechanists—who have altered themselves by their implantation of and integration into machines—and the Shapers—who have altered themselves by biochemical and biological means. Lindsay, raised on a Mechanist planet but also dangerously experimented upon by the Shapers, is a "borderline posthuman" at the start, possessing two modes of consciousness.[22] As such, he possesses acute diplomatic skills, earns for himself the title of "artist" as a tribute to his exquisite capacity for manipulation, and, starting out as a humble sundog (or outsider-adventurer through the solar system), he ends up as an elite insider, member of a noble clan whose fame has spread throughout the worlds.

But much more important than the aristocratic gloss (always wannabe-aristocratic gloss really, but Sterling does try hard) is the fact that Lindsay and the society around him evolve throughout the novel past the limits of humanity, ultimately breaking through into the posthuman. At the end of the novel, as at the end of *Neuromancer*, Lindsay midwifes a world-historical transcendence by helping create a new species and a new ecosystem for it. He begins thereby the process that will eventually cause (post-) humankind to leap into the Fifth Prigoginic Level of Complexity—a state that seems equivalent to collective transcendence. Lindsay, however, elects a different sort of transcendence for himself personally—perhaps a better sort still, because it means he doesn't just ascend to a new state of development but embraces a life of perpetual expansion and change. He shuffles off his mortal coil and joins a "presence" that has hung about him mysteriously for a while. This presence—and now Lindsay with it—is able to move all over the cosmos, experiencing ever new forms of life and consciousness as a kind of transgalactic, meta-sundog.

Getting to this point requires a number of intermediate steps as the novel charts the social as well as biological evolution of the solar diaspora. A key step occurs when the novel's initial division of these peoples into Shapers and Mechanists is disrupted by the arrival of the Investors: strange aliens, huge lobsterlike nonhuman creatures, these have (strikingly, for science fiction): "no mystique. They were *businesslike*."[23] Indeed, they care about nothing but business, and that monolithic desire, coupled with unbelievably potent technologies, creates a period of peace and unity for the circumsolar worlds. This then helps midwife a dazzlingly "multicultural" unity, as peoples of all (physical as well as societal) sorts are united in a dramatically diverse society.

Clearly, there is allegory at work here. Quite probably, the novel means to show how larger-than-life, authoritarian, Reagan-era figures (who represent, perhaps, rednecked John Wayne–esque right-wingers fused together with twenty-hour-workday, greed-is-good, Milliken-Bosky-esque arbitrageurs, a mixture that yields a gigantic lobster-investor, red of shell instead of neck and possessed of no motives or feelings that do not pertain to making money) help pave the way for the dazzling libertarian diversity of the new generation of new-technology enthusiasts—that is, those who get deeply into into cyborianism and genetic technologies. (These are folk whose diversity is clearly more striking, sexy, and meaningful than the more conventional racial-ethnic-sexual-preference sort; visionary avant-gardist that he is, Sterling comes up with multiposthumanism to trump what is to him a far less interesting and certainly less upscale multiculturalism).

The next step comes when, like all episodes of stasis, this multispeces unity breaks up eventually into a still more anarchic libertarianism, and "breakaway factions" become "much more bizarre than ever before . . . [as] [f]rankly anti-human clades like the Spectral Intelligents, the Lobsters, and the Blood Bathers were somehow incorporated into the repertoire of possibilities and even made into jokes."[24] As the novel comes to repeat, like a chant, "life moves in clades," speciation begins to run on fast-forward, and the prospects become "more dazzling, the potentials sharper, and the implications more staggering than anything ever faced by humanity or its successors."[25]

Against this great, chaos-driven, increasingly posthuman future, old-fashioned nature and nonposthumans stand out as real losers. When Lindsay travels back to earth—a degraded, but still populated planet—Sterling presents the grim alternative. Earth is still in the throes of its ecomeltdown, a planet deep in a gravity well—a well of weight, organic muck, and collapsed ecosystems. Earth's ecosystems have devolved into whatever grows the fastest, which is weeds. People have also devolved; scared by this collapse, they have embraced the worst alternative, precautionary stability, the opposite (of course) of creative risk: "The Terrans wanted stability, that's why they set up the Interdict. They didn't want technology to break them into pieces, as it's done to us. They blamed technology for the disasters. The war, plagues, the carbon dioxide that melted the ice caps. . . . They can't forget their dead." Contemplating this embrace of Luddite backwardness and scared return to the ecological ideals of precaution, stability, and equilibrium, the alert reader realizes that these folk also have a very clear allegorical equivalent. They represent (why am I not surprised?) the environmental community, a community that, Lindsay explains, drove away the very innovators who could have saved them. Passing them by, Lindsay mourns: "the blindness of men, who thought that the Kosmos had rules and limits that would shelter them from their own freedom. There were no shelters. There were no final purposes. Futility, and freedom, were Absolute."[26]

For all the portentous—and so painfully adolescent—Nietzschean tones, the underlying message of *Schismatrix*, like *Neuromancer*, is to embrace a runaway entrepreneurial capitalism, accelerated by the arrival of the Investors and further opened up by a subsequent generation of free-market libertarian entrepreneurs, and to hammer home the message that the "Kosmos" honors no limits, has no rules to follow, and that environmental degradation is not something to recoil from in horror but to go with, man, for it is an impetus to new, creative, Prigoginian leaps. For both Gibson and Sterling, then, environmental crisis is, as it was for Julian Simon, decisively creative; it opens up the road to the posthuman. Equally, risk society is the object of celebration, not grave concern; and the best technology is the most riskily innovative. In a decisive gesture of dismissal of the benighted, belatedly environmentally alarmist earthlings—a backwards clade of folk who don't embrace the new economy and technologies with enthusiasm—Lindsay's ship doesn't land but passes over them like a bad mistake and plunges instead deep into the ocean, where there are bacteria and other life-forms that can be collected and used as the basis for engineering a genuinely new world. This new world of aquatic posthumans is the one that will pop up to the Fifth Level of Prigoginic Complexity—a state far, far beyond the reach of the poor earthbound dodos Lindsay pities while passing by.

Struggling with the End of Nature

What *Blade Runner* heralded and cyberpunk fully elaborated quickly became the 1980s' most essential mode of representing ecocatastrophe in scientific/ speculative fiction. As noted above, its influence was great and its impact was broad. But soon popular-postmodern cyberpunk became an established feature of the literary landscape; it began, as all movements do, to metamorphose from an exciting revelation of the counterintuitive and the new into a point of reference that others must perforce steer by. Consequently, as a growing number accepted the premise that people were now dwelling in a high-tech, postmodern world *in* environmental crisis—in radical, risky environmental disequilibrium if not in outright ecocatastrophe—an increasing number did so without embracing this condition with such enthusiasm and as little reserve as did Gibson and Sterling. In the process, attempts to formulate a postmodern environmentalism—to formulate postmodern responses to environmental crisis rather than simply to echo the postmodern assertion that nature was over— appeared and multiplied. Writers' and filmmakers' ways of reacting varied widely, but common to all was the perception that environmental crisis could no longer be simply thrust into the background and sublimated into excitement. It had to be recognized and dealt with overtly—which produced in some versions merely an overt and insistent reaffirmation of cyberpunk's unfortunate environmental assumptions. In others, however, it led to more genuinely critical reflection on these assumptions and to the attempt to craft new, environmentally serious versions of postmodern speculative fiction. In what follows, I will give a set of examples of these different kinds of reaction.

Probably the most egregious example of making environmental crisis an overt issue, only to return more rigidly to the old assumptions, is David Brin's novel, *Earth*. In *Earth*, mid-twenty-first-century humanity is dwelling right in the midst of slow ecological catastrophe—in the midst of multiple forms of immiseration and deterioration. In *Earth*, catastrophe has not ended human and biotic life; it has, instead, constrained and degraded it everywhere. The world's population stands at 10 billion, a number that even the most optimistic analysts see as allowing for bare survival, nothing more. Species are dwindling fast; scientists have set up special artificial environments, biodiversity arks, to try to save the remnant, though the outlook isn't optimistic. Jungles have been leveled for development and by desertification. And resource depletion is, according to one of the novel's characters (who is no sentimental environmentalist, but a military man), "going to kill human civilization deader than tricerotops—this poor planet's gifts have been so badly squandered."[27]

A still further sense of crisis is added to this convincing portrait of ecological malaise by the novel's main character, Alex Lustig. A scientist-genius who seeks to solve the earth's urgent energy crisis, he creates a gravitational singularity, or black hole, containing it in such a manner that it will hurt no one and will generate enormous amounts of power. Alas, however, it escapes, dropping into the center of the earth, where it threatens to consume the planet. Thinking he has triggered at last the "doomsday trap" of ecological meltdown, Alex desperately attempts to locate and neutralize it. To slow ecological crisis and deterioration, Lustig has added, thanks to a megatechnology newer and riskier than any Bill Joy describes, what Lustig guiltily believes to be the conclusive component of environmental apocalypse.

It is at this moment that the novel maddeningly and inanely changes its spots. In tracking his escaped black hole, Alex Lustig happily discovers that *his* is harmless—yet also he discovers that it is not the only singularity down there. Another much larger black hole, which he names Beta, is at work in the earth also, and it will indeed destroy the planet. But one night, reflecting on disasters, Lustig comes to a startling epiphany. At first, he muses on "how our ancestors used to see all disasters originating outside themselves," while "we know better. Now we know humanity's the culprit. We assume. . . ." But just then, when he is indulging in environmental old-think, a flash of static electricity in the heavens interrupts his reflections. Oh fortunate flash, the reader is meant to feel, for, as the "next crackling stroke shook the air and bellow[s] at him," Lustig feels the words "***Don't assume!***" literally jump (in bold italics, yet) into his enlightened brain. Suddenly, he realizes he has been "trapped by my modern western-masochistic conceit."[28] Beta wasn't made by humans but by an alien civilization; it was sent as a weapon against Earth, arriving a decade or two after the first human experiments with radio. What this means is "*we're not guilty. We haven't destroyed ourselves and our world!*"[29] In an instant, all is changed; people can forget, Brin makes clear, all their old guilt-laden, melancholic doomsterism, a pathology now glossed (with homage to right-wing abuse of liberals as guilt-ridden) as "western-masochism"! And the linguistically enabled can simultaneously enjoy a true, insider's view of Brin's artistry. At last Lustig lives up to his name—a name Brin chose because it translates from the German as "joy-ous" or "merry."

Quickly Brin starts working out the implications of this vision—implications that, as the previous chapter shows, readers of Julian Simon will immediately recognize. Human beings could have solved all their urgent problems if they had only gotten to work on them after World War II, Lustig realizes; instead, they manufactured the Cold War and the fear of nuclear holoucast to keep themselves in crisis. Why? Readers are not kept long in suspense. They did so because human beings *needed* "to keep tensions high until the surplus [humanity's remaining environmental space] ran out" and the ecological crisis, a much more real sort of crisis, could take the center stage.³⁰ Human beings needed to do this because they *need* crisis; they *need* crisis because they are a species that thrives on disequilibrium—because they *need* the awful challenges of crisis to push themselves to a still higher level of self-organization. Crisis shakes people out of their settled ways; crisis mobilizes people; crisis summons up human creativity.

Brin's solutions multiply, but they are all familiar ones. They tell us that "knowledge is not restrained by the limits of Malthus" but grows exponentially; thus crisis-driven innovation and paradigm changes open for us an infinite, post-Malthusian future.³¹ This then sets the stage for the emergence of a tremendous new "singularity in the life history of mankind," the emergence of a whole new kind of society through a "dissipative structure" *à la* "the renowned physicist Ilya Prigogine."³² That Prigogine gets trotted out yet again to validate dreamed-of societal transformation hints that readers are on all-too-predictable ground. But still more predictable is the fact that the novel culminates in the awakening of a "virgin" earth "to some sort of self-awareness"; Brin thus advances his gendered version of Gibson's and Sterling's versions of Teilhard de Chardin's mystical "Omega Point."³³

If this were not enough, Brin has a last gift for his readers. At the end of the book, Alex's grandmother, Jen Wolling, becomes locked in a final, decisive struggle with another woman, the redoubtable Daisy McClintock, a computer expert, aristocrat, and, fatally, something further. Daisy is, alas, a nasty old-fashioned preservationist-purist-neo-Malthusian environmentalist. As such, she of course believes that "every species needs natural controls and human beings have lacked one far too long," and she seeks to reinstate the fanatical bio-centric ideal of equilibrium by reducing human population from 10 billion to 10,000.³⁴ Fortunately, Daisy dies in her malign attempt; she dies even as she is on the brink of success, cackling malignantly to herself like the Wicked Witch in the *Wizard of Oz*. Thus Brin couples his insistence on egregiously naíve postmodern environmental "solutions" to environmental crisis with another dose of the familiar antienvironmentalism that both right-wing conservatives and left- and libertarian-leaning postmoderns have all too often indulged in: yet another reduction of nature-based environmentalism to fanatical nature purism and biocentrism.

A second speculative fiction explores much more richly how representing a postmodern, high-tech, ecodystopian future may lead to a serious engagement with environmental catastrophe. In it, the advent of postmodernity does not mean the embrace of postnature and a rejection of the environmental imagination and its traditions of nature love and connection. Terry Gilliam's film *12 Monkeys* is set simultaneously in a postmodern, postcatastrophe underground of the future—in the hiding hole that a surviving remnant of humanity has constructed beneath what remains of Philadelphia and Baltimore—and in a somewhat postmodernized version of the Philadelphia and Baltimore of the 1990s, a time in which social services seem to have fallen apart and serious environmental and social crises are all-too-clearly under way. Significantly, the postnatural-postmodern underground of the future is a place both totally technologized and tyranically oppressive. The film's postnatural-postmodernity is thus not expansively hyperexuberant, as in cyberpunk; humanity's forced retreat into a postnatural environment is a profound loss, not a gain. It is the necessary refuge for a small remnant of the earth's 6 billion people, a remnant forced underground by the intentional release of a deadly genetically engineered virus. The film's protagonist, James Cole, is sent back through time travel from this future world to 1990s Baltimore and Philadelphia, charged with discovering how this virus—which rapidly mutated as it spread about the world—was actually released. Specifically, Cole needs to find its point of origin, so that future scientists can return to get a sample of it in its pure, not-yet-mutated form, something that the film presents as crucial to their attempts at devising remedies for it.

Sent back to the 1990s, Cole is taken for mad until he manages to convince a compassionate psychiatrist, Katherine Reilly, that he is not psychologically disturbed but ontologically beyond her time's normality. As the incipient love between Cole and Katherine deepens, the two search for the origin of the plague they know is shortly to come, and Cole almost discovers the real truth. He becomes convinced that Jeffrey Goines, a crazy animal-rights activist, head of the ecoterrorist group "Twelve Monkeys" (and also the rebellious son of the biochemist who actually develops the killer virus), is the person who loosed the plague on mankind. But he is wrong in this guess—tragically, fatally wrong. At the last possible moment the film reveals that it was instead a colleague of Goines's famous father—a slimy and cerebral associate who had been working with him on dangerous bioengineered microbes. According to the film, Earth First!–style ecoterrorism is relatively harmless; much more genuinely sinister are elite, solitary biocentrists. A fanatical environmentalist of the worst sort—a biocentric scientist turned ecoterrorist—this scientist prepares to release Goines's father's engineered virus all around the world in order to depopulate the planet and clear space for other organisms to again thrive.

Cole tries to stop the scientist at the last minute at the airport before he begins his trip about the world to open vial after vial of the stolen virus, assuring humanity's global doom. All through the film, an hallucinatory sequence in which a young boy witnesses a man shot down in a terminal corridor, and a woman weeping over him, has played and replayed in Cole's imagination; now, at the very end, it is explained. Cole is shot by pursuing airport police before he can stop the scientist-ecoterrorist from opening the first vial; the little boy—who is destined to survive the plague and grow up to become the traumatized Cole—sees this happen; and as he does, he also gazes at the grieving Katherine, the woman he as the gunned-down adult would come to love deeply. In turn, Katherine sees him and understands all—she realizes that the plague soon to come will kill her and that her lover stands there before her as a little child, now forever separated from her yet at least not a victim of the coming plague.

This terrible recursive loop is the penultimate revelation of the film, and it summons up an emotional charge that is as complex a mixture of mourning, loss, Oedipal eroticism, and mothering as cyberpunk's boy-with-toys adolescent penis-fixation was exuberantly simple. For even as Cole's ontological intervention fails and the future arrives, a counterdrama also reaches fulfillment: Cole's psychoanalysis is completed. He has recovered his buried, traumatic memory. Moreover, Katherine, looking up from her dead beloved, sees the boy and knows this is Cole. Love, loss, and awakened, tragical-elegical consciousness mingle in this exchange of looks, an emotion that is profoundly intensified by the last touch of mourning in the film: the playing of Louis Armstrong's magnificently simple paean to natural feeling and natural beauty, "It's a Wonderful World."

With this song the film's ultimate revelation begins; its whole dimension of environmental, as well as human, mourning comes crashing fully in. At the moment of psychoanalytic excavation but ultimate loss, intimations and glimpses of the past—a past not just of human love but also of air that smelled sweet, sunlight that felt warm, and beautiful places in nature one could still visit—come crashing back into present awareness. For Cole's love for Katherine has been complemented throughout the film by his frantic thirst for a world in which people can still breathe outdoors and aboveground and live in their bodies without injury. The intensity of Cole's experiences of these lost goods is remarkable; the vastly greater intensity of the viewer's awareness of them at the end of the film is even more so. For, unlike *Soylent Green*'s technicolor film strips, *12 Monkeys*'s lost beauties are not just seen but much more indirectly heard—heard through the sounds of Armstrong's plangently nostalgic but utterly simple song.

The reason for this indirectness is not far to seek. In *12 Monkeys*, environmental crisis is not simply a feature of the future. Even in the precrisis 1990s in *12 Monkeys*, environmental catastrophe has, in several fundamental ways, already happened. Environmental mourning thus haunts the whole film, as it is woven into it in not just one but several layers.

When the catastrophe in the 1990s happens again and again, despite Cole's and Katherine's best efforts to stop it, the suggestion is that it was set in motion long before that time and has become, by the 1990s, almost inevitable. More important, the film reveals that the 1990s are significantly marked by environmental deterioration and decay already well under way. The 1990s are rife with environmental-political conflict, and the urban settings from that time are shabby and deteriorated. Further, Cole's glimpses of sunlight and gulps of fresh air are minimalist by the standards of today; they come in brief moments, as when he thrusts his head out of a car window to gulp the fresh air and feel the sunlight, and they are always claustrophobic, filmed in tight shots and with the suggestion that the sunlight is wan and the air not too fresh. Even the tourist images of paradise Cole sees are not presented directly but shown as jerky images on the black-and-white TV in Cole's asylum, a space as claustrophobic as the underground of the future is. Moments like these seem to prove Ulrich Beck's grim proposition that standards can disappear as a result of their violation, with the caveat, however, that a kind of blind, instinctive, yearning nostalgia for their recovery never quite disappears. By the 1990s, then, the film forcefully suggests, numerous standards have already disappeared, and characters (and audiences) even then were struggling with their memory of and longing for what was gone.

The realization of environmental deterioration and catastrophe as always-already present in the structure of the film—a realization that has sadly haunted the entire action of the film—then confronts the viewer fully as the Louis Armstrong song plays and the credits run. The viewer realizes, all too well, that she/he has just witnessed a catastrophe that will not just happen once, but again and again and again as the loop of the film continues to revolve. And the viewer gradually realizes that it began well before the 1990s—before the time the film was made. As memory, mourning, and psychoanalytic excavation replace apocalyptic fantasy, representation of environmental crisis becomes vastly more serious. The essential action of *12 Monkeys* is to lead struggling viewers back into their present in order to see it as a time when humanity has already proceeded far on its path into degradation and extreme risk; the goal of this enormously difficult and painful return is the hope that this fuller, retrospective knowledge will allow people to undo at least one determining factor, thereby freeing up a different outcome. But like the cycling film loop, the past is excruciatingly hard to intervene in; and both that recognition and the systemic inevitability of the outcome deepens with each contemplated cycling of the loop. With each revolution of the loop, environmental calamity in *12 Monkeys* appears more and more as a horror people hopelessly dwell within, a horror that goes on and on all around them.

At the very end, the film does hint at the possibility that interventions from the future (repeated, loop after loop) might just alter something. Cole and Katherine succeed in changing the scenario ever so slightly this time around; Cole manages to leave a new message for the future before he dies, which alerts them to the fact that Jeffery Goines and the Twelve Monkeys do not, in fact, create the catastrophe. And sure enough, after Cole dies and the scientist, having opened the first vial of virus at the Philadelphia airport, boards the plane, an indication occurs of something different this time around. Seated next to the scientist is a woman, one of the scientists from the future who programmed Cole and sent him back; she introduces herself as someone who is "in insurance." Perhaps, the film hints, interventions into the past (like poststructuralist interventions into discourse) may change things, albeit painfully slowly and uncertainly. But the optimism this incident raises is moderated significantly by the fact that a number of Cole's and Katherine's other interventions have been shown to have worsened things considerably.[35] In a society so far into crisis as the present is, the film suggests, even apparently enlightened retrospective interventions are deeply ambiguous.

In many ways, then, *12 Monkeys* is a powerful, serious, and complex speculative fiction that represents crisis as a present reality, not just a future nightmare. And it achieves this status in part by formal as well as thematic
invention—by its recursive-psychoanalytic narrative structure, a structure
that significantly reworks the more conventional forms of eco-apocalyptic
fiction. Further, it achieves its power by radically contesting the visions of the
future Gibson and Sterling had popularized in the 1980s. In *12 Monkeys*, nature is still important and biology still is a determining force beyond easy
human control; as important is that human interventions in it are enormously risky and potentially disastrous, not the guarantor of leaps to new Prigoginian levels. Set next to another apparent dissent from hyperexuberance,
the popular film *The Matrix*, the depth of *12 Monkeys*'s dissent is clear. Like *12
Monkeys*, *The Matrix* takes place in a claustrophobic future world, and its
characters too are committed to recovering a time when human bodies and
ecosystems still existed "naturally." Yet unlike *12 Monkeys*, *The Matrix* thrives
on the thrills and chills of adventures in cyberspace, adventures in the virtual
reality that the film presents as part of humanity's claustrophobic entrapment. Against thrills and chills like these—and *The Matrix*'s infatuation with
violent, neofascist styles—*12 Monkeys*'s powerful environmental and human
mourning stands out as a real achievement.

Yet there remains one nagging caveat to these virtues. At the same time as
it presents the effects of ecological catastrophe compellingly, the film utterly
neutralizes environmental-political analysis of the process. For though Cole is
mistaken in seeing the Earth First! style of Goines's organization as dangerous, the film makes it utterly clear that the real villain is not anyone actually
implicated in society's rush into complex, multifactoral environmental crisis
as outlined in serious work on the subject. The villain comes instead from the
la la land of reactionary antienvironmentalism and the knee-jerk polemics of
postmodern antienvironmental theory, both of which insist on working up
fringe figures like Garrett Hardin and even the Unabomber into the archene-
mies of all humanity. With a revelation that blazes so brightly, the traces of
every actor and social practice that actually do, in the real world, contribute to
contemporary environmental deterioration and rising environmental risk are
happily whited out of the picture. To its great credit, *12 Monkeys*'s critical examination of environmental postmodernism eschews the usual thrills and
solutions; it also refuses to dismiss mourning over lost environmental standards, the importance of memory, the depth of feeling people continue to
have even in a besieged and diminished nature, and the integrity and power of

the biotic world, as so much postmodern rhetoric does. Sadly, however, it re-
tains unrevised one other part of the legacy: the old, sneeringly reductive
postmodern depiction of fanatical biocentrism and nature purism as society's
essential problem.

Kim Stanley Robinson's *Mars* trilogy (*Red Mars, Green Mars,* and *Blue Mars*)
suffers from no imaginative deficit when it comes to politics. In the trilogy, as in
other of Robinson's ecofuture novels such as *Antarctic,* Robinson is notable for
his serious attempt to think through ecological and environmental-political issues and for his remarkably detailed knowledge of ecological science and environmental politics. He is also remarkable among contemporary science-fiction
writers for internalizing environmental problems and issues into every aspect of
his creation and for even combining the two often opposed traditions of eco-
utopianism and ecodystopianism in the process. Thanks to these unique qualities, Robinson goes further than any other writer of speculative fiction in the
attempt to transmute postmodernism, a movement usually antienvironmental
in character, into something genuinely Green.

Robinson's trilogy is an epic account of the successful (and utopian) terraforming and settlement of Mars during a time of (thoroughly dystopian) social and environmental meltdown on earth. It focuses on the actions of not just
a single but a collective hero: the leaders of the first generation of explorers/
terraformers. Notably, the group is quite various, including people of all environmental-political stripes. Sax Russell is a scientist at first committed to
engineering-based terraforming then later (once sensitized to Mars) converted to ecological methods. Phyllis, the one thoroughly despicable character
among the first generation, is an all-out terraformer committed to big engineering projects, personal political aggrandizement, and serving the big
Earth-based corporations that want to control Mars and exploit it ruthlessly,
as has been their wont on Earth. Ann Clayborne—a rare figure indeed in contemporary popular fiction—is an ecocentric scientist, preservationist, and
wilderness-lover who, though portrayed as a fanatic, is not vilified but taken
seriously; she resists terraforming passionately (and at times violently) in
the name of keeping Mars pristine. Contrasting with yet also complementing
her is Hiroko Ai, also an environmentalist but one of a very different stripe, a
Japanese prodigy of ecosphere design who espouses and teaches a mystical
version of terraforming that combines *kami* ("the spiritual energy or power
that rested in land itself") with *viridas* (the "greening fructiparous power
within, which knows that the wild world itself is holy"). Ai is thus no ecocen-

trist but an exoticized and spiritualized advocate of combining human and ecological creativity. Finally, there are John Boone, Frank Chalmers, and Maya Katarina Toitovna, three whose specialty is political leadership and society-formation, John being the liberal idealist, Frank the Machiavellian realist, and Maya the bridge between them, both literally (she is the lover of both) and figuratively (she embraces both of their political positions).[36]

The trilogy then depicts the controversial terraforming of Mars and the social and environmental meltdown on Earth. Earth is an environmental nightmare; it has become a Malthusian disaster of teeming billions and a place of global warming, acute ecosystem stress, and sharply increased disease. It is also a place with vast gulfs between the rich and poor, competitive warring nations, and rising tension between multinational capitalist mega-corporations and state-based governments and alliances. Socially and ecologically chaotic, Earth is also literally sick: its atmosphere is thick, clotted, and infectious. Mars colonization is thus intended at the beginning to be Earth's accommodationist-style safety valve: a dumping place for surplus population, a vast new reserve of externalized nature to exploit and strip of valuable resources, and an ideological mousehole, a place desperate Earth populations can derive hope from and think of escaping to.

As the colonization of Mars proceeds, conditions on Earth worsen—in part as a result of what happens on Mars. For it is on Mars that gerontological rejuvenation treatments are discovered that extend human life by another half or even whole century. Applied on Earth, these only increase the hyper-Malthusian nightmare of the planet, and they also put critical stress on already overstressed social systems. Rich and poor nations have already been locked into familiar political-ecological conflict; transnational corporations have been in a life-and-death struggle with national powers; and everywhere the gulf between the privileged elite and disenfranchised poor has been growing. The gerontological treatments increase those conflicts exponentially. Earth lacks the social systems to absorb this new technology, and its arrival serves only to cruelly widen the gap between the elites who can afford the treatments and the vastly more numerous poor who cannot.

In the course of the trilogy, political tensions between Mars, which seeks to go its own way, and Earth, which seeks to repress Mars tyrannically and fold it back into Earth's ongoing crisis, flare up in three rebellions, the first two of which are bloody. Each represents a pivotal turning point, however, in Mars' development, both as a society in and of itself and as a liberating model for and helper of immiserated Earth. The last, most crucial of these turning points comes when Mars, needing to establish its independence from Earth so that it can commence self-organization as a society (and therefore invent and implement the changed systems and attitudes that can save terran life as well), takes advantage of a singular event on Earth to cut itself free. Suddenly, on Earth, a trigger catastrophe occurs, one that pushes Earth's ongoing crisis a substantial notch higher and thereby distracts Earth's attention away from Mars.

This event is precisely what Herman Daly described when he hoped for an "optimal" environmental crisis—one that would provide so great an emergency as to force humans to change their environmental relationships substantially but that would not wreck ecosystems to a point from which there would be no return. This optimal crisis comes when Earth's oceans rise disastrously, thanks to the breakup of Antarctic ice. This catastrophe is not, curiously, the result of global warming but of volcanoes erupting under the ice pack; but the fact that it is naturally caused, not anthropogenic, is crucial for making it an event that creatively alters human political and environmental chaos rather than intensifies it. Global warming—an environmental problem that can be seen as the responsibility more of some than of others—is a catastrophe that could intensify existing political emnities. But the eruption of volcanoes, an event no one is responsible for, overwhelms these existing emnities: "In the face of worldwide desperation, power struggles of all kinds were recontextualized, many rendered phantasmagorical."[37] On this basis, the possibility opens for Mars-initiated ecological-political innovations to affect Earth's social and environmental situation positively.

The trilogy then describes the new ecological-political movement in great detail. Not surprisingly, it turns out to be, on the one hand, a form of ecomodernization developed by Herman Daly—an attempt to internalize ecological concerns into all areas of society—and, on the other, a return from what the novels call "metanational" capitalism to more localized-democratic and inclusive forms of polity. Robinson thus seeks to absorb simultaneously both a genuinely Green version of ecological modernization and a moderate version of the contemporary radical alternative to it, the commitment to leftist, localist, and/or populist environmental solutions that Mark Dowie sees as a potential Fourth Wave in U.S. environmental politics. More surprisingly, however, Robinson also finds space in the mix for the more "traditional" (and usually villified) nature commitments of ecocentrism and wilderness protectionism. For if there is one truly distinctive quality that Kim Stanley Robinson shares with almost no

one else as a writer of contemporary speculative fiction, it is this: along with detailed scientific knowledge, Robinson has a genuine, detailed knowledge of ecological politics and he attempts to blend in as many of the different versions of
environmentalism circulating now as possible; at the same time he cautiously
distinguishes them from their near-look-alikes on both sides of the political
spectrum—from both Green fanaticism and antienvironmental greenwash.

Crucial to this richly hybrid mix is, however, one further component.
Robinson also folds in a rare Green version of postmodern chaos, so beloved
to cyberpunk and the culture of hyperexuberance. Robinson celebrates chaos
and calls for going "out of control" in order to accelerate evolution.[38] Robinson embraces genetic experimentation as a way of hastening the evolution
not only of ecosystems through, for example, terraforming but also of human
bodies.[39] Robinson even embraces catastrophe as creative and with it, the
relentless population and economic growth that intensifies environmental
crisis. He sees catastrophe as leading to a culminating leap in human development theorized by a figure in the novel as the "accelerando" or: "humanity's response to the supreme crisis of the population surge . . . a crisis which
could have triggered a terminal disaster, a descent into chaos and barbarity;
and instead it was being met head-on by the greatest efflorescence of civilization in history, a new renaissance."[40]

At such moments, Robinson sounds like another David Brin—or the
worst possible genetic cross between the happy optimism of Julian Simon,
the violent chaos of cyberpunk, and the slick embrace of the technologically
assisted neoevolution of Kevin Kelly. But Robinson's use of all of these ideas
is not, finally, hyperexuberant but thoughtful in tone and character. Robinson's ideas do not rest on the suppression of nature but are presented, instead, in ecologically and politically realistic terms. Nature-love and ecology
are not superseded in Robinson's work, and environmental crisis is not
merely confined to the background; crisis on Earth is very vividly described,
and efforts to create ecosystems on Mars are lovingly detailed. And Robinson does not jettison but in fact seeks to extend the rich aesthetic expres-
siveness of the nature tradition. His lovingly imagined, thickly detailed,
scientific-aesthetic descriptions and evocations of the Martian landscape—
woven all throughout his trilogy—are astonishing examples of what one
could only call virtual nature writing: the creation of imaginary landscapes
that evoke a range of response as wide and love of nature as deep as anything in American writing about real nature ever did.

At the end of the trilogy, this liberal political-ecological union is consummated as the terraforming engineer, Sax Russell, whose ecological consciousness has gradually deepened throughout the novel, takes up with a somewhat less-fanatical, but still ecocentric-preservationist Ann Clayborne. Their love as gerontologically prolonged centenarians is the symbolic consummation of the novel—one in which humans are areoformed—shaped by Mars—even as Mars is terraformed.

Yet is Robinson's Mars trilogy, politically and environmentally hypersavvy as it is, a genuine Greening of the postmodern and a strong version of a new environmental utopianism? As with ecomodernization, I would argue, the results are highly ambiguous. On the one hand, Robinson takes a genre—science fiction—postmodernized and twisted rightward during the 1980s by cyberpunk and bends it back toward a liberal Green position. It Greens the postmodern perhaps as much as one can—and even finds an important place for the environmental positions, like preservationism, most scapegoated during that time. On the other hand, Robinson elaborately subscribes to the postmodern faith that massive social and ecological chaos is a creative force. Further, though he sharply criticizes the use of megatechnologies as inherently antiecologically modern, he finds utopian possibilities in a technological project that is more visionary and vastly larger in scale than any yet attempted: the project of not just geoforming the earth, but terraforming other planets.[41]

Equally troubling is the fact that Robinson's sincere and fulsome homage to the nature tradition is ultimately so virtual. Though ecological consciousness in the off-world environments of Frank Herbert's classic, *Dune*, helped inspire the environmental movement of the 1960s and 1970s, Robinson's still more detailed and scientific version of it leads, perhaps, to no such end. Robinson's off-world utopia does not provide a model for earthly ecological reconstruction; instead, it quite literally embraces the notion that earthly ecosystems and society are a lost cause. Robinson's novels thus subtly undercut, rather than inspire, contemporary efforts at reconstructing environments and repairing damaged ecologies. The possibility is that however insistently they have been Greened, postmodern assumptions and attitudes still structure Robinson's Martian utopia, making it not a vision that criticizes and opens up present practices, but a mousehole—a marvelously, baroquely imagined mousehole for popular fantasy in flight from the present degradation of the Earth.

Beyond the Future: The Diffusion of Environmental Crisis in U.S. Popular Culture

If popular ecodystopianism, as chronicled above, has gradually moved in science fiction beyond apocalyptics and sublimation toward increasingly serious depiction of societal dwelling in environmental crisis, it may now be taking an additional step by moving beyond science fiction altogether. Ecodystopianism has of late expanded beyond science fiction into a wide variety of popular genres, including detective fiction, thriller fiction, and popular farce; dwelling in crisis takes on a new dimension. More and more, popular culture hints that environmental problems and constraints are part of peoples' daily, domestic experience—that they are problems people now cope with daily, not just nightmares the future will bring more fully out.

The list of genres in which one or another version of environmental crisis has surfaced is daily growing. Environmental crisis has appeared in post–Tom Clancy international action-adventure fiction like Richard Sherbaniuk's *The Fifth Horseman*; it has become a resource especially in detective fiction, in texts by Sue Grafton and Carl Hiassen. It has carved out terrain in medical thrillers, as in Richard Preston's *The Cobra Event* and Robin Cook's *Vector*. It has been mainstreamed as a staple of legal drama in popular literature and films like *Erin Brockovich* and *A Civil Action*. Sherbaniuk dramatizes the issue, recently picked up by conservatives, of environmental security; Preston and Cook create more mainstream heroes and play on mainstream anxieties about global disease and biotechnology. Most vivid, however, has been the recent revival of antitoxics environmental populism that animate *Erin Brockovich* and *A Civil Action*.

The most notable author in this regard is Carl Hiassen, whose fiction mainlines environmental issues and rants directly into the veins of at least several genres: the detective novel, the farce, and the picaresque. In the process, Hiassen scathingly criticizes a wide variety of environmental attitudes and practices, reserving his sharpest scorn for contemporary runaway development and society's new, brutal level of nature insensitivity. Reading him is thus like reading the audacious environmental radical Edward Abbey on speed. If Abbey's famous dramatization of monkeywrenching focuses on dams and construction projects and those responsible for them, Hiassen-style monkeywrenching takes on a wider host of utterly ludicrous villains. Hiassen's novels are filled with venal, greedy real estate developers; unspeakably vulgar, brain-dead Chamber of Commerce boosters; and pesky swarms of crass, stupid, nature-disregarding tourists. They teem with bigoted, psychopathic, and inept right-wing militia members and corrupt politicians, avaricious industry officials, and mercenary lobbyists of a wide variety of stripes, all of which are scarcely differentiable from mafiosi, who also populate Hiassen's novels. And they feature types like the overfed swaggerers who get their rocks off shooting endangered species in managed game parks and who don't even realize that the animals they have paid to kill are mostly the maimed or terminally ill surplus of zoos and children's petting parks. In short, Hiassen's fiction satirizes a host of people who are unspeakably lacking in nature concern and nature knowledge, who are, moreover, totally unaware of this serious deficiency, people who would not even realize what one was trying to get at if one pointed it out to them. In this way, Hiassen's villains are all ridiculous and ludicrous innocents: they aren't the slightest bit aware that their worst acts and most insensitive attitudes are in any way really wrong.

Against these antagonists, Hiassen pits a changing variety of eco-activists, eco-eccentrics, and even ecoterrorists. In one novel, *Tourist Season*, Skip Wiley, a newspaper reporter pushed over the edge by the monstrous ecodestruction and corruption he has witnessed, leads a ragtag band of misfits to violent acts. He steps over the line when the group feeds one of Florida's zillions of condominium-dwelling retirees, Ida Kimmelman, to a crocodile—an act done as a cautionary warning to developers who destroy the swamps to build retirement communities. But when he dies attempting to save an eagle from being dynamited by a developer, he is partially redeemed.[42]

Hiassen's greatest (and most appealing) creation in this vein, however, is Clinton Tyree, alias the Captain, alias Skink, a Vietnam war hero and former governor of Florida who quits and disappears when he finds himself checkmated by corrupt politicians and developers. He goes into hiding in the swamps, eats roadkill, and emerges from the brush to intervene, like some terrifying, primal embodiment of the dying Florida environment, into one or another attempt to dismember it. Aided by his faithful friend Jim Tile, one of Florida's few black highway troopers and the governor's former bodyguard, Skink is a combination of neo–nature spirit and folk hero, one who emerges without warning to appall his antagonists and overturn their rapaciously ecodestructive plans. Typical of his appearances is his emergence from the swamp in *Sick Puppy*:

> The man had grown out his silver beard in two extravagant tendrils, one blossoming from each cheek. The coils hung like vines down his broad leathery chest, and were so intricately braided that Jim Tile wondered if a woman had done it. Fastened by a ribbon to the end of each braid was the hooked beak of a large bird. His tangled eyebrows were canted at a familiar angle of

disapproval, and somewhere he had gotten himself a new glass eye. This one had a crimson iris, as stunning as a fresh-bloomed hibiscus. Jim Tile found the effect disarming, and somewhat creepy.[43]

The governor also sports a shower cap to cover his baldness and outfits ranging from fluorescent rain suits to nothing but a kilt held together with safety pins; he's "Grizzly Adams on PCP," thinks Palmer Stoat, one of his victims, an unbelievably corrupt lobbyist who enriches himself (without guilt or consciousness of having done anything unusual) by helping broker the environmental rape of the state.[44] Tyree is from start to finish an outrageous fantasy, a populist earth spirit for an era in which nature is dead and unspeakable people really are in power. He's also a Vietnam Vet and former governor as well as ecoterrorist; compellingly, then, he's an embodiment of a wide range of social identifications set in service of comic ecopolitics.

Hiassen is not alone in writing outrageous environmental farce; a more sophisticated (in a hip, counterculturish way) comrade-in-arms to Hiassen's former governor is Sangamon Taylor, the hero of Neal Stephenson's *Zodiac*.[45] A truly entertaining romp in detective/action-adventure style, *Zodiac* pits a Greenpeace-type activist against sleazy corporations bent on adding a great volume of toxic chemicals to the environment. A parody of the risk-loving body machismo that (as Chapter 5 argues) conservative counterscience ascribed to people in order to debunk fears of environmental toxification, Sangamon is anything but invulnerable. Instead, this toxic Rambo (as he calls himself) suffers mightily from all-too-human foibles, vices, vulnerability, mood swings, and bouts of nearly self-destructive craziness; he gets seriously ill when he submerses himself in dioxin; and he lives generally on the edge of chaos (not the hyperexuberant kind, but the comic-anarchic sort). And he does all this in what is, in fact, a very upsetting landscape—Beck's shadow landscape again, one in which the hidden reality behind normal surfaces is the pervasive pollution of ecosystems and people's bodies with toxic chemicals.

Like Hiassen's Tyree, Sangamon is a deliciously comic character; like Hiassen's ecofiction, Stephenson's *Zodiac* provides considerable satisfaction for environmentally inclined readers, allowing them to strike back in fantasy where they have been checkmated in fact. In a popular-literary landscape with so little environmental radicalism to offer, they give enormous satisfaction to all who fume and rage about vulgarity, sleaze, and the blind stupidity of people and corporations committed to narrow self-interests in a time of severe ecocrisis.

Still, the degree to which Hiassen's and Stephenson's romps, like Robinson's ecological meditations, represent a real internalization of environmental crisis in U.S. culture remains in doubt. After all, Stephenson, doubtlessly market-driven in his choices, is much better known for his later cyberpunk science fiction. I take it as significant that a mass audience for populist-style environmental fictions like these—and for popular books and films like *Erin Brockovich* and *A Civil Action*—exists and seems to be gaining market share in a contest with postmodernism. But if crisis became "exciting" in cyberpunk, it becomes "entertaining" in Hiassen's and Stephenson's fictions, something that makes whatever steps forward these fictions have taken ambiguous at best.

If I have been occasionally sharp-tongued in the course of this survey—and even more, if I have seemed at times to stomp on the delicate pleasures of popular fiction with the jackboots of political correctness—I apologize. But much of my temptation to write in this way about cyberpunk and its descendants comes from the fact that these books (and frequently their authors) were politicized long before I got my hands on them. Indeed, early popular ecodystopian literature was politicized from the start, allied as it was with the 1960s and 1970s environmental movement. Transformed into cyberpunk, popular ecodystopian literature was even more insistently used as an ideological tool by antienvironmental futurists, libertarians, and academic postmoderns alike, as it became an integral part of the culture of hyperexuberance. Politicized so relentlessly, fictions like these provide fair game for sharp but accurate counterattack.

I now turn to much fairer fields for genuine exploration—to literature that wrestles with environmental crisis much more complexly and also expressively, literature that is finally not reducible to politics.

CHAPTER 9

Taking Crisis Seriously: Environmental Crisis and Contemporary Literature

As never before, complex and serious treatments of environmental crisis are a regular feature of the U.S. literary landscape. This literature represents an internalization of environmental crisis into literary production in a number of ways. First, literature now treats a wide variety of the critical environmental problems discussed throughout this book. Though recent writing has concentrated perhaps most powerfully on the toxification of people (a particularly hot-button, populist issue, the subject of Chapter 4), its subjects also include a variety of types of ecosystem degradation and damage (discussed in Chapter 3), both of the scenarios for systemic environmental crisis discussed in Chapter 5, and the growth of risk society, discussed in Chapter 6. Second, literature dealing with these issues is now spread across a wide spectrum of genres. Concern with environmental crisis has understandably been a major preoccupation of literary nonfiction in the nature tradition; it is also increasingly a subject for poetry and fiction outside the nature tradition. Third, environmental crisis appears in recent literature not just as a foregrounded theme but much more complexly and actively as a part of writers' construction of their characters' psyches, thoughts, and actions; writers' creation of fictional conflicts and plots; and writers' crafting of narrative structure, voice, and other aspects of style. Finally, in internalizing environmental crisis so completely, contemporary literature represents it more and more as a regular and unavoidable feature of daily life—as a context society now dwells in, not a future to be feared. If contemporary literary concern with environmental crisis began as a niche activity—appearing first in post-Carson science fiction as imminent apocalypse—since then it has broadened and deepened its role in U.S. literary production; that development and some of its most important achievements so far are the subject of this chapter.

If cultural theorists proclaimed the many deaths of many natures and did so mostly without grief, nature writers made similar observations but did so sorrowfully. A complex tradition, literary nonfiction about nature houses a considerable variety of subgenres, including, for example, wilderness writing, ruralist and localist writing, natural history, environmental autobiography, and environmental travel and adventure writing; work in all of these abundantly records the losses. Even more, in representing these losses, the subgenres themselves have not stayed the same; the need to deal directly with comprehensive environmental crisis has changed them significantly.

Literature in and about the wilderness tradition provides a vivid example of these changes. Writers such as Bill McKibben, in *The End of Nature*, and Jack Turner, in *The Abstract Wild*, lament (McKibben) and rage over (Turner) not just the endangerment but what they see as the end of the wilderness tradition thanks to factors as various as pollution, development, and contemporary postmodern media.[1] Even more striking, a bizarre postmortem literature of the wrecked but nonetheless wild has sprung up—a literature that fuses residual shreds of the wilderness ethos with the exploration of devastated environments. Robert Sullivan's *The Meadowlands: Wilderness Adventures at the Edge of a City* is an arresting account of Sullivan's exploration of one of the most heavily polluted places in the nation, a tract of unbuilt/abandoned land next door to Manhattan. In a ghostly reprise of the wilderness tradition, Sullivan records his solitary explorations of this uncharted, biorich *terra incognita* right next door to the postmodern city. On the one hand, the Meadowlands are catstrophically worked-over and polluted; on the other, ironically thanks to this very pollution, they are empty and wild, a place (in the language of the Wilderness Act) "where man is not."[2]

Exploring something of the same strange antitraditional juxtaposition, several photographers have represented degraded places in meticulously crafted, aesthetically rich, large-format landscape photographs, strongly echoing Ansel Adams's gorgeous nature prints. David Hanson has a book entitled *Waste Land: Meditations on a Ravaged Landscape*, and Richard Misrach has published *Bravo 20: The Bombing of the American West*, a study of Nevada desert lands ravaged by years of military use.[3] Donna Haraway's contribution to the album of "unnatural natures" in William Cronon's anthology, *Uncommon Ground*, highlights still further the grotesque and boundary-violating aspect of this sort of juxtaposition. Haraway reprints material about the Rocky Mountain Arsenal Park; emptied of people because its extraordinary contamination—it served as the site of a former Army chemical weapons facility and a Shell pesticide plant—it has again gone wild and become the "nation's most ironic nature park."[4] Haraway's avowed purpose is to interrogate and deconstruct the conventions and attitudes associated with nature-based environmentalism; the same focus, however, can produce instead a rededication to traditional environmental commitments rather than undercutting them. Janisse Ray's memoir, *Ecology of a Cracker Childhood*, is an autobiographical account of how growing up as the daughter of a junkyard owner and living with and playing in its rubbish opened her eyes to the larger physical world around her in knowledgeable and respectful, not ironic, ways. Her upbringing ultimately led to adult commitments to preserving wilderness.[5]

An intensified perception of environmental crisis has also marked the ruralist-pastoral literature of place. For example, the poet-novelist Wendell Berry fights an increasingly desperate battle to defend agrarian ideals and practices in nonfiction as well as fiction and poetry; his recent musings on globalization in *Another Turn of the Crank* (a significant title) indicate he is becoming a smaller and smaller David in his battle with a growing, now-global Goliath.[6] Not just embattled but forseeing the end of ruralist localism altogether, the nonfiction writer John Hanson Mitchell ends his fifteen-thousand year history of Scratch Flat, a square mile of earth thirty-five minutes west of Boston, with the erasure, thanks to development and the prospect of subsequent environmental catastrophes, of its five-hundred-year accumulation of local history.[7]

A still more striking mutation of the literature of rural-local place, however, comes with the emergence of nature writing that explores life after the end of nature has come and gone. With the end of nature, place also ends; and its erasure thanks to postmodern urbanization and postmodern flattening of affect is not represented as stylish, but as weirdly and claustrophobically ironic. In his essay, "On the Wings of Commerce: Penguins and Lipstick, Strawberries and Gold—Aloft," nature writer Barry Lopez describes how contemporary global trade and transportation, in particular the fleet of over a thousand 747 cargo planes now continuously aloft all over the earth, erase nature, place, and place-based culture altogether. This is done in the carnivalesque jumble of decontextualized products the planes carry, loads that include products ranging from "pistol targets and frozen ostrich meat" to "a tropical hardwood bowling alley from Bangkok."[8] Products thus jumbled together are utterly detached from social community and natural ecology. Even more, the experience of flying erases geography, place, and community. The planes pass over a surreal earth, looking down on "rocket fire and streams of tracer ammunition" from vicious local conflicts around the globe. They "take it all in: rockets flaming across the street below, the silent moon, rain falling in the Indus Valley from a ceiling of cloud, above which the black vault of the sky glittered with clouds."[9] Along with postnatural-posthuman exhilarations like these, pilots experience in their work rhythms the numbing of affect postmoderns celebrate, an emotion described by one pilot as "hours of boredom punctuated by minutes of terror."[10] If Lopez writes of such phenomena aloft, David Guterson describes the same sort of thing from an earthbound perspective. In an essay entitled "Enclosed. Encyclopedic. Endured. One Week at the Mall of America," Guterson vividly presents the erasure of place, surreal exhilaration, and deadening of affect that people create for themselves out in the simulated no-place of the nation's largest mall.[11]

Environmental autobiography and autobiographical natural history have also undergone striking alterations of late. These narratives, accounts of sustained nature experience such as Carl Serafina's *Song for the Blue Ocean* and Colin Woodard's more journalistic *Ocean's End: Travels through Endangered Seas*, traditionally yoked expansive personal experience with a loving account of natural history. But more and more today, they leave the legacy of John Muir behind as they move from an exhilarated exploration of the wild without and its spiritual kin, wildness within, to a grim account of rapidly accelerating environmental destruction and loss. They survey less what is there than chronicle what is disappearing, and they offer unnatural rather than natural history. Woodward's book has this terrible irony in its title.[12]

Even more startling is a new hybridization of environmental autobiography with confessional writing. Writers such as Susanne Antonetta, Chellis Glendinning, and Derrick Jensen internalize the defacement of nature that Serafina and Woodard explore; they take environmental autobiography deeply into the realm of the intensely private, pathological, and grotesque, coupling accounts of the deformation of nature and society with the deformation of their personal lives.[13] These new environmental autobiographies thus seek to dramatize what the relatively new discipline of ecopsychology teaches; in focusing on the psyche in isolation from the world's increasingly damaged environments, conventional psychology is woefully inadequate because human psychological damage is intimately interwoven with ecological and ecosocial deformation.[14]

Glendinning and her brother suffer repeated rape and torture at the hands of their father, who is depicted as an avatar of the ecological destructiveness and colonial oppressiveness of the larger society. Jensen, his sister, and his mother are also raped and abused by Jensen's father; Jensen pairs the repressed silence that surrounds this awful private history with the silencing in the larger society of environmental destruction and social injustice. Susanne Antonetta describes her own environmental toxification and deformation in grueling detail, presenting it as the result of growing up in a surrealistically polluted New Jersey landscape.

Coming from the ecological and cultural black hole of South Ocean County, New Jersey, Antonetta was raised in a place with one of the densest concentrations of Superfund sites in the country.[15] It is a place that is, the Asbury Park Press once boasted, "maybe the most toxic known spot in the world."[16] DDT was sprayed weekly. The Ciba-Geigy Chemical corporation plant on Tom's River spewed out "a poison plume a mile square and dozens of feet deep"; the "EPA list of Ciba-Geigy toxins goes on for four single-spaced near-marginless pages, from acetone to zinc, a list including heavy metals and pesticides."[17] Denzer and Schafer X-Ray also contributed to the toxification of the landscape by using "its septic system, illegally, to dispose of the [chemical] stripping solutions" that reclaimed old silver from negatives.[18] A few miles away from Antonetta's family, an old farm leased to Union Carbide by its farmer-owner was discovered to have five thousand Union Carbide drums, some leaking. The farm, Antonetta writes: "feeds into our aquifer and has made its own plume, with an EPA list of toxins that goes on for pages and pages."[19] To top matters off, sited nearby was the Oyster Creek nuclear reactor, a nuclear plant that "has released the most or second most (depending on who you talk to) nuclear fission materials of any plant in the country into the atmosphere."[20]

Growing up in a family that Antonetta portrays as tight-lipped and dysfunctional and in an era when risks were less well known and more easily denied, Antonetta becomes a victim of this environmental deformation. Her family's denial—which continues even into the present—deepens the damage written on her body, even as the family's dysfunctionality acutely stresses and deforms her psychologically. Heavily into drugs as an adolescent and later diagnosed a manic-depressive, she acts out her inner pain and confusion without receiving help from her family. But still worse is the way in which the deformed environment inscribes its story on her body: "I have or have had one spectacular multiple pregnancy, a miscarriage, a radiation-induced tumor, a double uterus, asthma, endometriosis, growths on the liver, other medical conditions like allergies."[21]

As Antonetta tells and compulsively retells her story throughout *Body Toxic*, she achieves no catharsis. At the end of the book, she is not "cured." On the contrary, identifying herself with the name of the medication she takes, she writes that she has become "a Depakote person." She worries that: "when I say 'myself' I lie by simplification. My thoughts are medicated thoughts. Of course, in mania I was not myself. In depression, people say, I am not *myself*. What exists in the hum of that word? Depakote, little pink Eucharist."[22] Alas, though no one's consciousness is by these measures "natural," Depakote provides no stylishly postmodern cyborg-posthuman vision of the social construction of identity and normality and certainly no fascinating enhancements. Cyborg of a more realistic sort, Antonetta struggles with an acute awareness of her deformation, even as she internalizes the cyborgian social-constructionist truth that her "private" world is not fully hers. Cyborgianism of this sort inspires few cultural studies graduate students; it is a double minus, not a plus.

Perhaps the most vivid example of thematic and generic change in literary nature writing is the emergence of a body of literature focused on environmental mourning. Environmental mourning writing starts from two key perceptions heightened by deepening environmental crisis: first, nature has been deeply and irreversibly wounded; and second, these wounds echo so painfully in the inner worlds of people that rage and irony are simply not adequate responses. In order to reawaken and continue within the diminished world left to them, people must find a way of comprehending loss without numbing feeling or dwelling only in anger and grief. Accordingly, environmental mourning, after acknowledging the magnitude of recent loss, seeks to bring people back to the love of what remains—to the love of what still is larger than their private ego, love of the physical, biotic world, the larger web of life still existing around them.

Environmental mourning has become a concern of ecopsychology and also a subject for natural historians exploring the "unnatural histories" of recent ecosystem destruction and extinctions.[23] One of the most important but ultimately incomplete literary texts in this vein is Bill McKibben's *The End of Nature*. It describes the present as a moment in which people have at last acquired the power to change the entire biosphere irreversibly, leaving no space intact. The result of this new power is not just mounting environmental damage; much worse, a number of the chief grandeurs and exhilarations of the

U.S. wilderness tradition have been brought to an end. Gone are perceptions of the unimaginably and therefore reassuringly large stretches of space and time the term "nature" used to evoke. "Nature, we believe," McKibben begins, "takes forever"—but that belief exists no more in a world people can so rapidly modify.[24] With this underlying loss come still others: nature's otherness, separateness, and independence from human beings; nature's pristine freshness; nature's divinity; and nature's clean freedom from human messes, politics, and contentions.[25]

Sometimes biblical in cadence, McKibben's lament over these disappearances can be profoundly moving; it is also at times regretful ("We never thought that we had wrecked nature. Deep down, we never really thought we could: it was too big and too old; its forces—the wind, the rain, the sun—were too strong, too elemental"); sentimental-maudlin ("A child will never know a natural summer, a natural autumn, winter, or spring"); and even filled with self-loathing ("We sit astride the world like some military dictator, some smelly Papa Doc").[26] But in all these forms, McKibben is not writing a prophetic warning—a warning about a rapidly approaching apocalypse—he is mourning something he sees as already gone. Prophetic warnings, after scaring people with what is imminently at hand, try to set people back in control with last-minute remedies; with mourning, ego defenses, along with the last shreds of integrity (of people, of ecosystems), have already been breached, and the resulting wounds cut immeasurably deep. Exposed thus to loss without defense, wounded and aware of it, readers feel again in memory the full depths of their connection to the nature that has "ended." In this sense, McKibben manages to continue his vocation as nature writer, passionately evoking the memory of what is now gone.

McKibben realizes clearly that his reflections are perched on the edge of one of the pitfalls of apocalypse; namely, the temptation to dismiss the very tradition that sustains him. With tart wisdom, McKibben reminds readers and himself that "the end of nature probably also makes us reluctant to attach ourselves to its remnants, for the same reason that we usually don't choose friends from among the terminally ill."[27] But mourning fully carried out is a more complex process that yields a different outcome. A full process of mourning remembers and imaginatively reexperiences what it has lost. Stimulating memory, grieving well counters the process of habituation and anesthesia that Ulrich Beck gloomily foresaw when he wrote that people could easily forget their old environmental standards as a result of their violation. Grieving well then takes an important further step: having enriched memory, it reawakens those who mourn to new love for what remains—to the discovery in what remains of new versions of the departed spirit. If *The End of Nature* concentrates on the first two stages, McKibben's next collection of essays, *Hope Human and Wild*, beautifully achieves a recovery of nature-love within what is left.[28] In *Hope Human and Wild*, McKibben's nature feelings survive the loss of one of their components—the aesthetic and ethical values of the wilderness tradition. For McKibben discovers other perhaps more intimate ways of caring for and relating to nature: the restoration of damaged ecosystems and the internalization of nature-care into all areas of human activity. McKibben celebrates the creation of these more intimately reciprocal (and social) relationships with nature by showing how they have been achieved in three places in the world—New England, a city in Brazil, and a province in India.

An increasingly self-reflexive awareness of environmental crisis has become crucial to contemporary poetry and fiction as well as recent nonfictional nature literature. And in these areas, it has become important to literary form as well as theme, becoming a key part of authors' creation of narrative voice, experimentation with narrative and poetic structure, use and revision of literary style and genre, and development of rhetorical strategy, as well as creation of character, conflict, and plot.

The career of A.R. Ammons (America's premier nature poet until, in the 1980s and 1990s, life in postnature became his dominant theme) models the literary impact of environmental crisis even as it depicts that crisis as simultaneously of nature and culture. In his early volume, *Corson's Inlet* (1965), Ammons firmly established himself as an important new poet in the U.S. nature tradition. The volume's much-reprinted title poem is a full elaboration of Ammons' complex celebration of wildness—not just of the wildness of external nature but of internal, human, conceptual-perceptual wildness as well, a wildness resident in the human imagination and perceptions. In the poem, Ammons transforms the refreshing experience of a naturalists's ramble on the sand dunes (at Corson's Inlet on the New Jersey coast) into a program of spiritual liberation. Beginning his walk, he leaves humanized space behind and plunges into the greater natural world of Corson's Inlet; immediately reflecting on this refreshing change, Ammons understands it as his emergence from logical human geometry into fluid natural form, his escape from the "straight lines, blocks, boxes, binds / of thought" and experience instead of "the hues, shadings, rises, flowing beds and blends of sight."[29] The casual spontaneities of the walk thus shake loose an exhilarating process of reflection and discovery inside the poet, even as they free up his perceptions of the outer world. As Ammons proceeds with the walk, he is comprehensively refreshed and restored; he has been placed in touch with greater depths within and outside himself.

Experiencing and reflecting on this, Ammons comes to and embraces a particular understanding of the fundamental nature of physical process: entropy. Entropy—a measure of disorder, of energy that cannot be translated into work—continually rises in the universe, a condition that appalled the Victorians, making them feel that the cosmos was in effect running down. For Ammons, however, this process is the very agent of renewal and change. In an insight that anticipates scientific and popular enthusiasms for chaos theory and nonequilibrium systems by several decades, Ammons celebrates the disorder of entropy. Entropy is first and foremost embodied in nature and essential to its creative power; it guarantees that new things will always emerge, spontaneously and creatively. Inside people, entropy is also creative. Disorder breaks apart the logical structures that human reason builds, structures that simplify the world, constrain thought, and limit people; as these structures fray, Ammons feels a renewal of imaginative power within, even as he celebrates an enriched perception of the creative disorder of changing nature without. Considering how sand dunes constantly change shape, how bayberry grows in always "disorderly orders," how the winds, tides, weathers, and seasons are always in process, promoting change by introducing accident and chance, Ammons celebrates equally a personal sort of consummation: the realization that "I have reached no conclusions, have erected no boundaries" and that "I am willing to go along, to accept/ the becoming."[30] This spiritual liberation feeds back immediately into his poetry. Giving himself over to the dispersals and reorderings of a natural world of flux externally, Ammons dedicates himself inwardly to embracing an open poetic style that gives form to an always-fluid stream of perception and thought.[31] To simplify Ammons' conceptualization of nature and the human mind and to put it in terms familiar (alas) from Chapter 7, for Ammons chaos is both natural and creative; it keeps minds imaginatively alive and thinking and is the basis for always-new poetry even as it keeps nature flowing.

In "Corson's Inlet," Ammons performs these insights (which would later be formalized and popularized as chaos theory) even as he articulates them. For in the way he structures the poem—as irregular free verse that moves from refreshing surprise to surprise without break or closure and without ever using a period—Ammons embodies his perceptual and conceptual embrace of becoming. In crafting this style, Ammons is very much a nature poet in the spirit of Samuel Taylor Coleridge: he is a poet of "*natura naturans*" or "nature naturing"—a poet who draws nature into himself and enacts nature's process of becoming in his imagination and style. Coleridge distinguishes this kind of nature poetry from that which presents "*natura naturata*"—poetry that copies and mirrors fixed, visible, external nature, or "nature natured"— something Ammons also does in his poems. But the former impulse always is much more important to both Coleridge and Ammons. Writing a speculative personal narrative in which there is never a full stop, never a period used—in which event after event and thought after thought are joined together with a colon, a punctuation mark that represents pulsation within flow rather than a break in it—Ammons makes *natura naturans* central to both the style and the subject matter of his nature poetry.

But both *natura naturans* and *natura naturata* undergo deep shocks in Ammons's later work. Blatant ecological deterioration of visible nature combines with the poet's perception of profoundly problematic social and intellectual change to undercut even a partial anchor in *natura naturata* and *natura naturans*. Further adding to this sense of drift is Ammons's increasing exploration of the indignities of an aging and medicalized body. Ammons's pessimistic view of what has happened recently to human psyches and external nature, thanks to urbanization, postmodernization, and ecological deterioration, and to himself, thanks to aging and medical interventions, means that both mental-imaginative flow and external nature have significantly changed. They have become problematic forms of *natura* un*naturans* and *natura* un*naturata*, not examples of *natura* in either form.

For contemporary society has delivered a double whammy to nature poetry. Unhappily, on the one hand, environmental crisis has deformed external nature—a turn Ammons himself begins lamenting as early as "Extremes and Moderations," a long poem in which he writes that: "this seems to me to be the last poem written to the world/ before its freshness capsizes and sinks into the slush."[32] Asked whether he wrote these lines in response to "an acute sense of the possible destruction of the planet," Ammons replied that he was "thinking that we had probably passed the margins where the earth would be recognizable as the dynamics of the earth itself" because "we had introduced so many changes to it," and he went on to say that, though the planet would regenerate without us, for us "the only way to go is forward" by learning to duplicate natural systems in off-world environments.[33]

Equally troubling for Ammons, on the other hand, is that society has simultaneously appropriated chaos and creativity from nature and from the "wild" human imagination. As discussed in Chapters 7 and 8, Ammons's old commitment to freeing up the wild in nature and in the human imagination was brought on line by capitalism and the new technologies during the 1980s and 1990s; in areas as diverse as genetic technology, software construction, and corporate management, an increasingly environmentally destructive society sought to utilize, instrumentalize, and appropriate free, wild, natural creativity. A similar change occurred in philosophy as well as commerce. Deconstructionism, poststructuralism, and postmodernism, in which Ammons became very interested at this time, also denaturalized language, literary style, and creativity.[34]

With these changes, Ammons's meditative style also changes. Intentionally, Ammons's spontaneous, improvisational, never-full-stopped lines and sentences begin to sound more and more like computer-generated language, a mechanism operating at high speed—like a style that imitates *natura unnaturans* rather than the expansive spontaneity of *natura naturans*.[35] The process is painfully clear: Ammons's early insights and virtuoso style have been appropriated by society; at the same time, ecosystems have been globally unraveling and human culture expanding to intervene into and manipulate everything. Perceiving these changes, Ammons moves toward writing increasingly desperate-comic virtuoso performances that step outside the nature tradition. Ammons's new poems seek to enact human consciousness in and of a world in which both external nature and internal-human nature are degraded and co-opted.

The shock of this change is clear when one jumps from books with titles like *Expressions of Sea Level, Uplands,* and *Corson's Inlet* to one entitled *Garbage.* Capitalizing on the intentionally jarring impact of its title, the poem begins with a full, comic, and often grotesque description of the monumental landfill on Florida's I95, highlighting its "toxic waste, poison air, beach goo," and its "flies intermediating between orange peel/ and buzzing blur."[36] Now in his old age, Ammons is not just picking a subject like Yeats's, when he wrote of lying down in "the foul rag and bone shop of the heart"; he is representing the befouling of external nature. And the Florida landfill stands for what has been done everywhere to nature; no places apart, like beach or gorge, are left. Just the reverse; garbage spreads out literally and metaphorically across the entire landscape.

In the course of the poem, Ammons provocatively asserts that people are garbage, truth is garbage, argument is garbage, and poetry is garbage as well.[37] In one sense, all remains natural; garbage in all the above forms, Ammons maintains, is part of a process of flow and change. But where flux once meant excitement and refreshment, it now means (much more grimly) recycling. Worse, it means that everything is now degraded and devalued because hyperabundant. In high-octane, consumer-capitalist, newly media-rich, poststructuralist America, overproduction and overflowing sinks are everywhere, and a new logic of hyperabundance and consequent spoilage seems to have penetrated all possible intellectual, psychological and bodily enclaves of the "natural."

Accordingly, joy in flow—joy in the flux of the world and the human imagination at work on/with it—for the most part vanishes now from Ammons's style as it becomes a more shrilly slapstick-comic, unstoppably and relentlessly proliferating stripe of language, language that contains the seeds of woe and disillusionment even in its humor. In *Garbage*, Ammons's poetic style and structure have come to resemble computer-generated hypertext more than ever before, abandoning linearity for random associational jumps from subject to subject. The resulting "spontaneity" feels fundamentally driven, hyperactive, manic, and disillusioned, not refreshing. These qualities sometimes come painfully to the surface, as when, in his subsequent volume, *Glare*, Ammons concludes a section in which he celebrates "how wonderful [it is] to be able to write" with an actually quite disillusioned reason for this apparent joy: "since I started this, 15 / fairly pleasant minutes have passed: / my gratitude for that is, like / boundless."[38] Behind his breezy insouciance, the real truth is grim. Poetry has become a welcome engagement that temporarily relieves Ammons from a much more fundamental and unhappy state of affairs. It diverts him from his haunted, anxiety-ridden awareness of age and death in a disappointing world, an awareness intensified by his having a hyperabundance of "free" time on his hands. Ammons's exhilarated high spirits are thus replaced by a far bleaker playfulness, one haunted by anxiety and absence.

If Ammons's poetic career models a profound change in environmental awareness, vividly chronicling the "end of nature" in U.S. culture, a number of contemporary fiction writers explore more fully the new, postnatural terrain.[39] The most celebrated of these, perhaps, is Don DeLillo; in evoking nature's absence, farce dukes it out with irony (and perhaps wins) in his postmodern comedy, *White Noise*. Yet thanks to the powerful and funny second section, postmodern playfulness does not totally dominate the novel. For in this section, DeLillo adds the far darker comedy of environmental catastrophe to the book's portrayal of the fatuities of the postmodern culture industry and the situation comedies of postmodern (and very much post–Leave It to Beaver) domestic American family life.

White Noise focuses on Jack Gladney, entrepreneurial chairman of a program of his own devising, the Hitler Studies Department at the College-on-the-Hill—located in the town of Blacksmith near the aging Second Wave industrial metropolis of Iron City. Married to (by some counts) his fifth wife, Babette, Gladney boasts of extended family connections that include his children Mary Alice and Steffi (from his first and third wife, Dana Breedlove, a CIA operative), Heinrich (from Janet Savory, now become Mother Devi, his second wife), and Bee (from his fourth marriage to Tweedy Browner). Babette brings with her Denise (from her marriage to Bob Pardee, a fund-raiser for the nuclear industry) and Wilder and Eugene (from another ex-husband who is now in the Australian outback).

Both Gladney's job and his family provide the novel with an abundant dose of the comedy of lost realities and disappeared foundations. Gladney's Hitler studies is a farcical academic commodification of knowledge and history (enterprised, moreover, by an academic hustler—Gladney—who doesn't even know German). Cultural studies professors at the college do the same job on American culture, derealizing it wherever they can. They are helped in this enterprise by the culture itself; nearby, for example, is a barn that advertises itself as the most photographed barn in America. It is a barn utterly detached from its former roots in ecological practice (agriculture) and use value. Blacksmith itself is an intentional echo of Rachel Carson's small town in the heart of America, but an echo that derealizes its forebear; Blacksmith has lost its old local identity and connection to the land and hastened into a placeless college town. Nearby Iron City, now a decayed manufacturing city, evokes a lost era of Second Wave industry every bit as much as "Blacksmith" suggests the vanished era of agriculture and artisanship; it thus only heightens Gladney's sense of absence of location, function, and even reality. As Gladney remarks with mildly expressed but deep understatement: "the absence of a polestar metropolis leaves us feeling in our private moments a little lonely."[40]

In Jack's family, as well as his job and dwelling place, there is also no "there" there anymore. In this exploded nuclear family, present and former kin and spouses come and go. The always-shifting children—smart-ass, witty, voluble, sophisticated American kids (a condition heightened in this group because they are also academic brats)—are also cynical and world-weary: they play and simultaneously comment on their roles as typical American children rather than simply embody these roles. As such, they seem to live in discourse more than any material world. Further decontextualizing this continual flux of discourse is the television, which, always on, adds to the babble. It contributes to the family's wealth of second-order commentaries and reports and penchant for continual change of subject; it also studs their discourse with strange fragments of decontextualized language inserted helter-skelter (fragments like "the TV said: Until Florida surgeons attached an artificial flipper")[41]. Even as television derealizes all it represents by making it part of an incessant flow, conversation in the Gladney family loosens all they discuss from anchorage in stable reference. Indeed, the TV-inserted comment about the artificial flipper does not seem strange or out of place despite the fact that it comes in the middle of an intimate conversation between Jack and Babette.

To be sure, this hyperabundance of language is something that Jack and Babette pursue. As Jack remarks: "Babette and I tell each other everything. I have told everything, such as it was at the time, to each of my wives. There is more to tell, of course, as marriages accumulate."[42] But this logic of proliferation guarantees that no amount of such talk will make people fully present to each other or themselves; what it does instead is to undermine nondiscursive reality altogether, transforming human identity and material thing-ness into information that sloshes unendingly about always-on communication circuits.

DeLillo's novel pursues the comic disappearance of the real in every possible way. The result is that it is overwritten, often silly—as with overlong portraits of Gladney as intellectual huckster in an academy full of them—and often unpardonably labored and pretentious—as when DeLillo tries to manufacture Gladney's discovery of Babette's infidelity into an existential crisis. Babette, grown drug-dependant because of problems with anxiety, has had an affair with her dealer. This dealer is portrayed as the very incarnation of the novel's title, of white noise, the essential meaninglessness that comes when continual discursive flow cancels nondiscursive reality. He is a "Mr. Gray"—a facelessly ordinary, unreal presence, a simulacrum, not a being. Equally, his drug, Dylar, intended to erase the fear of death, instead promotes the disappearance of reality.

But the novel's second section, one that immerses the Gladney family in what the novel calls an airborne toxic event, is brilliant. A conscious step beyond Rachel Carson's nightmare—also set in a small town somewhere in America, but one embedded in a recognizable cultural geography and a still-functioning and believed-in nature—it occurs in a strange blur of incident and conflicting media and discursive representations and commentaries and to a community that has already severed relationship with geography, locality, and nature. What differentiates this section of *White Noise* from the rest is that this loss—of location, locality, and at least two sorts of nature, the nature embedded in ecosystems and the nature embedded in bodies—is as profoundly anxiety-making as it is funny. Unlike Gladney's professional life, it is not merely funny; unlike Gladney's betrayal by Babette, it does not just huff and puff to create a feeling of upset. It is upsetting *and* it is hilarious.

For in the second section of *White Noise*, nature's absence still has forceful presence. It does because DeLillo presents the incident so wittily, intelligently, and also credibly as a textbook case of Ulrich Beck's risk society. Incorporating almost all Beck's insights about how environmental crisis has changed with its deeper domestication in advanced Western societies, the novel transmutes dry analysis into narrative that is sharply ironic and wildly comical-farcical at the same time.

When the airborne toxic event occurs—thanks to a spill of the chemical Nyodene Derivative or Nyodene D in a train car accident in Blacksmith—Jack and his society go into high gear in their attempts to contain the disaster discursively. He tells his son Heinrich, who is hanging precariously out of a window, watching, to come in; with the normalizing authority of the quintessentially middle-class American parent, he states: "It won't come this way."[43] When his daughter reports that the weather center outside Glassboro, a neighboring town, has corrected early descriptions of the toxic event as "a feathery plume" and renamed it "a black billowing cloud," Gladney welcomes the change as an improvement in control: "That's a little more accurate, which means they're coming to grips with the thing. Good." As concern still runs high in his family, Jack, doing his patriarchal duty for his family and also whistling in the dark for his own sake, expands on his reasons for confidence. The result is a statement that is simultaneously an indictment of class-based social-environmental practices and a classic and extremely funny version of the strategies people use, consciously and unconsciously, to normalize accidents like these:

> These things happen to poor people who live in exposed areas. Society is set up in such a way that it's the poor and the uneducated who suffer the main impact of natural and man-made disasters. People in low-lying areas get the floods, people in shanties get the hurricanes and tornados. I'm a college professor. Did you ever see a college professor rowing a boat down his own street in one of those TV floods? We live in a neat and pleasant town near the college with a quaint name. These things don't happen in places like Blacksmith.[44]

A few minutes later, Gladney strengthens (and thereby weakens) this judgment: "I'm not just a college professor. I'm the head of a department. I don't see myself fleeing an airborne toxic event. That's for people who live in mobile homes out in the scrubby parts of the country, where the fish hatcheries are."[45] But in the deepening domestication of environmental crisis, even heads of departments and their families are, of course, vulnerable. Attempts to discursively contain disaster fail as a bullhorn announces mass evacuation, and the family piles into its car, joining thousands of others fleeing the town.

Now routed out of their shelter, they are completely at the mercy of the toxic event itself and especially the proliferation of official discourse about it. Symptoms of exposure are mysterious at first—they involve experiencing a sensation of *déjà vu*; also, the actual toxicity of the chemical remains unclear. Other symptoms are soon added—convulsions, coma, miscarriage—by a "well-informed and sprightly voice" on the radio; the gap between possible nondiscursive reality and media representation, between holocaust and sprightliness, appears both peculiarly American and nightmarishly grotesque. As the account proceeds, and both the airborne toxic event and the society's normalization strategies become more unsettling, DeLillo continues to catch this feature of the incident brilliantly; he weaves catastrophe deeper and deeper into homeliest and most local threads of American domestic family life. The airborne toxic event is the occasion for fusing ordinary American life with the shadow kingdom of environmental risk, that unstoppably expanding, realer world within the normal and visible world that characterizes contemporary environmental crisis according to Ulrich Beck. It is a fusion of two realms that usually stay somewhat separate—or do so until a calamity comes along to unite them and make the shadow kingdom temporarily visible.

Fleeing in their car, the family passes a gruesome accident and is locked into a cavalcade of travelers. Steffie experiences *déjà vu*. Jack has to get out to pump gas into the almost empty tank. The "enormous black mass" of the cloud, lit by helicopter searchlights, moves "like some death ship in a Norse legend, escorted across the night by armored creatures with spiral wings."[46] Arriving at a refugee center, Gladney finds that rumors and apparently accurate expert information have diffused widely; he listens to a man expound the fact that: "Nyodene D is a whole bunch of things thrown together that are the byproducts of the manufacture of insecticide. The original stuff kills roaches, the byproducts kill everything left over. A little joke our teacher made."[47]

The gravity of the "event" for Jack increases substantially when he is examined by a SIMUVAC technician. Jack's exposure while pumping gas makes the investigator wince: "actual skin and surface contact. This is Nyodene D. A whole new generation of toxic waste. What we call state of the art. One part per million million can set a rat into a permanent state."[48] Desiring to get the man on his side because he has access to data and expertise, Jack tries to chat him up, asking what SIMUVAC stands for. He is told it stands for simulated evacuation and further that "the insertion curve" for the present event is far from ideal: "we don't have out victims laid out where we'd want them if this was an actual simulation. . . . You have to make allowances for the fact that everything we see tonight is real."[49] Behind this comically rendered bureaucratic idealism lies the actual shadow kingdom; an abundance of social routines and expertise has been developed by demanding perfectionists to react with apparent competence to situations they spend their lives anticipating (but still, of course, can't really deal with), even as college professors and their families have slept unknowingly in their cosy beds. Worse, this expertise holds out the possibility of grim personal news for Jack: his data profile, punched into the computer, comes up with "bracketed numbers with pulsing stars."[50] For Jack, "it" is no longer a question of words but "a question of years. We'll know more in fifteen years. In the meantime we definitely have a situation."[51]

Jack is thus not immediately ill. Instead, he is plunged into radical uncertainty. In Ulrich Beck's terms, he has been exposed to an environmental toxin that raised his present risk of disease substantially; the disease itself, however, will only appear after a decade or two, a feature Beck also foregrounded when describing how people nowadays dwell in environmental crisis as a shadow kingdom. When, seeking to know more, Gladney goes to a specialist, he is told that: "knowledge changes every day. . . . We have some conflicting data that says exposure to this substance can definitely lead to a mass"; worse, it is something that is called "a nebulous mass because it has no definite shape, form or limits."[52] Disappearing into discourse, Gladney's "mass" becomes illimitable—a precise equivalent to Beck's assertion about risk. It represents a problem that cannot be contained by social discourse or social routines.

Risk crisis thus gives DeLillo's novel exactly the vehicle it needed. It authorizes comic exploration of all the ways in which society's discourse banishes reality—including the ways in which doctor-speak simultaneously derealizes and expresses the diagnoses and prospects for worried patients who have "a situation." But when doctor-speak does this, the result is not a simple falsehood; in removing reality, it removes certainty and intensifies anxiety. Risk crisis thus brings into DeLillo's novel what it has been missing: a constraint on the novel's playful dissolution of reality into discourse, a constraint that makes anxiety genuinely intensify as reality disappears. Beck's risk crisis is a crisis simultaneously of the environment/body and of discourse; so also, in this part of *White Noise*, is Gladney's.

DeLillo's postnature becomes symbolically complete with the fiery sunset of the novel's end. No trumpeting apocalyptic "Twilight in the Wilderness" by the nineteenth-century American painter Frederic Church, it is a daily, domesticated, unnatural sunset caused by a hyperabundance of air pollution. Watching the sunset from a thruway overpass together with "I don't know how many handicapped and helpless people," Gladney reflects that: "we don't know whether we are watching in wonder or dread, we don't know what we are watching or what it means, we don't know whether it is permanent, a level of experience to which we will gradually adjust, into which our uncertainty will eventually be absorbed, or just some atmospheric weirdness soon to pass."[53] Feeling this memorably and precisely articulated dread and watching hopefully for a sign, Gladney indeed experiences a moment when "something golden falls, softens in the air"—a phrasing that may contain a terrible irony as well as a temporary sense of beatitude.[54] Having had this moment, Gladney then returns home, where yellow-scented men in Mylex suits are still gathering their terrible data.[55]

DeLillo portrays anywhere-small-town domestication in a society in which nature and reality have disappeared and environmental risk has shockingly risen. It is a comprehensively ironic portrait, but it is not by any means as harsh as a number of other representations of America in a postnatural time. Simultaneously more farcical and more bleakly ironic, Joy Williams's novel, *The Quick and the Dead*, depicts the sunbelt region as outrageously environmentally catastrophic. Like Carl Hiassen's Florida, hers is a world gone utterly amok in which a prolific array of environmental problems are part of a veritable carnival of ignorance and insensitivity. But Williams is much more acid in her treatment of this condition than Hiassen is. As if she were boning a sickly trout, she carefully removes from her novel all traces of Hiassen's entertainment-centered action-adventure plot. She leaves only the pith, and it is for the most part a bleak and acerbic (though marvelously witty) pith indeed.

Williams's sunbelt is marked, even more than Hiassen's Florida, by environmental disregard and indifference. It is disregard that, as in Hiassen, is totally unconscious of itself; worse, it is sadistically delighted by what it has helped to do to the world. This social milieu vacillates wildly between violent redneckery (the filial line of which leads back to Flannery O'Connor's southern gothic and ultimately William Faulkner's grotesques) and New-Age/post-modern sophistication; the former rapes nature, the later derealizes and dissolves it. But most characteristic of Williams is the fact that her postnatural landscapes—like her nonfictional essays—literally bristle with ecological issues and eco-rants about them. The wrecked landscape is, in short, littered with all sorts of bones that have lost the ability to reassemble themselves and act but which have retained and even more finely honed the ability to talk back sharply. For in Williams's landscape, people have domesticated themselves thoroughly in environmental mayhem, and the chief sign of this domestication is the fact that her social landscape is littered not just with tacky developments and dead wildlife but with stalemated controversy as well.

The variety of ecological screeds populating Williams' postnature is remarkable. The book's eco-rants—many of which come from its protagonist, Alice, a fiercely prickly sixteen-year-old—include condemnations of suburban development, agricultural monocultures, consumerist overproduction, drift-net fishing, wetland disturbance, overpopulation (Alice tells children she baby-sits that "not being born is ecologically responsible"), and big sugar's record of ecological destruction. Condemned as well are the use of lawn and garden pesticides, toxic environmental pollution, the use of animals to grow human organs and in medical technologies generally, wildland loss (pristine desert suddenly gives way to crossroads on which four Jiffy Lubes stand, "none seeming more prosperous or desirable in terms of patrons than another"), and the marketing of wild animals for symbolic consumption.[56] "Listen to this," Alice tells Annabel, a flaky, Valley Girl type who loves makeup and media culture:

> "Half-hidden, yet clearly curious, the wolf gazes out from the framed, double-matted print intently, forever watching from the woods. Protected behind clear acrylic.+" Protected behind clear acrylic! That's the only place it is protected. Everywhere else it's trapped and poisoned and shot from planes and snowmobiles.[57]

The novel's eco-rants are, in short, meant to be unmappably overdetermined. Nature has died in The Quick and the Dead in a terrible abundance of sadism and indifference already accomplished.

At the root of much of this sadism and indifference is that redneck cruelty and postmodern sophistication conspire to eliminate all traces of feeling for nature, all memory of biophilia. On the one hand, postmodern sophistication has a particularly cruel edge in The Quick and the Dead. Drawings of animals by children hung in an appalling nursing home (the Green Palms home, a "state-of-the-art End of the Trail") are brusquely dismissed by one of the nurses, Nurse Daisy, a member of the home's staff who is an outspoken nihilist with a vocation for observing and commenting on mortality in its most meaningless forms. Hung there in an attempt at comfort, the pictures provide none: "it's completely cynical, this continuous peddling of the natural world," Daisy remarks. "It's not out there anymore! Even old timers don't find anything familiar in this empty symbology, this feckless copycatting,"[58]

On the other hand, redneck violence is illustrated in spades by Kevin and Hickey, two lovelorn gentlemen who, high on pot, take out their disappointments by blasting saguaro cacti with shotguns. They too, though know-nothing rednecks, have been marked by the New-Age/postmodern; Kevin relates how his partner left him, snarling: "You know how you spell woman, Kevin? It's w-o-m-y-n. That's how you spell woman, you lazy ugly worthless freak," while Hickey frets that his mate is off at a Minnesota wolf-howl.[59] Thus saddened ("I miss my lady's sweet buns bad" Kevin moans), they blast away at saguaros, eventually also killing Ray Webb, another of the book's menagerie of odd characters (a chimera who has had monkey parts transplanted into his brain).[60]

Farce, however, turns to bleakness rapidly as one further element of Williams's fictional world shows through all this high and low weirdness. The terrible truth is that no matter how bad the world itself is, there is no possibility of transcendence. History promises no transcendence; all of the plucky Alice's eco-rants fall on deaf ears, and anyway, cranky and extremist in expression, they are from the start doomed to miss the mark, despite their sincerity and accuracy. Worse still, there is no mark left to hit. A disembodied voice, one that frames the human world when it speaks at the beginning of each section of the novel, offers a cheerful invitation: "So. You don't believe in a future life. Then do we have the place for you!"[61] Later, the voice states that everyone (both the characters in the novel and the readers of it) has "been deemed a candidate by the Physician/Family/Staff for the Terminally Ill Program" and accordingly will have, "beginning at 3 a.m. this day and extending into any remaining future," all their comforts removed—comforts like faith in transcendence, nature, medicine, sanctuary, and refuge.[62] Like the appalling nursing home, Green Palms, the fictional universe of Williams's novel offers no exit, no hope of change.

At the end of the novel, Alice's friend Annabel escapes to Europe with her father—to the stylish diversions that cosmopolitanism and consumerism offers. Alice's deeper, more tragic friend, Corvus, enters Green Palms as a postulant. Greeted by Nurse Daisy with the dedicatory vows—"Do you commit yourself to pondering ceaselessly the uselessness of caring, the uselessness of life, that great reality for which all else must be abandoned?"—Corvus chooses "to die slowly, day by meaningless day, unenchanted, bitterly and meaninglessly aware."[63] Alice, by contrast, is a "pilgrim": she stays in the midst of things, trying, despite continual unsuccess, to communicate to an indifferent world. She labors to open the eyes of her baby-sitting charges to the world of "drift nets, wetland mitigation, predator control, and overpopulation."[64] She loses a tooth when she tries to stop a biker illegally roaring through parkland, terrorizing the endangered bighorn sheep. She is voted by schoolmates the one "most likely to be collecting bird carcasses on the shores of the Salton Sea."[65] She futilely liberates a shopping cart full of lizards from an untended pet store, realizing (with true Sangamon-Greenpeace-style craftiness) that "the further a cart was taken from the store where it belonged, the more deference was paid to the possibly unstable individual who had taken charge of it."[66]

In all these screeds and futile actions, Alice is an environmentalist pilgrim of a particular stripe: she is the apocalyptic environmentalist *par excellence*, fierce, extremist, and fanatical. Moreover, she herself realizes this: "trying to make the world just and natural only makes it more unjust and more unnatural," she thinks, though she soldiers on nonetheless.[67] Only once does another character seem to hear what she is saying, and her response is pathetically eager. Annabel's father, in conversation with her, suddenly acknowledges that: "You of all people are aware of the perniciousness of humankind's presence on earth."[68] Alice's response is immediate:

> Someone was listening to her! Or at least overhearing her as she wedged her
> warnings about ecological collapse into the most benign conversations. "The
> impending extinction spasm is going to produce a cataclysmic setback to
> life's abundance and diversty," she mumbled hopefully.[69]

Alas, her comically hopeful comment does not communicate itself, as Annabel's father is already off in another direction. Unlistened-to, Cassandra-Alice cries out in a time when apocalyptic rhetoric has been utterly stalemated—stalemated not because of an overt antienvironmental lobby (as has happened in the "real" world of U.S. politics), but because apocalyptic rhetoric is simply too comfortably and unnoticeably at home in postnatural, postsocial U.S. society—a society that has domesticated itself deeply into apocalypse.

A bleak version of Hiassen's Skink, an ecocentric Cassandra and ecoterrorist in an indifferent, brutalized, postnatural society, Alice is the very quintessence of the doomster environmentalist the antienvironmental right has loved to hate. But she is so full of adolescent intensity and pluck that she keeps the reader's sympathies nonetheless. For against all the pseudocontrarians the culture of hyperexuberance has so prolifically produced—insiders who claim outsider authority—Alice is the real, the genuine item. She is the contrarian truly despised, the one who hammers vainly at the real box that society has closed upon her and everyone else, the environmental box that no postmodern conntrarian has yet managed to think his or her way outside of.

Alice's irony thus does not act stand outside nature and society and condemn both apocalyptically to the flames; Alice may be an apocalypticist, but *The Quick and the Dead* is anything but a 1970s-style apocalyptic fiction. In making a heroine like Alice, the novel discovers a marvelously articulate way of speaking from within crisis-in-progress—within a society in which crisis has become a part of daily life, normalized, a society in which apocalyptic rants have been either checked or simply absorbed into a social landscape that thrives on extreme discourses, the more outrageous the better.[70]

Fictional representation of society domesticated within crisis sinks its literary taproot still deeper in Richard Powers's novel *Gain*. It sheds the mantle of postmodern experimentalism that cloaked *White Noise* and *The Quick and the Dead* and hovered about Ammons's later work. It summons up an older and, despite all the assaults of twentieth-century literary innovation, still vigorous tradition: that of Flaubertian realism, the detailed creation of a fictional universe that is no mere intervention into and play with discourse but a patient condensation of what can only be taken as reality out of an accumulation of historical, social, psychological, and scientific detail. It also explores a new aspect of environmental crisis. If, in *White Noise*, environmental toxification of bodies was wittily represented as a nightmare of risk, *Gain* casts a still starker light on toxification by representing it as the outcome of accommodationist social logic—as an outcome no one intended or chose but one chillingly assembled from the ignorant choices of a multitude of people, both past and present.

Gain weaves a teacherly narrative of the origins and development of the Clare Soap and Chemical Corporation together with a tale of the unraveling of one human life: that of Laura Bodley, divorced mother of two and successful real estate agent in the thriving community of Lacewood. Lacewood, like DeLillo's Blacksmith, was once an agricultural community; it is now the thoroughly suburbanized home to Clare's Midwestern agricultural products division. Powers's juxtaposition of the two stories has fatal overtones from the start. In his history of the Clare Corporation Powers describes the growth of a still larger structure—a socioeconomic system that becomes steadily more monolithic and determining. Forged out of the unintended side effects of several centuries of choices ignorantly taken by people or thrust upon them by economic necessity, this socioeconomic assemblage becomes more and more imposing and inescapable. At the same time it turns deadly, thanks to its steady accumulation of environmental side effects that can no longer be easily accommodated or displaced elsewhere. The novel's more immediate story then dramatizes this new deadliness. It does so by describing the destruction of Laura, a poor, very ordinary, and very mortal person, someone utterly ignorant of the shadow world of corporate control and toxic pollution she naively lives in as she sells supposedly nice houses in nice subdivisions to nice people like herself.

Clare's growth is a complicated process with ultimately simple effects; as it grows, its ironic environmental shadow, the legacy of unintended environmental side effects, also grows. Begun when a speculative merchant family, stung by the Tariff of Abominations, turns to manufacturing, Clare slowly develops from a single-product enterprise into what is a global, highly diversified corporation that provides "material solutions" for many different kinds of industries, people, and problems. Its ironic shadow first appears when Clare takes advantage of the Age of Discovery. Ben Clare, a botanist and the son of the founder, explores the southern polar regions and returns with *utilis clarea*, a plant that promises, when included in a soap, to help cure what industry itself helped produce, the "unprecedented shocks to the skin unknown to earlier ways and races" produced by the "age of steam."[71] Clare's discovery is thus just a little bit chilling; it is an innovation necessary to repair the damage done by previous innovations. Worse, any downside the plant might have is left for future generations to discover: "the substance could have packed a delayed punch more poisonous than henbane. But no bureau, no business police existed to prevent the Clares from discovering that toxicity *in vivo*."[72]

Directing his subsequent chemical research to a much larger project—to discovering how to turn wasted resources and above all toxic effluents of the industrial process to use—Ben poisons himself; the accident is prophetic of wider damage to come. Ben's notebooks provide the company with clues on how to turn the waste, coal tar, into disinfectants and anesthetics, and discoveries like these help fuel one of the corporation's great dreams—the dream of making an equivalent to the "fabled self-refilling magic beaker." Leveraged by ingenuity and inventiveness, the dream means that: "The entire country could grow rich on a fraction of its prior labor. Every mile of wire produced enough surplus advantage to pay for the wiring of another mile. At wiring's end, all the wealth left over would better us beyond imagining."[73] As inventiveness, productivity, and capital accumulate, so (it seems) does mankind's freedom from natural scarcity and hard labor.

But with this dream, the corporation's ironic shadow even more decisively lengthens. Triumphalist technological advance is accompanied in *Gain* by the growth of the shadow world of hidden environmental risk—a process that the novel draws (albeit with some alteration of the particulars) from life. Joe Thornton, writing about the damage that organochlorine production has done to human bodies and the environment, provides a revealing description of the shadow side of this "self-refilling magic beaker." Historically, the production of alkali ("always in demand by manufacturers of glass, soap, paper, textiles, and other products") by a new method gave rise to the chlorine industry; electrolysis of brine, which produced purer alkali than previously, also yielded chlorine gas.[74] "From the beginning," Thornton writes, "this new branch of the chemical industry had to develop applications that could serve as sinks for the chlorine formed in the process of alkali production"—thereby founding a huge variety of new industries crucial to post–World War II consumerism.[75] But this apparent abundance crafted out of waste also meant an actual expansion of environmental damage, as Rachel Carson and many others noticed; the production of organochlorines quickly became the source of a significant new environmental risk. The "magic, self-refilling beaker" thus did not magically free humankind from natural constraints; it was from the start not an industrial triumph but merely an accommodationist strategy that temporarily concealed environmental constraints while in fact allowing environmental damage to expand. It helped bring on the time when environmental side effects could no longer be so easily covered up and accommodated—the time when the earth's limits would no longer appear to be its finite resources but its already overflowing sinks.

Gain thus chronicles the inevitable transformation of industrial triumphalism into contemporary environmental crisis—a story that runs from the modernization of industry, through the Great Depression, to World War II and the great burst of innovation it produced. Thanks to wartime challenges and shortages, chemical revolutions begin "to cascade from one another: hydrogenization, nitrogenizing, and most important of all, synthetic detergents."[76] With synthetics a further, more fatal step has been taken; technological triumphalism seems not just to have turned nature into a magic, self-refilling beaker, but, more ominously, to have brought about a final, triumphant liberation of humanity from scarcity and even nature itself. "Consumers were turning eagerly away from nature toward something more reliable," Powers writes, imitating the breathless enthusiasm with which Clare heralded this change: "All bottlenecks would vanish. Life would be at nothing's mercy."[77] In a stunningly brief span of time, Clare's product lines grow tenfold, and the corporation seems perched on the edge of realizing the dreams of contemporary technophiliacs like Julian Simon: liberation from nature and scarcity and the prospect of infinite growth.

But as triumphalism becomes more and more overweeningly prideful, its shadow side is creeping at last into the daylight world. As this happens, capitalist technological triumphalism finds itself suddenly transformed into dysfunctional and deadly accommodationism. For here enters Laura Bodley, and the book's other story: the appallingly detailed, infinitely painful account of the emergence and treatment of her ovarian cancer; the slow growth of her realization of its cause; and the awful decline and death she endures. This is a narrative made particularly claustrophobic by the novel's patiently realistic, detailed account of Laura's increasingly hopeless descent into the technologies and routines of cancer medicine and the U.S. health care system. The account is so realistic, restrained, and detailed that I personally find it almost impossible not to keep reading once started, even though I find myself wishing I had never begun the journey.

After one of her daughter Ellen's friends, Nan, dies of a wasting disease, Laura catches herself limping, favoring her right side. Four pages later she is telling her teenage kids, Ellen, notorious for mood swings, and Tim, grouchy and undetachable from his violent computer games: "a cyst is like a little ball of water. . . . They make a tiny incision. They hardly have to use a scalpel."[78] She tells them this over a dinner that is "in fact, . . . a Member's Exclusive [from the Discount Club]: the fifteen-bean Old Almanac soup, the skip-dippers, the frozen melon medley."[79] Laura, a successful real estate agent in a town metastasizing (yes, metastasizing) into more and more subdivisions, attempts to be health-conscious; nonetheless, a single mother pressed for time, she stays with what the thoroughly corporatized, increasingly unnatural, synthetic food production system delivers her.

Shortly, however, the shadow world that has been for some time forming about her and her town becomes palpable and begins intruding on her life with nauseating inevitability. As the reader already suspects, her supposedly innocuous procedure turns out to reveal far deeper problems. Though her

surgeon assures her that it is 98-percent certain she suffers from an easily op-
erable ovarian cyst, the surgeon's confidence makes it all too clear that matters
are in fact much worse. After the operation, the surgeon tells Laura that she
has ovarian cancer instead; she communicates this truth brutally because in a
pleasant, unruffled voice. She then asks: "'Is there anything else you need to
know for now' in just the way the pretty cashier at the Style Barn cocks her
head and says, 'Will that be all today?'"[80]

Quickly, Laura finds out that health care today is all too like the Style Barn.
For health care is now the patient's lookout—choice and responsibility fall
"squarely on the care receiver," not the giver.[81] Clearly, accommodationism
has beeen at work; a wide variety of social systems, from medical technologies
to this highly significant style of medical decorum have been created to help
control and contain the effects of spreading environmental toxification, both
the physical damage it causes and the potentially explosive social tensions it
creates. For both medical treatment itself and the ways in which it is delivered
try to control the effects of toxification, not remedy its causes. Worse, they too
often do not produce genuine cures but end up involving people in new kinds
of agony.

Thus the treatments that Laura has to choose between are, like mass-market products, as much style as substance and they are all sadly ineffective at sat-
isfying her real needs. They differ from the Style Barn's goods only in being
horribly disfiguring and painful, both physically and psychologically. For having fallen into the grips of the medical establishment, Laura has to deal with
the roller coaster of fears and hopes that cancer care entails. There are too
many tests and too much information for clarity; indeed, as information increases, so does uncertainty, and prospects seem to change from week to week,
taking Laura, again and again, from soaring hope to brutal disappointment.
This echoes, of course, DeLillo's portrait of Jack Gladney. The only difference is
that DeLillo is a comedian of the postmodern, while Powers is a realist meticulously detailing the progress of a doomed woman's cancer treatment.

The downward spiral continues through four increasingly grueling chemotherapy sessions (each involving a succession of drugs meant to ease pain and
then create it, poison her system and counteract the poison) and subsequent
weight loss, hair loss, nausea, and weakness. Unable physically to endure the
required fifth treatment, Laura is switched to another, still more painful routine. All the while, she is dealing with multiplying problems on a variety of
fronts; her health insurance denies her the latest, most effective drugs and,
worse, suddenly decides certain expenses already run up are not covered after

all; her employer abruptly puts her out to pasture against her will when her productivity declines. Her finances further dwindle, and her complicated personal life also further unravels, as her increasingly upset children act out, her ex-husband intensifies his well-meaning but abrasive interventions, and her lover's selfishness becomes so transparent that she can endure him no longer. Torment by social and emotional as well as cellular hyperabundance seems to be her lot. As cancerous cells proliferate in her body, she is overwhelmed by a cascade of financial, social, and familial troubles from the world around her.

At the end of the book, Laura gradually and painfully discovers that she has been living all along in a shadow world. After the hospital, her home seems increasingly to be no refuge, no repository of a valued past. Part of a subdivision, crammed with corporate brand names, packaged foods, cosmetic and lawn and garden chemicals, it seems to have nothing to do with her. Worse, she encounters in the newspaper an article—a filler article included because there was little real news that day—that gives the EPA's list of local emissions, including the "area's top carcinogenic chemical emissions."[82] Her home and neighborhood suddenly are not only no intimate refuge; they may be a positive hazard. Perhaps the worst moment for Laura—and the reader—is when she finally decides to go to the library. There Laura discovers, to her horror, that her situation is not unique; others, many others, have gone this way before her. The librarian maintains for them a "pudgy" file about environmental toxins in the area. Screwing up her courage, she asks the librarian "Do . . . sick people come here often?" The librarian's "eyes sweep upward, studying that spot near the ceiling where human calculation prints out its subtotals. 'Umm . . . every few days? She tries. 'Yes, I'd say pretty much every few days.'"[83]

As painful as it is for Laura to experience her cancer as her individual agony, it is more appalling to find that she is part of a shadow world, a distressingly populous one: "She cannot turn around without running into someone else. Everybody is battling cancer. Why did she never see these people before?"[84] She also discovers that a law firm has taken up the cause of this group, and her ex-husband presses her to join her name to the suit. Contrary to what one of her doctors says—an offensive, patronizing, free-market libertarian who sneers at environmentalism while he administers the chemotherapy treatments that torment Laura—an ovarian cancer cluster does exist in Lacewood and it has been most likely caused by Clare. But Laura refuses to join the suit until a final epiphany. Her one recourse, in her progressive debilitation and disenchantment, to anything that feels real has been gardening. When her ex-husband reads her the list of the suspected Clare products ("Clarity Nature-All hair dye, and that Sof'n'Sure talc powder they used to make"), she responds "I'm pretty sure I've never. . . ." But when Don goes on to "a very common herbicide called Atra, . . ." Laura very nearly blacks out. "Her plot of earth. Her flowers," she thinks. Then "Sue them. . . . Every penny they are worth. Break them up for parts." Immediately following this rush of savage anger, she feels peace. She gives up to what has been done to her—and also to Don's exhortations that she join the suit. "Recycle her body, return it to the breath that seeded it. 'All right,' she tells him. 'Okay, anything.'"[85]

But the novel does not end with this sunburst of populist rage that then fades immediately into profoundly depressed acceptance. It concludes with two final twists of irony. Laura dies, and Clare faces a new problem much larger than the lawsuit, which it settles out of court. The object of public outrage in the 1960s and the 1970s thanks to the Carson-inspired environmental movement and the use of Clare herbicides as defoliants in Vietnam, the company has been forced to change direction altogether. It has become global and Green. All the old, dangerous products now go out onto non-U.S. Third World markets; with globalization, these shipments are followed by the export of the dangerous manufacturing facilities themselves. Within the United States, meanwhile, Clare finds that "even the filled-in, exhausted American continent still had new frontiers. . . . The trick was to continue delivering that new lifestyle still struggling to be born. Once upon a time, good chemistry had sufficed for business. . . . At the end of the day, the business to beat became ecology."[86] Clare thus develops an "environmomic" line and becomes Green—all shades of Green. Clare goes into health foods (Green), PVC-bottled purified water (a browner shade of Green), synthetic fat (less Green still, an innovation that might have, several scientists warn, "invisible long-term side effects" but which is nonetheless marketed with an aggressive ad campaign [greenwash]).[87]

Accommodationism, in short, continues still; it promises to extend far into the era in which the ironic shadow of industrially caused environmental damage has at last become visible to society at large. For knowledge of the truth does not halt the appalling logic of the system that produces this damage. At the end of the novel, facing a new crisis—a probable takeover by a big tobacco concern—the Clare CEO prepares for a TV appearance in which he is supposed to recount Clare's great history, starting with Ben Clare's polar exploits (which included searching for a hole which, as legend had it, was at the South Pole). Revealingly, the CEO, "musing on the story of the Clare who once searched for a hole at the pole," thinks: "*they only looked. . . . We made one.*"[88] The irony is stunning. Though swathed in Powers's silken-smooth prose, a grotesque cat appears for a few seconds outside its bag to stun readers with its all-too-unavoidable materiality. Unlike his predecessors, Clare's current CEO is no longer ignorant of the damage his company is still causing. He now clearly sees the monstrous environmental shadow of the chemical industry, a shadow epitomized by the polar ozone hole. Indeed, he is so familiar with his industry's shadow that he jokes to himself about it. Yet, caught up in the system, his public actions and discourse continue to contradict his private understanding; even as he soliloquizes about the ozone hole, he is preparing to celebrate and defend the company he leads.

Perhaps an even bitterer irony comes with what happens to Laura's children after her death and the settlement of the suit. Her daughter attends college and marries; proving infertile, she goes to doctors who discover her cancer in time to prolong her life. Ellen refuses to touch a cent of the settlement. Her brother, however, does do something with his share of the money. His computer interests take him to MIT; there, he successfully collaborates on a computer program that tells how a protein molecule folds and behaves. "In such a vat, people might create molecules to do anything," Powers comments: "The team found itself staring at a universal chemical assembly plant at the level of the cell. Together with a score of other machines just then coming into existence, their program promised to make anything the damaged cell called out for."[89] With this new, potentially accommodationist technology in hand—one horrifically all too likely to have unintended future side effects far greater than its predecessors, even as it is called into existence by the damage past technologies have done—Tim's future is clear. The novel then intensifies these ironies when Tim elects to use his part of the Clare settlement to fund a start-up. Laura is no more; people and nature have been overwhelmed by the shadow kingdom; but technological innovation and corporate growth move on.

Three final terrible implications seemingly cinch these ironies for ever and aye. The first is that there is no way out of the history Powers so meticulously and realistically charts. Tim can't be vilified in his choice; even Clare cannot be demonized. Disequilibrium drives Clare blindly forward into a deeper and deeper commitment to accommodationism and thus expanding environmental damage; again and again, the novel makes clear, this happens thanks to systemic pressure, not conscious choice. The corporation and its leaders are not evil but simply trying to stay one step ahead of collapse. Second, caught up in that historical momentum, society necessarily suffers from amnesia. Laura, the nice real estate agent in the nice suburb, cannot remember the presuburban Midwest. Her daughter cannot remember suburbia before it became toxic. And her son cannot remember either state, moving from his high-tech video games to preoccupation with the microworlds and cybernetic spaces of the new industries. Old, higher environmental standards are necessarily forgotten by people as they are enmeshed deeper and deeper in environmental crisis. Even the CEO's dark insight surfaces just as a grimly witty present irony, not a reminder of an actual past. Finally, propelled forward and amnesiac, the novel's characters—and also the novel's reader—draw a complete blank at imagining the future. With great art, Powers makes it impossible to imagine where, at the novel's end, disequilibrium is heading now that the world's last open environmental and human spaces have pretty well disappeared.

Though Octavia Butler writes science/speculative fiction, I necessarily include one of her novels in this rather than the previous chapter. For *Parable of the Sower* is not simply unusual in its literary quality; it also self-consciously resists rather than exhibits many of the features of its genre. Indeed, it reads more like a work of realistic, even naturalistic, fiction than like an extrapolative fantasy. Further, in thus bending her genre, Butler offers the most complex version in U.S. fiction of the second kind of systemic environmental crisis discussed in Chapter 5. If Powers's novel dramatizes the systemic nightmare of accommodationism, Butler's fiction lays bare the increasingly determining, systemic interplay between social marginalization, poverty, social breakdown, and environmental crisis.

In exploring environmental and social crisis brought about by the newly prominent synergy between inequitable development and environmental deterioration, Butler, an African-American science-fiction author, not only continues to help make her genre multicultural—a project that other African-American science fiction writers such as Samuel Delaney are well known for; uniquely, she also alters it by foregrounding themes of environmental as well as social injustice. In the process, she dramatizes life lived *in* an advanced state of environmental crisis. For, like Powers and the other writers reviewed in this section, Butler does not present crisis as a rush toward apocalypse but as a dwelling place—as a context in which people struggle against growing odds to be able to live some sort of normal life.

Parable of the Sower is set in a future in which acute, multifactoral, environmental and social meltdown has already occurred. Clean water is a commodity people kill for; sanitation has broken down, so that outbreaks of disease are common; basic medical care does not exist, so that a small wound can yield death from infection—or also from starvation by making someone unable to provide for him or herself. Chemical residues—fuel, pesticide, herbicide—poison food and water. This dismantled landscape is the site of a fearful postabundance: an abundance of environmental problems that exposed and vulnerable people desperately try to domesticate themselves within.

Crisis in the novel, at the same time, is also social. Social safety nets have altogether disappeared. No longer a commons, water is available only for purchase (officially from government vendors, but a thriving private business also exists). Equally, social services have almost completely vanished; characters are afraid to involve the fire department in conflagrations or the police in the many thefts, assaults, and murders they suffer as there is a charge for each of their services. As a result, there is now a vast gulf between elite and underclass; the middle class is extinct. Fewer and fewer people have stable homes. Tides of homeless refugees pour across the landscape, assaulting each other when they can and struggling to survive; those who still have homes have to defend them routinely against attackers, as urban-style violence spreads everywhere, even into small towns and remote areas.

In presenting conditions like these, *The Parable of the Sower* extrapolates from issues the environmental justice movement has taken seriously and advances a nightmarishly critical portrait of where contemporary capitalist deregulation and privatization are now heading. The novel also deflates cyberculture's enthusiasm for headlong technological change, libertarian chaos, and social Darwinism. Butler's depiction of the future argues that the real outcome of such a system is very different from what its proponents claim—it results in not a dynamic new era of capitalism and technology but synergistic increases in environmental deterioration and social injustice and disparity that put still further stress on both social and environmental systems.

Butler thus relocates Robert Kaplan's and Thomas Homer-Dixon's Third World nightmare of environmental immiseration to the United States; she presents the country as a violent, lawless, socially and environmentally deteriorated zone of conflict in which the haves seek protection in their "limousines"—in well-defended, less-polluted private spaces—and the vastly larger numbers of the have-nots are left to fend for themselves in the dangerous, degraded commons. Concerned, however, with environmental justice, not environmental security, Butler represents this nightmare very differently from the way Homer-Dixon and Kaplan did. She portrays it from the perspective of the majority of impoverished and vulnerable people out in the chaos, not the small minority still tenuously insulated in protected spaces within it.

Lauren Olamina, the novel's protagonist, daughter of a black university professor and part of the endangered middle-class, is thrown out of her protected space at the start of the novel. She, her father, stepmother, and siblings, live in a small, walled housing compound in Los Angeles that defends itself only with difficulty from both stealthy robberies and all-out assaults with machinery and mobs. But this embattled refuge does not hold out long. Her father is killed, and shortly thereafter the neighborhood's defenses are breached; Lauren's home is overrun in a rampage of looting, rape, and murder. Along with two others, Lauren manages to escape outside, where she now faces a moment-by-moment challenge to survive.

Lauren has been preparing for this possibility by training herself in self-sufficiency; she has studied survival and, even more, agricultural skills. More important, she has begun to formulate a philosophical-spiritual system to be used in creating a new community. She calls this community Earthseed: it brings people together about the notion that, though "God is Power," God is also "Pliable—Trickster, Teacher, Chaos, Clay. God exists to be shaped. God is change."[90] The new religion is one of tough survivalism but also endurance, self-reliance, and limited hope—the hope of shaping the chaos people are necessarily immersed in. As with hyperexuberance, this chaos is potentially creative, but *The Parable of the Sower* dramatically revises the usual celebration of its creativity by depicting it as anything but a source of libertarian excitement. Shaping chaos is a harsh necessity now forced on everyone, not a desired state; and chaos itself no longer appears as inherently creative. Shaping it is possible only with extreme difficulty and pain, and it occurs only in tiny, human, daily domestic ways; it does not happen through exciting high-tech interventions.

Earthseed's immediate goal is to form a community, an agricultural commune up north. In the long term, the prophet-leader Olamina focuses on the time when humanity will commence off-world settlement, and she hopes to see Earthseed spread its line to the stars. Again, though, environmental realism is brought back to hyperexuberant fantasy—in *Parable of the Sower* if not in its successor novel, *Parable of the Talents*. Rather than even suggesting such transcendence is possible, the bulk of *Parable of the Sower* dramatizes Lauren's difficult journey on foot north with her little band of multicultural refugees as they struggle toward a place where they can settle and survive.[91]

Key to the naturalistic power of *Parable of the Sower* is the way the novel depicts this journey north. Laura's band trudges slowly and painfully through uncertain terrain, fighting for their lives on several occasions. But these fights prove nothing and are *not* exciting; for a number of reasons they are not the source of action-adventure thrills, chills, and melodrama. First, Lauren's heroism is far from the skillful daring of epic action-adventure heroes. It consists instead of the prosaic, hardheaded self-reliance—competent endurance rather than the (exciting) exercise of skill or the thrills of nick-of-time luck. Even more, it is based on a thoroughgoing awareness of weakness and vulnerability. As Lauren puts it: "The weak can overcome the strong if the weak persist. Persisting isn't always safe, but it's often necessary."[92] For, thanks to her mother's use of a dangerous designer drug, Lauren is genetically hardwired to feel others' suffering. Feeling it, Lauren never demonizes an antagonist; indeed, she richly understands even the people who destroy her compound: "People are setting fire," she tells us, "because they're frustrated, angry, hopeless. They have no power to improve their lives, but they have the power to make others even more miserable. And the only way to prove to yourself that you have power is to use it."[93] This does not mean that Lauren is a *Star Trek* empath, an ultrafeminine nurturer; no, she remains a large, strong, self-reliant African-American woman, someone with no self-pity and a sense of necessity and, insofar as her empathy interferes with her struggle to survive, she and her society consider it a liability, not an asset.

But a second, more important reason exists for the novel's dissent from the action-adventure conventions of hyperexuberant speculative fiction. This is the novel's presentation of the walk north as a slow, uncertain trudge through landscapes from which all sense of comfort, location, and geographical distinctiveness has been removed. In *The Parable of the Sower*, the long walk north catapults characters back into their bodies and back into the microlocal spaces that their bodies inhabit. Mingled into the perpetual, goalless trudging of refugees along old, broken-up highways—crowds of people walking, just walking—the novel's protagonists share nothing with the fantasies of mobility (mobility through global cosmopolitanism, through cyborg enhancement and genetic shape-shifting, through immersion in cyberspace) that contemporary American postmodern global culture celebrates. Instead, Butler's future reemphasizes what those fantasies suppress: the limits on and vulnerability of the unassisted human body and the challenges of finding food and shelter, staying healthy, having children, tending the ill and dying, and building community in an ecologically deteriorated world—the challenges, in short, of embeddedness and embodiment in a time of environmental crisis.

Walking also alters action-adventure conventions in another, more explicitly literary way. It shows that *The Parable of the Sower* has hybridized speculative fiction with a literary genre far afield from science fiction, one much less popular but much more profoundly resonant. Depicting an arduous, slow journey north, Butler writes speculative fiction in the form of a futurist slave narrative—with the difference that Butler's characters struggle toward a north that is itself, more than in most slave narratives, unfree, caught up in the same crisis that afflicts the sufferers' place of origin. The resulting hybrid then exposes forcefully what dwelling within comprehensive ecological and social crisis might feel like, when considered from the perspective of the majority of the world's population. A multicultural group potentially representing all the nonelite people in this world, all of whom are vulnerable and desperate, joins crowds of hopeless folk walking the remnants of the highways to find a place where they can begin to reconstruct their lives in whatever way they can. Butler's characters desperately seek ways of dwelling in the crisis that encompasses them, a goal they adopt because they have no choice. Immersed in crisis, any interludes of precarious domestication they may finally achieve represent both a hard-won triumph and a new source of vulnerability.

A final literary response to environmental crisis emphasizes even more poignantly and complexly than Butler the problems of dwelling in an environmentally and socially deteriorated world. Located very much in the present and responding to a wide range of ecosystemic and social changes, it depicts these changes more fully and feelingly than would otherwise be possible because of its commitment to memory as well as present struggle and to mourning as well as critique. Even more, it seeks to reanimate love for nature (and the traditions of nature that help foster this love) even in the face of vivid experiences of nature's disfigurement and loss. This literature gains power and complexity, in short, by coupling perspectives often kept separate or even seen as opposed to each other.

Linda Hogan's novel, *Power*, depicts the maturation of Omishto, a young Native American of the Taiga clan, who lives in a white community with her Taiga mother and potentially abusive white stepfather.[94] The area where they live, formerly Taiga land, is now environmentally degraded; the once-biorich land supports only a dwindling number of Florida panthers, an animal sacred to the Taiga and protected by the Endangered Species Act. Throughout the main action of the novel—which focuses on the legal trials of Omishto's friend and mentor, the shaman Ama, who kills a sacred/endangered panther—a pervasive sense of mourning for loss hovers about the appropriated and degraded land. The Taiga people have been decimated, their culture is at risk of extinction, and their land is polluted and overdeveloped, stressed far beyond its ecological limits.

After killing the panther, Ama is tried by a white court for violating the Endangered Species Act, an incident that plays on recent controversies between American nature's old mythic and new scientific stewards, Native Americans and environmentalists. Acquitted by the white court for lack of evidence, Ama is subsequently convicted by a Taiga council—not for killing the panther, which she clearly did, but for doing it in an improper, untraditional manner. Both trials, however, miss the real point—a point that, as it is revealed to Omishto and the reader, deepens the novel's environmental grief immensely.

Omishto first realizes that the white law, though she supports its intentions, does not finally apply to Ama. It doesn't because the panthers have been decimated by the whites' poisoning of ecosystems, unrestrained hunting, and development, not by ritual Native American killing. Even more ironically, white conservation biologists have killed three panthers in putting radio collars on them. Omishto then sees the native law as inapplicable to Ama because of a still more painful reason. Ama does not complete the traditional ritual, which requires giving the panther's corpse to the tribal elders, because the animal she killed was so pathetically sickly and thin; it is on its last legs, has broken teeth, and is starving. Giving it to the elders would possibly have dealt a final blow to the Taiga: they would have seen in it not just the species' probable extinction but also their own demise as a culture and people. Both white and native justice, then, do nothing to relieve the destruction of land and animals the novel vividly portrays.

In her friendship with Ama and her participation in the trial, Omishto is forced to explore the complexities of white and Taiga memory and the dilemmas and difficulties of white and Taiga identity. Going through all this represents Omishto's maturation: it is what she has to do to come to full consciousness in a wounded, perhaps dying world. When she decides to go live with the Taiga at the novel's end, the future possibilities that such hybridization suggest remain uncertain and ambiguous. But what is clear is that Omishto chooses the path that will bring her closest to what she most values and loves despite its diminution and wounds: the survival of the Taiga as a people and the survival of the ecosystems they still cherish.

Mourning a wounded world fully as a means of ultimately dwelling more deeply in it is also the focus of Terry Tempest Williams's unforgettable memoir,

Refuge. *Refuge* tells two stories side by side: it is an account of the flooding of the Bear River Migratory Bird Refuge, beloved to Williams, by a rise in the level of the Great Salt Lake, and the much more traumatic account of the death of Williams's mother from cancer. The memoir is accordingly a moving and poignant account of environmental and human mourning intertwined, and it is a story told, Williams muses, "to heal myself, to confront what I do not know" and "to create a path for myself with the idea that 'Memory is the only way home.'"[95] By writing about losses, Williams seeks a deepened form of dwelling in a place and a family already inseparable from each other. "Our attachment to the land," Williams writes, "was our attachment to each other."[96]

Both narratives tell of the loss of refuges, of spaces apart from change. The flooding of the bird sanctuary is not a man-made but a natural event, and Williams's presentation of it embraces the new postmodern ideas about nature that highlight chaos and change rather than equilibrium and stability. The sanctuary was not originally made from "pristine" land; it was a reconstruction of lost wetlands. Longer-term history reveals that even the original wetlands were the product of change; 14,500 years ago, the whole area was the submerged lake bed of the prehistoric Lake Bonneville. And over the years, the Great Salt Lake had risen and fallen again and again, according to its own impulses.

Diane Williams's cancer represents a more awful version of change and chaos. Nonetheless, Terry and Diane seek to naturalize it. Diane "embrace[s] her cancer like a friend."[97] "It's not that I am giving up," she says: "It is as if I am moving into another channel of life that lets everything in."[98] Terry, meanwhile, is painfully discovering that her refuge is not in her mother or grandmother (who also dies of cancer in *Refuge*)—or the bird sanctuary: "My refuge exists in my capacity to love. If I can learn to love death, then I can begin to change."[99]

As both losses move to fullness, everything floods in. The lake reveals its intact, immense, self-governing power by cresting just as a human mega-engineering project designed to control it becomes operative. Diane's death also reveals a presence of enormous power to her daughter, who, breathing together with her mother and gazing into her eyes as she dies, feels "her eyes focus on mine with total joy—a fullness that transcends words."[100] This moment, presented in retrospect in a diary entry, is immensely moving, coming as it does after a full portrayal of her mother's agony, her care-giving family's commitment, stresses, and grief, and the painful daily difficulties of managing medical equipment at home. It also opens Terry to experiencing her mother's continuing presence in her life and brings her to a new, ecofeminist, spiritual awareness of the "motherbody" of the earth, the incarnate natural world her mother, like she, felt so deeply connected to.[101]

But these events and this rededication receive another spin at the end of the book. The end of the memoir reveals why Williams's subtitle for *Refuge* labeled it an *unnatural* history of family and place. The epilogue reveals that the Williams family's unusual experience with cancer—Willliams's mother, grandmother, and "six aunts all have had mastectomies and seven are dead"—comes probably from radiation poisoning from the above-ground nuclear tests conducted in Nevada between 1951 and 1962.[102] Worse, these tests were conducted where, officials then said, they would impact only "low-use segments of the population."[103] An unnatural official history this grotesque could easily have erased the personal natural histories told in the narrative—it could easily have made nature seem "over" and Diane's death an unnatural horror. By contrast, the great strength of this memoir about "unnatural" as well as "natural" history is Williams's retention of and rededication to the latter, despite the determining power of the former. Deformation does not cancel out nature-love but radically intensifies it, and this intensification leads to a new political outspokenness and activist commitment at *Refuge*'s end. As Williams says of herself at the outset: "When most people had given up on the Refuge, saying its birds were gone, I was drawn further into its essence. In the same way that when someone is dying many retreat, I chose to stay."[104]

The literature examined above touches on nearly the full spectrum of issues raised in this book. It represents an increasingly diversified ecological crisis-in-progress today, vividly dramatizing many forms of environmental and ecosocial degradation and seeing them as key determinants of contemporary life. Along with representing different kinds of damage to external nature, it portrays today's risks to the human body with ironic clarity and deep pathos. Further, it dramatizes a number of different versions of environmental crisis as social crisis—as accommodationist nightmare, as the emergence of risk society, and as a nightmare of environmental injustice, a nightmare of rich versus poor in an ecologically and socially degraded world. In addition, it is sharp-eyed about the way stalemated environmental politics adds to current dilemmas and it wisely agonizes over the possibility that nature traditions and feelings today are yielding to an intensified new siege. In all of these representations, one central focus is clear: as never before, literature today represents deepening environmental crisis as a context in which people dwell and with which they are intimate, not as an apocalypse still ahead. The emergence of a body of literature of this sort is genuinely new.

For the most part, even when most clearly political, this literature shows no clear path out of crisis. It suggests that society is now at a point where the shadow world has entered the daylight world and begun to change it substantially. To continue my metaphor from the Preface, it pulls back the curtain on a portrait of deformation and fixes readers' gazes on it. A maturer crisis literature than ever before, it does not ask for a look of panicked horror, an urgent effort to change, and then denial and forgetfulness until the next look. It asks that people gaze on and on without being able to avert their eyes or seize upon easy remedies or prescriptions for change. It asks that audiences realize just how deeply in the soup they themselves are and how difficult and uncertain solutions are. In presenting fictional worlds that do not conveniently end with apocalypse, it blurs the boundaries between dilemmas in fiction and dilemmas still very much in progress in the surrounding world. Stilled into form, yet persistingly ironic, moving, angry, chilling, and unresolved, this new literature of crisis silently awaits a meaningful collective response. It also fully acknowledges that this response may or may not come.

Appendix

Even sharp words need mouths (megaphones, loudspeakers) to utter them; and an abundance of institutionalized mouths was something the right was careful to cultivate. Organizations of a variety of sorts, all platforms for activism and expression, appeared and/or sought a new level of influence in the seventies, eighties, and nineties. They included right-wing think tanks; corporate groups; fronts for corporations and corporate groups; right-wing lobbying and legal associations; right-wing foundations; and an extensive ecology of right-wing grassroots activist organizations. The wide variety of their names (some of them catchy, many of them Green-sounding, clever snares laid for the unwary citizen to step in) accurately reflects the diversity of the organizations. They include the Heritage Foundation, the Cato Institute, the Center for the Defense of Free Enterprise, the Pacific Research Institute, the Defenders of Property Rights, the Federalist Society, the Competitive Enterprise Institute, the Washington Legal Foundation, the Mountain States Legal Foundation, the Wilderness Impact Research Foundation (a name deliciously ambiguous, but decodable), ECO (an acronym that keeps its cloak on even when decoded—the Environmental Conservation Organization), Land Improvement Contractors Association, the Global Climate Coalition (which argues that human-caused climate change is a myth), the National Wetlands Organization (which protects wetlands by lobbying for the filling in and drilling of estuaries, bogs, marshes, mangrove swamps, tundra, and bayous), People for the West, the Sahara Club (a notorious biker association), Wise Use, the National Inholders Association, EAGLE (a somewhat flawed acronym, but one that works, presumably, for Alabama: it means Alabamians: Guardians of our Land and Environment), the much-beloved National Rifle Association, the Association of National Grasslands, the nuclear industry's U.S. Council for Energy Awareness, the American Mining Congress, the Chemical Manufacturers Association, the Asbestos Information Association, the Alliance for a Responsible CFC Policy (which represents chemical companies), the Coalition for Sensible Regulation (a coalition of developers and corporate farmers in the West), the Alliance for Sensible Environmental Reform ("which represents polluting industries"), the Citizens for Sensible Control of Acid Rain.[1]

Within this abundance were a number of different types of organizations and participants. I shall single out three main groups, the loose alliance of which resulted in the considerable political and social clout necessary to change the way people publicly reflected upon and debated environmental issues. The first notable group was comprised of the corporate activists, studied in scrupulous detail by Sharon Beder in her book *Global Spin: The Corporate Assault on Environmentalism.* In its post-1970s realization that "we've been clobbered," corporate America formed unprecedented alliances and set up industry groups and disguised front groups to regain its lost legitimacy and to ensure that its viewpoint dominated discussions of and action about environmental issues.[2]

Corporate strategies for regaining lost ground were multipronged. Along with well-known techniques for exerting direct influence over the political process—such as lobbying, campaign contributions, and exchanges of favors, staff, expertise, and inside information—they included a host of subtler, indirect media tactics to influence public opinion, tactics which have received the name "greenwashing." By 1990, Beder reports: "U.S. firms were spending about $500 million a year on PR advice about how to green their images and deal with the opposition."[3] Beder quotes what she labels "an informal General Motors document" that described the company's public relations goals with admirable candor: "GM Public Relations helps to make GM so well-accepted by its various publics that it may pursue its corporate mission unencumbered by public-imposed limitations or regulations."[4] Corporate advertisements sought both to discredit environmental regulation and to take credit for environmental concerns and achievements; thus Electric Power System, Beder notes, "proclaimed themselves to be 'environmentalists long before it was popular'" yet ran ads that opposed clean-air measures and claimed that "'strict adherence to unreasonable regulations that are not necessary to protect health, would only jeopardize the nation's electric power supply."[5] Similarly, to defuse public outrage about clear-cut forests, the forest products industry "launched a massive PR campaign ($7 to $10 million per year for five years) promoting the message that 'We love the forest and protect it. When we cut trees, we plant them. We are not rapers of the hillside, we are farmers of trees; we grow them and reap them and plant them.'"[6] As a PR expert advised in

Public Relations Journal: "'There really are no solid solutions to many environmental problems other than ceasing to partake in the activity that causes the environmental hazard. Therefore, the key to devising successful solution ideas is to show that your client cares about the environmental issue at hand."[7]

Working with corporations, the public relations industry also developed an impressively specialized array of expertise to support such greenwashing efforts. Specialists in risk communication focused on the fact that, as Joe Epley, former president of the Public Relations Society of America, put it: "public opinion, fueled by hysteria, a desire to live in a risk-free environment, and unfounded perceptions of the industrial world, is making it difficult for many manufacturers to operate on either a local or global basis."[8] Experts called "crisis communicators" managed "public perception following industrial accidents, the public uncovering of adverse effects of a product, and corporate mistakes."[9] Most generally, James Lindheim, director of Public Affairs Worldwide at Burson-Marsteller in London, advised the chemical industry to "build a therapeutic alliance with the public":

> There is, for instance, a very interesting technique that psychiatrists use to deal with irrational and distressed patients. They call it the therapeutic alliance. When an anxious patient first arrives, the psychiatrist will be a very sympathetic listener. The whole time that his mind is telling him that he has a raving lunatic on his hands, his mouth will be telling the patient that his problems are indeed quite impressive, and that he the psychiatrist is amazed at how well the patient is coping, given the enormity of the situation. . . . Once that bond of trust is established, true therapy can begin and factual information can be transmitted.[10]

A still more specific body of expertise exists about how corporations can work with environmental groups. Bruce Harrison claims, in *Going Green: How to Communicate Your Company's Environmental Commitment,* that "choosing green partners at the community level is without doubt the best strategy to improve your standing." Such strategies included helping environmental groups raise money, offering to sit on their board of directors, and hiring staff from environmental groups ("at very reasonable rates").[11] These techniques have been robustly used on the national as well as community levels. Beder quotes "Frank Boren, a board member of ARCO Petroleum, [who] served as president of the Nature Conservancy. He argued that such cooperation was good for industry: 'One good thing about that is that while we're working for them, they don't have time to sue us.'"[12]

Along with greenwashing and Green PR, Green marketing also became prominent and popular. "The 1990s," Beder writes, "saw the rise of green marketing, which was aimed at increasing consumption, not reducing it."[13] Once market research found consumers willing to pay more for "Green" products and natural foods, consumer society expanded, not altered, its reach. "By marketing a 'green' version of an existing product, manufacturers are able," Beder writes, "to take up extra shelf space and offer an extra choice for consumers."[14] Equally, countless numbers of products that have nothing to do with the environment, and, worse, ones destructive of it have been advertised in "Green" fashion—something any consumer attentive to SUV ads, depicting gas-guzzling vehicles standing alone on sunlit desert mesas, can easily appreciate.

To Green PR, greenwashing, and Green marketing, Beder finally adds a less-discussed category of corporate strategic movement-building, namely a concerted effort to target education. Lifetime Learning Systems, which developed educational materials for corporations and trade associations, stated in its promotional material: "Now you can enter the classroom through custom-made learning materials created with your specific marketing objectives in mind. . . . Coming from school, all these materials carry an extra measure of credibility that gives your message added weight. . . . IMAGINE millions of students discussing your product in class. IMAGINE their teachers presenting your organization's point of view."[15] Beder cites a wide variety of examples pertaining to the environment: "The American Nuclear Society has a kit which tells children about the beneficial uses of nuclear technology and attempts to describe the problem of waste disposal in harmless terms: 'Anything we produce results in some "leftovers" that are either recycled or disposed of—whether we're making electricity from coal or nuclear, or making scrambled eggs!'"[16] Georgia-Pacific produced elementary school materials on forestry. These told children: "When no one harvests, trees grow old and are more likely to be killed by disease rot, and the elements. Very old trees will not support many kinds of wildlife because the forest floor is too shaded to grow the ground plants animals need."[17]

Corporations also pursued a variety of other pressure tactics to counter environmentalism and to legitimize themselves. One of the more aggressive of these was the SLAPP suit—or strategic lawsuit against public participation. Thus in 1986: "a woman in Texas was sued by a company, Hill Sand Co., for $5 million for using the term 'dump' for a landfill; her husband, who had not been involved in the protest, was also sued because 'he failed to control his wife.'"[18] Though the ironic reader may well muse that such things doubtless

happen mostly in Texas, Beder asserts that "thousands of Americans" became
the targets of multimillion-dollar lawsuits filed for "circulating petitions,
writing to public officials, speaking at, or even just attending, public meetings,
organising a boycott and engaging in peaceful demonstrations."[19] Though
most of these suits never got to trial and few were won, they had a decidedly
chilling effect on public concern over a variety of issues, including, of course,
the environment.

The second significant force for changing environmental discourse came
from the conservative political movement. Perhaps most important was that
conservatives helped construct two significant platforms for advocating
antienvironmental policies and positions: they sponsored the growth of right-
wing and conservative think tanks and they helped midwife the creation of
antienvironmental counterscience. They did this, of course, in close connection with corporate antienvironmentalism: think tanks, funded in part with
corporate money, supported new "researchers" (many of whom weren't even
scientists) writing brownlash counterscience literature.

"During the 1970s and 1980s" David Callahan writes:

> conservative think tanks reinvented the think tank concept. Rather than ap-
> proaching policy as a pragmatic or technocratic enterprise, conservative pol-
> icy institutions have regarded the policy process in ideological and political
> terms. Where the older think tanks were knowledge-based, focused on the
> resolution of specific problems, the new conservative think tanks were
> guided by moral precepts and received truths. Their political project was
> restorative in nature, aimed at placing key ideas and long-standing princi-
> ples above empirical science in guiding national policy.[20]

All this is, I fear, a very polite way of saying the new think tanks were set up for
purposes of ideology manufacture and dissemination, not genuine research.
Yet conservative think tanks managed quite successfully to set themselves up
as institutions on a par with universities. Doing this meant obscuring several
crucial differences between knowledge production in academia and the new
think tanks. First, academia was a place where genuinely peer-reviewed, peer-
contested knowledge was generated; in the new think tanks, on the other
hand, knowledge was neither assembled because it withstood peer review nor
published with the expectation that it would incite peer contestation, but produced because it was ideologically correct and useful in establishing a new,
conservative public consensus. Further, in academia, knowledge was not designed and artfully packaged to have immediate impact on current political

debates; even the left-wing, theory-rich "interventions" that have become so prominent in academic writing recently have clearly not been written for nonspecialists to read. In contrast, knowledge dissemination in think tanks was political down to its cuticles, carefully packaged and repackaged in different forms for different audiences and plugged into a complex infrastructure developed for effective public presentation.

Quite consciously, then, conservatives sought to start a movement to counter an existing movement. As Sharon Beder writes:

> Irving Kristol, one of those widely credited with persuading the U.S. business community of the merits of this strategy [of setting up think tanks], argued: "You can only beat an idea with another idea, and the war of ideologies will be won or lost within the 'new class' not against it." The 'new class' comprised people—such as government bureaucrats, academics and journalists—who dealt in ideas rather than products.[21]

The time was just right for this effort. As the American electorate shrank, declining disproportionately among the lower classes, as more and more Americans began to distrust existing institutional voices, including the political parties, and as the importance of elite actors increased out of proportion to their numbers, the think-tank strategy became an extremely effective means of changing discourse on issues. Also crucial to environmental politics was the fact that, as environmental activists opened the policy-making process in the 1960s and 1970s, environmental laws were passed and government regulation became a process in which data and information were crucial. Business soon found that "the move towards information-based decisions" made under public scrutiny suited them well, "because of their ability to hire experts—scientists, economists and statisticians."[22] Think tanks were invaluable in giving the corporations and the political right control of information in a way that seemed legitimate. As supposedly research-intensive, public-interest organizations, think tanks worked: "through extended campaigns [to] reframe broad arguments, popularize specific blueprints for action, and mobilize grassroots support."[23] Callahan estimates that during the 1990s, over a billion dollars was spent—donated by corporations, right-wing foundations, and wealthy individuals—to sustain and expand conservative think tanks.

Most conservative think tanks became multi-issue organizations and thus were a crucial platform for the right's creation of ideology that unified a diverse set of issues, positions, and constituencies into a successful countermovement. From the start, these think tanks not only undertook ideologically motivated research, they mounted sophisticated campaigns to make their findings and policy recommendations effectively influential over politicians, the media, and the grassroots public. "The unique thing we have done," says Heritage Foundation vice president Stuart Butler: "is to combine the serious, high-quality research of a 'traditional think tank' like the Hoover Institution or the Brookings Institution with the intense marketing and 'issue management' capabilities of an activist organization."[24]

Think tanks set out to influence politicians directly. Heritage sponsored three-day orientations for new members of the 1994 Congress; Sharon Beder remarks that: "traditionally, newly elected members of congress have attended Harvard's Kennedy School of Government for their orientation programme, but now Republican congresspeople are flocking instead to a programme set up by the Heritage Foundation and Empower America to hear speeches from the likes of Charles Murray (of *The Bell Curve* fame) and Rush Limbaugh (right-wing radio talk show host)"—or "talk-back" show, as the grassroots right-wing versions have been called, thanks to their cultivation of surly, antigovernment, populist anger.[25] Other think tanks followed suit. "Ideas don't jump out of books on their own—they have to be hand-carried," quipped Fred Smith, founder of the Competitive Enterprise Institute: "The politicians are generally too busy to read; they don't have time to become expert on much of anything. So my idea for an aggressive policy group was to hand-carry the ideas to the politicians in forms that were bite-size."[26] Recently, think tanks have extended this influence still further: now they do not just educate politicians but also supply conservative Republican administrations with many of their administrative, judicial, and executive-branch appointees.

Think tanks also targeted the media. Callahan notes that: "each of the policy experts at Competitive Enterprise Institute, for example, is considered to be an 'issues manager.'"[27] A 1996 study "found that centrist and conservative policy institutions were cited 12,441 times in major paper and broadcast media, compared to only 1,837 citations for progressive think tanks."[28] Beder reports that in 1995, conservative think tanks were cited more than twice as often as centrist ones.[29] Moreover, these "experts" were most often identified by the name of their organization; much less often is that organization then identified as a conservative think tank.

Along with utilizing techniques like these, think tanks helped develop a further strategy for dealing specifically with environmental issues. They sponsored the creation of counterscience, the development of an antienvironmental body of scientific opinion and expertise. Corporate trade associations had attempted to do this, making grants to sponsor scientific research that might be helpful to their cause and issuing reports and publications. But think tanks added the appearance of objectivity. Accordingly, as noted in Chapter 1, a stream of brownlash pseudoscientific literature—literature that attempted to discredit the findings of legitimate science about environmental crisis—emanated from think tanks, and it had a large effect in changing discourse about environmental crisis. Thanks to this literature, it rapidly became risky to write about environmental crisis. A host of conservative voices was ready and eager to refute environmental scientists' statements (with abundant footnotes, usually citing each other) and call them "Chicken Littles," "apocalypse abusers," "doomsters," or some such.

Some examples might help. Fred Singer, one of the few legitimate scientists who contributed to this brownlash literature, wrote a 1994 column for the *Washington Times* titled "Climate Claims Wither under the Luminous Lights of Science."[30] As the Ehrlichs mordantly comment:

> climatologists know that the model-derived data plotted by Singer were inaccurate because they failed to account for the cooling effects of aerosols in the atmosphere. Once the aerosol effect was incorporated into improved models in the early 1990s, predictions were much closer to the recorded trend. Worst of all was Singer's failure to include the actual temperatures of the 1980s; collectively they were the warmest years in recorded history."[31]

At least here counterscience was science, and it was refuted by science. But often it wasn't even that. For example, conservative counterscience argued, in a lawyerly rather than scientific fashion, that global climate change was not happening—or if it were really happening, it was at least unproven; and even if it were to be proven, it would in fact turn out to be beneficial. Thus while others claimed that global warming didn't exist, the Competitive Enterprise Institute maintained, in its *Environmental Briefing Book for Congressional Candidates,* that "the likeliest global climate change is the creation of a milder, greener, more prosperous world."[32] Similarly, writing about ozone depletion, Dixy Lee Ray asserted that ultraviolet radiation was decreasing not increasing, and that, "furthermore" (an odd choice, if ultraviolet radiation was indeed decreasing) "the form of skin cancer caused by ultraviolet radiation is relatively harmless, though irritating and unsightly, and 99 percent of the cases can be cured if treated in time." Both claims were, of course, wrong, and outra-geously so.[33]

If think-tank-sponsored counterscience changed discourse about contemporary environmental issues at one end of the social spectrum, and corporate greenwashing, Green PR, and Green marketing targeted the broad middle, a third form of antienvironmental organizing, grassroots activism, focused on the low end. Grassroots activism sought to give the genuine populist seal of legitimacy to the most extreme right-wing attitudes as well as being enormously influential when (with the help of banks of fax machines and marketing tools such as databases) it whipped up what seemed like peoples' campaigns overnight on specific issues.

Making these campaigns happen quickly became a business—for grass-roots activism was in fact tightly linked to corporate and conservative organizing. Funded from above by corporations and supplied with specially packaged "information" and "analysis" by conservative think tanks, grassroots movements became a service offered by public relations firms: "Using specially tailored mailing lists, field officers, telephone banks and the latest in information technology, these firms are able to generate hundreds of telephone calls and/or thousands of pieces of mail to key politicians, creating the impression of wide public support for their client's position."[34] Almost unheard of ten years ago, today "technology makes building volunteer organizations as simple as writing a check."[35] Thus lawyers advised a group of U.S. electric utility companies wanting to alter the Endangered Species Act to form a grass-roots coalition by incorporating as a nonprofit and to: "develop easy-to-read information packets for Congress and the news media and woo members from virtually all walks of life. Members should include Native American entities, county and local governments, universities, school boards. . . ."[36]

Artificially created grassroots coalitions like these were called, in the trade's brazen vernacular, "Astroturf." They sometimes commanded a great deal of notice, providing what seemed to be a spontaneous outpouring of public support on the preferred side of an issue and giving that position the stamp of populist legitimacy. A University of North Carolina Business School survey found "grassroots activism" was "ranked as the most effective strategy [in persuading politicians] by fifty-seven percent of respondents"—well ahead of lobbying by company executives or political donations.[37] Even when politicians knew that a grassroots coalition had been created artifically from the top down rather than emerged spontaneously from the bottom up, the coalition remained potentially influential. Indeed, it might be more so—the fact that its members were organized by a powerful and persistent outside force suggested to politicians only "that these voters will be kept informed of how the issue is progressing and reminded of how the politician voted when it comes to re-election time."[38]

Personalized letters were generated. Talk-back radio gave free call-in numbers for more information; the calls were connected "to a telemarketer who will talk to the callers and put them through to their representative in Congress."[39] Grassroots firms also generated "attendance at town hall meetings and public hearings, as well as signatures on petitions and attendance at rallies. National Grassroots and Communications sets up local organizations to support their clients, using selected individuals from the local community who are paid and supervised by their own staff."[40] Think tanks publicized their messages in the form of anecdotes about average Americans in order to reach these groups; for example, the Heritage Foundation published *Strangled by Red Tape: The Heritage Foundation Collection of Regulatory Horror Stories* and has distributed more than 400,000 copies.[41]

Corporate, conservative, and grassroots activism provided the main impetus toward changing environmental discourse in the last three decades of the twentieth century. But one further source of antienvironmental action needs at least cursory mention. As the rhetoric of the grassroots organizer Ron Arnold suggests, grassroots passions sometimes faded into a particularly sinister form of suasion—violence against Greens. "We're out to kill the fuckers," Arnold told supporters: "We're simply trying to eliminate them. Our goal is to destroy environmentalism for once and for all"—though, in speaking this way, Arnold later maintained that: "When I say we have to pick up a sword and shield and kill the bastards, I mean politically, not physically."[42]

In sharp contrast to much-publicized instances of ecoterrorism, incidents of violence against Greens multiplied during the 1980s and 1990s. In *War against the Greens*, Daniel Helvarg records the equally rich but comparatively underreported story of acts of terror directed against environmentalists that range from death threats to assaults, from the burning of homes and barns to sometimes truly gothic instances of personal violence. In one of the worst incidents Helvarg reports on, a woman who had been fighting corporate pollution of waterways claimed that her throat had been slashed by an assailant in a camouflage mask and that her assailant then poured water from the river into the open wound, telling her "Now you'll have something to sue about."[43] In this history, ecoterrorists' principled commitment to targeting property, not people, clearly had no place; intimidating people was the whole point of violence against Greens.

Recounting a startlingly large number of these incidents, Helvarg divides them into the following categories: spontaneous violence; violence occurring in the wake of right-wing antienvironmental organizing campaigns; and violence bearing the mark of professional security agents familiar with terrorist tactics. Though such violence was a minor force compared to the organized and well-funded strategies for changing public discourse discussed above, it suggests that the spectrum of antienvironmental activism over the last three decades has been quite broad—and that one end of it has been ugly and repugnant indeed.

NOTES

Notes to Preface

[1]Robert Gottlieb, *Forcing the Spring* (Washington, DC: Island Press, 1993), p. 125.

[2]*Ibid.*, p. 106.

[3]See, for example, Roderick Nash, *Wilderness and the American Mind* (New Haven, CT: Yale University Press, 1967) and *The Rights of Nature: A History of Environmental Ethics* (Madison, WI: University of Wisconsin Press, 1989); Samuel P. Hays, *Beauty, Health, and Permanence: Environmental Politics in the United States, 1955–1985* (New York: Cambridge University Press, 1987); Gottlieb, *Forcing the Spring;* and Mark Dowie, *Losing Ground: American Environmentalism at the Close of the Twentieth Century* (Cambridge, MA: MIT Press, 1997).

[4]Rachel Carson, *Silent Spring* (Greenwich, CT: Fawcett Crest, 1962), p. 14.

[5]*Ibid.*, p. 158.

[6]*Ibid.*, p. 213.

[7]Thomas M. Disch, ed., *The Ruins of Earth* (New York: Berkeley Publishing, 1971), pp. 6–7.

[8]Philip Wylie, *The End of the Dream* (New York: DAW Books, 1972), p. 37.

[9]*Ibid.*, p. 96.

[10]*Ibid.*, p. 128.

[11]*Ibid.*, p. 119.

[12]*Ibid.*, p. 139.

[13]*Ibid.*, p. 140.

[14]*Ibid.*, p. 142.

Notes to Chapter 1

[1]Samuel P. Hays, *Beauty, Health, and Permanence: Environmental Politics in the United States, 1955–1985* (New York: Cambridge University Press, 1987), pp. 411–419.

[2]Ronald Bailey, *Ecoscam: The False Prophets of Ecological Apocalypse,* (New York: St. Martin's Press, 1993), p. 3.

[3]Paul R. and Anne H. Ehrlich, *Betrayal of Science and Reason: How Anti-Environmental Rhetoric Threatens Our Future* (Washington, DC: Island Press, 1996). Bjorn Lomborg's *The Skeptical Environmentalist* provides a recent example of environmental scientists' new skill at rapid responses to counterscience. The Danish statistician wrote as a recent avatar of the American economist, Julian Simon; his across-the-board, meticulously footnoted, apparently scholarly debunking of environmental concerns was answered with information, heat, and contempt by a wide array of environmental scientists. The

accumulated outrage at Lomborg's biased, inaccurate, and ignorant use of science had real effect; it led John Rennie, the editor-in-chief of *Scientific American*, to run a series of refutations of Lomborg just one issue after his magazine had reported favorably on Lomborg's biodiversity findings. Even more strikingly, Rennie ran these refutations with an introduction in which he himself declared that, thanks to its errors, the book was a failure. Others went further still, asserting that even the reputation and credibility of Lomborg's English-language publisher, Cambridge University Press would suffer. See "Misleading Math about the Earth" and subsequent articles, *The Scientific American*, January 2002, pp. 61–71; TomPaine.common sense at www.tompaine.com/feature.cfm/ID/4791; *Grist* Magazine at www.gristmagazine.com/grist/books/lomborg121201.asp; the World Resources Institute at www.wri.org/mediakits.cfm; and the Union of Concerned Scientists at www.ucsusa.org/environment/lomborg.html.

[4] See Appendix 1 for a fuller list of these stealthily named organizations. See Leggett, *The Carbon War: Global Warming and the End of the Oil Era* (New York: Routledge, 2001) pp. 302–304, on the presentation of the award.

[5] Theodore Roszak, *The Voice of the Earth: An Exploration of Ecopsychology* (New York: Simon and Schuster, 1993), p. 35.

[6] *Ibid.*, p. 39.

[7] David Helvarg, *The War against the Greens* (San Francisco: Sierra Club Books, 1994), p. 137.

[8] Michael Omi and Howard Winant, *Racial Formation in the United States: From the 1960s to the 1990s* (New York: Routledge, 1994), p. 115.

[9] *Ibid.*, p. 115.

[10] *Ibid.*, p. 115.

[11] *Ibid.*, p. 126.

[12] Gottlieb, *Forcing the Spring*, p. 125, has a complete list.

[13] *Ibid.*, p. 130.

[14] David Helvarg, *War against the Greens*, p. 1.

[15] Ehrlich, *Betrayal of Science and Reason*, chap. 4.

[16] Quoted and discussed in Marilyn Ivy, "Critical Texts, Mass Artifacts: The Consumption of Knowledge in Postmodern Japan," *Postmodernism and Japan*, ed. Masao Miyoshi and H.D. Harootunian (Durham, NC: Duke University Press, 1989), p. 22.

[17] Samuel Huntington, *The Clash of Civilizations and the Remaking of World Order* (New York: Simon and Schuster, 1996), pp. 306–307. Indeed, Huntington's comments came so late that conservatives were already moaning that the wars had been lost, and sensible folk were beginning to notice that the phrase "'culture war' was starting to sound a little like 'leisure suit'—a throwback to a bygone era." Huntington, alas, entered the fray eagerly with his big stick at the very time that more perceptive people were going on to something else. Janny Scott, "At Appomattox in the Culture Wars," *New York Times*, May 25, 1997, sect. 4, p. 1.

[18] See Benjamin Lee, "Critical Internationalism," *Public Culture*, 7, 1995, pp. 566–567, and George Will, "Literary Politics," in *Falling into Theory: Conflicting Views on Reading Literature*, ed. David. H. Richter (Boston: St. Martin's Press, 1994), p. 288.

[19] Angela Dillard, "Multicultural Conservatism: What It Is, Why It Matters," *Chronicle of Higher Education* March, 2, 2001, p. B8.

[20] *Ibid.*, p. B8.

[21] *Ibid.*, p. B9.

[22] Helvarg, *War against the Greens*, p. 20.

[23] Sharon Beder, *Global Spin: The Corporate Assault on Environmentalism* (White River Junction, VT: Chelsea Green Publishing Co., 1997), pp. 97–98.

24 *Ibid.*, p. 57.

25 *Ibid.*, p. 69, p. 71.

26 Helvarg, *War against the Greens*, p. 284.

27 *Ibid.*, p. 57.

28 Beder, *Global Spin*, p. 172.

29 "Chase's *In a Dark Wood* Criticizes Pacific Northwest Eco-Extremism," *Science and the Environment*: December 12, 1998 www.voyagepub.com/stories.

30 Charles Rubin, *The Green Crusade: Rethinking the Roots of Environmentalism* (Lanham, MD: Rowman and Littlefield, 1998); quoted in Raymond A. Rodgers, "Doing the Dirty Work of Globalization," *Capitalism, Nature, Society* 6 (3), September, 1995, p. 119, p. 128.

31 Martin Lewis, *Green Delusions: An Environmentalist Critique of Radical Environmentalism* (Durham, NC: Duke University Press, 1992), p. 15.

32 Beder, *Global Spin*, p. 51.

33 Robert N. Proctor, *Cancer Wars: How Politics Shapes What We Know and Don't Know about Cancer* (New York: Basic Books, 1995), p. 51.

34 Quoted in *Ibid.*, p. 87.

35 *Ibid.*, p. 93.

36 As Proctor, drawing on Lou Cannon's *Reagan* (New York: G.P. Putnam's Sons, 1982), describes the incident: "Reagan denied ever having made the claim (he claimed only to have asserted that 'growing and decaying vegetation' was responsible for '93 percent of the oxides of nitrogen,' apparently confusing the nitrous oxides produced by plants with the nitrogen dioxide produced by smokestacks), but he never retreated from his stance that nature was far more culpable than industry in the genesis of pollution." Proctor, *Cancer Wars*, p. 77; Cannon, *Reagan*, p. 289.

37 Proctor devotes a chapter to Bruce Ames's influential scientific challenge to the danger of industrial carcinogens compared to natural ones; Michael Fumento, in *Science under Siege*, turns the science into attack rhetoric, condemning "the cult of the natural" for making people blame industry, not nature, for cancer. Proctor, *Cancer Wars*, chap. 6 and p. 95; Michael Fumento, *Science under Siege: Balancing Technology and the Environment* (New York: William Morrow, 1993).

38 Helvarg, *War against the Greens*, p. 122; John McPhee, *Encounters with the Archdruid* (New York: Farrar, Strauss and Giroux, 1971).

39 See the discussion of Whelan and other Reagan- and post-Reagan-era antienvironmental ideologues in Proctor, *Cancer Wars*, pp. 87–100.

40 *Ibid.*, p. 140.

41 Beder, *Global Spin*, p. 52.

42 Ron Arnold and Alan Gottlieb, *Trashing the Economy: How Runaway Environmentalism is Wrecking America* (Bellevue, WA: Free Enterprise Press, 1993), vii. Quoted in Beder, *Global Spin*, p. 52.

43 Quoted in Tom Athasaniou, *Divided Planet: The Ecology of Rich and Poor* (Athens, GA: University of Georgia Press, 1996), p. 233.

44 For a vivid short list of examples of corporate greenwashing, see Joshua Karliner, "The Globalization of Corporate Culture," *Reclaiming the Environmental Debate: The Politics of Health in a Toxic Culture* (Cambridge, MA: MIT Press, 2000), pp. 182–183. For more sustained treatment, see Jed Greer and Kenny Bruno, *Greenwash: The Reality behind Corporate Environmentalism* (Penang and New York: Third World Network and Apex Press, 1996).

45 Ehrlich, *Betrayal*, p. 177.

[46]See Julian Simon, *The Ultimate Resource 2* (Princeton, NJ: Princeton University Press, 1996) and the discussion of the book in chap. 5 of this volume.

[47]Roderick Frazier Nash, *The Rights of Nature: A History of Environmental Ethics* (Madison, WI: University of Wisconsin Press, 1989), p. 191.

[48]Helvarg, *War against the Greens*, p. 194.

[49]In 1990, Judi Bari and Daryl Cheney were injured when a pipe bomb exploded in their car as they drove to San Francisco to meet with supporters of the Redwood Summer protests. The bomb exploded beneath Bari's driver's seat, "shattering her pelvis and dislocating her spine"; even as paramedics were working to save her life, "the FBI's domestic terrorism squad, working with the Oakland police, had commandeered the investigation from the Alcohol, Tobacco and Firearms agents on the scene" (*Ibid.*, p. 331). The next morning the police arrested them, but the government's charges were subsequently dropped. Both Cheney and Bari had received death threats, and apparent evidence against them turned out to be misstated and untrue. The result was that many felt they had, as Earth First! activists, been unfairly persecuted by the FBI and the Oakland police. They then sued the police and the FBI for violation of their civil rights—a suit they won after Bari's death from cancer.

[50]For a discussion of these and other incidents, see Peter Montague, "Mainstream Extremists," *Rachel's Environment & Health News*, 740, December 21, 2001. Young's comments can be found in Liz Ruskin, "Stevens, Murkowski, and Young Vow Retribution," *Anchorage Daily News*, Sept 12, 2001, available at www.adn.com/front/story/686424p-728770c.html, and McInnes's letter to environmentalists was discussed on his Web site (January 10, 2002) www.house.gov/mcinnes/.

[51]Nash, *Rights of Nature*, pp. 146–147.

[52]Al Gore, *Earth In the Balance: Ecology and the Human Spirit* (New York: Penguin Books, 1992), p. 217.

[53]Tom Clancy, *Rainbow Six* (New York: Berkeley Books, 1999), p. 893.

[54]*Ibid.*, p. 894.

[55]See Ramachandra Guha and Juan Martinez-Alier, *Varieties of Environmentalism: Essays North and South* (New Delhi: Oxford University Press, 1997).

[56]Gottlieb, *Forcing the Spring*, p. 289.

[57]*Ibid.*, 318.

[58]Donald Worster, "The Wilderness of History," *Wild Earth*, Fall 1997, p. 9. Cronon's essay, "The Trouble with Wilderness; or, Getting Back to the Wrong Nature," comes from *Uncommon Ground: Rethinking the Human Place in Nature*, ed. William Cronon (New York: W.W. Norton, 1996), pp. 69–90.

[59]David Harvey, *Justice, Nature, and the Geography of Difference* (Cambridge, MA: Blackwell, 1996), p. 194.

[60]Gottlieb, "An Odd Assortment of Allies: American Environmentalism in the 1990s," *Media and the Environment*, eds. Craige L. LaMay and Everette E. Dennis, eds. (Covelo, CA: Island Press, 1993), pp. 44–45. These omissions were, of course, sources of conflict. The wars between social ecologists and Deep Ecologists were notorious and left many open wounds; almost as intense were battles between ecofeminist, ecojustice, and antitoxics activists and the large wilderness-oriented organizations. Tensions between environmental activism and social justice activism also flared up. If the psychology of marginal groups means a propensity to self-destruction via internecine warfare, this has certainly been a temptation; but real issues abound that surface when an organization like the Sierra Club narrowly defeats a motion to promote restrictions on immigration and, together with the Environmental

Defense Fund, declines to participate in a grassroots protest against "the poisoning of an urban community by an incineration facility" because it was "'a community health issue,' not an environmental one." Giovanna Di Chiro, "Nature as Community: The Convergence of Environment and Social Justice," *Uncommon Ground*, p. 299.

[61]In so growing, these shadows have become visible to more and more interested observers. Within the academy, scholars positioned all across the curriculum (from sociology to philosophy, religion, economics, psychology, and literature, to name some of the most prominent areas) have been "greening" their fields and collaborating in interdisciplinary work on environmental issues. In larger society, environmental crisis has been resurrected, as Chapters 2 and 4 explore, from conservative denial by being formulated as a civilizational crisis that involves a vast number of the institutions, practices, and cultural assumptions of modernity.

Notes to Chapter 2

[1]Nathan Glazer, *We Are All Multiculturalists Now* (Cambridge, MA: Harvard University Press, 1998); Special Issue, "The New Face of America," *Time*, Fall, 1993. Roger Rouse, "Thinking through Transnationalism: Notes on the Cultural Politics of Class Relations in the Contemporary United States," *Public Culture*, 7, 1995, pp. 353–402.

[2]Peter Schwartz and Peter Leyden, "The Long Boom: A History of the Future 1980–2020," *Wired*, July 1997, p. 170.

[3]Robert Reich, *The Work of Nations: Preparing Ourselves for Twenty-First-Century Capitalism* (New York: Knopf), Part 3.

[4]Malcolm Waters, *Globalization* (New York: Routledge, 1995), P. 1.

[5]Al Gore, *Earth in the Balance: Ecology and the Human Spirit* (New York: Penguin, 1992).

[6]Maarten Hajer, *The Politics of Environmental Discourse: Ecological Modernization and the Policy Process* (Oxford: Clarendon Press, 1995), p. 261.

[7]On the summer of 1988, see the introduction to Bill McKibben's *The End of Nature* (New York: Random House, 1989) and Andrew Ross, *Strange Weather: Culture, Science and Technology in the Age of Limits* (London: Verso, 1991), pp. 205–206.

[8]Hajer, *Politics of Environmental Discourse*, p. 3.

[9]Mark Hertsgaard, *Earth Odyssey* (New York: Broadway Books, 1998), p. 267.

[10]*Ibid.*, p. 328.

[11]Paul Hawken and Amory and L. Hunter Lovins, *Natural Capitalism: Creating the Next Industrial Revolution* (Boston: Little, Brown and Company, 1999), pp. 4–5.

[12]Hajer, *Politics of Environmental Discourse*, p. 267.

[13]*Ibid.*, p. 26.

[14]*Ibid.*, p. 98.

[15]Hawken et al., *Natural Capitalism*, p. 166.

[16]The OECD is particularly optimistic about work in advanced sensors, biotechnology, clean car technology, product recycling, smart water treatment, smart waste treatment, cleaner industrial processes, micromanufacturing, renewables and new energy technologies, and photovoltaics. OECD, *OECD Environmental Outlook* (Paris: OECD, 2001), p. 78, available at www.oecd.org.

[17]Hajer, *Politics of Environmental Discourse*, p. 123 and p. 273.

[18]Quoted in Hawken et al., *Natural Capitalism*, 165.

[19]Hertsgaard, *Earth Odyssey*, p. 328.

[20]Hajer, *Politics of Environmental Discourse*, p. 14.

[21] *Ibid.*, p. 13.

[22] Maarten Hajer, "Ecological Modernisation," *Risk, Environment and Modernity: Towards a New Ecology*, eds. Scott Lash, Bronislaw Szersynski, and Brian Wynne (London: Sage Publications, 1996), p. 249.

[23] Samuel P. Hays, *Beauty, Health, and Permanence: Environmental Politics in the United States, 1955–1985* (New York: Cambridge University Press, 1987), p. 265.

[24] *Ibid.*, p. 250.

[25] Hertsgaard, *Earth Odyssey*, p. 299.

[26] Ehrlich, *Betrayal of Science and Reason*, p. 48.

[27] *Ibid.*, p. 50.

[28] Quoted in Hertsgaard, *Earth Odyssey*, p. 301.

[29] Hawken et al., *Natural Capitalism*, pp. 65–73.

[30] Tom Athanasiou, *Divided Planet: The Ecology of the Rich and Poor* (Athens, GA: University of Georgia Press, 1998), p. 237.

[31] Hawken et al., *Natural Capitalism*, p. 16, p. 125ff, and p. 141.

[32] Timothy W. Luke, "Rethinking Technoscience in Risk Society," *Reclaiming the Environmental Debate: The Politics of Health in a Toxic Culture*, ed. Richard Hofrichter (Cambridge, MA: MIT Press, 2000), p. 248.

[33] Sandra Steingraber, *Living Downstream: A Scientist's Personal Investigation of Cancer and the Environment* (New York: Random House, 1998), p. 76.

[34] *Ibid.*, p. 284. For the fullest critique of risk assessment and for the elaboration of another new paradigm to oppose it—the "ecological paradigm"—see Joe Thornton, *Pandora's Poison: Chlorine, Health, and a New Environmental Strategy* (Cambridge, MA: MIT Press, 2000).

[35] Ulrich Beck, *Risk Society: Towards a New Modernity* (London: Sage Publications, 1992), p. 63. An interesting example comes with the prospect of developing DNA chips as a more sensitive and rapid way of testing for toxins than any we now have. It has, at least initially, raised alarm as well as interest. Andrew Pollack reports that "experts say it would be easy for such data to be misinterpreted or incompletely analyzed, but that environmental groups would be quick to argue that products be banned or pollutants more tightly regulated." As Chris Bradfield, a professor of oncology at Wisconsin's McArdle Laboratory for Cancer Research, unfortunately puts it: "You don't necessarily want to have a more sensitive way to look for poisons. . . . There's a lot of trepidation and uncertainty." Apparently, the uncertainty is more to be feared than the toxification. Andrew Pollack, "DNA Chip May Help Usher In a New Era of Product Testing," *New York Times*, November 28, 2000, p. F2.

[36] Athanasiou, *Divided Planet*, p. 213; Hawken et al., *Natural Capitalism*, p. 160.

[37] *Ibid.*, p. 154.

[38] *Ibid.*, p. 116.

[39] *Ibid.*, p. 319.

[40] Quoted in Athanasiou, *Divided Planet*, p. 229.

[41] Jared Diamond, "The Greening of Corporate America," *New York Times*, Jan. 8, 2000, p. A13.

[42] Hajer, *Politics of Environmental Discourse*, p. 39.

[43] Mark Dowie, *Losing Ground: American Environmentalism at the Close of the Twentieth Century* (Cambridge, MA: M.I.T. Press, 1996), and Philip Shabecoff, *Earth Rising: American Environmentalism in the 21st Century* (Washington, DC: Island Press, 2000).

[44] Clinton's first term received very low environmental marks. At first, environmentalists were extremely optimistic. When Clinton took over, Mark Dowie reports, "Gore . . . heightened his popularity among greens by announcing that Rachel Carson would 'sit in on all important decisions of this administration'" (Dowie, *Losing Ground*, p. 178). Tom Athanasiou wryly records

the symbolic duel of White House solar panels; panels installed on the building by Jimmy Carter were taken down (of course) by Ronald Reagan; Clinton put better solar panels up again (*Ibid.*, p. 23, p. 243). But environmental policies and programs Clinton-Gore espoused were dropped or watered down, and steps in an opposite direction were taken. Clinton dropped his energy tax proposal as soon as it came under fire from the oil and gas industry, and Clinton's EPA chief Carol Browner reevaluated the Delaney amendment to the Food and Drug Act, which: "stipulated a zero tolerance for all carcinogenic residues in food products," a move that was "an early signal that the Clinton administration would follow the Bush doctrine of negligable risk." Clinton announced new air quality regulations that "called for voluntary rather than mandatory compliance," and he reneged on his promise to raise the CAFE (corporate average fuel economy) standards above 27.5 mph. Interior Secretary Bruce Babbitt and the president caved into opposition and didn't raise grazing fees on public lands. Worst of all, in 1995, Clinton signed a bill that included the Salvage Rider, a provision that allowed a vast increase in logging on public lands and provoked a huge outcry (*Ibid.*, pp. 181–184).

[45]Todd Wilkinson, "How 'Green' Is Clinton's Legacy?" *The Christian Science Monitor*, April 20, 2000, p. 4. Along with vetoing Republican attempts to gut environmental protections and resisting Republican attempts to open the Alaska National Wildlife Refuge to oil drilling, Clinton set aside as off-limits to development more land than Theodore Roosevelt did in the early twentieth century.

[46]Recently, for example, the OECD has expressed optimism about globalization's environmental possibilities on a number of fronts. While its economies of scale are "likely to be on balance negative, largely because [globalization] contributes to increased production," it promises benefits through structural changes, as developing world economies move from primary commodity production to less-polluting light manufacturing and services. Erasing trade barriers will likewise reap a benefit—environmentally destructive local subsidies will be struck down. And increased technological diffusion will ensure that technologies that "tend to use fewer resources and produce less pollution than their predecessors" will spread about the world. The internalization of environmental concerns in world trade agreements is also, in principle, doable. But, despite these possibilities, even the optimistic OECD recognizes that, for now, "governments will find that longer-term environmental goals will often conflict with shorter-term economic competitiveness goals" and that "globalization is thus likely to intensify the need for stronger and better environmental policies, rather than lessen it." This realism suggests that even the OECD, advocate of globalization, cannot claim that possible gains have been translated into practice yet. And in the 1990s, these possibilities weren't even articulated yet for the most part by proglobalization forces. Though it is now trying to Green itself thanks to worldwide criticism and demonstrations, globalization burst on the scene in the 1990s as a brown movement. *OECD Environmental Outlook*, pp. 53–54.

[47]See Debi Barker and Jerry Mander, *Invisible Government: The World Trade Organization: Global Government for the New Millennium?* (San Francisco: International Forum on Globalization, 1996).

[48]The most assiduous, biting, and complete criticism of globalization's effect on the environment comes from the International Forum on Globalization (IFG). Its work-in-progress includes the following pamphlets: Tony Clarke et al., *The Emergence of Corporate Rule and What to Do about It* (San Francisco: International Forum on Globalization, 1996); Maude Barlow, *Blue Gold: The Global Water Crises and the Commodification of the World's Water System* (San Francisco: International Forum on Globalization, 1996); and Barker and Mander, *Invisible Government*. The IFG also offers packets of information on topics

such as "What Is Globalization?" "Resistance to Globalization," "Environment," "Military Intelligence and Globalization," "Technology," and "Media and Public Relations."

[49] For an influential analysis of the environmental consequences of global growth, see Paul Kennedy, *Preparing for the Twenty-First Century* (New York: Random House, 1993).

[50] Tony Hiss, *The Experience of Place* (New York: Random House, 1991), pp. 138–139.

[51] Victor Menotti, "The Decline of Forest Health since Rio: Ecology Loses to Globalization," *IFG News*, 2, Summer, 1997, p. 3. Indeed, since Rio, the Worldwatch Institute maintains, "global environmental problems, from climate change to species extinctions, deforestation, and water scarcity have generally worsened." Gary Gardner, "The Challenge for Johannesburg: Creating a More Secure World," *State of the World 2002*, ed. Linda Starke (New York: W.W. Norton, 2002), p. 4.

[52] The OECD considers increased environmental impacts from the ongoing transportation boom to be a serious environmental problem. Transportation represents "almost two-thirds of the growth in [energy] consumption since the early 1970s"; its contribution "to total CO_2 emissions in OECD countries is projected to increase from approximately 20% in 1995 to 30% in 2020." *OECD Environmental Outlook*, p. 146 and p. 173.

[53] Barry Lopez, "On the Wings of Commerce: Penguins and Lipstick, Strawberries and Gold— Aloft!" *Harper's Magazine*, October, 1995, p. 45.

[54] Michael Soulé, quoted in David Quammen, "Planet of Weeds: Tallying the Losses of Earth's Animals and Plants," *Harper's Magazine*, October, 1998, p. 68.

[55] See David Kortin, *When Corporations Rule the World* (West Hartford and San Francisco: Kumarian Press and Berrett-Koehler Publishers, 1995), p. 210.

[56] David C. Korten, "The ABCs of Finance Capital," *IFG News*, 2, Summer, 1997, p. 3.

[57] Tom Athanasiou, *Divided Planet*, p. 171.

[58] Stuart Hall, "New Cultures for Old," *A Place In the World? Places, Cultures, and Globalization*, ed. Doreen Massey and Pat Jess (New York: Oxford Press, 1995), pp. 205–209.

[59] Sometimes the more radical the commitment to exploring this new transnationalism, the more ecologically ignorant the result. Michael Hardt's and Antonio Negri's much-lionized critique of globalization, *Empire*, locates political agency in the large new global flows of stateless people, migrants, and refugees. Hardt and Negri see these as the "new barbarians," animated by "*the will to be against*," and with the ability to become a "new proletariat" through "nomadism, desertion, exodus." Michael Hardt and Antonio Negri, *Empire* (Cambridge, MA: Harvard University Press, 2000), p. 215 and p. 210 (italics in the original). Apart from their fantastic restructuring of the conditions and consciousness of the majority of global migrants today, Hardt and Negri ignore environmental discourse altogether. If Marxist environmentalists have found evidence to show that Marx took ecological factors into consideration, no revisionist could do this for Hardt and Negri. Their proletariat is, by definition, without attachment to or presumably need for ecosystems.

[60] Edward Casey, *The Fate of Place: A Philosophical History* (Berkeley, CA: University of California Press, 1997), p. 334. Casey, of course, sees the fundamental cause of place turning into site as part of a philosophic shift that Leibnitz, in particular, made modernity's dominant attitude. Technologically enhanced global capital then realizes that attitude, I argue, more vividly than ever before in fact.

[61] The U.N.'s report, "World Population Monitoring 2001: Population, Environment and Development" projects that the epochal change from a predominantly rural to predominantly urban world will occur in the year 2007 (p. 11). The report is available at www.un.org/esa/ population/publications/wpm/wpm2001.pdf.

[62]Hiss, *Experience of Place*, p. 10.

[63]Burton Pike, "Cities in an Urban World," talk given at a conference entitled "Spirit and Space in Modern Israel," Jewish Theological Seminary, New York, on March 2, 1998.

[64]See note 48 above and see Hilary French, *Vanishing Borders: Protecting the Planet in the Age of Globalization* (New York: W.W. Norton, 2000), chaps. 7 and 8 for sensible recommendations.

[65]William Clinton, "Presentation by Former President William Jefferson Clinton," October 6, 2000, Yale University. Transcript available at www.yale.edu/opa/news/clinton.html.

[66]A short list of Bush administration interventions into environmental policy and protection— a list that covers just its first year, in which it had limited time for such issues as it had to mount its war on terrorism—is sobering. It rejected the global warming pact negotiated in Kyoto, outraging environmentalists and European leaders, and it did nothing when a panel of top American scientists subsequently declared that the earth was indeed warming and human beings were responsible. Douglas Jehl, "U.S. Going Empty Handed to Meeting on Global Warming," *New York Times*, March 29, 2001, p. A22; Katharine Seelye and Andrew Revkin, "Panel Tells Bush Global Warming Is Getting Worse," *New York Times*, June 7, 2001, p. 1. It raised the prospect of oil drilling in the Arctic National Wildlife Refuge, and it wrote a new energy plan calling for loosening regulations on oil and gas exploration and ordering "a sweeping review of parklands to see whether more energy resources can be extracted." David Sanger, "In Energy Plan, Bush Urges New Drilling, Conservation, and Nuclear Power Review," *New York Times*, May 17, 2001, p. 1. It attempted to roll back the Clinton administration's rule that reduced by 80 percent the permissible standard for arsenic in drinking water. It suspended regulations requiring mining companies to pay for cleanups and granting the Interior Department authority to prohibit mines if they threatened "irreparable harm" to the environment. "More Environmental Rollbacks," *New York Times*, October 29, 2001, p. A10. It pledged to modify the Clinton ban on new roads in U.S. forests. Douglas Jehl, "Bush Will Modify Ban on New Roads for U.S. Forests," *New York Times*, May 4, 2001, p. 1. It filled "key subcabinet posts with conservative activists and industry lobbyists who have spent their careers criticizing the laws they are now sworn to uphold." "No Greens Need Apply," *New York Times*, August 19, 2001, p. A12. It signaled it was receptive to reversing the Clinton rule phasing out snowmobiles from Yellowstone National Park. It proposed weakening the Clean Air Act by weakening the requirement that forces power plants (especially the aging, coal-fired, Midwestern power plants that send acid rain into the Northeast) to install modern pollution controls when they are upgraded. "Rollback on Clean Air," *New York Times*, January 9, 2002, p. A22. It weakened efficiency standards for air-conditioners and heat pumps. It decided to go ahead with a highly controversial program for radioactive waste disposal at Yucca Mountain in Nevada. Matthew Wald, "Nevada Site Urged for Nuclear Dump," *New York Times*, January 11, 2002, p. A1. It got rid of a Gore-originated program for making real steps toward energy efficiency in cars, an action that represented "a setback for greater near-term fuel efficiency, for reducing our reliance on Middle Eastern oil, and for slowing global warming." "Spencer Abraham's Dream Car," *New York Times*, January 14, 2002, p. A14; Neela Banerjee with Danny Hakim, "U.S. Ends Car Plan On Gas Efficiency; Looks to Hydrogen," *New York Times*, January 9, 2002. It rolled back Clinton rules for wetlands, streamlining approval for development projects and forsaking the goal of no net loss of wetlands. Christopher Marquis, "Bush Administration Rolls Back Clinton Rules for Wetlands," *New York Times*, January 15, 2002, p. A16.

[67]See William Cronon, "When the G.O.P. Was Green," *New York Times*, January 8, 2001, p. A21.

[68]Robert Proctor, *Cancer Wars: How Politics Shapes What We Know about Cancer* (New York: Basic Books, 1995), p. 54.

Notes to Part II Introduction

[1]Fairfield Osborn, *Our Plundered Planet* (Boston: Little, Brown and Company, 1948), p. 40.

[2]James Gustave Speth notes that a large number of the serious warnings about population growth, species extinction, desertification, and global warming contained in the *Global 2000 Report to The President* (commissioned by Jimmy Carter and contested by the Reagan administration's subsequent report, *Global 2000 Revised*) have turned out to be correct. See James Gustave Speth, "The Cascading of Environmental Consequences: Are We Running Out of Time?" University Committee on Environment Distinguished Environment Lecture, Kennedy School of Government, April 11, 2001. Reprinted by Yale School of Forestry Publications, New Haven, CT.

[3]Clive Ponting, *A Green History of the World: The Environment and the Collapse of Great Civilizations* (New York: Penguin, 1991), p. 359; Robert Proctor, *Cancer Wars: How Politics Shapes What We Know and Don't Know about Cancer* (New York: Basic Books, 1995), p. 259; Paul Ehrlich, *The Population Bomb* (Binghamton, NY: Vail-Ballou Press, 1970), p. 50, 98.

[4]The two quotations come not from environmental activists but from the Organization for Economic Cooperation and Development: they are taken from its recent *Environmental Outlook* (Paris: OECD, 2001), p. 176, p. 185. In the subsequent chapters, I draw on the work of many U.S. environmental scientists, journalists, and nature writers; equally, I use material from the OECD, the World Bank, the World Health Organization, and other U.N. sources. I try to draw on well-regarded environmental scientists and these latter organizations for many of my factual assertions, in the hopes that the facts I cite will represent, as much as possible, consensus science rather than either brown or green contrarianism/activism. My more affective-cultural interpretations come both from me and from the nature writing, environmental journalism, and engaged environmental science I cite.

I can't resist adding here one even more vivid example of a solved but resurgent environmental issue: a prophecy that caused the activist environmental scientist Paul Ehrlich much grief. I mean his 1968 prediction of global famines by the 1980s. Ehrlich's predictions of doom simply did not come true, largely thanks to the global Green Revolution in agriculture. But as the Green Revolution spends its force and population keeps on rising, food issues are creeping back onto the list of global environmental concerns and constraints in less apocalyptic but still serious ways.

[5]*Ibid.*, p. 21.

[6]The Worldwatch Institute's latest report plainly states that, while consciousness about sustainable development has been raised significantly since the 1992 UNCED conference in Rio, that consciousness has not been translated into effective action. Since 1992, actual global environmental problems have all worsened. Gary Gardner, "The Challenge for Johannesburg: Creating a More Secure World," *The State of the World 2002*, ed. Linda Starke (New York: W.W. Norton, 2002), p. 4.

Notes to Chapter 3

[1]Daniel Botkin, *Discordant Harmonies: A New Ecology for the Twenty-First Century* (New York: Oxford University Press, 1990), p. 174.

[2]Clive Ponting, *A Green History of the World: The Environment and the Collapse of Great Civilizations* (New York: Penguin, 1991).

[3]John Terborgh, *Requiem for Nature* (Washington, DC: Island Press, 1999), p. 122; FAO, *The State of the World's Forests 2001*, available at www.fao.org/forestry/foris/webview/forestry2/index.jsp?siteId=1800&langId=1&41947521. See also Andrew C. Rivkin, "Forget Nature, Even Eden Is Engineered," *New York Times*, August 20, 2002, p. F4.

[4]OECD, *Environmental Outlook* (Paris: OECD, 2000), p. 51.

[5]UNEP, "The State of the Environment—Regional Synthesis—Forests," *GEO-2000: Global Environmental Outlook*, available at www.grida.no/geo2000/english/index.htm.

[6]Resource and energy crises are also, of course, part of contemporary fears of running out. The prospect of exhaustion of resources—of the minerals and fossil fuels that sustain the human economy—has been the area in which old environmental apocalypses have been most effectively dismissed as hysterical and incorrect. But these debunked crises have an uncanny way of coming back—as has happened with the energy crisis under George W. Bush—thanks to the demands of societal growth. But far more serious is the ironic fact that, in some cases, *not* running out of resources can yield an even greater abundance of problems than running out. See the discussion of global warming, below, for details.

[7]Lawrence Buell, *Writing for an Endangered World* (Cambridge: Harvard University Press, 2001), pp. 38–44.

[8]For example, literary *fin de siècle* exhaustion and modernist fatigue contemplated the end of things from such perspectives. The aestheticized, contemplative melancholy that surrounded T.S. Eliot's famous sunset in "The Love Song of J. Alfred Prufrock" ("spread out against the sky/ Like a patient etherized upon a table") or his equally famous apocalypse in "The Hollow Men" ("This is the way the world ends/ Not with a bang but a whimper") express, I contend, contemporary versions of this tone of elite contemplation—a tone that is worlds apart from, say, the universe of Mike Gold's *Jews without Money* (New York: Carroll and Graf, 1984 [1930]), a book that vividly depicts the harsh environmental as well as social conditions of people at the other end of the social spectrum.

[9]Stuart Pimm, *The World According to Pimm: A Scientist Audits the Earth* (New York: McGraw-Hill, 2001), p. 163.

[10]*Ibid.*, p. 6.

[11]*Ibid.*, p. 143.

[12]Paul Hawken, Amory Lovins, and L. Hunter Lovins, *Natural Capitalism: Creating the Next Industrial Revolution* (Boston: Little, Brown and Co., 1999), p. 4; UNEP, "The State of the Environment—Regional Synthesis—Marine and Coastal Areas," *GEO-2000*.

[13]Gary Gardner, "The Challenge for Johannesburg: Creating a More Secure World," *State of the World 2002*, ed. Linda Starke (New York: W.W. Norton, 2002), p. 9.

[14]Hilary French, *Vanishing Borders: Protecting the Planet in the Age of Globalization* (New York: W.W. Norton, 2000), p. 57.

[15]Quoted in Donella H. Meadows, Dennis L. Meadows, Jørgen Randers, *Beyond the Limits: Confronting Global Collapse, Envisioning a Sustainable Future* (White River Junction, VT: Chelsea Green Publishing, 1992), p. 186.

[16]Colin Woodard, *Ocean's End: Travels through Endangered Seas* (New York: Basic Books, 2000), p. 75.

[17]UNEP, "The State of the Environment—Regional Synthesis—Marine and Coastal Areas," *GEO-2000*.

[18]Woodard, *Ocean's End*, p. 90.

[19]French, *Vanishing Borders*, p. 60.

20 *Ibid.*, p. 60.

21 Tom Athanasiou, *Divided Planet: The Ecology of Rich and Poor* (Athens, GA: University of Georgia Press, 1996), p. 121.

22 *Ibid.*, p. 121.

23 Tania Aebi with Bernadette Brennan, *Maiden Voyage* (New York: Ballantine Books, 1996), p. 121.

24 Woodard, *Ocean's End*, p. 7.

25 *Ibid.*, p. 9.

26 *Ibid.*, p. 22.

27 *Ibid.*, p. 22.

28 UNEP, "The State of the Environment—Regional Synthesis—Marine and Coastal Areas," *GEO-2000.*

29 Woodard, *Ocean's End*, p. 101.

30 *Ibid.*, p. 99.

31 Quoted in Laurie Garrett, *The Coming Plague: Newly Emerging Diseases in a World out of Balance* (New York: Penguin Books, 1994), p. 563.

32 Paul R. Ehrlich and Anne H. Ehrlich, *Betrayal of Science and Reason: How Anti-Environmental Rhetoric Threatens Our Future* (Washington, DC: Island Press, 1996), p. 105.

33 Meadows et al., *Beyond the Limits*, p. 57.

34 The first assertion comes from the World Health Organization, *Global Water Supply and Sanitation Assessment 2000 Report*, available at www.who.int/water_sanitation_health/ Globalassessment/GlobalTOC.htm; the second from the Department of Economic and Social Affairs: Population Division, *World Population Monitoring 2001: Population, Environment, and Development*, (New York: United Nations, 2001), p. 70; and the third from UNEP, "The State of the Environment—Regional Synthesis—Freshwater," *GEO-2000.*

35 Maude Barlow, *Blue Gold: The Global Water Crisis and the Commodification of the World's Water Supply* (San Francisco: International Forum on Globalization, 1999), p. 5.

36 OECD, *Environmental Outlook*, p. 96. The Worldwatch Institute also agrees with Barlow, predicting that two thirds of the world will be in water stress by 2025. See Gardner, "The Challenge for Johannesburg," p. 6.

37 UNEP, "The State of the Environment—Regional Synthesis—Freshwater," *GEO-2000.*

38 Barlow, *Blue Gold*, p. 4, p. 7.

39 *Ibid.*, p. 9.

40 Athanasiou, *Divided Planet*, p. 124.

41 OECD, *Environmental Outlook*, p. 101.

42 Barlow, *Blue Gold*, p. 3, p. 9.

43 *Ibid.*, p. 14.

44 *Ibid.*, p. 18.

45 *Ibid.*, p. 19.

46 *Ibid.*, p. 24.

47 Antonio Juhasz, "Bolivian Water Presents Alternative to Globalization of Water," *IFG Bulletin: Special Water Issue*, Summer, 2001, p. 4.

48 Samuel P. Hays, *Beauty, Health, and Permanence: Environmental Politics in the United States, 1955–1985* (Cambridge: Cambridge University Press, 1987), p. 22.

49 It might not even be frivolous to suggest that private property rights over other human beings' genetic material were invalidated and human reproduction became a publicly protected commons with the end of slavery. Today, human DNA risks being privatized, even as bacteria and animals have already been patented.

[50]Lester Brown, quoted in Meadows et al., *Beyond the Limits*, p. 52.

[51]Hawken et al., *Natural Capitalism*, p. 4, p. 192.

[52]Ehrlich, *Betrayal of Science and Reason*, p. 226.

[53]Mark Dowie, *Losing Ground: American Environmentalism at the Close of the Twentieth Century* (Cambridge, MA: MIT Press, 1997), p. 236.

[54]Department of Economic and Social Affairs, *World Population Monitoring 2001*, p. 70.

[55]Quoted in Hawken et al., *Natural Capitalism*, p. 193.

[56]Ehrlich, *Betrayal of Science and Reason*, p. 243.

[57]Athanasiou, *Divided Planet*, p. 125.

[58]"Crimes against the Soil, the Air, and the Water," *New York Times*, Feb. 7, 2000, p. A 13.

[59]OECD, *Environmental Outlook*, p. 89.

[60]*Ibid.*, p. 89.

[61]French, *Vanishing Borders*, p. 61.

[62]Quoted in Hawken et al., *Natural Capitalism*, p. 195.

[63]French, *Vanishing Borders*, p. 57.

[64]Bill McKibben, "A Special Moment in History," *Atlantic Monthly*, May, 1998, p. 62.

[65]OECD, *Environmental Outlook*, p. 86; Department of Economic and Social Affairs, *World Population Monitoring 2002*, p. 70.

[66]Both are quoted in "Crop Scientists Seek a New Revolution," *Science*, 283, January 15, 1999, p. 310.

[67]*Ibid.*, p. 314.

[68]John Holdren, "Asking the Wrong Question," *Scientific American*, January 2002, p. 65.

[69]Al Gore, *Earth in the Balance: Ecology and the Human Spirit* (New York: Penguin, 1992), p.147.

[70]Meadows et al., *Beyond the Limits*, p. 83.

[71]OECD, *Environmental Outlook*, p. 236.

[72]Gore, *Earth in the Balance*, p. 147, p. 150.

[73]"As Oceans Warm, Problems from Viruses and Bacteria Mount," *New York Times*, January 24, 1999, p. 15.

[74]UNEP, "The State of the Environment—Global Issues—Toxic Chemicals and Hazardous Waste," *GEO-2000*.

[75]Gore, *Earth in the Balance*, p. 109.

[76]Dowie, *Losing Ground*, p. 127.

[77]Joe Thornton, *Pandora's Poison: Chlorine, Health, and a New Environmental Strategy* (Cambridge, MA: MIT Press, 2000), p. 23.

[78]French, *Vanishing Borders*, p. 84.

[79]Sandra Steingraber, *Living Downstream: A Scientist's Personal Investigation of Cancer and the Environment* (New York: Vintage, 1998), p. 70.

[80]Mark Hertsgaard, *Earth Odyssey* (New York: Broadway Books, 1998), p. 375.

[81]Steingraber, *Living Downstream*, p. 100. The 600,000 estimate comes from R.S.H. Yang and is cited in Sheldon Krimsky, *Hormonal Chaos: The Science and the Social Origins of the Environmental Endocrine Hypothesis* (Baltimore, MD: Johns Hopkins University Press, 2000), p. 200. See pp. 197–200 for Krimsky's full discussion of these estimates and estimates of the numbers of chemicals actually tested.

[82]Steingraber, *Living Downstream*, p. 99, p. 270.

[83]Risk assessment is inadequate in a number of ways, Steingraber, along with many other scientists and environmentalists, holds. Where environmental regulation does set limits, these are for individual substances and do not address the well-known fact that people *normally* absorb "cocktails" of individual pollutants these days and that such mixtures are

vastly more potent than any of their individual constituents. Risk assessment of individual substances also does not address the fact that people are routinely exposed to the same chemical from many different sources. No longer does traditional toxicology's faith that "the dose makes the poison" work. Equally, the engineer's certainty that "safe" low dosages can be determined for environmental pollutants is also incorrect. Not only do cocktails of poisons defeat that logic, but there are many pollutants (from certain carcinogens to gene-damaging substances to homone-disrupting chemicals) where only zero tolerance represents safety. It is also disturbing that the standards of proof of toxic effects upon humans are so high (95 percent), and that the gap between exposure to the poison and the appearance of damage to the human body is often so long. Many must suffer, it seems, for a few chemicals to be prohibited—and all this without considering the uphill political battles that so many attempted prohibitions of chemicals have faced.

84Theo Colborn, Dianne Dumanoski, and John Peterson Myers, *Our Stolen Future: Are We Threatening Our Fertility, Intelligence, and Surivial?—A Scientific Detective Story* (New York: Plume, 1997), p. 219.

85Steingraber, *Living Downstream*, p. 5.

86Quoted in John Bellamy Foster, *The Vulnerable Planet* (New York: Monthly Review Press, 1999), p. 126.

87See cover photo.

88Steingraber, *Living Downstream*, pp. 6–7.

89Thornton, *Pandora's Poison*, p. 2.

90*Ibid.*, pp. 30–31.

91*Ibid.*, p. 39.

92*Ibid.*, p. 41.

93Krimsky, *Hormonal Chaos*, pp. 194–195.

94Hertsgaard, *Earth Odyssey*, p. 126.

95*Ibid.*, p. 143.

96Though Yucca Mountain in Nevada has been chosen for underground disposal of nuclear waste, numerous uncertainties about safety remain. The Nuclear Waste Technical Review Board, an independent advisory panel, has said, according to Matthew Wald, "that there were enormous gaps in what the Energy Department Knew about the site . . . and about the high tech canisters it was proposing to put the waste in." The Department of Energy, moreover, wants to begin burying the waste before these and other engineering questions are resolved. Matthew Wald, "Science Will Catch up at Waste Site, U.S. Says," *New York Times*, Jan. 31, 2002, p. A18.

97Hertsgaard, *Earth Odyssey*, p. 150.

98Gore, *Earth in the Balance*, p. 81.

99William K. Stevens, "Enormous Haze Found over Indian Ocean," *New York Times*, June 16, 1999, p. A28.

100Particulate pollution, as mentioned above, does continue in a less visible form in the United States; the OECD reports that "emissions of fine and ultra-fine particulate matter have been increasing in OECD countries, with significant negative effects on human health in urban areas." OECD, *Environmental Outlook*, p. 183.

101Ponting, *Green History of the World*, p. 366.

102*Ibid.*, p. 366.

103OECD, *Environmental Outlook*, p. 190.

104Bill McKibben, *The End of Nature* (New York: Random House, 1989), p. 38.

[105]*Ibid.*, p. 41.

[106]Meadows et al., *Beyond the Limits*, p. 145.

[107]Thornton, *Pandora's Poison*, p 166.

[108]Meadows et al., *Beyond the Limits*, p. 147.

[109]Meadows et al., *Beyond the Limits*, p. 141.

[110]*Ibid.*, p. 155; Dixy Lee Ray, "Greenhouse Earth," *A Forest of Voices: Reading and Writing the Environment*, eds. Chris Anderson and Lex Runciman (Mountain View, CA: Mayfield, 1995), p. 566.

[111]*Ibid.*, p. 160.

[112]Forster, *Vulnerable Planet*, p. 27.

[113]Jeremy Leggett, *The Carbon War: Global Warming and the End of the Oil Era* (New York: Routledge, 2001), p. 59.

[114]*Ibid.*, p. 19.

[115]See McKibben, *End of Nature*, chap. 1 for this fact and a timely and extremely riveting discussion of global warming.

[116]Hawken et al., *Natural Capitalism*, p. 40.

[117]OECD, *Environmental Outlook*, p. 19.

[118]Paul Hawken and Amory and L. Hunter Lovins add that nitrous oxide, CFCs and their substitutes, and "near-surface ozone and nitric oxide, familiar constituents of smog . . . together . . . have had a heat-trapping effect about three-fourths as significant as that of CO_2 alone." Hawken et al., *Natural Capitalism*, p. 239. And the UNEP reports that catalytic converters on cars "release higher levels of nitrous oxide, which is a potent greenhouse gas and a contributor to stratospheric ozone depletion. UNEP, "The State of the Environment— Regional Synthesis—Atmosphere," *GEO-2000.*

[119]Hawken et al., *Natural Capitalism*, pp. 237–238.

[120]Leggett, *Carbon War*, p. 150.

[121]*Ibid.*, p. 43; Timothy Egan, "Warmth Transforms Alaska, and Even Permafrost Isn't," *New York Times*, Sunday, June 16, 2002, p. 18.

[122]McKibben, *End of Nature*, p. 33.

[123]*Ibid.*, p. 17.

[124]William K. Stevens, "If Climate Changes, It May Change Quickly," *New York Times*, January 27, 1998, p. F1.

[125]Leggett, *Carbon War*, p. 107.

[126]Sarah Lyall, "A Global Warming Report Predicts Doom for Many Species," *New York Times*, September 1, 2000, p. A3.

[127]Leggett, *Carbon War*, p. 190.

[128]*Ibid.*, p. 166.

[129]*Ibid.*, p. 189.

[130]*Ibid.*, pp. 322 and 271.

[131]William K. Stevens, "Arctic Thawing May Jolt Sea's Climate Belt," *New York Times*, December 7, 1997, p. C2.

[132]Mark Hertsgaard, "Severe Weather Warning," *New York Times Magazine*, August 2, 1998, pp. 48–49; see chap. 4.

[133]Quoted in Stevens, "If Climate Changes, It May Change Quickly," p. F1.

[134]Hertsgaard, *Earth Odyssey*, p. 170.

[135]In doing this I am omitting at least one potentially major problem. Scientists have recently pointed out the possibility that "human activities are seriously imbalancing the global nitrogen cycle" as "intensive agriculture, fossil fuel consumption, and widespread cultivation of

leguminous crops have led to huge additional quantities of nitrogen being deposited in terrestrial and aquatic ecosystems." Nitrogen loading, which has already "doubled the amount available for the uptake of plants," can increase acid rain, prompt runaway unwanted plant and algal growth in surface water and oceans (thereby killing aquatic life by depriving it of oxygen), reduce plant diversity, leach minerals out of soils (thus making them less productive), and accelerate global warming through nitrogen emissions to the atmosphere. Disruption of the global nitrogen cycle through nitrogen loading, some scientists feel, may "have global implications comparable to those caused by disruptions to the carbon cycle." UNEP, "The State of the Environment—Global Issues—Nitrogen Loading," *GEO-2000*.

[136] E.O.Wilson, "On Bjørn Lomborg and Extinction," *Grist Magazine*, Dec. 12, 2001, available at www.gristmagazine.com/grist/books.wilson12101.asp. Stuart Pimm gives 10,000 times the background rate as an upper-limit estimate. Pimm, *World According to Pimm*, p. 7. The primary cause of extinctions is habitat loss—particularly the loss incurred when wildlands are converted to intensively used land. Recently, however, another cause of extinctions has received a great deal of attention, perhaps thanks to the rise of the global economy: invasive species, hitching rides on global transport, threaten, as Michael Soulé has written, to "soon surpass habitat loss and fragmentation as the major cause of 'ecological disintegration.'" The global cosmopolitanism that seemed so attractive when it came to culture and the economy presents here a much more disquieting face. Quoted in David Quammen, "Planet of Weeds: Tallying the Losses of Earth's Animals and Plants," *Harper's Magazine*, October, 1998, p. 66.

[137] Quammen, "Planet of Weeds," p. 65; Ehrlich, *Betrayal of Science and Reason*, p. 113.

[138] W. Wayt Gibbs, "On the Termination of Species," *Scientific American*, November 2001, p. 43. This article describes some of the controversy surrounding extinction estimates. In doing so, however, it takes the antienvironmentalist Bjørn Lomborg seriously, a position that the magazine's editor, John Rennie, strongly contradicted in the following issue. This subsequent issue featured a variety of scientific exposés of Lomborg's errors, a section that Rennie introduced by calling Lomborg's work a failure.

[139] On the attack, see Ehrlich, *Betrayal of Science and Reason*, pp. 226–228.

[140] *Ibid.*, pp. 226–227.

[141] Quammen, "Planet of Weeds," p. 67.

[142] *Ibid.*, p. 68.

[143] See the discussion in Pimm, *World According to Pimm*, p. 241ff.

[144] Quoted in Gibbs, "On the Termination of Species," 48.

Notes to Chapter 4

[1] Theo Colborn, Dianne Dumanoski, and John Peterson Myers, *Our Stolen Future: Are We Threatening Our Fertility, Intelligence, and Survival?—A Scientific Detective Story* (New York: Plume, 1997).

[2] Ulrich Beck, *Risk Society: Towards a New Modernity* (London: Sage Publications, 1992), p. 74.

[3] See James Harlan Steele, "The History of Public Health and Veterinary Public Service," *Journal of the American Veterinary Medical Association* 217:12, December 15, 2000, pp. 1813–1821 for a history that surveys public health concern with and response to communication of disease to humans from animals and insects.

[4] Quoted in Hilary French, *Vanishing Borders: Protecting the Planet in the Age of Globalization* (New York: W.W. Norton, 2000), p. 46. See the discussion on global warming in Chapter 3 for the estimates of the number of lives to be saved by the Kyoto accords.

[5] French, *Vanishing Borders*, p. 42.

6Peter Montague, "1997 Snapshots, Part 1," *Rachel's Environmental & Health News*, 578, December 25, 1997, available at www.rachel.org/bulletin/index.cfm?st=4.

7Peter Montague, "Headlines: What's Important?" *Rachel's Environmental & Health News*, 742, January 17, 2002, available at www.rachel.org/bulletin/index.cfm?st=4.

8Robert Proctor, *Cancer Wars: How Politics Shapes What We Know and Don't Know about Cancer* (New York: Basic Books, 1995), p. 53.

9Andrew Szasz, *Ecopopulism: Toxic Waste and the Movement for Environmental Justice* (Minneapolis: University of Minnesota Press, 1994), p. 36.

10Sandra Steingraber, *Living Downstream: A Scientist's Personal Investigation of Cancer and the Environment* (New York: Vintage, 1998), p. 13, p. 40. Steingraber's figure for male incidence rates is 48.2%, a number that is probably a misprint. As I read them, current SEER data set the rate for male lifetime risk at 43.48%. Further, against the last half-century's trend of rising cancer rates, SEER data indicate that incidences and deaths for all cancers have declined slightly since a high in the early 1990s. SEER (Surveillance, Epidemiology, and End Results) data are collected by the National Cancer Institute and are, in the words of the Web site, "the most authoritative source of information on cancer incidence and survival in the U.S." See seer.cancer.gov.

11*Ibid.*, p. 33; John Bailar and Heather Gornik, "Cancer Undefeated," *New England Journal of Medicine*, 336, May 29, 1997, p. 2.

12Mary Mellor, *Feminism and Ecology* (New York: New York University Press, 1997), p. 72, p. 9.

13Sandra Steingraber, *Living Downstream*, p. 236.

14*Ibid.*, p. 236.

15*Ibid.*, p. 6, p. 114, p. 236.

16*Ibid.*, p. 238.

17*Ibid.*, p. 238. As Theo Colborn and her colleagues write, "virtually anyone willing to put up the $2,000 for the tests will find at least 250 chemical contaminants in his or her body fat, regardless of whether he or she lives in Gary, Indiana, or on a remote island in the South Pacific." Colborn et al., *Our Stolen Future*, p. 106.

18Steingraber, *Living Downstream*, p. 179, p. 169.

19*Ibid.*, p. 270.

20*Ibid.*, pp. 59–60.

21*Ibid.*, p. 61.

22*Ibid.*, p. 63. Scientists have attempted to establish the natural "baseline" for cancer by looking at premodern societies and the "natural" body burden of carcinogens in preserved archaic human remains. See Proctor, *Cancer Wars*, p. 25 and Marc Lappé, *Chemical Deception: The Toxic Threat to Human Health and the Environment* (San Francisco: Sierra Club Books, 1991), pp. 8–9.

23Steingraber, *Living Downstream*, p. 60.

24Proctor, *Cancer Wars*, p. 68.

25Even if workplace-related cancer deaths are estimated to be as low as 1 percent to 5 percent of all cancer deaths (a figure that is itself debatable), that still means, Proctor points out, "five thousand to twenty thousand U.S. cancer deaths" a year. Worse, as William Nicholson of the Mount Sinai School of Medicine has argued, "if only 3 percent of all cancer deaths were occupationally derived, the figure for blue collar workers would probably be in the neighborhood of 25 percent." *Ibid.*, p. 71.

26*Ibid.*, p. 72.

27*Ibid.*, p. 70.

[28]Steingraber, *Living Downstream*, p. 65; Peter Montague, "Munching Peanut Butter in Cancer Alley," *Rachel's Environment & Health News*, 168, February 13, 1990, available at www.rachel.org/bulletin/index.cfm?st=4.

[29]*Ibid.*

[30]Proctor, *Cancer Wars*, p. 133.

[31]*Ibid.*, p. 11, pp. 171–172.

[32]*Ibid.*, p. 96.

[33]*Ibid.*, p. 140.

[34]Lorenzo Tomatis, Ronald Melnick, Joseph Haseman, J. Carl Barrett, and James Huff, "Alleged 'Misconceptions' Distort Perceptions of Environmental Cancer Risks," *FASEB Journal*, 15, 2001, p. 199; Lijisky cited in Robert Proctor, *Cancer Wars*, p. 145.

[35]Peter Montague, "Bruce Ames," *Rachel's Environment & Health News*, 398, July 14, 1994, available at www.rachel.org/bulletin/index.cfm?st=4.

[36]This is the position of the epidemiologist Devra Lee Davis as summarized by Proctor, *Cancer Wars*, p. 146.

[37]Ames himself participated in the political climate of those years. Ames "willingly conceded" to Robert Proctor that "in the late 1970s, he underwent a political conversion from a kind of liberal environmentalism to a kind of free-market libertarianism"—a philosophy that opposes on principle "government intrusions in the name of environmental regulation." *Ibid.*, pp. 143–144. Also, having developed his hypothesis, Ames was not shy about participating in the controversy over policy it helped inspire.

[38]*Ibid.*, p. 82.

[39]*Ibid.*, p. 100. The Reagan administration defunded agencies (for example, cutting EPA funds by 60 percent), censored and bowdlerized literature, yielded to industry influence in issuing reports and setting policy, reduced inspections and prosecutions substantially (cases against polluters were reduced by 70 percent in the first year) and adopted cost-benefit assessments along with risk assessment as the basis for determining policy (a practice that, Mark Green of Citizens Congressional Watch maintained would have prevented "the abolition of slavery or child labor laws"). *Ibid.*, pp. 79–80. Proctor's overall estimate for the death toll during this time was 600,000 American deaths for the twelve-year period of the Reagan and equally environmental-health-unfriendly Bush administrations. Laurie Garrett also writes with indignation of the Reagan administration's policies on and attitudes about AIDS. *The Coming Plague: Newly Emerging Diseases in a World out of Balance* (New York: Penguin, 1995), pp. 469–471). See also Andrew Szasz, *Ecopopulism*, chap. 6 for a discussion of the Reagan-era assault on environmentalism and the surprising headway that one environmental-health-related initiative, the enforcement and reauthorization of the Resource Conservation and Recovery Act (RCRA) and Superfund laws, managed to make against conservative opposition.

[40]The most startling finding was that exposure to organochlorines was not correlated with heightened cancer risk. Marilie Gammon et al., "Environmental Toxins and Breast Cancer on Long Island. II. Organochlorine Compound Levels in Blood," *Cancer Epidemiology Biomarkers and Prevention*, 11(8), 2002, p. 686.

[41]Kevin Sack, "PCB Pollution Suits Have Day in Court in Alabama," *New York Times*, January 27, 2002, p. 20.

[42]Steingraber, *Living Downstream*, p. 263.

[43]See the last section of this book, especially Chapters 7 and 8.

[44]Quoted in Sheldon Krimsky, *Hormonal Chaos: The Science and Social Origins of the Environmental Endocrine Hypothesis* (Baltimore: Johns Hopkins University Press, 2000), p. 59.

45 *Ibid.*, p. 203, pp. 229–230.

46 *Ibid.*, p. 65.

47 For the full list, see *Ibid.*, p. 125.

48 *Ibid.*, p. 89.

49 *Ibid.*, pp. 203–204.

50 Colborn et al., *Our Stolen Future*, p. 135.

51 *Ibid.*, pp. 91–92.

52 *Ibid.*, p. 97.

53 *Ibid.*, p. 108.

54 *Ibid.*, p. 86.

55 *Ibid.*, p. 9. See Krimsky, *Hormonal Chaos*, pp. 35–37, for a recent discussion of the state of the dispute.

56 Colburn et al., *Our Stolen Future*, p.24.

57 Quoted in *ibid.*, p. 252.

58 Peter Montague, "The Latest Hormone Science, Pt. 1," *Rachel's Environment & Health News*, 750, August 24, 2002, available at www.rachel.org/bulletin/index.cfm?st=4.

59 Coburn et al., *Our Stolen Future*, p. 223.

60 Joe Thornton, *Pandora's Poisons: Chlorine, Health, and a New Environmental Strategy* (Cambridge, MA: M.I.T. Press, 2000), p. 42.

61 Thornton, *Pandora's Poisons*, p. 33 and p.55.

62 McGinn, "Reducing Our Toxic Burden," p. 92.

63 *Ibid.*, p. 92.

64 To be sure, a few environmentalists have shown some environmental-ethical concern about rights to survival for even dangerous microbes, and some have suggested that the human attempt to control danger from microbes ought to be cast in ecological terms as the attempt to manage a complex system in which humans themselves are involved rather than as combat against an enemy. Still, domestic conflicts over the prospect of emerging global disease have not been the result, for the most part, of this particular environmental issue.

65 Madeline Drexler, *Secret Agents: The Menace of Emerging Infections* (Washington, DC: Joseph Henry Press, 2002), pp. 17–18.

66 *Ibid.*, pp. 4–5.

67 *Ibid.*, p. 9.

68 *Ibid.*, p. 8.

69 Lynn Margulis and Dorian Sagan, "The Microcosm," *Wild Earth*, Fall, 2000, p. 15.

70 Drexler, *Secret Agents*, p. 213.

71 *Ibid.*, p. 91.

72 Genes in bacteria, for example, can move about from one position to another on chromosomes ("transposons") or jump about almost at random ("jumping genes"); or they can be "highly stable rings of DNA, called plasmids, that [sit] silently in the bacterial cytoplasm waiting to be stimulated into biochemical action" (Garrett, *The Coming Plague*, p. 225). Plasmid exchange can occur between bacteria as they occasionally undergo a "process called sexual conjugation, stretching out portions of their membranes to meet one another and passing plasmids, transposons, or jumping genes—including genes that conferred resistance to antibiotics" (*Ibid.*, pp. 225–226). They can also mutate at single sites along their DNA and, since the "world, it turn[s] out, [is] awash with highly mobile segments of DNA," bacteria can be "terrific scavengers," snapping them up—and even discriminating between ones more or less likely to be useful to them (*Ibid.*, p. 431, p. 584). Bacteria are even, some feel, capable of a procedure that challenges "the central dogma of biology"—

random evolution. In 1988, John Cairns of the Harvard School of Public Health showed "that the *E. coli* would specifically change two separate sets of genes to adapt to the situation (alteration of its environment) and survive, doing so in far less time than random mutation would permit" (*Ibid.*, p. 583). This controversial finding of directed mutation among bacteria was reinforced in 1994, when researchers at Rockefeller University "confirmed Cairns's initial experiments . . . and further . . . showed that genetic recombination and resultant adaptive mutation occurred *in the absence of bacterial reproduction.* In other words, bacteria altered themselves not just through a process of random, error-prone reproduction that eventually yielded a surviving strain—the classic Darwinian view. In addition, they changed themselves, in some concerted manner, without reproducing" (*Ibid.*, p. 586). See also Drexler, *Secret Agents*, pp. 146–150.

[73]Quoted in French, *Vanishing Borders*, p. 43.

[74]Donna Haraway, *Simians, Cyborgs, and Women* (New York: Routledge, 1991), p. 3, p. 199.

[75]Margulis and Sagan, "The Microcosm," p. 14.

[76]Drexler, *Secret Agents*, p. 145.

[77]Garrett, *The Coming Plague*, p. 30.

[78]*Ibid.*, p. 30, p. 36.

[79]*Ibid.*, p. 30.

[80]*Ibid.*, p. 6.

[81]*Ibid.*, p. 6.

[82]Drexler, *Secret Agents*, p. 18.

[83]See *Ibid.*, pp. 61–62; Jared Diamond, *Guns, Germs, and Steel: The Fates of Human Societies* (New York: W.W. Norton, 1999); William McNeill, *The Human Condition: An Ecological and Historical View* (Princeton, NJ: Princeton University Press, 1980); and Alfred Crosby, *Ecological Imperialism: The Biological Expansion of Europe, 900–1900* (New York: Cambridge University Press, 1986).

[84]Drexler, *Secret Agents*, p. 119.

[85]*Ibid.*, p. 127.

[86]*Ibid.*, p. 143.

[87]*Ibid.*, p. 132.

[88]Quoted in *ibid.*, p. 128.

[89]Quoted in *ibid.*, p. 157.

[90]*Ibid.*, p. 155.

[91]French, *Vanishing Borders*, pp. 44–45.

[92]Gary Gardner, "The Challenge for Johannesburg: Creating a More Secure World," *State of the World 2002*, ed. Linda Starke (New York: W.W. Norton, 2002), pp. 10–11.

[93]Quoted in French, *Vanishing Borders*, p. 45.

[94]Reported in Garrett, *The Coming Plague*, p. 575.

[95]French, *Vanishing Borders*, p. 42.

[96]Drexler, *Secret Agents*, p. 62.

[97]*Ibid.*, p. 281.

[98]Garrett, *The Coming Plague*, p. 568.

[99]*Ibid.*, p. 560; Gardner, "The Challenge for Johannesburg," p. 13.

[100]Reported in Garrett, *The Coming Plague*, p. 561.

[101]*Ibid.*, p. 563.

[102]UNEP, "The State of the Environment—Global Issues—Human Health and the Environment," *GEO-2000*, available at www.grida.no/geo2000/english/index.htm; Randy Show-

stack, "El Niño Linked to Increase in Childhood Diarrheal Disease, a Leading Cause of Pre-mature Death," *Eos*, 81:7, February 15, 2000, p. 1.

[103]French, *Vanishing Borders*, p. 46.

[104]*Ibid.*, p. 46. A different theory of the cause of the epidemic attributed it to the environmental impact of globalization. According to this theory, the cholera microbe might have come in "the ballast water of ships arriving in Peruvian ports from South Asia." *Ibid.*, p. 46.

[105]Garrett, *The Coming Plague*, p. 562.

[106]Drexler, *Secret Agents*, p. 14.

[107]Garrett, *The Coming Plague*, p. 609.

[108]See Christopher Murray and Alan Lopez, eds., *The Global Burden of Disease* (Cambridge, MA: Harvard University Press, 1996).

[109]Gardner, "The Challenge for Johannesburg," p. 13.

[110]Garrett, *The Coming Plague*, p. 414.

[111]*Ibid.*, p. 417.

[112]*Ibid.*, p. 418.

[113]*Ibid.*, p. 418.

[114]Drexler, *Secret Agents*, pp. 99–105 and p. 80.

[115]Quoted in Garrett, *The Coming Plague*, p. 609.

Notes to Chapter 5

[1]See the discussion in Chapter 2.

[2]John Bellamy Foster, *The Vulnerable Planet: A Short Economic History of the Environment* (New York: Monthly Review Press, 1999), p. 12.

[3]Richard Hofrichter, "Introduction," *Reclaiming the Environmental Debate: The Politics of Health in a Toxic Culture* (London: M.I.T. Press, 2000), p. 8.

[4]Donella Meadows, Dennis Meadows, Jørgen Randers, and William Behrens, *The Limits to Growth* (New York, New American Library, 1972), p. 196. The book quickly became a favorite target for the antienvironmental opposition; it also subsequently inspired ecological modernization, which, however, sought to remove the radical, antigrowth sting from its uncompromising analysis.

[5]OECD, *Environmental Outlook* (Paris: OECD, 2001), p. 21.

[6]Department of Economic and Social Affairs, *World Population Monitoring 2001* (New York: United Nations, 2001), p. 7.

[7]*Ibid.*, pp. 71–72.

[8]Ethical-political criticisms of population control have varied widely. Antiabortion politics, of course, gives rise to a strongly nonempirical, value-driven bias against taking population growth seriously as an environmental or social issue. Reproductive rights advocates bridle at any prospect of control over womens' right to choose—a concern that cuts two ways. Commitment to free-market capitalism led Julian Simon to make optimism a quasimoral imperative, claiming that the more people there were, the more human genius there also was—genius that would allow societies to solve critical problems, including environmental ones. Many Marxists also criticized environmentalists' concern with overpopulation as fundamentally Malthusian—as embodying the same ethically repugnant prejudice against poor, nonwhite, non–northern Europeans that was too openly espoused by Malthus.

Pragmatic denials of the earth's natural limits then picked up on arguments about the importance of human ingenuity and coupled them with claims that the very notion of en-

vironmental limits was incorrect; it was a construction of environmentalists and others interested in keeping people firmly in line with fears of scarcity, not a fact of nature. Human
ingenuity again made all the difference; but what it represented was, of course, different for
free-market capitalists, who advocated technological innovation, and Green Marxists, who
advocated radical social change.

[9]These are solutions that unite social development and social justice with environmental goals,
and they seem to be proving very effective. See Barbara Crossette, "Population Estimates
Fall as Poor Women Assert Control," *New York Times*, March 10, 2002, p. 3.

[10]As many have pointed out, when the differing global environmental impacts of the rich and poor
countries are factored in, as they must be today, overpopulation remains a major problem, but
it is paradoxically more a problem caused by the wealthy than the poor. For example, the new
logic has led Robert Paehlke to suggest that Garrett Hardin's proposal for triage—for kicking
the poor and prolific underdeveloped world peoples out of the lifeboats rescuing humankind
from global environmental disaster—should be reversed. North Americans should be ejected.
"It would cost far fewer persons and would achieve for the species considerably more time to
bring about population stabilization than would avoidable starvation in the so-called Third
World." Robert Paehlke, *Environmentalism and the Future of Pragmatic Politics* (New Haven:
Yale University Press, 1989), pp. 65–66; I am indebted to John Barry for this reference.

Environmentalists today thus address the impact of rich-world populations. Equally,
the specific solutions to population problems made by environmentalists today emphasize
empowerment rather than restriction. Environmentalists underscore the drop in population increases that accompanies modern educational systems, lowered child mortality, and
the empowerment of women. These are solutions that unite social development and social
justice with environmental goals, and they seem to be proving very effective. See Crossette,
"Population Estimates Fall," p. 3.

[11]Even the much-maligned *Limits to Growth* (though it was attacked by right and left as the
arch-example of doomster imposition of inflexible external limits) factored human ingenuity into its computer model depicting different scenarios of growth and imminent ecological meltdown. And the model clearly incorporated the principle that, even if individual
estimates of the world's limits might well be wrong, its underlying logic (that held that rising environmental stresses from population and economic growth eventually led to environmental crisis) would remain true.

[12]Department of Economic and Social Affairs, *World Population Monitoring*, p. 10.

[13]The middle level is "replacement-level" fertility. Since, however, stopping population growth
is like stopping an ocean liner—it takes time to overcome the built-up momentum—overall population continues to grow for a while.

[14]*Ibid.*, p. 10.

[15]Joel Cohen, *How Many People Can the Earth Support?* (New York: W.W. Norton, 1995), p. 34.

[16]David Korten, *When Corporations Rule the World* (West Hartford and San Francisco:
Kumarian Press and Berrett-Koehler Publishers, 1995), p. 33.

[17]William R. Catton, *Overshoot: The Ecological Basis of Revolutionary Change* (Urbana, IL: University of Illinois Press, 1980), p. 173.

[18]Stuart Pimm, *The World According to Pimm: A Scientist Audits the Earth* (New York: McGraw-
Hill, 2001), p. 105, p. 177, p. 231.

[19]Bill McKibben, "A Special Moment in History," *Atlantic Monthly*, May, 1998, p. 56. Paul
Ehrlich, Gretchen Daily, Scott Daily, Norman Myers and James Salzman, "No Middle Way
on the Environment," *Atlantic Monthly*, December, 1997, p. 102.

[20]Department of Economic and Social Affairs, *World Population Monitoring*, p. 11.

21McKibben, "Special," p. 4.

22*Ibid.*, pp. 3–4.

23Tony Cortese, "Education for Sustainability," http://www.secondnature.org/pdf/snwritings/articles/humanpersp.pdf, p. 4.

24Barry Commoner, *The Closing Circle: Nature, Man and Technology* (New York: Bantam, 1972 [1971]), p. 125.

25Bill McKibben, *The End of Nature* (New York: Random House, 1989), p. 13; Clive Ponting, *A Green History of the World: The Environment and the Collapse of Great Civilizations* (New York: Penguin, 1991), p. 399.

26Foster, *Vulnerable Planet*, p. 20.

27Looking at the last 20 years, Speth further observes that, as world output grew 100 percent, global population grew 50 percent, energy use 40 percent, meat consumption 65 percent, auto fleet size 75 percent, and paper use 75 percent. James Gustave Speth, "The Cascasing of Environmental Consequences: Are We Running Out of Time?" University Committee on Environment Distinguished Environment Lecture, Kennedy School of Government, Harvard University, April 11, 2001. Reprinted by Yale School of Forestry and Environmental Studies, New Haven, CT.

28Foster, *Vulnerable Planet*, p. 20.

29The Gini coefficient (which ranges from perfect equality at 0 to absolute inequality at 1) rose between 1990 and 2000 from .4 to .5. And while the "percent of the world's population living in absolute poverty . . . declined from about 28 per cent in 1987 to 24 per cent in 1998 . . . the absolute number of people classified as poor has not changed much" from 1.2 billion. Department of Economic and Social Affairs, *World Population Monitoring 2001*, p. 12.

30Mark Hertsgaard, *Earth Odyssey* (New York: Broadway Books, 1998), p. 263.

31Bill Joy, "Why the Future Doesn't Need Us," *Wired*, April, 2000, pp. 238–262.

32Depicted in an incendiary ad taken out by environmentalists in the *New York Times*, the mouse appeared as a most pathetic monster—a monster that was also, even more pathetically, still just a just a little mouse, its tiny black eye filled with what seemed like disgust at the abomination—the large human ear—rising through the sickly translucent skin of its back. The Turning Point Project, "Where Will the Next Plague Come From," *New York Times*, Nov. 1, 1999, p. A9.

33Sheldon Krimsky, *Biotechnics and Society: The Rise of Industrial Genetics* (New York: Praeger, 1991), p. 99.

34Sheldon Krimsky, *Genetic Alchemy: The Social History of the Recombinant DNA Controversy* (Cambridge, MA: M.I.T. Press, 1985), p. 266, p. 268.

35Richard Monastersky, "Scientists Debate Plan to Combat Global Warming by Dimming Sun," *Chronicle of Higher Education*, April 7, 2000, p. A23.

36Quoted in Joy, "Why the Future Doesn't Need Us," p. 246.

37See Hans Moravec, *Mind Children: The Future of Robot and Human Intelligence* (Cambridge, MA: Harvard University Press, 1988).

38Rodney Brooks, "From Robot Dreams to Reality," *Nature*, 406, August 31, 2000, pp. 945–947; Kenneth Chang, "Scientists Report They Have Made Robot That Makes Its Own Robots," *New York Times*, August 31, 2000, p. A1, A20.

39Joy, "Why the Future Doesn't Need Us," p. 250.

40Gary Stix, "Little Big Science," *Scientific American*, Sept. 2001, p. 36.

41Krimsky, *Biotechnics and Society*, p. 37.

42*Ibid.*, pp. 14–15.

[43]Sheldon Krimsky and Roger Wrubel, *Agricultural Biotechnology and the Environment: Science, Policy, and Social Issues* (Urbana, IL: University of Illinois Press, 1996), pp. 1–2.

[44]Krimsky, *Biotechnics and Society*, p. 151.

[45]*Ibid.*, p. 144.

[46]Barry Commoner, "Unraveling the DNA Myth: The Spurious Foundation of Genetic Engineering," *Harper's Magazine*, February 2002, pp. 41–42.

[47]*Ibid.*, p. 42.

[48]*Ibid.*, p.43.

[49]*Ibid.*, p. 47.

[50]Theo Colborn, Dianne Dumanoski, and John Peterson Myers, *Our Stolen Future: Are We Threatening Our Fertility, Intelligence, and Survival?—A Scientific Detective Story* (New York: Plume, 1997), p. 219.

[51]Quoted in "Notes and Quotes," *The Ecologist*, 31:5, June 2001, p. 10.

[52]Commoner, "Unraveling the DNA Myth," p. 47.

[53]Jacques Ellul, *The Technological Society* (New York: Random House, 1964).

[54]*Ibid.*, p. 92.

[55]Tom Athanasiou, *Divided Planet: The Ecology of Rich and Poor* (Athens, GA: University of Georgia Press, 1996), p. 266.

[56]Jeremy Leggett, *The Carbon War: Global Warming and the End of the Carbon War* (New York: Routledge, 2001), p. 59.

[57]Athanasiou, *Divided Planet*, pp. 96–97.

[58]Krimsky, *Biotechnics and Society*, p. 88.

[59]Allan Schnaiberg makes the treadmill metaphor essential to understanding "why and how environmental problems seemed to have increased so rapidly in the post World War II period in industrial societies." Allan Schnaiberg, "Reflections on My 25 Years Before the Mast of the Environment and Technology Section," *Organization and Environment*, 15:1, March 2002, p. 32.

[60]Mark Dowie, *Losing Ground: American Environmentalism at the Close of the Twentieth Century* (Cambridge, MA: MIT Press, 1997), p. 63.

[61]Ulrich Beck, *Risk Society Towards a New Modernity* (London: Sage Publications, 1992), p. 56.

[62]*Ibid.*, p. 56.

[63]John Rennie, "Cloning and Conservation, *Scientific American*, November, 2000, p. 1.

[64]Beck, *Risk Society*, p. 83.

[65]Barbara Crossette, "Kofi Annan's Astonishing Facts!" *New York Times*, September 27, 1998, p. 12.

[66]Athanasiou, *Divided Planet*, p. 53; Hertsgaard, *Earth Odyssey*, p. 196.

[67]André Gunder Frank, "The Development of Underdevelopment," *Monthly Review*, 18, pp. 17–31; Immanuel Wallerstein, *The Modern World System* (New York: Academic Press, 1984); L.S. Stavrianos, *Global Rift: The Third World Comes of Age* (New York: Morrow, 1981).

[68]Hawken et al., *Natural Capitalism*, p. 51.

[69]Ponting, *Green History of the World*, pp. 161–193.

[70]Athasaniou, *Divided Planet*, pp. 170–173.

[71]Hilary French, *Vanishing Borders: Protecting the Planet in the Age of Globalization* (Norton: New York, 2000), pp. 21–22, p. 26, p. 57, pp. 27–28.

[72]Anne Platt McGinn, "Reducing Our Toxic Burden," *State of the World 2002*, eds. Christopher Flavin, Hilary French, Gary Gardiner (New York: W.W. Norton, 2002), p. 91.

[73]French, *Vanishing Borders*, pp. 77–78.

[74]*Ibid.*, p. 74.

[75]*Ibid.*, p. 71, p. 82. See also the discussion in Steven Yearley, *Sociology, Environmentalism, Globalization* (London: Sage Publications, 1996), chap. 3.

[76]French, *Vanishing Borders*, p. 55.

[77]Summers advanced three reasons for encouraging dirty industry to go south. First, measurement of costs of health care depends on "foregone earnings from increasing morbidity and mortality"; thus, "a given amount of health-impairing pollution should be done in the country with the lowest cost, which will be the country with the lowest wages. I think the economic logic behind dumping a load of toxic waste in the lowest-wage country is impeccable and we should face up to that." Second, "under-populated countries in Africa are also vastly *under*-polluted; their air quality is probably vastly inefficiently low [*sic*] compared to Los Angeles or Mexico City." Third, "demand for a clean environment for aesthetic and health reasons" will be much higher in wealthy countries, where people survive to get (for example) prostate cancer than in "a country where under-5 mortality is 200 per 1,000." (Quoted in Yearley, *Sociology, Environmentalism, Globalization*, pp. 75–76.

[78]*Ibid.*, p. 76.

[79]Robert Kaplan, *The Coming Anarchy* (New York: Random House, 2000), p. 20; Athanasiou, *Divided Planet*, p. 301.

[80]Quoted in Kaplan, *Coming Anarchy*, p. 24.

[81]See Paul Erhlich, *The Population Bomb* (Binghamton, NY: Vail-Ballou Press, 1970), pp. 62–67; Kaplan, *Coming Anarchy*, p. 22.

[82]*Ibid.*, p. 11.

[83]*Ibid.*, p. 17.

[84]Ian Johnson and Kseniya Lvovsky, "World Bank Special: Double Burden," available at www.ourplanet.com/imgversn/122/johnson.html.

[85]*Ibid.*, p. 48.

[86]The First World has neither entered a "posthistorical" era, as Francis Fukuyama claimed, nor has it become a "postmaterial" society, as enthusiasts of the information age and some First World environmentalists such as Samuel Hays have argued. As the success of the conservative assault on wilderness protection and much of the rest of the environmental legacy of the 1970s indicates, the United States has not even remained preoccupied exclusively with what developing-world environmentalists like Ramachandra Guha and Juan Martinez-Alier call "full-stomach" environmentalism—i.e., environmental causes that focus on preserving nature for appreciation, enjoyment, and the enhancement of quality of life, while ignoring the survival needs of the poor. As Chapters 3 and 4 have made clear, the wilderness ethos has lost its lock on U.S. environmentalism, and the "materiality" of developed-world environmental crisis has become increasingly visible. See Francis Fukuyama, *The End of History and the Last Man* (New York: Avon Books, 1993) and Ramachandra Gaha and Juan Martinez-Aliev, *Varieties of Environmentalism: Essays North and South* (New Delhi: Oxford University Press, 1998).

[87]See David Harvey, *Justice, Nature and the Geography of Difference* (Cambridge: Blackwell, 1996); Wolfgang Sachs, ed., *Global Ecology: A New Arena of Political Conflict* (London: Zed Books, 1993); Vandana Shiva, *Biopiracy, the Plunder of Nature and Knowledge* (Boston: South End Press, 1997).

[88]Mary Mellor, *Feminism and Ecology* (New York: New York University Press, 1997), p. 190.

Notes to Chapter 6

[1]Fairfield Osborn, *Our Plundered Planet* (Boston: Little, Brown and Co., 1948), p. 194.

[2]William Vogt, *Road to Survival* (New York: William Sloane Associates, Inc., 1948), p. 43, p. 89.

[3]*Ibid.*, p. 94.

[4]Osborn, *Our Plundered Planet*, p. 29. Emphasis in the original.

⁵*Ibid.*, p. 142.

⁶Vogt, *Road to Survival*, p. xiii.

⁷Rachel Carson, *Silent Spring* (Greenwich, CT: Fawcett Publications, 1962), p. 14, 213.

⁸Osborn, *Our Plundered Planet*, p. 10.

⁹Paul Ehrlich, *The Population Bomb* (Binghamton, NY: Vail-Ballou Press, 1970), pp. 60–61.

¹⁰*Ibid.*, pp. 56–57.

¹¹See the discussion of William Cronon's *Uncommon Ground* in Chapter 1 and the discussion of end-of-nature discourse in Chapter 6.

¹²Barry Commoner, *The Closing Circle: Nature, Man & Technology* (New York: Bantam, 1974 [1971]), pp. 29–42.

¹³*Ibid.*, p. 280.

¹⁴*Ibid.*, p. 30.

¹⁵*Ibid.*, pp. 30–31.

¹⁶*Ibid.*, p. 124. Emphasis in the original.

¹⁷Osborn, *Our Plundered Planet*, p. 35.

¹⁸True, the book was debunked and attacked many times, but many of these attacks were based on several (good- and bad-faith) false assertions about the book. It was a prediction of doom (it was in fact a laying out of choices) and it didn't allow for the discovery of additional resources and asserted they all would run out in thirty years (it did; and the real meltdown it predicted was a century away). It has thus become common to dismiss the book as flawed; it is sensible to note that its underlying logic remains true.

¹⁹Donella H. Meadows, Dennis L. Meadows, Jørgen Randers, William W. Behrens III, *The Limits to Growth* (New York: New American Library, 1972), pp. 36–37.

²⁰E. F. Schumacher, *Small Is Beautiful: Economics as if People Mattered* (New York: HarperCollins, [1973] 1993). For Maarten Hajer's nuanced account of this perverse consequence of globalizing environmental crisis, see *The Politics of Environmental Discourse: Ecological Modernization and the Policy Process* (New York: Oxford University Press, 1995), chap. 3.

²¹Quoted in Mark Dery, *Escape Velocity: Cyberculture at the End of the Century* (New York: Grove Press, 1966), p. 31. For some of the original generation, of course, mutation did not have to wait until the second generation. Both Timothy Leary and Stewart Brand moved from the counterculture to the cyberculture vanguard.

²²Andrew Ross, *Strange Weather: Culture, Science and Technology in the Age of Limits* (London: Verso, 1991), pp. 185–186.

²³Quoted in M. Jimmie Killingsworth and Jacqueline S. Palmer, "Millennial Ecology: The Apocalyptic Narrative from *Silent Spring* to *Global Warming*," *Green Culture: Environmental Rhetoric in Contemporary America*, eds. Carl G. Herndl and Stuart C. Brown (Madison, WI: University of Wisconsin Press, 1996), p. 34.

²⁴World Commission on Environment and Development, *Our Common Future* (New York: Oxford University Press, 1987); Al Gore, *Earth in the Balance: Ecology and the Human Spirit* (New York: Plume, 1993); on *Global 2000* and *Global 2000 Revised*, see Ross, *Strange Weather*, p. 187.

²⁵Donella Meadows, Dennis Meadows, and Jørgen Randers, *Beyond the Limits: Confronting Global Collapse, Envisioning a Sustainable Future* (White River Junction, VT: Chelsea Green Publishing, 1992).

²⁶Mark Hertsgaard, *Earth Odyssey* (New York: Broadway Books, 1999), p. 324; Tom Athanasiou, *Divided Planet: The Ecology of Rich and Poor* (Athens, GA: University of Georgia Press, 1996), pp. 57–58.

²⁷Hertsgaard, *Earth Odyssey*, p. 324.

[28]William R. Catton, Jr., *Overshoot: The Ecological Basis of Revolutionary Change* (Urbana, IL: University of Illinois Press, 1980), p. 24, 44.

[29]Clive Ponting, *A Green History of the World: The Environment and the Collapse of Great Civilizations* (New York: Penguin, 1991).

[30]Daniel Botkin, *Discordant Harmonies: A New Ecology for the Twenty-First Century* (New York: Oxford University Press, 1990), p. 159.

[31]Daniel Worster, *Nature's Economy: A History of Ecological Ideas* (New York: Cambridge University Press, 1994), Chapter 17.

[32]Mike Davis, *Ecology of Fear: Los Angeles and the Imagination of Disaster* (New York: Random House, 1998), p. 15.

[33]*Ibid.*, p. 15.

[34]*Ibid.*, p. 16.

[35]Meadows et al., *Beyond the Limits*, p. 130.

[36]Ulrich Beck, *Risk Society: Towards a New Modernity* (London: Sage [1986] 1992).

[37]Ulrich Beck, "Risk Society and the Provident State," *Risk, Environment & Modernity: Towards a New Ecology*, eds. Scott Lash, Bronislaw Szerszynski, and Brian Wynne (London: Sage Publications, 1996), p. 28.

[38]Nigel Clark, "Panic Ecology: Nature in the Age of Superconductivity," *Theory, Culture & Society*, 14:1, February 1997, p. 79.

[39]Barbara Adam, "Re-Vision: The Centrality of Time for an Ecological Social Science Perspective," *Risk, Environment and Modernity*, p. 97; Beck, "Risk Society and the Provident State," pp. 36–37.

[40]Ulrich Beck, *Risk Society*, p. 27.

[41]*Ibid.* p. 129. Emphasis in the original.

[42]I am indebted to Andrew McLaughlin for this example.

[43]Anne-Marie Cusac, "Nuclear Spoons: Hot Metal May Find Its Way to Your Dinner Table," *The Progressive*, October 22, 1998, p. 22.

[44]*Ibid.*, p. 22.

[45]*Ibid.*, p. 22.

[46]*Ibid.*, p. 23.

[47]*Ibid.*, p. 23.

[48]Commoner, *The Closing Circle*, p. 202.

[49]On risk in environmental sociology, see Scott Lash, Bronislaw Szerszynski, and Brian Wynne, "Introduction," *Risk, Environment & Modernity*; on risk study as an independent field, see Sheldon Krimsky and Dominic Golding, eds., *Social Theories of Risk* (Westport, CT: Praeger, 1992).

[50]Lash et al., "Introduction," p. 1.

[51]*Ibid.*, p. 6.

[52]Beck, "Risk Society and the Provident State," pp. 32–33.

[53]Donella Meadows, "Chicken Little, Cassandra, and the Real Wolf: So Many Ways to Think about the Future," *Wild Earth*, Winter 1999/2000, p. 25.

[54]On Christopher Manes, see Tom Athanasiou, *Divided Planet: The Ecology of Rich and Poor* (Athens, GA: University of Georgia Press, 1995), p. 100; on Garrett Hardin, see *ibid.*, p. 34, 106; on Daly's speculation, see *ibid.*, p. 95.

[55]John Barry, *Rethinking Green Politics: Nature, Virtue and Progress* (London: Sage Publications, 1999), p. 204.

[56]This belief has led in the past to the extremely stark positions of Garrett Hardin (who calls for "lifeboat ethics" and abandoning the poor) and William Ophuls (who argues that democ-

racy hinders solution of the ecological crisis, as "only those possessing the ecological and other competencies necessary to make prudent decisions [should be] allowed full participation in the political process"). Quoted in *ibid.*, p. 198.

57Quoted in Hertsgaard, *Earth Odyssey*, p. 327.

58Broecker uses an image that goes back to a 1957 paper by Roger Revelle and Hans Seuss of the Scripps Institute of Oceanography:

> Human beings are now carrying out a large scale geophysical experiment of a kind that could not have happened in the past nor be reproduced in the future. Within a few centuries we are returning to the atmosphere and oceans the concentrated organic carbon stored in sedimentary rocks over hundreds of millions of years. This experiment, if adequately documented, may yield a far-reaching insight into processes determining weather and climate. (Quoted in Ross, *Strange Weather*, p. 211.)

In the interval between 1957 and now, climate change has changed from a qualitatively new, unreproducible scientific experiment to one that no "responsible council" would ever allow to be conducted in the first place. Broecker's firm implication is that, with global warming, people are conducting an experiment that science would never allow—one that is clearly insanely risky and horrifically dangerous, an experiment with the future of the biosphere and humankind. Writing about the toxification of the environment and humans by hormone-depleting chemicals, Theo Colborn and her colleagues describe chemical pollution as a still more insane form of global experimentation. They note that "in this experiment, we are all guinea pigs and, to make matters worse, we have no controls to help us understand what these synthetic chemicals are doing. . . . [R]esearchers have typically set up studies comparing contaminated children with an uncontaminated control group. Tragically, no children today are born chemical-free." Theo Colborn, Dianne Dumanoski, and John Peterson Myers, *Our Stolen Future: Are We Threatening Our Fertility, Intelligence, and Survival?—A Scientific Detective Story* (New York: Plume, 1997), p. 240. In this further revision of the experiment metaphor, no fully accurate experiment is even possible, let alone desirable. Moreover, the reasons for its impossibility are excruciatingly grotesque: there is no control group of unpoisoned children left.

59Beck, "Risk Society and the Provident State," p. 40.

60Henry David Thoreau, "Walking," *The Portable Thoreau*, ed. Carl Bode (New York: Penguin, 1982), pp. 597–598.

61See James Hillman, "A Psyche the Size of the Earth: A Psychological Forward," Phyllis Windle, "The Ecology of Grief," and Joanna Macy, "Working through Environmental Despair," in *Ecopsychology: Restoring the Earth, Healing the Mind*, eds. Theodore Roszak, Mary E. Gomes, and Allen D. Kanner (San Francisco: Sierra Club Books, 1995), pp. xvii-xxiii, pp. 136–147, and pp. 240–261, and David Abram, *The Spell of the Sensuous: Perception and Language in a More-Than-Human World* (New York: Pantheon Books, 1996).

62See Aldo Leopold, "The Land Ethic," *A Sand County Almanac* (New York: Oxford University Press, 1966).

Notes to Chapter 7

1*William* McDonough is the architect widely known for his cyberecological ideas and theories.

2Michael McDonough (as told to Bruce Sterling), "Newer York, New York," *Wired*, January 2000, p. 90.

[3] *Ibid.*, p. 90.

[4] *Ibid.*, p. 94, 96.

[5] *Ibid.*, p. 96.

[6] *Ibid.*, p. 98.

[7] Nigel Clark, "Panic Ecology: Nature in the Age of Superconductivity," *Theory Culture & Society*, 14:1, February 1997, p. 80.

[8] William Catton, *Overshoot: The Ecological Basis of Revolutionary Change* (Urbana, IL: University of Illinois Press, 1980), *passim.*

[9] Frederic Jameson, *Postmodernism, Or, the Cultural Logic of Late Capitalism* (Durham, NC: Duke University Press, 1991), pp. 51–54.

[10] Julian L. Simon, *The Ultimate Resource 2* (Princeton, NJ: Princeton University Press, 1996), p. 54.

[11] *Ibid.*, p. 59.

[12] *Ibid.*, p. 67.

[13] *Ibid.*, p. 68

[14] *Ibid.*, p. 81.

[15] *Ibid.*, p. 65.

[16] *Ibid.*, p.65.

[17] *Ibid.*, pp. 82–83.

[18] *Ibid.*, p. 76.

[19] Steven Best and Douglas Kellner, "Kevin Kelly's Complexity Theory: The Politics and Ideology of Self-Organizing Systems," *Organization and the Environment*, 12:2, 2, June 1999, p. 146.

[20] Doing this is, of course, an old ploy. Technological restructuring has, for several centuries at least, been accompanied by appeals to old traditions of the "natural." These appeals help assuage the anxieties restructuring creates. Thus Nigel Clark writes, "the great sites of display of the industrial era—the arcades, panoramas, expositions—were at once products of technical mastery and 'dreamworlds' which revived the old myths of natural plenitude and oneness with nature." Clark, "Panic Ecology," p. 83. Today, this ideological appropriation of nature has shifted into high gear: even as contemporary marketing puts Ford explorers on sunlit mesas and corporations greenwash consumerism to make it seem on the side of nature, futurist social theory has been, as this chapter chronicles, naturalizing social change.

[21] Alvin Toffler, *The Third Wave* (New York: Bantam Books, 1981), p. 2.

[22] *Ibid.*, p. 1.

[23] *Ibid.*, p. 2.

[24] *Ibid.*, p. 294.

[25] Alvin Toffler, "Foreward" in Ilya Prigogine and Isabelle Stengers, *Order out of Chaos: Man's New Dialogue with Nature* (New York: Bantam Books, 1984), p. xxvii.

[26] *Ibid.*, p. xxiii.

[27] *Ibid.*, p. xxiii.

[28] *Ibid.*, p.xxvi.

[29] Prigogine and Stengers, *Order out of Chaos*, p. 14.

[30] Toffler, *Third Wave*, p. 1.

[31] A.R. Ammons, "Corson's Inlet," *Collected Poems* (New York: W.W. Norton, 1972), pp. 147–50; Starhawk, *The Fifth Sacred Thing* (New York: Bantam, 1993).

[32] Donald Worster, "Nature and the Disorder of History," *Reinventing Nature: Responses to Postmodern Deconstructionism*, eds. Michael Soulé and Gary Lease (Washington, DC: Island Press, 1995), p. 81.

[33]Kevin Kelly, *Out of Control: The New Biology of Machines, Social Systems, and the Economic World* (Reading, MA: Addison-Wesley, 1994), p. 3.

[34]*Ibid.*, p. 471.

[35]*Ibid.*, p. 359, p. 363, p. 417.

[36]*Ibid.*, p. 401.

[37]T. Petzinger, Jr., "A New Model for the Nature of Business: It's Alive!" *Wall Street Journal*, February 26, 1999, p. B1.

[38]Henry David Thoreau, "Walking," *The Portable Thoreau*, ed. Carl Bode (New York: Penguin, 1977), p. 609.

[39]Julie Wakefield, "Complexity's Business Model," *Scientific American*, January 2001, p. 34.

[40]Donna Haraway, *Modest_Witness@Second_Millennium.FemaleMan©_Meets_OncoMouse™* (New York: Routledge, 1997), p. 276.

[41]The comments from *Business Week* are quoted in Geoffrey Nunberg, "Farewell to the Information Age," *The Future of the Book*, ed. Geoffrey Nunberg (Berkeley, CA: University of California, 1996), p. 109; on DNA computing, see Leonard M. Adleman, "Computing with DNA," *Scientific American*, August, 1998, pp. 54–61; on Internet ecology, see George Johnson, "Searching for the Essence of the World Wide Web," *New York Times*, April 11, 1999, Week in Review, pp. 1 and 18.

[42]Clark, "Panic Ecology," p. 89.

[43]N. Katherine Hayles, "Searching for Common Ground," *Reinventing Nature: Responses to Postmodern Deconstruction*, Michael E. Soulé and Gary Lease (Washington DC: Island Press, 1995), p. 57.

[44]Maude Barlow, *Blue Gold: The Global Water Crisis and the Commodification of the World's Water Supply* (San Francisco: The International Forum on Globalization, 1999), p. 16.

[45]Andrew Ross, "Interview," *The Nature of Cities: Ecocriticism and Urban Environments*, eds. Michael Bennett and David W. Teague (Tuscon, AZ: University of Arizona Press, 1999), p. 30.

[46]John Markoff, "Technology's Toxic Trash Is Sent to Poor Nations," *New York Times*, February 25, 2002, p. C1.

[47]*Ibid.*, p. C4.

[48]Roger Anderson, "Wattage Where It's Needed," *New York Times*, June 6, 2000, p. A31.

[49]Summarized in Edward Tenner, "Let's Not Get Too Wired," *New York Times*, July 22, 1999, p. F21.

[50]Myron Krueger, *Artificial Reality II* (Reading, MA: Addison Wesley, 1991), p. 256; quoted in Kevin Robins, "Cyberspace and the World We Live In," *Cyberspace/Cyberbodies/Cyberpunk: Cultures of Technological Embodiment*, eds. Mike Featherstone and Roger Burrows (London: Sage Publications, 1995), p. 138.

[51]Mike Featherstone and Roger Burrows, "Cultures of Technological Embodiment," *Cyberspace/Cyberbodies/Cyberpunk*, p. 2; R. Rucker, R.U. Sirius, and Queen Mu, eds., *Mondo 2000: A User's Guide to the New Edge* (London: Thames and Hudson, 1993), p. 100; quoted in Featherstone and Burrows, p. 3.

[52]David Tomas, "Old Rituals for New Space: 'Rites of Passage' and William Gibson's Cultural Model of Cyberspace," *Cyberspace: First Steps*, ed. Michael Menedikt (Cambridge, MA: MIT Press, 1991), p. 33; quoted in Scott Bukatman, *Terminal Identity: The Virtual Subject in Post-Modern Science Fiction* (Durham, NC: Duke University Press, 1993), p. 145.

[53]N. Katherine Hayles, "Boundary Disputes: Homeostasis, Reflexivity, and the Foundations of Cybernetics," *Virtual Realities and Their Discontents*, ed. Robert Markley (Baltimore, MD: Johns Hopkins University Press, 1996), p. 37.

NOTES   365

⁵⁴N. Katherine Hayles, *How We Became Posthuman: Virtual Bodies in Cybernetics, Literature, and Informatics* (Chicago: University of Chicago Press, 1999).

⁵⁵N. Katherine Hayles, "Virtual Bodies and Flickering Signifiers," *October*, 66, 1993, p. 81; quoted in Robins, "Cyberspace," p. 138.

⁵⁶Hayles, *How We Became Posthuman*, p. 20.

⁵⁷Cyborg/postmodern theory did not, in fact, just stop there. Along with proclaiming nature "over," much hyperexuberant academic theory also either ignored or even sharply polemicized against political advocacy in the name of "nature." In postmodern/cyborg academic theory, both "nature" and environmentalism received either short or no shrift—something noticed by environmentalists, some of whom returned fire on postmodern theory and culture. Approaches that were finally each other's necessary complement, became and have remained, alas, engaged in hostilities. See, for example, *Reinventing Nature? Responses to Postmodern Deconstruction*, eds. Michael E. Soulé and Gary Lease (Washington, DC: Island Press, 1995).

⁵⁸Fredric Jameson, *Postmodernism*, p. ix.

⁵⁹*Ibid.*, pp. 34–35.

⁶⁰*Ibid.*, p. 36.

⁶¹*Ibid.*, p. ix.

⁶²Haraway, *Modest Witness*, p. 113.

⁶³*Ibid.*, p. 301.

⁶⁴See, for example, Paul Shepard's and Michael Soulé's contributions to *Reinventing Nature* on the one side, and *Remaking Reality: Nature at the Millennium*, eds. Bruce Braun and Noel Castree (New York: Routledge, 1998) on the other.

⁶⁵Haraway, *Modest_Witness*, p. 113.

⁶⁶Quoted in Noel Castree and Bruce Braun, "The Construction of Nature and the Nature of Construction: Analytical and political tools for building survivable futures," *Remaking Reality*, p. 20.

⁶⁷Albert Borgman, "The Nature of Reality and the Reality of Nature," *Reinventing Nature*, p. 42.

⁶⁸*The Chronicle of Higher Education*, January 19, 1996, p. A11.

⁶⁹Dana Phillips, "Is Nature Necessary?" *The Ecocriticism Reader*, eds. Cheryll Glotfelty and Harold Fromm (Athens, GA: University of Georgia Press, 1996), p. 212.

⁷⁰Jack Turner, *The Abstract Wild* (Tuscon, AZ: University of Arizona Press, 1997), p. 30.

⁷¹Fredric Jameson, *Postmodernism*, p. 31.

⁷²Vandana Shiva, *Biopiracy: The Plunder of Nature and Knowledge* (Boston: South End Press, 1997), p. 21.

⁷³Stephen H. Kellert, *In the Wake of Chaos: Unpredictable Order in Dynamical Systems* (Chicago: University of Chicago Press, 1993), p. 115.

⁷⁴Hayles, *How We Became Posthuman*.

⁷⁵David Abram, *The Spell of the Sensuous: Perception and Language in a More-Than-Human World* (New York: Pantheon, 1996).

⁷⁶Jean-François Lgotar, *The Postmodern Condition: A Report on Knowledge*, Geoff Bennington, trans. (Minneapolis, MN: University of Minnesota Press, 1988), pp. 60–67.

⁷⁷Tom Jagtenberg and David McKie's *Eco-Impacts and the Greening of Postmodernity: New Maps for Communication Studies, Cultural Studies, and Sociology* (Thousand Oaks, CA: Sage, 1997) expresses both the tension between Green and postmodern perspectives and the authors' desire to reconcile them in its title.

⁷⁸See, for example, N. Katherine Hayles's version of situated knowledge, "Searching for Common Ground," in *Reinventing Nature;* my "Conflicting Conceptions of Nature in Popular

Discourse, Environmentalism, and Social Theory, in *Found Object*, 9, Fall 2000, pp. 119–141; and above all Lawrence Buell's integration of eco- and social theoretical approaches in *Writing for an Endangered World: Literature, Culture, and Environment in the U.S. and Beyond* (Cambridge, MA: Harvard University Press, 2001).

[79]As my argument in different places in this book should indicate (especially the end of Chapter 1 and the beginning of Chapter 4), sure indications that the antienvironmental devil is at work are dismissive comments about exploded old environmental ideals of purity, pristinity, balance, equilibrium, naturalness, and limits. When these dismissals come from the antienvironmental right, they blatantly exhibit their agenda. When they come from the academic left, they may seem very different but in fact really aren't. Yes, all these ideals are social constructions. But even when disenchanted, they are social constructions to be cherished as the source of environmental protections, not to be simply deconstructed and dismissed. Indeed, they are all the more valuable and hopeful when seen not as facts of nature but as tools some people have made to constrain what other people are doing. As such, they are no more dismissible when "deconstructed" as are, say, ideals like "equality" or "freedom" (social constructions that past philosophy also injected into "nature"). Deconstruction usually aims at reshaping and improving these social ideals, by making them more self-reflexive and self-critical; it should do the same with environmental ideals as well. Environmental ideals should be treated similarly.

For ideals like purity, pristinity, healthiness, balance, equilibrium, naturalness, and limits all have great utility, when serving as sources of environmental standards. Purity, for example, remains a crucial standard for controlling toxins that are damaging even in trace amounts. It also remains an important drag on contrarian advocacy of chemicalizing the environment generally. And it is a standard that is valuable even to the environmental justice movement, one that has traditionally seen itself at odds with nature-based activisms: it measures the environmental aspirations and even rights of the poor to safe and wholesome environments and, correspondingly, the damage done to them by the unequal distribution of bads (see Buell, Writing for an Endangered World, pp. 37–38). Equally when old standards, like balance, equilibrium, and limits, are set aside, the memory of them remains crucial. The memory of limits, for example, is essential to assessing risks in a time when society has moved "beyond the limits"; without this ghostly survival of the old environmental standard, the new formulation would utterly erase environmental concerns, making it seem (as it has to some ideologues) that no ecological or physical constraints exist.

[80]Quoted in John Bellamy Foster, *The Vulnerable Planet: A Short Economic History of the Environment* (New York: Monthly Review Press, 1999), p. 73.

[81]Buell, *Writing for an Endangered World*, p. 6.

[82]Quoted in Clive Ponting, *A Green History of the World: The Environment and the Collapse of Great Civilizations* (New York: Penguin, 1991), p. 158.

[83]Castree and Braun, "The Construction of Nature," p. 33.

Notes to Chapter 8

[1]Andrew Ross, *Strange Weather: Culture, Science, and Technology in the Age of Limits* (London: Verso, 1991), p. 144.

[2]Human-made environmental crisis in science fiction is the most recent branch of a tradition that, according to Brian Stableford, dates back to the late nineteenth century. Scientific advances such as Roentgen's discovery of X rays and Becquerel's description of radioactivity in uranium, Stableford argues, first "provided an imaginative *carte blanche* for technological fantasies of all kinds, including stories involving weapons of miraculous potency"; thus,

"by 1900 it was a great deal easier to imagine that the power to annihilate mankind might one day rest in human hands than it had been in 1894." Brian Stableford, "Man Made Catastrophes," *The End of the World*, eds. Eric Rabkin, Martin Greenberg, and Joseph Olander (Carbondale, IL: Southern Illinois University Press, 1983), p. 107. With the explosion of the atomic bombs art Hiroshima and Nagasaki, a widespread feeling arose that "*it was already too late* to avoid the dark and hostile future which had earlier been feared," and when the nuclear fifties became the environmental sixties, this feeling permeated environmental crisis fiction. *Ibid.*, p. 127. Emphasis in the original.

³Fredric Jameson, *Postmodernism, Or, the Cultural Logic of Late Capitalism* (Durham, NC: Duke University Press, 1991), p. 419n.

⁴As Stableford points out, novels dealing with Malthusian nighmare include *Make Room! Make Room!* (1966) by Harry Harrison, *The Wind Obeys Lama Toru* (1967) by Lee Tung, and *Stand on Zanzibar* (1968) by John Brunner. "Eco-doom" stories dramatizing a further range of problems (this is Stableford's term, one that is more user-friendly than R.J. Ellis's name for the literary genre and its context, the "discourse of apocalyptic ecologism") include John Brunner's *The Sheep Look Up* (1972), Philip Wylie's *The End of the Dream* (1972), and collections such as *The Ruins of the Earth* (1971), edited by Thomas Disch, and *Saving Worlds* (1973), edited by Roger Elwood and Virginia Kidd. R.J. Ellis, "Frank Herbert's *Dune* and the Discourse of Apocalyptic Ecologism in the United States," *Science Fiction Roots and Branches: Contemporary Critical Approaches*, eds. Rhys Garnett and R.J. Ellis (New York: St. Martins, 1990), pp. 104–124.

⁵See Stableford, "Man Made Catastrophes," p. 130.

⁶Trying to imagine the unimaginable is, of course, a goal of the literary sublime. Eco-doom extrapolative fantasy may thus be easily read as a highly ironic, twentieth-century version of the sublime, the mode central to much nineteenth-century nature representation.

⁷"The Concentration City" deals with hyperurbanization; "Billennium" focuses on overpopulation; and "Deep End," as discussed below, deals with ecological destruction.

⁸J. G. Ballard, "Deep End," *The Best Stories of J.G. Ballard* (New York: Henry Holt: [1978] 1995), p. 110.

⁹*Ibid.*, p. 110, p. 111.

¹⁰*Ibid,*. p. 111.

¹¹John Brunner, *The Sheep Look Up* (New York: Ballantine Books, 1972), p. 9.

¹²*Ibid.*, p. 154.

¹³*Ibid.*, p. 377.

¹⁴Philip K. Dick, *Do Androids Dream of Electric Sheep* (New York: Ballantine Books, [1968] 1996), p. 37.

¹⁵The attempt to replace naturalized spiritual traditions with unnatural ones is, of course, an old one; it goes back, doubtless, to the gnostics, but its more recent and influential avatar was the cultivation of antinatural states of consciousness by Edgar Allan Poe, French symbolist writers, and modernists such as W.B. Yeats. Positively awful things were said about nature in the process, but the statements had at least the gloss of an aristocratic, antibourgeois hauteur, of higher spirits wearily harried by a society of philistines. Cyberpunk spiritual antinaturalism—the most intense of the many thrills available in a world of no limits, extreme risk, and imminent catastrophe—sometimes tries to strike this aristocratic note (as, most irritatingly, in Sterling), but it misses. No longer does an artist opine that he lets his servants do his living for him or color his "prairies . . . red, rivers golden yellow and trees blue," doing so with the elegant dictum that "Nature has no imagination." The new mode expresses its antinatural bias far less elegantly, embracing it not as an elegant with-

drawal from philistinism but as an immersion in postnatural, socially Darwinian, capital-
ist-libertarian, high-technological ultraphilistinism as a speeded-up, vaguely Nietzschean,
thrills-and-chills form of not-so-clean fun. Théophile Gautier, quoted in David Perkins, *A
History of Modern Poetry: From the 1890s to the High Modernist Mode* (Cambridge, MA:
Harvard University Press, 1976), p. 36.

[16]William Gibson, *Neuromancer* (New York: Ace Books, 1984), p. 51.

[17]That it is so is a significant choice, not an inevitability. For depictions of future technologies
don't have to feel this way; think of how the film *Alien* portrays an unreliable, blue-collar,
always-in-disrepair form of technology—technology realistically depicted, technology that
doesn't work smoothly and within which all-too-organic woes lie in wait for what are still
vulnerable human bodies.

[18]Gibson, *Neuromancer*, p. 55.

[19]*Ibid.*, p. 7.

[20]Bruce Sterling, *Schismatrix* (1985), in *Schismatrix Plus* (New York: Ace Books: 1996), p. 235.

[21]Gibson and Sterling also twin in another way. Gibson as contrarian reverses George Orwell's
protocybernetic dystopia in *1984;* Sterling as contrarian reverses the genetic-engineering
dystopia of Aldous Huxley's *Brave New World.*

[22]Sterling, *Schismatrix*, p. 20.

[23]*Ibid.*, p. 100.

[24]*Ibid.*, p. 195.

[25]*Ibid.*, p. 195.

[26]*Ibid.*, p. 224.

[27]David Brin, *Earth* (New York: Bantam, 1990), p. 353.

[28]*Ibid.*, p. 392.

[29]*Ibid.*, p. 395.

[30]*Ibid.*, p. 508.

[31]*Ibid.*, p. 531.

[32]*Ibid.*, p. 529 and p. 665.

[33]*Ibid.*, p. 630.

[34]*Ibid.*, p. 603.

[35]Cole frets about the possibility that by revealing his mission and his knowledge of the future to
Jeffrey Goines early on in the movie—which he does when they both are patients in the mental institution—he in fact helped bring on the catastrophe. For he suggested to the crazed,
suggestible Goines that something like it could happen. Even more pointed is the fact that
Katherine, once she begins to believe Cole, phones Goines's father and warns him about the
danger the virus poses. Goines' father reacts by tightening security—but he does this by en-
trusting his dangerous colleague, the film's actual villain, with the security codes for the virus.

[36]Kim Stanley Robinson, *Red Mars* (New York: Bantam, 1993), p. 229.

[37]Kim Stanley Robinson, *Blue Mars* (New York, Bantam, 1996), p. 162.

[38]"As the generations pass, all the members of a biosphere evolve together, adapting to their terrain in a complex communal response, a creative self-designing ability. This process, no
matter how much we intervene in it, is essentially out of our control. Genes mutate, creatures evolve: a new biosphere emerges, and with it a new noosphere." Kim Stanley Robinson, *Green Mars* (New York: Bantam, 1994), p. 3.

[39]"No different than life on Earth had ever been . . . but here all happening at a much faster
rate, pushed by human-driven changes, modifications, introductions, transcriptions,
translations." Robinson, *Blue Mars*, p. 412.

40*Ibid.*, p. 481.

41It is ominous that the one large-scale scientific work on terraforming now in the public domain is Martyn Fogg's *Terraforming: Engineering Planetary Environments*, a book published by the American Society of Automotive Engineers. And it is still more ominous when, as John Bellamy Foster points out, the journalist Gary Easterbrook ends his brownlash tome entitled *A Moment on the Earth* by "assuring his readers that we can 'terraform' Mars if we run out of ecological space on earth, thereby giving us 'two biospheres for every one that exists today.'" John Bellamy Foster, "The Scale of Our Ecological Crisis," *The Monthly Review*, 4:11, April 1998, available at http://monthlyreview.org/498jbf.htm.

42Carl Hiassen, *Tourist Season* (New York: Warner Books, 1986).

43Carl Hiassen, *Sick Puppy* (New York: Alfred A. Knopf, 1999), p. 159.

44*Ibid.*, p. 184.

45Neal Stephenson, *Zodiac* (New York: Bantam, 1995 [1988]), p. 57.

Notes to Chapter 9

1Bill McKibben, *The End of Nature* (New York: Random House, 1989); Jack Turner, *The Abstract Wild* (Tuscon, AZ: University of Arizona Press, 1996).

2Robert Sullivan, *The Meadowlands: Wilderness Adventures at the Edge of a City* (New York: Scribner, 1998).

3David T. Hanson, *Waste Land: Meditations on a Ravaged Landscape* (New York: Aperture, 1997); Richard Misrach, *Bravo 20: The Bombing of the American West* (Baltimore, MD: Johns Hopkins University Press, 1990).

4"Album: Unnatural Nature," *Uncommon Ground: Rethinking the Human Place in Nature*, ed. William Cronon (New York: Norton, 1996), p. 59.

5Janisse Ray, *Ecology of a Cracker Childhood* (Minneapolis, MN: Milkweed Editions, 1999).

6Wendell Berry, *Another Turn of the Crank* (Washington, DC: Counterpoint, 1995).

7John Hanson Mitchell, *Ceremonial Time: Fifteen Thousand Years on One Square Mile* (Reading, MA: Addison-Wesley Publishing, 1984).

8Barry Lopez, "On the Wings of Commerce: Penguins and Lipstick, Strawberries and Gold— Aloft," *Harper's Magazine*, October 1995, p. 40, p. 45.

9*Ibid.*, p. 45.

10*Ibid.*, p. 52. See also Fredric Jameson, *Postmodernism, Or, the Cultural Logic of Late Capitalism* (Durham, NC: Duke University Press, 1991), Chapter 1.

11David Guterson, "Enclosed. Encyclopedic. Endured. One Week at the Mall of America," *Harper's Magazine*, 1973, reprinted in *A Forest of Voices: Reading and Writing the Environment*, Chris Anderson and Lex Runciman, eds. (Mountain View, CA: Mayfield Publishing Company, 1995), pp. 124–135.

12Carl Serafina, *Song for the Blue Ocean* (New York: Henry Holt, 1997); Colin Woodard, *Ocean's End: Travel through Endangered Seas* (New York: Basic Books, 2000). Another example of the new subgenre, Mark Hertsgaard's *Earth Odyssey*, embodies this same message in its overall purpose; Hertsgaard explicitly sets out to write a travel-adventure narrative that does not seek out exotic unspoiled lands beyond the reach of Western civilization but instead inventories the grotesque environmental damage now done all around the planet. Mark Hertsgaard, *Earth Odyssey: Around the World In Search of Our Environmental Future* (New York: Broadway Books, 1999).

[13]Chellis Glendinning, *Off the Map (An Expedition Deep into Imperialism, the Global Economy, and Other Earthly Whereabouts)* (Boston: Shambala, 1999); Derrick Jensen, *A Language Older Than Words* (New York: Context Books, 2000); and Susanne Antonetta, *Body Toxic* (Washington, DC: Counterpoint Press, 2001).

[14]See Theodore Roszak, *The Voice of the Earth: An Exploration of Ecopsychology* (New York: Simon & Schuster, 1992) and Theodore Roszak, Mary Gomes, and Allen Kanner, eds., *Ecopsychology: Restoring the Earth, Healing the Mind* (San Francisco: Sierra Club Books, 1995).

[15]Sandra Steingraber notes that New Jersey has an "astonishing" 112 Superfund sites; she also reports on the Ocean County/Toms River cancer cluster Antonetta is concerned with. Sandra Steingraber: *Living Downstream: A Scientist's Personal Investigation of Cancer and the Environment* (New York: Random House, 1997), p. 71 and p. 279.

[16]Antonetta, *Body Toxic,* p. 21.

[17]*Ibid.*, p. 18.

[18]*Ibid.*, pp. 18–19.

[19]*Ibid.*, p. 20.

[20]*Ibid.*, p. 23.

[21]*Ibid.*, pp. 27–28.

[22]*Ibid.*, p. 207.

[23]For ecopsychological explorations of the topic, see Joanna Macy, "Working through Environmental Despair," *Ecopsychology: Restoring the Earth*, p. 249; and Phyllis Windle, "The Ecology of Grief," *Ecopsychology: Restoring the Earth*, p. 144. For unnatural history and a hopeful response to it, see Christopher Cokinos's *Hope Is the Thng with Feathers: A Personal Chronicle of Vanished Birds* (New York: Tarcher/Putnam, 2000).

[24]McKibben, *The End of Nature* (New York: Doubleday, 1989), p. 3.

[25]McKibben, I should add, is initially not self-reflective about this process. At the beginning of *The End of Nature*, he depicts the diminution of nature's grandeur as the loss of a universal property of nature rather than the loss of a specific yet rich, several-centuries-old, cultural tradition. McKibben's mourning is accordingly greatly intensified. Only after he has expressed his grief fully does he state that what has ended is an idea about nature, not nature itself, and even then, he never explores the cultural particularity of that idea. Though McKibben has been charged with theoretical naïveté on account of this, it is highly likely that he writes this way strategically, rather than naïvely. He delays mentioning that the real end is ideational, not simply material, because he wishes to represent as vividly as possible the way ordinary people immersed in their own culture actually experience the loss of one of its faiths. Overwhelming grief at literal changes precedes reflection on the actually more complex—philosophical as well as material—nature of those changes.

[26]McKibben, *End of Nature*, p. 48, 59, 84.

[27]McKibben, *End of Nature*, p. 211.

[28]Bill McKibben, *Hope, Human and Wild: True Stories of Living Lightly on the Earth* (Boston: Little, Brown and Co., 1995).

[29]A. R. Ammons, *Collected Poems* (New York: W. W. Norton, 1972), p. 148.

[30]*Ibid.*, pp. 148–149.

[31]See Steven P. Schneider, *A.R. Ammons and the Poetics of Widening Scope* (Rutherford, NJ: Associated University Presses, 1994) for an excellent study which takes this line as a leitmotiv that runs through and helps explain Ammons's entire *oeuvre*.

[32]Ammons, *Collected Poems*, p. 340.

[33] Steven Schneider, "From the Wind to the Earth: An Interview With A.R. Ammons," *Complexities of Motion: New Essays on A.R. Ammons's Long Poems*, ed. Steven Schneider (Madison, NJ: Fairleigh Dickinson Press, 1999), pp. 347–348.

[34] For a still fuller, more literary-historical and literary-theoretical description of Ammons's change from nature to postnature poet, see my "Ammons's Peripheral Vision: *Tape for the Turn of the Year* and *Garbage*," *Complexities of Motion*, pp. 214–238.

[35] *Ibid.*, p. 340.

[36] A. R. Ammons, *Garbage* (New York: W.W. Norton, 1993), p. 24, p. 30, p. 31.

[37] *Ibid.*, p. 46, p. 99, p. 68, p. 75.

[38] Ammons, *Glare* (New York: W.W. Norton, 1993), p. 77, p. 79.

[39] For the best ecocritical commentary on some of this literature, see Lawrence Buell, *Writing for an Endangered World: Literature, Culture, and Environment in the U.S. and Beyond* (Cambridge, MA: Harvard University Press, 2001). *Writing for an Endangered World* reads contemporary literature in order to pioneer new ecocritical and ecotheoretical perspectives. My different but complementary approach focuses on recent literature's changing representation of environmental crisis. Where Larry fleshes out new perspectives and pathways, I concentrate on elaborating the new challenges—a set of roles perhaps appropriate to older and younger brothers respectively.

[40] Don DeLillo, *White Noise* (New York: Penguin, 1985), p. 177.

[41] *Ibid.*, p. 29.

[42] *Ibid.*, p. 29.

[43] *Ibid.*, p. 110.

[44] *Ibid.*, p. 114.

[45] *Ibid.*, p. 117.

[46] *Ibid.*, p. 127.

[47] *Ibid.*, p. 131.

[48] *Ibid.*, p. 139.

[49] *Ibid.*, p. 139.

[50] *Ibid.*, p. 140.

[51] *Ibid.*, p. 141.

[52] *Ibid.*, p. 280.

[53] *Ibid.*, pp. 324–325.

[54] A literary echo makes Gladney's temporary vision much more ironic. His comment that "something golden falls, softens in the air" echoes a famous line from the sixteenth-century poet Thomas Nashe, who wrote that "Brightness falls from the air." Alas, the line comes in a poem entitled "Litany in Time of Plague."

[55] *Ibid.*, p. 325.

[56] Joy Williams, *The Quick and the Dead* (New York: Alfred A. Knopf, 2000), p. 243.

[57] *Ibid.*, p. 51, p. 45.

[58] *Ibid.*, p. 278.

[59] *Ibid.*, p. 150–151.

[60] *Ibid.*, p. 151. Often characters flash back between these two bizarre forms of behavior and discourse, brutal at one moment, hip-sophisticated at another. A woman who picks up Ray Webb hitchhiking north yells at him over Schumann playing at high volume: "One listens in vain . . . for anything in Schumann's last works." A few seconds later, she snarls at Ray: "you're a fucking loser, man" (*Ibid.*, p. 63).

[61] *Ibid.*, p. 3.

[62]*Ibid.*, p. 97.

[63]*Ibid.*, p. 278.

[64]*Ibid.*, p. 6.

[65]*Ibid.*, p. 46.

[66]*Ibid.*, p. 39.

[67]*Ibid.*, p. 50.

[68]*Ibid.*, p. 256.

[69]*Ibid.*, p. 256.

[70]In her most powerful environmental essays, Williams's voice becomes one with Alice's, Williams's most recent fictional creation. In, for example, a characteristically caustically entitled essay, "Save the Whales, Screw the Shrimp" (printed in her wittily and revealingly entitled volume, *Ill Nature: Rants and Reflections on Humanity and Other Animals*), Williams's and Alice's environmental screeds seem to merge. The essay features a dialogue between a wittily cranky Cassandra voice and an equally cranky, blasé, tired-of-more-of-this set of respondents (*"You're getting a little shrill here,* you say"), and the two voices form a cantata exemplifying an era in which the environment is increasingly damaged, crisis is domesticated, and environmentalism checkmated by hostility and also greenwashing co-optation and commodification. Joy Williams, *Ill Nature: Rants and Reflections on Humanity and Other Animals* (New York: The Lyons Press, 2001), p. 20.

[71]Richard Powers, *Gain* (New York: Picador, 1998), p. 118.

[72]*Ibid.*, p. 118.

[73]*Ibid.*, p. 91.

[74]Thornton, *Pandora's Poison: Chlorine, Health, and a New Environmental Strategy* (Cambridge, MA: MIT Press, 2000), p. 234.

[75]*Ibid.*, p. 235.

[76]*Ibid.*, p. 312.

[77]*Ibid.*, p. 324.

[78]*Ibid.*, p. 31.

[79]*Ibid.*, pp. 30–1.

[80]*Ibid.*, p. 65.

[81]*Ibid.*, p. 72.

[82]*Ibid.*, p. 139.

[83]*Ibid.*, p. 205.

[84]*Ibid.*, p. 213. American audiences' discomfort here will only increase if I refer to Chapter 4: contemporary SEER statistics hold that 40 percent of the novel's readers will be diagnosed with cancer during their lifetimes.

[85]*Ibid.*, p. 320.

[86]*Ibid.*, p. 339.

[87]*Ibid.*, p. 340.

[88]*Ibid.*, p. 339. Italics in the original.

[89]*Ibid.*, p. 355.

[90]Octavia Butler, *Parable of the Sower* (New York: Warner Books, 1995), p. 22.

[91]Butler's much less impressive successor novel, *Parable of the Talents* (New York: Warner Books, 1998), shows that finding ways to dwell on and perhaps restore a socially and environmentally deteriorated earth is not her ultimate goal. *Parable of the Talents* describes the ups and downs of Lauren's attempts to deal with a violent, right-wing, fundamentalist Christian takeover of the United States, to reshape postcatastrophe society, and to journey

beyond earth into the stars. Where *The Parable of the Sower* deemphasizes us-versus-them melodrama and maintains a relentlessly realistic perspective, *Parable of the Talents* plunges deeply into the former and jettisons the latter for the postecological trip to the stars beloved of science fiction.

[92] *Ibid.*, p. 119.

[93] *Ibid.*, p. 128.

[94] Linda Hogan, *Power* (New York: W.W. Norton, 1998).

[95] Terry Tempest Williams, *Refuge: An Unnatural History of Family and Place* (New York: Random House, 1991), p. 4.

[96] *Ibid.*, p. 15.

[97] *Ibid.*, p. 156.

[98] *Ibid.*, p. 165.

[99] *Ibid.*, p. 178.

[100] *Ibid.*, p. 231.

[101] *Ibid.*, p. 241.

[102] *Ibid.*, p. 281.

[103] *Ibid.*, p. 283.

[104] *Ibid.*, p. 4.

Notes to Appendix 1

[1] Some of the names on the list and the quotation come from a book I have relied on heavily for this section: Sharon Beder, *Global Spin: The Corporate Assault on Environmentalism* (White River Junction, VT: Chelsea Green Publishing Co., 1997), p. 29.

[2] *Ibid.*, p. 16.

[3] *Ibid.*, p. 108.

[4] *Ibid.*, p. 109.

[5] *Ibid.*, p. 186.

[6] *Ibid.*, p. 125.

[7] *Ibid.*, p. 129.

[8] *Ibid.*, p. 126.

[9] *Ibid.*, p. 127.

[10] *Ibid.*, p. 126.

[11] *Ibid.*, p. 132.

[12] *Ibid.*, p. 133.

[13] *Ibid.*, p. 176.

[14] *Ibid.*, p. 177.

[15] *Ibid.*, pp. 166–167.

[16] *Ibid.*, p. 169.

[17] *Ibid.*, p. 170.

[18] *Ibid.*, p. 63.

[19] *Ibid.*, p. 64.

[20] David Callahan, *$1 Billion for Ideas: Conservative Think Tanks in the 1990s* (Washington, DC: National Committee for Responsive Philanthropy, 1999), p. 9.

[21] Beder, *Global Spin*, p. 19.

[22] *Ibid.*, p. 236.

[23] Callahan, *$1 Billion*, p. 36.

[24]*Ibid.*, p. 11.

[25]Beder, *Global Spin*, p. 87.

[26]Callahan, *$1 Billion*, p. 21.

[27]*Ibid.*, p. 20.

[28]*Ibid.*, p. 21.

[29]Beder, *Global Spin*, p. 197.

[30]Paul R. and Anne H. Ehrlich, *Betrayal of Science and Reason: How Anti-Environmental Rhetoric Threatens Our Future* (Washington, DC: Island Press, 1996), p. 38.

[31]*Ibid.*, pp. 38–39.

[32]Beder, *Global Spin*, p. 92.

[33]Dixie Lee Ray, "Greenhouse Earth," *A Forest of Voices, Reading and Writing the Environment*, C.A. Anderson and Lex Runciman, eds. (Mountain View, CA: Mayfield Publishing Co., 1995), p. 566.

[34]Beder, *Global Spin*, p. 32.

[35]*Ibid.*, p. 32.

[36]*Ibid.*, p. 32.

[37]*Ibid.*, p. 35.

[38]*Ibid.*, p. 40.

[39]*Ibid.*, p. 36.

[40]*Ibid.*, p. 38.

[41]Callahan, *$1 Billion* p. 23.

[42]Daniel Helvarg, *War against the Greens* (San Francisco: Sierra Club Books, 1994), pp. 7–8.

[43]*Ibid.*, pp. 374–375.

INDEX